AMERICAN DRAMATISTS IN THE 21ST CENTURY

Related Titles

ANXIOUS MASCULINITY IN THE DRAMA OF ARTHUR MILLER AND BEYOND: SALESMEN, SLUGGERS, AND BIG DADDIES
ISBN 978-1-3502-7111-1
Claire Gleitman

THE METHUEN DRAMA GUIDE TO CONTEMPORARY AMERICAN PLAYWRIGHTS
ISBN 978-1-4081-3479-5
Edited by Martin Middeke, Peter Paul Schnierer, Christopher Innes and Matthew C. Roudané

MODERN AMERICAN DRAMA: PLAYWRITING 2000-2009
ISBN 978-1-4725-7147-2
Julia Listengarten and Cindy Rosenthal

STAGING AMERICA: TWENTY-FIRST-CENTURY DRAMATISTS
ISBN 978-1-3502-0092-0
Christopher Bigsby

TRAGEDY SINCE 9/11: READING A WORLD OUT OF JOINT
ISBN 978-1-3500-3562-1
Jennifer Wallace

VISIONS OF TRAGEDY IN MODERN AMERICAN DRAMA
ISBN 978-1-4742-7693-1
Edited by David Palmer

AMERICAN DRAMATISTS IN THE 21ST CENTURY

OPENING DOORS

Christopher Bigsby

methuen | drama
LONDON • NEW YORK • OXFORD • NEW DELHI • SYDNEY

METHUEN DRAMA
Bloomsbury Publishing Plc
50 Bedford Square, London, WC1B 3DP, UK
1385 Broadway, New York, NY 10018, USA
29 Earlsfort Terrace, Dublin 2, Ireland

BLOOMSBURY, METHUEN DRAMA and the Methuen Drama logo are
trademarks of Bloomsbury Publishing Plc

First published in Great Britain 2023
This paperback edition published 2024

Copyright © Christopher Bigsby, 2023

Christopher Bigsby has asserted his right under the Copyright, Designs and
Patents Act, 1988, to be identified as author of this work.

For legal purposes the Acknowledgements on p. vi constitute
an extension of this copyright page.

Cover design: Ben Anslow
Cover image: (L-R) Nikki Crawford, Samuel Ray Gates, Shannon Dorsey, and
Chinna Palmer in Fairview at Woolly Mammoth Theatre (© Teresa Castracane Photography)

All rights reserved. No part of this publication may be reproduced or transmitted in any form or
by any means, electronic or mechanical, including photocopying, recording, or any information
storage or retrieval system, without prior permission in writing from the publishers.

Bloomsbury Publishing Plc does not have any control over, or responsibility for, any third-party
websites referred to or in this book. All internet addresses given in this book were correct at the
time of going to press. The author and publisher regret any inconvenience caused if addresses have
changed or sites have ceased to exist, but can accept no responsibility for any such changes.

A catalogue record for this book is available from the British Library.

Library of Congress Cataloging-in-Publication Data
Names: Bigsby, C. W. E., author.
Title: American dramatists in the 21st century : opening doors / Christopher Bigsby.
Description: London ; New York : Methuen Drama, 2023. | Includes index. |
Summary: "Analyzing the work of 7 American playwrights whose careers began in the present century, each chapter of this book focuses on a different playwright: David Adjmi, Julia Cho, Jackie Sibblies Drury, Will Eno, Martyna Majok, Dominique Morisseau and Anna Ziegler. In addition to covering all their works, and providing a sense of their critical reception, Bigsby also includes brand new interviews with the playwrights themselves, and exclusive discussions of unpublished works, the texts having been supplied by the authors. Bigsby argues that the diverse range of racial, religious, gendered, and, in several instances, immigrant backgrounds from which these playwrights come means that they all see America from a different perspective. These playwrights differ in their styles but share an interest in identity, as well as a desire to break the fourth wall, often seeing the audience as intimately involved with the work on stage. Their careers have all advanced through development, staged readings, and small venues to major stages, and they have picked up many awards along the way (including Pulitzers, Obies and in one case a McArthur 'Genius Grant'). The book, therefore, is in part an account of how North American theatre works from the point of view of those who commit to the challenging task of making their living by writing for it. At a time when, as a result of the Covid-19 pandemic, theatre has been under greater pressure than ever, it is a reminder of what a present tense art has to offer, as it holds a mirror up to a society ever concerned with its own sense of itself in a changing world"– Provided by publisher.
Identifiers: LCCN 2022029777 | ISBN 9781350340480 (hardback) | ISBN 9781350340527 (paperback) | ISBN 9781350340497 (epub) | ISBN 9781350340503 (ebook) | ISBN 9781350340510
Subjects: LCSH: American drama–21st century–History and criticism. | Dramatists, American–21st century–Interviews. | LCGFT: Literary criticism. | Interviews.
Classification: LCC PS353 .B53 2023 | DDC 812/.609–dc23/eng/20221004
LC record available at https://lccn.loc.gov/2022029777

ISBN:	HB:	978-1-3503-4048-0
	PB:	978-1-3503-4052-7
	ePDF:	978-1-3503-4050-3
	eBook:	978-1-3503-4049-7

Typeset by Integra Software Services Pvt. Ltd.

To find out more about our authors and books visit www.bloomsbury.com
and sign up for our newsletters.

CONTENTS

Acknowledgements		vi
Introduction		1
1	David Adjmi: The outsider	5
2	Julia Cho: Love, loss and memory	29
3	Jackie Sibblies Drury: Staging race	55
4	Will Eno: A touch of Beckett	83
5	Martyna Majok: On displacement	113
6	Dominique Morisseau: Poet of Detroit	137
7	Anna Ziegler: Time passing	165
Notes		198
Index		211

ACKNOWLEDGEMENTS

I gratefully acknowledge the kindness of Julia Cho, Jackie Sibblies Drury, Martyna Majok and Anna Ziegler who provided me with copies of their work

INTRODUCTION

The American theatre has changed in recent years. Doors have opened that were if not closed then only ajar, even as a national debate about identity has become more central than ever. First- and second-generation immigrants have used the stage to explore the nature of their relationship to a country whose motto, until replaced by In God We Trust, was E Pluribus Unum. The writers considered here include a Syrian-Jewish American, Korean American, Jamaican American, Polish American and Haitian American. Women have increasingly claimed centre stage. In the 2019–20 season, eight out of the ten (in fact fourteen because of ties) of the most produced plays in America were by women, while twelve out of twenty (in fact twenty-two because of ties) of the most produced playwrights were also women. In 2022, Lynn Nottage had three plays on Broadway. There is a reason that women predominate in this study.

An increasing number of theatres have sought to give space to new writers whose path to success has often involved staged readings, development and productions in small, sometimes unnervingly small, spaces though reviewers, for whom such would once have fallen below the radar, are now inclined to keep a watchful eye. This includes *The New York Times*. Along the way, as the size of audiences grew, the writers considered here have all picked up awards from the kind of grants and fellowships which enabled them to put food on the table and maintain confidence in themselves, to national and international recognition, including Pulitzer Prizes. Dominque Morisseau won the McArthur so-called genius grant worth $625,000. In the years since 1981, playwrights have been honoured just sixteen times by the McArthur Foundation. Of these, fourteen are either women or members of a minority group, again an emphasis reflected in *Contemporary American Dramatists*. Though this is a book about playwrights, it also reflects the changing nature of the society they address.

If doors have opened, in 2020–1 they closed as the Covid pandemic took hold. Many lost their lives, economies suffered and restrictions were imposed. The theatre was not immune. A few companies responded by taking productions online, but most entered a period of enforced hibernation. A few closed down completely, never to re-open. Online versions were clearly a boon, but they were also a reminder that an essential element of theatre is presence. A present-tense art, it takes place in the presence of audiences who breathe the same air (hence the restrictions), occupy the same moment, respond to those on stage as those on stage respond to them. Though individuals bring their own experiences, convictions, feelings to bear, they are also responding to those around them. Theatre is social, whether in a small space where exposure is unavoidable, or Broadway's sometimes cavernous auditoria. An online play is impervious to audiences. Time is not shared nor, usually, is the experience. In a sense audiences become voyeurs, observers rather than full participants.

Audiences in the theatre, of course, are not one thing. They have different reasons for attending, looking for different things, consenting to enter the lives of others to a differing extent, leaning back in their seats to be entertained, or leaning forward, captured by something more than the moment. They are, however, present, having signed up to an implied contract which finds them seated alongside strangers and exposed to a story whose unfamiliarity becomes familiar. As the director and theatre theoretician Herb Blau remarked, theatre is a ratification of the social. He quotes Virginia Woolf's remark, 'No audience. No echo. That's part of one's death,' as he does John Ashberry's 'For we never knew, never knew what joined us together.' He quotes, too, from Woolf's final novel, *Between the Acts*: 'There was nothing for the audience to do … They were silent … Their minds and bodies were too close, yet not close enough.'[1] At the end of the play (a pageant) mirrors are turned on them by the performers.

Mirrors are turned on the audiences by all the playwrights considered here who write plays in which characters engage directly with audiences, the fourth wall proving fully permeable. In a Will Eno play a character counts the number in the audience. Dominique Morisseau even posts what she calls Rules of Engagement, in theatres or programmes, in which she exhorts those attending to be a full part of the drama, declaring, 'Please be an audience member that joins with others and allows a bit of breathing room. Exhale together. Laugh together. Say "amen" should you need to. This is community.' Community, indeed, celebrated and threatened, is another link, the question being what constitutes it in a country which simultaneously celebrates and distrusts difference. In Jackie Sibblies Drury's *Fairview* the audience is invited on stage, or at least some of them are, as racial divisions are confronted, thereby becoming its subject.

This is not an echo of 1960s and 1970s works in which audiences were embraced, berated, coerced, liberated, radical groups even taking to the streets in a demonstration of their relevance and commitment. What is at stake in the work of those I discuss is the nature of community in a culture in which experiences may differ radically, an attempt to bridge that gulf, a bid for intimacy originally, perhaps, facilitated by the nature of the venues in which they worked. There is acknowledgement of the nature of theatre, its processes and artifice, even as its virtues are made manifest. Direct address to the audience, like the Shakespearian soliloquy, like the first-person narrative of the novel, allows the playwright to enter the mind and sensibility of a character under pressure.

This has been, and continues to be, an exciting period in the American theatre. *Contemporary American Dramatists* offers an account of some of today's most compelling playwrights. The American theatre is not Broadway, with its forty-one theatres seating five hundred or more, the evidence for that to be found in the careers of these writers, even as it remains a place seen, by some, as an ultimate validation. Sixty-five per cent of those attending Broadway productions are tourists, while some 80 per cent of those productions are musicals. It does have its loyal devotees, 28 per cent of all tickets being bought by those who attend fifteen or more productions,[2] while 68 per cent of audiences are women. The average ticket price in 2022 was $113. By contrast, tickets at Chicago's Goodman Theatre can be bought for between $15 and $40, while students can pick up tickets for $10. People's Light, where Dominique Morisseau's *Mud Row* was staged, charged $40–45.

The American theatre thrives in small theatres, in communities, though not without a struggle. It seeks new audiences, listens out for new voices, stages a debate with the society beyond its doors, challenging, celebrating, exploring, failing, succeeding. Sometimes the playwrights move to Off Broadway and Broadway. More significantly, their plays are presented across the country. Broadway shows still travel. In 2019, you could see *Hamilton* in twenty-three cities. But so, too, do the plays considered here. The Theatre Communications Group lists seven-hundred-member theatres, in forty-seven states. There are just short of 1,900 community theatres in America. In 2019, over 7 million attended not-for-profit theatres. Now recovering from the pandemic, theatre is live, and alive.

CHAPTER 1
DAVID ADJMI: THE OUTSIDER

> I think the theater has a moral obligation to start telling these other kinds of stories.[1]
>
> David Adjmi

Whatever the subject of his plays, they are, David Adjmi has confessed, rooted in aspects of himself and his experiences. 'I write plays', he has said,

> Because I have to exorcise certain things. It's like I'm trying to reach for one thing, but I'm also trying to expel something else inside of myself. There are things in my unconscious that need to come out. Some sort of demon or dark side of myself. I thought I was going to write a comedy after *The Evildoers* because that was a very dark play. I thought I would write something kooky and fun, and then *Stunning* took this hairpin turn. I have this fantasy of being Noel Coward and I really want to do frothy light things. And yet I'm always undone because I always encounter the hard wall of reality.

Even *Marie Antoinette*, which features the last Queen of France before the Revolution, combined 'drawing room elements' with 'German tragic elements' and is 'really a play about America and … people in my life'.[2] No matter how far he travels, he always seems to come back to himself generating drama from his own contradictions and finding in them echoes of a society apparently so assured but equally capable of contradiction and a level of self-destruction.

His insecurities are plain from his interviews, his sense not only of staring into society from the outside but also of looking at his own life with the same sense of unease. He has said that 'I've been in dark places … because I've pushed myself to look at things that can't easily be repaired or healed.'[3] In a way he writes himself into existence, assuming the guise of characters whose grasp of events is not as secure as it seems, sensing that something is not quite in place, their identities under threat. They are seldom quite what they appear, a fluid style reflecting psychological and social flux. He moves from the carefully constructed and artfully deceptive assurance of the woman in *Elective Affinities*, blind to, or consciously suppressing, the entropy which threatens both herself and her society, to a queen who clothes herself in imperial certainties only to find her world subverted, dissolving in the face of external threats and internal disturbances. When he turns to farce, as in *3C*, he revels in the permeability of boundaries, the arbitrary nature of distinctions, simultaneously mocking those who presume themselves to carry authority while sensing that farce may, indeed, characterize an existence in which nothing is really secure. His name, Adjmi, he has explained, derives from the Arabic name for outsider or exile, and there is a sense in which that applies to his own sense of outsiderness, his time in therapy an attempt to locate himself.

A surprising number of American playwrights owe something to the British theatre, either beginning their careers in the UK or receiving a boost there. Ayad Akhtar has said that 'I would say that in the UK there is a social commitment to the theatre. The audiences are well versed in the form … The Brits have a national writer [Shakespeare] – we don't even have a national writer – and their national writer is a playwright!' They 'have an exposure to a rich performative language. In the U.S. nobody goes to plays, unless they live in New York. There isn't a national obsession or a national interest in the theatre, so it just creates a different kind of petri dish. The petri dish of British theatre is overflowing with rich abundance that just can't be rivalled.'[4] Clearly, this is more than a little over the top. The British, in truth, are not obsessed with the theatre while there is a world beyond New York, more especially when it comes to the fostering of new work. Even so, not only did the Edinburgh Festival prove receptive to American plays, but small theatres and major companies alike welcomed them. While still a graduate student, and before attending the Juilliard in New York, Adjmi received a commission from the Royal Court Theatre which led to the production of *Elective Affinities* in 2005, nine years before its American premiere at New York's Soho Rep.

Elective Affinities, a monologue delivered by a wealthy WASP woman 'of the Brooke Astor, Gloria Vanderbilt ilk,'[5] called Alice, on the face of it seems an unlikely first play from Adjmi given his background, a gay Sephardic Jew whose family had originally come from Syria, though that would become more relevant with his later play, *Stunning*. His parents had lived in Nashville and were 'southern Jews, very assimilated'. They had subsequently moved to Midwood in Brooklyn. Though they were not particularly religious, they sent him to the yeshiva, a Jewish institution which focusses on the study of religious texts, though he has confessed that he had never opened a Bible or attended a synagogue, nor could he speak Hebrew. His fellow pupils were Sephardic Jews (Jews from the Mediterranean area), children of rabbis and for the most part well off. His father's business, in the Bronx, having not done well, his store having been robbed seventeen times in its first year, leading to him becoming bankrupt, he was on financial aid and aware, as were his fellow pupils, that his clothes did not match theirs. His consciousness of the value placed on wealth and material goods would later be satirized in *Stunning* in which he would return to this world in a comedy which edges towards the tragic. He did not fit in, even being suspended for eating non-kosher food, though he committed other offences.

He later recalled that 'there was an enormous amount of racism in my immediate family, and at school. There was one girl who was African American in the yeshiva … she didn't last very long. If you were Sephardic, you thought you were better, you had nicer clothes.' His fellow pupils were essentially trying to dream the American dream even as they kept a distance from a country which offered to accommodate them at the price of assimilation. The school, though, was also 'incredibly homophobic. It's really hard when there are no models for it. The only gay Sephardic Jew was I guess Isaac Mizrahi [a fashion designer] … a Syrian Jew who also went to yeshiva of Flatbush. And he dropped out.'

Having started out in Honours classes, 'by the time I left I was in the dumb class. It was … horrible. And eventually I just left. I dropped out of school my junior year.' He was an outsider even among outsiders. As he explained, when he was in high school,

> I thought, I can just fix it; I was seeing a therapist who was like, 'You can fix yourself.' So, I [thought] okay, I'll just do it, I'll move to Ocean Parkway, I'll work in an electronic

shop, I'll have kids and somehow just make it work. Until it was like, it's not going to happen … I always felt so invisible and just not part of the discourse.⁶

His family were not happy with the fact that he was gay, were, indeed, not happy with one another, his father leaving home only later, equally mysteriously, to return, at least for a while, still with a fondness for vodka, subsequently re-discovering a religion he had never really discovered in the first place, encouraging his son to follow suit, whose bar mitzvah had originally seemed no more than a kind of ritual theatre. His religious period was short as was his attempt at relationships with girls, beginning to feel, if not yet acknowledge, that he was more attracted to boys. Later, his therapist 'tried to do a conversion on me to make me into a bisexual and get married off. That didn't work, but I tried, I tried.' It was 'like some gigantic sedimentary rock I carry, like some of the trauma of that'.⁷ As a measure of that trauma, he would later consult a psychic healer at $150 for twenty minutes. It was as though he were suffering from a disease and seeking a cure, though from what exactly? Peace of mind has seldom come cheap in America, though in his case it seemed beneficial.

As he has explained, 'I felt Other within the Other … I felt my sense of alterity very excruciatingly. I am a gay, eccentric, arty person. In the world in general, I feel weird. But in this community – which has a very specific set of codes, values, and structure – I felt suffocated.'⁸ An edict by rabbis in the Syrian-Jewish community, he told Felicia R. Lee in *The New York Times*, banned intermarriage with non-Jews even if the non-Jews converted, a process which they regarded as 'fictitious and valueless'.⁹

Threatened with expulsion, he pre-empted those who had sought to prescribe his behaviour, clothes, convictions, feeling that 'They'd devised a reality for me to step into, but I could just as easily step out of it. I could build a new reality. I could make it anything I wanted.' His feelings of exile were 'transmuted into freedom'.¹⁰ It is tempting to feel that that is what he would subsequently do, not least in creating fictions, plays, which would indeed constitute a new reality.

For all his Jewish background, *Stunning* aside, he explained that 'I mainly write about WASPS' though, 'ultimately, I write about people who are outsiders and then impersonate insiders' as he himself had done at yeshiva. For him, playwrights were outsiders almost by definition. In his case, though, there were other reasons for his sense if not of alienation then of marginalization, and whatever the subject of his plays might be he never strays far from his own experiences. As he has said, while other writers choose to invent, 'I'm working through things in my plays, and I can't really write things unless I have a very, very deep, molecular connection to the material.'¹¹ He grew up largely surrounded by women – his mother, sisters, and cousins – and that is reflected in his plays. It was his mother who introduced him to theatre and art, he later recalling a production of *Sweeney Todd* which left him shaken but suddenly aware of what drama could do.

From the yeshiva he moved uptown and upmarket, going to the private York Prep then on East 85th Street, with its British headmaster who had founded it. Adjmi prepared by teaching himself more acceptable pronunciations than had passed in Brooklyn. He was now able to take courses not available at Jewish schools, including on drama, taught by an actress, the first text he studied being *A Streetcar Named Desire*, Blanche appealing to him because she was 'like me, sensitive and poetic and desperate to re-create herself … she was like me, an outsider, a sensitive person crushed by reality'.¹² His recreation even took the form of adopting a French accent when, for a while, he worked at an expensive clothing store, as he did a Southern one when challenged for smoking on the subway while wearing an expensive cowboy hat. As he explained, 'I became a different person ... The self was an endless burden, like a giant piece of luggage you were forced to haul around. But what if there was a way to remove the burden? What if you could just erase the self you had, as though it were a drawing in pencil, and start over?' (175)

After school, he enrolled at the University of Southern California to study film where his reinvention seemed to be in the direction of being as masculine as the fraternity boy-men he encountered, along with those who surfed on drink, drugs, and pornography: 'I ceded my wants and desires for everyone around me so I could be part of life', (190) though it was here he had his first homosexual encounter.

He then transferred to Sarah Lawrence, in Westchester County, New York, deciding that he wanted to be 'a serious person', having found it difficult to see himself in the regular glare of the California sun. It was at Sarah Lawrence that he finally came out as gay. He majored in philosophy, learning that, for Nietzsche, the self was 'an audacious forgery'. On a visit to New York, he saw John Guare's *Six Degrees of Separation* recognizing something of himself in the protagonist, a man masquerading as who he was not, so upset that, in tears, he stayed in the theatre when others had left, suddenly aware of the power of theatre to talk directly to him. It was crucial in his decision to be a playwright, just as it was a new psychoanalyst who rejected the notion that he could be 'cured' of homosexuality by becoming bisexual. Because of this he felt 'able to heal'. (258)

It was, though, a philosophy teacher who told him that if he had ambitions to be a playwright then he should begin immediately. He graduated in 1996, in 2002 beginning three years studying for an MFA in the Playwrights Workshop at the University of Iowa, while there writing two comedies, *Doppelgangbang* and *Woody Allen's Fall Project*. At the same time, his account of other budding playwrights had a certain irony about it, one writing a play (clearly based on Adjmi) about a gay Jew eaten by a mountain lion, while another 'wrote Afro-womanist collages patterned on the work of Ntozake Shange, and always cast Kendra (the only black woman on the program) as "Witchgrass" or "Calendula" or something you could get at an apothecary.' It seemed to him that all of them were 'psychodevelopmentally falling apart', having suffered a variety of traumas (296). He himself consulted the most recent in a long line of analysts. Whether because of that or not, after failing to write anything, he felt suddenly inspired submitting the resulting play minutes before the deadline, to his surprise finding it selected for a full production. To his equal surprise, it was well received.

At Iowa, beyond the full-time faculty, he was exposed to visiting writers, including Athol Fugard, but it was the workshop format that he found particularly valuable. While there, he wrote *Strange Attractors*, in its form, he explained, based on Ibsen's *A Doll's House* though contemporary in its concern with sexual transgressions, his turn to Ibsen a desperate throw of the dice when he found himself stuck. At its centre is the figure of Betsy, scarcely an intellectual, with a fondness for shopping, married to an MTV executive, and with a liking for sado-masochistic sex. 'I'm not a provocateur,' Adjmi insisted, 'but I do need to clear space for the possibility of pissing people off. Once I know I can piss people off with impunity, I know I'll be able to say what I have to say.'[13]

Following a series of readings and workshops, it opened at the Empty Space Theatre in Seattle in 2002. It was this that would lead the Royal Court Theatre to offer him an international playwright residency. There he was asked to write a short play for their human rights festival which they called 'Letters from America', not something he felt ready to undertake. In a state of panic, until then having had a torrid time at the Julliard as part of the Julliard Playwrights Programme (which had produced David Auburn and David Lindsay-Abaire whom he had known at Sarah Lawrence), where what was to have been his first class coincided with the attack on the Twin Towers, he came up with some 350 pages, which hardly qualified for the word 'short'. Buried within it, though, was a woman who would become Alice and the makings of what would become a monologue, *Elective Affinities*, which received a staged reading at the Royal Court in 2002 and a production by the Royal Shakespeare Company in 2005, the latter part of a double bill (with Brett Neveu's *Eric LaRue*) under the title *Postcards from America*. He was dismissed from the Julliard because, a letter explained, he had been unresponsive to their teaching style. It stalled him for two years.

He had, however, won a prize and used the money to live in Berlin, where he not only watched plays at the Volksbuhne but studied German plays, explaining that 'I love the German Romantics because they have an innate understanding of the fracturedness of human feeling and intellect. The tones are constantly shifting – like Rubato [speeding up and slowing down rhythm at will] in music. The plays are tempestuous and precarious and unstable, you don't know where they're going from moment to moment.'[14] It was an education that would explain elements of his work. On his return, he founded a theatre company called the Vinegar Tom Players, commissioning a group of playwrights to come up with a play inspired by a German *Sturm und Drang* text feeling that what was missing from the American theatre was a sense of primal energies. By way of payment, he told Heidi Schreck, he offered them a pie of their choice.[15]

In 1809, Goethe published a novel called *Elective Affinities*. It proposed the impact on an aristocratic couple's marriage of being exposed to the presence of others, drawing a parallel to chemical reactions (in *Arcadia*, Tom Stoppard updated it, relating relationships to the second law of thermodynamics). Perhaps there is a nod to Goethe in Adjmi's play in so far as Alice's husband is German, his and her name being Hauptmann. It is closer in spirit, though, to Robert Browning's monologues, particularly 'My Late Duchess' in which the speaker slowly and unconsciously reveals aspects of his character. The printed text of *Elective Affinities* is barely eleven pages long, but then 'My Late Duchess' runs to only forty-six lines. Both, though, manage, by indirection, to create a portrait in which the narrator is oblivious to what he or she has revealed.

Alice lives in an opulent home and greets an implied visitor required to do nothing but listen. She exudes an air of entitlement. When it was finally staged in New York in 2011, it was presented not in a theatre but initially on the second floor of an elegant Fifth Avenue town house on the Upper East Side, in a room dominated by a large black sculpture, before the audience was summoned to an upper floor. They had all received special invitations saying, 'Mrs Alice Hauptmann would like to extend her cordial invitation to an informal gathering hosted at her home. Fine teas will be brewed, and sandwiches and lady fingers enjoyed.'

As the audience, restricted to thirty in its New York premiere, waited for their hostess to arrive, they were treated to a pianist playing Chopin before ultimately being greeted, with a calculated hauteur, by a woman coldly assured, any sense of familiarity to be quickly dispelled. She was, after all, there to speak to those permitted, on sufferance, to glimpse a world surely distant from their own, and not to engage with them. Propinquity only served to underline a social distance to be preserved, along with the presumption of a social code to be respected even as cracks in her assurance slowly become apparent, her room a kind of prison even as she asserts that it is the focus of culture and a social hierarchy. Her love of art, it transpires, is a love of what it represents, not least the wealth which enables her to purchase it and the taste which it embodies. The world is as she asserts it to be, morality itself at her behest. Hers is an imperial self in a country which itself has an imperial conviction that its values have primacy. There were only twelve performances, Zoe Caldwell, who doubted she could remember the lines, reading from the script.

It is a monologue not simply in terms of a theatrical convention but because she requires no reply as she reveals her prejudices, free associates, contradicts herself, exposes her insecurities. She plainly needs an audience otherwise seemingly marooned in a place where taste predominates over other values, albeit not a taste shared by her husband who, like the father in Tennessee Williams's *The Glass Menagerie*, has fallen in love with long distance. He travels a lot, she says. Their only trip together had been to Disney World, clearly at odds with her cultural presumptions. Otherwise, we learn, he is 'cross' with her, 'furious', and regards her as 'monstrous'. There is, in other words, a reason this is a monologue. Her husband's absence is a presence in the play. Nor, we learn, is he the only one she alienates.

She seems 'almost of another era', her world seemingly hermetic. Certainly, she has not travelled, her knowledge of other cultures deriving from visits to museums where everything is suitably contained, aesthetic rather than social. She has installed a piece of sculpture of a kind that leads her husband to storm out, not least because she wishes it to be '*big* because the *world* is big, and I want to see that bigness in the confines of this *one* room in this *one* house'. (269) The truth would seem to be, though, that for her the room is her world. As she says, 'I prefer to stay where I am and have the world come to me. It's very arrogant I know; I'm *terrible*.' Just how terrible, and in which way, slowly becomes apparent.

She is, a stage direction suggests, 'very charming', though her charm, it emerges, does not extend to her views, her generosity seemingly restricted to the expensive chocolates on view. Her damaged relationship with her husband she puts down to the fact that 'everyone is so cross around me, but people are just peevish these days'. (271) Why they might be cross gradually becomes apparent. Her account of watching nature programmes on television, in which gazelles and other 'animals eat each other alive … with tendons coming apart, and blood and gore', (270) suggests something of her own predatory views, favouring the torturing of prisoners while declaring 'who wants to use torture? *No One*, that's who. *Nobody* does, it's *unpleasant* … I was merely stating that … the FBI could, should and *would* use it.' (271) One of her defining characteristics is not to be aware of her own contradictions, or not to care.

At the same time, she sees herself as a victim. She and her husband had wanted children but were unable to: 'I surrendered. I accepted my fate … like one of those gazelles … when they're captured by some predator … they just sort of tilt their heads back … like this … I was like one of those gazelles.' Even so, she says, popping a chocolate into her mouth, she has had 'a very nice life … I mean I *feel* happy. I've always considered myself a happy person. I've always *been* happy.' Qualification follows qualification, as for evidence she invokes tea drinking which makes her feel 'edified *spiritually*'. (273) The italicized words, strung together, are telling: *terrible, No One, Nobody, unpleasant, would, feel, been, spiritually*. These are the words she emphasizes. 'I've managed to find spiritual fulfilment in material *things*', she declares, seemingly without irony.

The passage about the gazelle, Adjmi has confessed, came directly from something one of his teachers at the Julliard had said, he being anxious to ingratiate himself with someone who until then had been hostile. Beyond that 'Alice was a self-portrait ... in some respect, I was writing a cautionary tale to myself. I was that gazelle, who would sacrifice what was fragile and beautiful in itself because it believed it was doomed and wanted its struggle to be over.'[16]

Adopting the voice of her friend, Deirdre, she presents her as asking whether it is right 'to violate certain ideals with the intention of upholding those ideals, I mean do you really think that's OK?' only to reply, in her own voice, 'if you want to live in a civilized society, then I guess it *has* to be OK', (275) explaining that she could never torture Deidre because she loves her or, rather, 'I prefer you to other people', this being precisely what Goethe explored in *Elective Affinities*. For her, the whole discourse of human rights 'is sort of a joke ... as if *all* human beings have some innate value' while in fact, '... nature is very cruel. Nature confers no rights'. (276)

Something has happened, supposedly a terrorist attack, which has provoked the conversation, but while others are grief stricken, lacking the language with which to express their feelings, she insists that 'I *do* have the language ... Eliminate them ... Kill them, kill every last one' (278) as Conrad's Kurt in *The Heart of Darkness* had called out 'exterminate all the brutes', and, interestingly, when Frances Ford Coppola finished *Apocalypse Now*, based on *The Heart of Darkness*, and with his marriage in a state of collapse, he planned to make a series of four films based on Goethe's *Elective Affinities*. Alice, by now, '*trancelike, almost evangelical*', continues, 'Kill every living thing, so nothing remains, *nothing*, nothing, kill *every*thing, kill *everyone*, then sow the earth with *salt* ... so nothing grows there *ever* again.' (278)

After a short pause, however, she smiles brightly and momentarily returns to the topic of marriage recalling that her mother had told her that intimate relationships benefit from the presence of a third person, territory also explored by Goethe. Somehow the conviction that love is 'double sided' leads her to declare that foreigners, political prisoners and terrorists, 'have value ... not innate value but the value I assign them', this echoing the relationship she has with those she purports to love. Her indifference to others, she suggests, is what makes her partial to those she assumes to be close to her, the elective affinities of the title, except by this time it is clear that for her no one has value beyond that which she is prepared to assign them.

Behind the bland civility, the teacups and chocolate, the fine art and chatter of museums, is not so much indifference, though, as contempt hence her ready sanctioning of cruelty. The world does, indeed, only seem to render up meaning as refracted through Alice's warped sensibility. She is her own artwork, akin to the menacing sculpture she commissioned which is 'a little terrifying'. (269) She has shaped herself to her own requirements, vaguely registering the hostility she generates, the relationships which in the end mean little to her, other people being no more than satellites circling her undaunted narcissism. The monologue is her natural form since she requires no intervention, no contradiction. With no children, an absent husband and supposed friends who exist only to be parodied or defeated in her mind, she stands in an isolation which is moral no less than physical.

Beyond her, however, surely lie those others prepared to sanction torture, secure in their own certainties, whose awareness of the world beyond is a product not of knowledge but of images. Outside the confines of this elegant house lies a complexity to be rendered simple by a rhetoric which is hermetic and self-justifying. Beyond America is a world to be symbolized by the 'black, hulking ... *mass*' (269) of the statue, designed as a homogeneous representation of what cannot be acknowledged in its particularities, George W. Bush's War on Terror being a battle against an abstract noun. The dark humour of *Elective Affinities* is generated by Alice's lack of self-knowledge, her casual contradictions, her misplaced confidence in herself as slowly, layer by layer, her performances are stripped away finally leaving nothing but a lonely woman unwilling to accept the depth of her isolation or the profundity of her failures. She seems the epitome of the American dream, at least in so far as she does indeed find spiritual fulfilment in things, even as her pursuit of happiness has led her to a spiritual cul de sac, happiness, ultimately, being a concept, which evades her.

She is, in fact, not truly 'of another era', except in her belief that manners are a virtue, form trumping substance. Her views are disturbingly congruent with those then being deployed by a president, and those who surrounded him, for whom torture was declared legal and whose view of a threatening world beyond the confines of a nation confident in its supremacy was one of unconsidered violence. Her Darwinian view of the world, in which the strong prevail, and those who have attained status stand justified, is echoed by those determining national policy. The achievement of *Elective Affinities* lies in the fact that what prevails in 'this *one* room in this *one* house' (269) also does so in the society of which it becomes a symbol. Adjmi has said that his plays 'aren't black comedies' even as he explains that

> comedy deepens and expands the dark elements, but the two elements – farce and tragedy – are both there and have equal presence ... I think people in general are broken, atomised ... We don't know how to listen to what's actually going on with us, we're not taught how to experience ourselves, that's why we end up inflicting so much harm on people.[17]

Alice clearly inflicts pain, does not listen, has no understanding of herself or others.

For Adjmi, *Elective Affinities* is 'about a woman confronting certain choices that she's made, certain relationships that she's had at the end of her life. And, I guess, realising that what she thought was real isn't real and she doesn't always know how to defend it.'[18] Brief though it was, it prompted an enthusiastic review from the *New York Times*, Ben Brantley praising its 'flirtatious artistry'[19] while *Time Out*'s David Cote noted its 'eloquent, perverse core of coolly rationalized cruelty'.[20] For John Heilpern, in *The New York Observer*, it was a 'brilliant monologue'.[21] It might be thought that responses were initially to the fact that the monologue was delivered by four-time Tony Award winner Zoe Caldwell, but when the part was played by the equally accomplished Marian Seldes (who was to die three years later of Alzheimer's) responses were equally enthusiastic, Seldes's work with Edward Albee, particularly in *Three Tall Women*, perhaps being useful preparation for Adjmi's play.

New York, of course, was seeing his play out of sequence, six years after its Royal Shakespeare opening. With *The Evildoers* (Yale Rep, 2008) he was back in the world of the privileged, one of two married couples living on the Upper East Side, the other relegated to the country. They drive a Hummer, eat in the best restaurants, buy only the finest food, preferably with a French name, use only the finest luggage, stay at the best hotels, discuss marriage, love and friendship, usually with a glass or two to hand, though with an undertone of anxiety about their lives. They attend classical concerts, are familiar with literature and theories of the self, if not quite sure what might constitute their own selves. They throw ideas around, are articulate even as their articulacy can desert them finding it difficult to hold ideas in their mind for long or using language less to communicate than to avoid the intimacy they claim. Words, as a character observes, 'can do violence'.²² So they do. Sometimes they slice with the precision of a scalpel, at others they are blunt weapons, calculated to do damage.

These are characters who appear secure. They are achievers, even if they are unsure what those achievements might amount to. Everything, it seems, is in place, relationships reassuringly assumed, sustained over time, except there is an undercurrent of uncertainty, insecurity. Assurances are challenged, sudden doubts obtrude. They look for faith, aware that something is absent from their lives, conscious of a void which they hesitate to inhabit or even identify. On the surface all seems what it has ever been, though largely because they have not chosen to examine relationships, beliefs, which they assumed rather than interrogated. Now, however, a crisis is precipitated, sudden changes threaten their sense of an equanimity which has anyway been contingent, a product of habit as much as conviction. A rug is pulled from under them. They invade one another's territory as they had not before. Even their own identities prove insecure, all being of an age when questions are asked if never quite in expectation that they will or could be answered. Betrayal, desertion, false epiphanies interrupt what had anyway been a steady progression down a path to no certain destination.

The printed version begins with more than three pages of introductory material in which Adjmi offers unusually elaborate descriptions of the characters and the style of presentation which, as he says, undergoes 'rather tortuous shifts'.²³ Jerry Thernstrom, he explains, 'possesses the old-world affectations and speech of an older WASP-y type, as well as the glow of narcissism and self-containment that is specific to New York psychoanalysis', a subject on which he had a certain expertise having undergone various therapies as a result of being in what he has called 'dark places'. Jerry's wife, Carol, is a 'wedding planner who is intensely cynical about marriage. She is quick-witted, fashionable, controlling, meticulous (i.e., *compulsive*), self-conscious, literate, and wears all this kind of breast-plate or armor.'

Jerry's best friend from school, Martin, an anaesthesiologist, while having warmth and an apparent openness, is '*Intensely* emotional' developing 'a deep, agonizing, insatiable longing' throughout the course of the play, as well as 'a profound – and finally *pathological* need to connect to people, to himself, to something authentic and rooted'. His wife, Judy, is 'fragile, under-confident and somewhat neurotic', as she 'works to conceal her obsessiveness and neuroses ... Her respect for decorum is a default.' (145–6)

It is interesting that he should feel the need to spell out what becomes clear as the play unfolds. The paradox is that he gives depth to those who in many ways lack it, none of them being really rooted, performing roles as if they are, indeed, coterminous with those roles. There is a degree of cynicism in a psychiatrist who says he does no more than hold a mirror to people, while charging a high price as evidence of authenticity, or a marriage planner who does not believe in marriage, her own having fractured in a way not acknowledged. There is an absence at their centre as, it seems, there is in the society of which they are a part and in which they seem paradigms of achievement. As in *Who's Afraid of Virginia Woolf?* they are walking what's left of their wits, their very articulacy deployed as a fencing foil, or to facilitate evasion. As Adjmi has said, in '*The Evildoers* ... the quest for integrity and self-understanding leads to ... awful isolation and ... even insanity'. The characters are 'lost inside their roles', while 'this sense of falseness is so-deep-veined it cannot be shaken, and the more deeply Jerry and Martin try to discover themselves in their quest for "authenticity," the more lost they get.'²⁴ Beyond them lies a society about the same business, declaring an integrity easily compromised.

The play begins in a restaurant where the four are gathered to celebrate Jerry and Carol's anniversary. They are guests of their friends, Martin and Judy, even as friendship proves no more meaningful than marriage. By this stage, they have all had a deal to drink, their conversation rapid-fired if disjointed, non-sequiturs underlining the degree to which they are each following the logic, or illogic, of their own thoughts or discrete emotional states. The alcohol has evidently removed their inhibitions, as in Albee's play, and a certain hostility has invaded dinner table chatter. Not unnaturally, marriage is one topic, but it quickly becomes apparent that this is nothing to celebrate. Carol, who persistently refuses her husband's attempt to fill her glass, offer her food, or kiss her hand, in the face of Martin's assertion that for most people marriage is sacred, insists that 'For "most people" a marriage licence has all the stature of a *parking* ticket … it means *nothing* … nobody gives a *shit*.' (157) When he challenges her, she reminds him that he is an anaesthetist, as if that were an equivalent.

Nonetheless, she sees her own class as in some sense a defence against the vulgarity, the middlebrow tastes and moral decay of America even as she rejects what seems to her to be a fashionable apocalyptic vision: 'WE hold it up – "we" being the intelligentsia, the cultured elite, progressive thinkers! … we're like *barges*: and we're holding up these big pyramids of *garbage*' but 'one day the garbage started to *multiply* … and now we're all just SINKING. But sinking can go on for a long time, we can go on like this in*definitely*.' (161) These, then, with their collapsing marriages, broken friendships, coruscating contempt, are the last defence against the incipient anarchy which otherwise they seem to exemplify.

Jerry, equally, diagnoses what he calls the 'WHOLE PROBLEM', namely that 'people don't want to *know* each other' because 'people aren't *authentic* … they're all circling this – terrible abyss of uh uh pain'. Like Carol, he sees themselves as representing a defence even as their relationships are infected with the same gravitational pull towards the void, his language having a reflexive circularity: 'it's *our* job to get *inside* of that … because … if we can't *enter* people's suffering then *we* suffer. Because we're disconnected from their lives: and *their* lives *are* our lives – but we don't want to see that. And then we *inflict* suffering!' But then, he confesses, 'What can *any* of us do I don't *know* I just keep *con*jugating the problem.' (164) Carol is not wrong in calling this '*bullshit*', even though she is herself fluent in that language.

Judy, like Honey, in *Who's Afraid of Virginia Woolf?* is timid, anxious to deflect disturbing truths, easily crushed. In the face of Carol's cynicism, she has no defence beyond an artificial smile. She and Martin have moved to the country for reasons yet unspecified, but it is apparent that this move has not been a success.

This discordant quartet expose an essential loneliness at the heart of each of them. Marriage, friendship, are terms hollowed out by experience as Tom Lehrer, in his ironically titled song 'Bright College Days', spoke of sliding down the razor blade of life, not so irrelevant given that Jerry and Martin will later reminisce about their school days. Theirs is a pain transmuted into aggression. Self-doubt becomes assertion, even as their interventions in the conversation wander aimlessly, half-formed theories, ten cent philosophies, intercut with personal abuse, self-revelation. Their future, it seems, lies behind them.

As the scene edges towards its conclusion Martin turns on Judy, with a sudden outburst of bitterness which leaves her shaking and hysterical: 'you think I'm going to hit you? Maybe I should – because it's what you want … being that we're all in *love* and we're *married* and we're little strumming *lovebirds*, with honey just *dripping* of our beaks, RIGHT?' (168) As Judy stutters out a response, however, there is a radical stylistic shift as, to the accompaniment of sudden loud music, the space begins to transform. The title of the play is displayed, and Adjmi indicates that '*the chaos of the argument is parlayed into the transition*', as Jerry and Carol change into night clothes and Martin is seen pouring a bucket of champagne over his head to simulate the rain from which he will shortly appear as, two weeks later, at three in the morning, he arrives at Jerry and Carol's apartment. The music stops, replaced by the sound of a speeding train. The seams of the play are starting to pull apart, mirroring the lives of those at its centre.

Having left Judy, Martin has discovered that he is gay striking up a relationship with a man on the subway, himself a married man. It leaves him with a feeling of release but also guilt and a sense of pain at abandoning his wife. A drunken Jerry seeks to console him with an increasingly absurd attempt to suggest that suffering is itself a tonic, desperately reaching for metaphors, invoking babushkas and quarks, until his efforts collapse as he himself loses touch with what he is saying even as Martin suddenly kisses him. The first act ends as the sound of a train and whistle recurs until it is '*unbearably loud*'.

The second act begins in Judy and Martin's home in Fleetwood, Pennsylvania, a small country town. Their belongings are, for the most part, still in boxes. Carol is on hand seemingly to console Judy who has been in hospital and whose reading runs to *Brave New World*, along with accounts of mass killings. The daughter of abusive parents, she has been told by her doctor to pretend that one of them at least had been good. For her part, Carol barely seems to listen, insisting that mothers naturally love their children except those who drown them, as detached from Judy's suffering as she appears to be from her own life, except that there comes a moment, back in her home, when she loses the baby she has been carrying.

Meanwhile, Martin has become ever stranger, his mind a tumble dryer of random ideas as he tries to make sense of the vacancy in his own life which has led him down the path to his present confusions, making further sexual advances to Jerry. They both scream at each other, loud music cutting in '*as the style has tilted somewhat, gets manic, compressed*'. There is, Adjmi indicates, '*complete chaos*'. (223)

For his part, Jerry is left adrift, desperate for a reassurance which he wishes to call love. When, in their bedroom, following his disturbing encounter with Martin, he looks for a gesture of affection from Carol because 'You're my wife,' she replies, 'you don't have a *wife* you have a well-filled liquor cabinet. You have a DVD collection. You do not. Have. A wife.' (225) He declares love and demands it in return, before dropping to his knees and burying his face in her stomach, a gesture described in the stage directions as 'an act of grace', though in truth it is hard to see it as such.

Before he leaves, ejected by the couple who had taken him in, Martin declares that he has thrown Carol's ring, the ring which has featured throughout the play as a symbol of love, or love's frailty, into the East River. He is the T.S. Eliot character who enters to disrupt the lives of those he encounters, in his case, though, with villainous intent. Carol, it turns out, has lost her baby because he gave her apricots laced with a chemical which would provoke a miscarriage. This prophet of truth is a murderer who acts as he does because he believes suffering to be the key to understanding.

Carol, for all her disengagement from the life of others, slowly emerges not only as the most intelligent and articulate of the quartet but the one with the tightest grip on reality. When accused by the increasingly crazed Martin of having a faulty world view, she replies, 'What "world view" SANITY is not a fucking WORLD VIEW it's the fucking SUBSTRATE of human existence.' (235) Learning what he has done, she collapses in tears. For the only time in the play,

Adjmi indicates, '*possibly for the first time in her adult life – Carol cries, and her crying carries with it currents that eddy backward with the force of her entire history*', (237) a tough call for an actress.

What follows is a gothic touch as, in kissing her, he bites out her tongue, in expiation cutting off his own finger. She runs off, followed by Martin, before Jerry returns, oblivious to what has happened, only to sit and read a magazine whose headline reads: 'Salman Rushdie declares jihad on Harper Collins.' (240) Whatever may be happening in the outside world, however, would seem an extension of what happens in a play in which a suspect faith inspires violence.

The final act, set a few hours later, takes an even stranger turn, metaphors having become literal as things fall apart in what seems a more general apocalypse. Judy's house having burned down, she takes refuge with Jerry, both unaware of what has happened. She is described, perhaps understandably, as looking like Elsa Lanchester in *The Bride of Frankenstein*, who played both Mary Shelley and the Monster's mate, Judy being a mate, though now divorced from a man who has transformed into a monster. Jerry is now detached from reality, even the discovery of an abandoned tongue failing to register as does news of Carol's death, she having meanwhile thrown herself into the river. When Martin fails to rescue her, he returns to the apartment and kills himself with a knife.

Time, Adjmi explains, '*starts to warp, slow down*', and '*the world breaks open*'. A scream '*comes, faraway, hollow, distant*' before getting '*louder, higher*' reduplicating with '*multiple tracks*'. Beyond the window, the rain which has fallen throughout has created a flood as both Martin and Carol come back to life. Adjmi is hardly wrong when he refers to an '*impossible reality*', as Jerry reads from the Bible lines from *Corinthians* referring to the end of the world when the dead will arise, and all will be changed. Indeed, Judy now appears, wearing a wedding dress, '*the Ideal Judy*'. 'This all,' we are told in a stage direction, 'has the tenor of a dream ... The walls start to shake' as Carol returns from her river death having '*developed the tragic, shattered nobility of someone who's been stripped of all vestments of civilization*' even as a '*disconsolate sadness*' is exposed while Jerry utters '*a garbled, fevered prayer*'. (262–4)

What begins with a search for identity and authenticity leads to the collapse of both, the play's structure and style reflecting that. Beneath the civilities, themselves barely sustained, is a whirlpool of banalities presented as philosophical positions. The various shocks delivered at intervals – a sudden conversion to homosexuality, a severed tongue, off-stage and on-stage deaths – seem to be designed as adrenaline injections increasing momentum towards an apocalypse. Even the structure implicit in plot is abandoned. Language disintegrates, Jerry reduced from an articulate person to a stuttering wreck oblivious to the disasters which play out before him, ending with a smile at odds with the collapse of all form.

What had appeared to be one kind of play turns into another. It is a difficult trick to pull off, the elaborate stage directions offering a critical commentary as the play devolves into a kind of synesthesia of effects. There are colour changes, surface brightness dulling, while sound is amplified as character is pressed to extremes. He wrote the play while living in Germany, and it is not hard to feel the influence of Sturm und Drang (storm and stress), which originally derived from a play of that name by Friedrich Maximillian Klinger set during the American Revolution concerned with emotion and subjectivity as opposed to rationalism, and with ideas of structure subordinated. Here, in *The Evil Doers*, is another American Revolution, the play's title seemingly deriving from George W. Bush's determination, five days after 9/11, to rid the world of evil doers, goodness presumed to nestle at the heart of America even as it was being subverted by his immediate actions.

Sturm and Drang is concerned with shocking audiences and provoking emotional responses. Much the same could be said of *The Evil Doers*. It made reviewers understandably uneasy, on solid ground when considering the first part of the play but unsure as it departed from familiar territory. What, after all, are we to make of the dead rising, of discarded tongues, characters who are deconstructed, sound underscoring an increasing hysteria? Ironically, at a time when America was supposedly finding common ground against an external enemy, Adjmi was staging a society imploding of its own self-regard, a vacuous attachment to style, spiritually adrift, self-consuming. Jerry's smile as his world collapses becomes emblematic, the pursuit of happiness ending in a rictus grin.

For the most part reviewers found themselves limping in some laps behind, perhaps not surprisingly having difficulty in accepting, or even referring to, a sudden stylistic shift perhaps with faint echoes of Susan Glaspell's *The Verge* or grand Guignol. Charles Isherwood, in *The New York Times*, while granting that Adjmi was 'certainly skilled at writing dialogue that both captures and softly lampoons the fluid eloquence and showy wit that poisons the air at Manhattan restaurants and dining rooms' seeking to 'drive home the point that the country's privileged classes have been chattering away about thread counts while Rome burns', thought that as the play progressed 'its mixture of high ambitions and lurid details begins to curdle', and that 'his quasi-apocalyptic, quasi-mystical and wholly grotesque analysis of the national malaise lacks both subtlety and sense'.[25] For Frank Rizzo, in *Variety*, it was 'Adjmi's anxiety attack of a play', in which, he jokingly remarks, the playwright 'bites off more than he can chew'.[26] Adjmi, though, saw himself as committed to exploring a form of theatre which could incorporate startling images, disorient by stylistic shifts. As he remarked, 'I feel like my generation is assimilating methods from performance companies of the 1970s and '80s like Richard Foreman and the Wooster Group.'[27] That same year there was a workshop production of *Caligula* at the Soho Rep, a play which he now considers unfinished, never sorting it out to his own satisfaction and which he consequently is not considering for publication.[28]

With *Stunning*, which he wrote three years after leaving the Julliard, Adjmi turned away from the world of WASPS, though not from the wealthy, to his own community with a play which took him five years to write. He had begun it, as he had others, including *The Evil Doers*, back in Berlin, in the aftermath of 9/11. As he has explained, 'This is a play about my background ... It is terrifyingly – and sometimes ludicrously – autobiographical. It is about where I come from and about a community – Syrian/Sephardic/American/Jewish/whatever – that is truly marginalized and not really represented in the mainstream media or otherwise.'[29] Indeed he doubted that anyone would be interested in a play focussing on such a small and specific community. 'I thought,' he confessed, that he might only be able 'to put this on at my mum's house with flashlights ... I did it as a caprice, a joke.'[30]

It is, indeed, set in his home territory of Ocean Parkway in the Midwood area of Brooklyn, one scene precisely located at number 929, in fact the address of a childhood friend. As he points out in describing this setting, it is 'a very affluent, largely Jewish area'. It features, at its heart, the newly married sixteen-year-old Lily Schwecky, a Syrian Jew, admittedly unsure of that identity, a drop-out from yeshiva, and her maid, Blanche, who claims to be a graduate of Brown University. The characters are conflicted, their contradictions laid out in Adjmi's descriptions of them in which the word 'but' recurs. Thus, Lily's mind works quickly, '*but* her thoughts are incredibly scattered'. She is a follower, '*but* it's more out of a need for connectedness than an innate passivity'. Blanche is damaged '*but* maintains a great sense of irony and dry humor'. Lily's husband, Ike, is controlling, brute and bumptious, '*but* there's something fragile in him, broken'. Lily's older sister, Shelly, has a 'stentorian quality, *but* naturalizes this by cultivating "girl" preoccupations'. Her husband, Jojo, is basically 'a good guy *but* limited'[31] (my italics).

In an interview with *The New York Times*, he explained something of that dualism. 'I think,' he said, 'on one level, it's about people who rely on this bulwark of appearance. They try to create this hard wall of surface to suffice for their wounds – personal wounds, cultural wounds, historical wounds. It's like an Edith Wharton novel about the repressive forces of culture and how we internalize that stuff and how it erases us from ourselves.'[32] In truth, it is more like a Tennessee Williams' play, a fact which becomes evident in the final act. Indeed, what could be more Williams-like than his description of the play as 'asking for empathy for people who are wounded', a play in which 'power supplants love' and characters 'can't make themselves vulnerable for various reasons: family, politics, race, sex'.[33]

As with *The Evil Doers*, this is a play with a mixture of styles and tones which are, he says, to be 'deliberate *and drastic*'.[34] And, indeed, they are. Where that play had started with an Albee-like confrontation, *Stunning* begins as what seems a frothy comedy as Lily, her sister Shelly, and Claudine, play cards, all dressed similarly in a community which he describes as characterized by its provincialism and insularity, their clothes an indicator of their wealth. Colour is drained from a set which is scattered with mirrors reflecting not only those who look in them but, beyond that 'the themes of illusion, imitation, deception', (6) to which could be added reversal as transformations are affected and the play edges towards the tragic as its focus changes.

Their gossip may invoke divorce, a Down's syndrome baby, suicide, but it is interspersed with comments on chip dip, bracelets, the names of stores and face cream as if they were equivalents. These are people who have personal trainers, tennis coaches, take cooking lessons at the Ecole, have a French manicurist. The word 'stunning' is a catch-all, applied to appearance, a holiday, a house, a word therefore evacuated of meaning, an equivalent of awesome. Lily has just returned from her Caribbean holiday in Aruba, where her skin has darkened making her defensive about her appearance, in denial of her Syrian heritage and hence identity. Married at sixteen, she suddenly declares 'I miss Mommy and Daddy.' (19) This is the child who in the course of the play will grow up even as her new knowledge will eventually lead her to recognize her isolation, like Stella in *A Streetcar Named Desire* pregnant and married to a man given to sudden acts of violence, who has driven out another woman, deeply illusioned and destructive.

Lily's new house is decorated in several shades of white, with a paint pot in every room to maintain its whiteness, while bleach is to hand. It has a minimalism which, Adjmi observes, '*is that of the arid, philistine, nouveau riche*', though his instruction that a fishbowl should be inhabited by '*a lonely confused little goldfish swimming in circles*', (20) a metaphor for this hermetic social world, must have presented casting difficulties. The fish is called Kitty which Lilly claims derives from her reading of Anne Frank's diary, another example of her tendency to blend the frivolous with the serious.

Into this white world, in which Lily is determined to insist on her own whiteness, her appearance notwithstanding ('I tan easily'), comes the significantly named Blanche (significant both because of the meaning of the name and its reference to Blanche Dubois whose role in some ways she plays), though her clothes, in contrast to Lily's, are brightly coloured while she is African American. She is to be a maid, and is evidently in need of a sanctuary, though why is not immediately apparent. Lily is thrown by her race and colour having hoped for a Puerto Rican since she had been raised by one, in a sense never having escaped the nursery. However, to her surprise, Blanche turns out to be fluent in Spanish and thus acceptable provided she agrees to answer to the name of her childhood maid. Already, though, she has come up against a woman prepared to challenge her, particularly when it comes to her racial background. What matters to Lily is appearance, and not only in terms of her own background. As she says, 'when people come to my house I want things to appear a certain way … everything is white that's how I want things to be Stunning stunning *white*'. (26) Ironically, Arabic music cuts in as the scene ends.

Lily's sister Shelly, who becomes pregnant because it is 'nice being pregnant just to glow', (37) pleased that the foetus evidently has 'no disfigurement', is dismissive of Blanche, suddenly invoking the n word, Blanche freezing and Lily feeling deeply uncomfortable.

The radical change which comes about is that Blanche, who at forty-three is implausibly seeking a job as a teacher, becomes a teacher to sixteen-year-old Lily, introducing her to classical music, semiotics, wine appreciation, a world beyond that delineated by her Ocean Parkway home. More radically, she reveals herself as a lesbian and the two are drawn to one another, Lily being convinced that she is bi-sexual, the age gap mirroring that between Lily and Ike. Though her husband wants children, she takes birth control pills, aware that to become pregnant will be to be trapped in the world represented by her sister. Suddenly, she has a sense that there is a way out.

Meanwhile, Lily's husband Ike, older than her, insensitive, arrogant, steals money from the company founded by his brother-in-law even as Lilly plans to run away with Blanche who implies that she has a job offer from Northwestern University, that she graduated Phi Beta Kappa with a 3.94 GPA, and is personal friends with leading Black intellectuals. For the first time Lilly finds love, or believes she does, and there is something between them.

It is Blanche who claims that Lily does not know who she is and urges her not to 'let these people decide your life for you, don't be a victim! *You* make the decision, *you* do it.' When she adds, 'You could make yourself a whole other person', however, the stage direction indicates that she is '*very, very* vulnerable'. (59) Why? Because, we learn later, that is precisely what Blanche herself has done. Were her parents called White when her name is Blanche? Was she abused? Was she adopted when she was twelve? Did she later live in a homeless shelter? Why does she carry a gun? The last is a hint at what is eventually revealed, a lesson she has evidently learned, that

> the world's a dangerous *place* … you don't know what it's like. You can be hurt and *never* recover. You think you can end it but it don't end … You can walk out that door but you never really leave! You think you do – but you come back to the *same thing* again and again! You need to meet it head on.
>
> (109)

The lessons may be valid, but she is a false teacher, having constructed herself, burrowing down into this place, forging a relationship to her own advantage. She takes money from Lily claiming it is to pay off her student loan but when Lily believes the two can run off together, and tells her sister, Blanche insists that she must explain that this had been a joke, her entire history, we are told in a stage direction, suddenly catching up with her, though what that history really is, is not yet clear. Feeling betrayed, Lilly demands the money back, walking out leaving Blanche dismayed, herself now abandoned. She picks up a rag and begins to clean a mirror, spraying it with Windex. As she does so, Adjmi indicates, 'she catches her reflection in the mirror. She is transfixed by her own image. She stretches out her arm as if holding a gun. She sprays the Windex ... Sprays again. Again. Again, again, faster and faster as the liquid drips down the mirror and her face becomes a blur.' (15) Her constructed identity begins to dissolve.

The focus now shifts from Lily to Blanche, the final act being entitled *Para Los Muertos* (Flowers for the Dead), the street seller's cry in *A Streetcar Named Desire*, Ike now playing the role of Stanley Kowalski, Blanche effectively becoming Blanche Dubois. Where Stanley had thrown a radio out, Ike merely turns it off but, like Stanley, has been investigating her past, employing someone to do so. He flourishes a photograph of her father, who used to work in textiles but was ruined ('he had greatness in him,' he remarks, a reference to Willy Loman's description of Biff in *Death of a Salesman*). She had not, he has discovered, studied at Brown or any college: 'you act like you're so much better than me. You're not even *educated*.' (121) Her response, aimed at him, and true of him, is equally true of her, and a contradiction of the lesson she had offered to Lily, 'You thought you could be anything you wanted. Tried to make yourself a whole other person. Kicked screamed all you wanted. Din matter. It's the System. (*To herself*) You don't got a choice in it. Don matter what you do. Gonna crush you anyhow.' (121)

Blanche has tried to exist within her imagination. Black and gay, she is an outsider, a drifter hiding from her own failure but also from a past to which she can no longer relate. Beyond that, she is hiding from something else. The reason she has come to this all-white house, Ike now explains, is that she had tried to shoot her own father, stories of abuse perhaps being real. He attacks her, as Stanley did Blanche Dubois, in this case pushing her head into a can of white paint, a Black woman whose identity is thus erased even as Ike desperately declares, 'We *are* white, people of Spanish descent are *Caucasian*'. (122) Yet he is aware that on some level he has lost, Blanche having stirred more than an urge to knowledge in Lily. He looks in the mirror and sees a stranger staring back, aghast at what he has done, what he has become.

Blanche is now to be ejected from the house, Lily, pregnant, no longer avoiding commitment, settling for what she has, even as she realizes what is about to be lost to her. Blanche pays back some of the money she has accepted, confessing that it was not to pay off student debt but, more ominously, a loan from those who were threatening her. In a split scene, Lily and Ike count the money while Blanche spins off into a reverie, as her counterpart had in *Streetcar*. Ike seeks to re-establish a relationship with his wife, but she has a new-found autonomy indistinguishable from solitariness and his temper cuts across a real reconciliation. Lily and Blanche see a ghost invisible to others, in a house supposedly haunted. As the morning comes a car horn sounds as a cab arrives to take Blanche away but she is not led out on the arm of a doctor or nurse, having now lost touch with reality. She does not find the comfort of strangers having shot herself, seen lying on the floor in a pool of blood. There is no comfort for Lily either. She has been changed irrevocably. The car horn continues to sound as she goes upstairs to the man with whom she will continue to live but, like Stella, in *Streetcar*, now with knowledge that life cannot be the same, that the past lives on into the present, itself a ghost not to be exorcised.

It is hard to think of a more violent volte-face from light comedy to a tragic sense of life and in truth it is hard to accept such a sharp transition, as Lily goes from a teenage airhead, for whom life consists of surfaces and who barely has a grasp on the world, cocooned in the closed world of wealthy Sephardic Jews in denial of their identity, to a woman who has found new depths of knowledge and suffering, discovering love in the most unlikely place, though the gay love in this play, as in *The Evildoers,* does, as Adjmi has hinted, reflect something of his own experience.

The characters are deliberately set up as caricatures, albeit responsible for their own unquestioning acceptance of the values of their community, and this makes it more difficult to follow their journeys towards self-knowledge. It is Blanche, though, who emerges as the central figure, a confidence trickster (an echo of the protagonist of *Six Degrees of Separation*) intent above all to deceive herself, most alive when inventing her world. Her parading of knowledge is in part to ensnare Lily but also integral to the architecture of her fantasies. This is who she wishes to be, and who, at moments, perhaps she is. She is the Black maid, required to change her name to become acceptable, mocking her status, a storyteller with a moral purpose at the same time as her motives lack a moral core. That the lessons she offers serve to consolidate the identity she wishes to embrace does not invalidate the effect they have on Lilly the recipient of a knowledge which will, though, leave her with a sense of discontent and loss as she discovers and loses the love she sought.

In a sense these are characters lost to themselves but in search of themselves, except that Lilly's sister and friends represent what they are leaving behind. Blanche is a Black woman literally whitewashed, but Ike and Lilly pursue the same imperative, living in a white house with white paint to hand should any mark betray the truth, anxious to reject the suggestion that they are themselves anything but white.

Adjmi has said,

> I had written a play I believed was unproduceable. Not only did I skewer a community no one had ever heard of, but it was crazily stylized: it clashed together genres and tones in a way that was not exactly in vogue. It was bleak, it was harsh, and there was no redemption in it anywhere … I knew no artistic director in New York who would put on this sort of bleak, crazy play. It wasn't marketable, and the American theatre was driven by the desires of subscribers,

but that fact released him. 'The writing was intensely cathartic – I sobbed uncontrollably writing the end … I cried for my characters and my family and the whole brutal, broken world.' Despite his concerns, the play received readings by the New York Theatre Workshop and the Manhattan Theatre Club before a production at Lincoln Centre, where he had seen *Six Degrees of Separation* and where he had been dismissed from the Julliard. The production sold out and was extended, several times.

The play did not go well with many from his own community, those he called the Syrians, for whom he was Benedict Arnold, but reviewers praised much about the play while being uncertain about its change of direction, what was seen as a descent into melodrama. For *backstage*, 'By the time we reach the headshaking conclusion, it's hard to recognize the exhilarating voice that had spoken from the stage earlier in the evening.'[35] *Curtain Up* was concerned with what seemed a schizophrenic denouement. Jason Zinoman, in *The New York Times*, found the change of tone and style difficult while Hilton Als, in *The New Yorker*, had problems with the figure of Blanche. As with *The* Evildoers, Adjmi was intent to disrupt the expectations which he himself had raised, to deny what might have been the easy satisfactions to be derived from the fast-paced comedy with which *Stunning* begins, the play itself being concerned with fabricated identities, and this from a man who described his own as an experimental identity. *The Washington Post* chose it as one of its top ten plays of the year while it attracted full houses in its extended run at Lincoln Center.

In January 2014 David Adjmi found himself in the Southern District Court of New York defending a play that had been staged, in June 2012, by the 104-seat Rattlestick Playwrights Company in the West Village, but not since. He was suing a company which had sent a cease-and-desist order to him on the opening night of the production. The play was *3C*, a parody of a television sitcom that had originally run from 1977 to 1984, though re-runs would continue in the ensuing decades. To be sure, characters and plot were closely based on the original: *Three's Company*. There were, it was claimed, in fact seventeen points of similarity. The show, based on the British sitcom *Man about the House*, featured three roommates in a Santa Monica apartment – a florist, Janet Wood; a secretary, Chrissy Snow; and Jack Tripper, a cookery school student who has passed out in the bathroom following a party and who is persuaded to become their roommate, overcoming the objections of their landlord when they persuade him that Jack is gay. All those elements are, in truth, retained in Adjmi's play precisely because he sets out to parody the original and the values implicit in what was otherwise simply a farce at a time when the attitude towards women and gays was different. And it was as a parody that Adjmi, with the support of an impressive list of fellow writers (Tony Kushner, Edward Albee, John Guare, Stephen Sondheim and Aaron Sorkin among others), and a law firm which took the case on a pro bono basis, sought to justify his work having been prevented from authorizing productions or publication.

The ruling, when it came, accepted that plot, premise, characters, sets and even scenes were copies of the original but found that '*Despite the many similarities between the two, 3C is clearly a transformative use of Three's Company.*' It used those elements to '*turn Three's Company's sunny 1970s Santa Monica into an upside-down, dark version of itself*. Though the company, it acknowledged, '*may not like that transformation*', it was a '*transformation nonetheless*'.[36] For its part, the company had insisted that the play's production might damage the original and hence its financial interests. In a statement, the president of DLT Entertainment expressed surprise and disappointment saying that the decision had been arrived at without seeing the play, a somewhat curious objection given that it had ensured that there were no productions to see.

3C is named for the apartment number where the action takes place. It does, indeed, follow the basic plot of the original, with effectively the same cast of characters as the original, a farce full of verbal and physical comedy. Again, there are two flatmates, Linda and Connie, who enrol a third, Brad, who has to masquerade as gay to fool the intrusive and disapproving landlord, except that here that landlord, Mr. Wicker, is given to sexual assaults to which one of the women acquiesces, while Brad does have sexual feelings for his friend Terry who, in turn, is a misogynist.

The apartment is a mess, with a discarded condom. Coke is snorted and a set piece turns on what is mistaken to be a blow job. Mr. Wicker tells a series of vulgar anti-gay jokes while his wife is constantly on the edge of hysteria. None of these elements, of course, could have made their way onto network television except that Adjmi's farce is designed to underscore the casual sexism and homophobia then acceptable in the guise of situation comedy. The problem he sets himself is to present characters who are caricatures, skating across the surface of life, lacking self-awareness, figures for whom nothing is serious, life a game without consequences, while insisting that there are depths to them, that they have tears to shed, insecurities to acknowledge, pain beneath the mask given that they are their masks and that the rules of farce militate against feeling. Psychological and physical pratfalls are there to amuse. Yet here, at one moment, blood does flow, blows are struck, games expose feelings which they deny.

The notes to the published version underscore the degree to which he sees the play as more than a parody, a glance back at the mores of a different time and the caustic elements which passed unnoticed in mass market comedy. *3C*, he asserts, 'is so much about panic and existential terror in the face of a toxic world. On the surface it seems kind of flat and lowbrow, but it's a reverse *trompe l'oeil* – the flatness is illusion. And for the play to work in production this tension between the surface banality and this underlying anxiety/horror must be present.' It is, he says, 'not exactly a comedy' and 'not really a drama, though it is in many ways an exploration of human anguish'. The play, he confesses, is 'so flipped out by the human condition that it doesn't quite know how to feel about itself'. It is hard to disagree. It does, indeed, like several of his plays, have 'mercurial shifts in tone' between scenes and 'between beats,'[37] and that can be difficult to follow.

The problem is to convey what lies below the surface banality. At one stage the characters play a game called Faces. In this they challenge one another to provide the appropriate face to convey an emotion, but the real challenge is to combine two emotional states: mania with an undercurrent of calm, anguish with an undercurrent of sexiness. Reverse the terms, and that is what Adjmi is aiming at. The brittle brightness and inconsequential banter of *Three's Company* are to be invaded by doubts, reversals, a vague sense, on the part of his characters, of insufficiency. The problem is that he is so accomplished at writing farce that even given the sudden shocks – an overt sexual assault by Mr. Wicker, a fight between Brad and Terry, the Asperger outbreaks of Mrs. Wicker, the revelation of Brad's homosexuality, the sudden erotic longing of Linda, the crude anti-gay jokes – there is a risk of the human anguish being vitiated.

It is extremely funny and moves with the kind of speed which is the essence of farce. For Adjmi, the 'anxiety gets shunted into a sort of wild hydroplaning speed in the dialogue that is punctuated with abrupt shifts, and increasingly frightening gaps and silences'. There needs, he suggests, to be a 'level of anguish, that sort of gravity. It should feel disorienting.' (np) So it does, but it is difficult to feel the gravity, the disorientation being at the service of comedy, the essence of farce being that pain, social embarrassment, violations are drained of menace. Admittedly, in the hands of Joe Orton it had an anarchistic charge. He wrote plays which ridiculed authority, revelled in subversion. In *3C* that caustic element is less evident as audiences are invited to laugh at the unreconstructed values and language of unreconstructed characters situated both at a specific time and in the context of a genre laughably unaware of its social assumptions. It is true, though, that those values have clearly survived into an age in which, in 2017, a history of sexual aggression was exposed on the part of those involved in theatre and television as much as any other field.

The liberal comedy of the sitcom *The Cosby Show*, which began in the year that *Three's Company* ended, retrospectively provoked a different response when Cosby was accused of sexual assaults. Suddenly a show which had celebrated the family was suffused with irony. It could be argued that in so far as, in 3C, audiences are invited to laugh at the attitudes expressed in a series now nearly thirty years in the past, this might imply a reassuring sense that such values had now been transcended, except that sexism has plainly survived the moment while, for Adjmi, the casual homophobia of *Three's Company* clearly left its mark. While he has said that 'I don't have a big gay play in me' he has also confessed that '3C maybe was my big gay play ... It was me re-enacting my trauma watching the show "Three's Company" when I was a little boy and going, "What is this?" It seemed like being gay was a joke and I thought, "Wait, am I gay? Oh, no, I'm a joke."'[38] As in all his plays, his own situation is never far away whether in comedies or tragi-comedies.

Critical responses were markedly divided. John Lahr, writing in *The New Yorker*, found it 'smart and well written' while 'The psychological stasis that Adjmi captures with such skill is the bright doom of an unexamined life.'[39] Larry Kunofsky, in the *New York Theatre Review*, described it as the best play he had seen all year, 'Absolutely outstanding theatre.'[40] The *Time Out* review by David Cote found it 'bitterly funny and inventive.'[41] On the other hand, for Charles Isherwood, in *The New York Times*, it veered 'maladroitly between lampooning the dopey style of the original and thrashing through dank psychological waters', wandering 'aimlessly from scene to scene, with random incident piling on random incident',[42] Marilyn Stasio, in *Variety*, dismissing it as a one-note joke. There was a feeling that Adjmi was trying to have his cake and eat it, exposing sexist and homophobic language while getting laughs along the way, though that, of course, was his point, the unease it created in audiences, no less than reviewers, being precisely what he wished to generate.

Remarkably, David Adjmi wrote six plays in eighteen months, ending with *Marie Antoinette* in 2006. Following his eighteen-month writing spree, however, nothing happened. His work had generated no money and he confessed to feeling angry and neglected, deciding to abandon the theatre. No one, it seemed, wanted his plays while the appearance in that same year of Sophia Coppola's film, also called *Marie Antoinette*, seemed to seal the fate of his own play. Indeed, it would be six years before it received its premiere at the Yale Repertory Theatre, and seven before reaching New York. He had, he confessed, felt burned out by his burst of activity. He had also been ill, a condition exacerbated by the emotional toll taken by writing about characters in pain, dying. He admitted sobbing as he wrote, getting overwhelmed with the emotion invested in texts so close, in many respects, to himself.

Only a year later, however, interest suddenly flared. He quickly revised those early works and won a $50,000 Whiting Award as an emerging playwright. It would be eight years, however, before he told an interviewer that he was beginning to write for the theatre again, his attention having switched elsewhere, including to a long-gestating memoir, while three years on from that interview still no new play had appeared as he tried his hand at screenplays and television pilots.

Writing, for him, was not a comfortable experience, not least because it led him back to his own sensitivities and anxieties. As he has confessed, 'The intensity of my emotions when I'm writing can sometimes overwhelm my characters, and I confuse my experience when I'm writing with the characters.'[43] His plays are part exploration, part therapy, part exorcism. Even in *Marie Antoinette*, while insisting that 'I didn't insert myself totally in it', he added,

> What I feel for her is this feeling of lostness ... She's trying to feign being something but she doesn't know if she is. She's coming into her womanhood and trying to understand her sexuality. She tries to be entertaining, but she's actually quite lost. There's so much forlornness and anguish in her ... I came to empathize with a lot of what she was feeling ... She can't be responsible really because she doesn't understand herself. She doesn't feel a whole person. She feels like she is a lost regressed child. I am very interested in that.[44]

The play had its origin when he was working at the MacDowell Colony in Peterborough, New Hampshire, founded at the beginning of the nineteenth century, a writers' colony consisting of thirty-two studios where writers from Thornton Wilder and James Baldwin to Suzan-Lori Parks and Michael Chabon have been given a place to work for up to eight weeks, rent free. Adjmi was himself writing a play based on a Henry James novella for Soho Rep, where he was part of their Writer/Director Lab. It was not working. Then he came across a passing reference to 'Versailles or something' (he is vague about precisely what) in Mary Gaitskill's *Veronica*, though the novel, her first in a decade and a half, was set in the 1980s and involves a character married to a bisexual who passes on HIV before dying. It is, though, partly set in Paris and, as Meghan O'Rourke, writing in *New York Times*, explains, moves around in time and is 'a masterly examination of the relationship between surface and self, culture and fashion, time and memory',[45] not wholly irrelevant to Adjmi's play. The reference was enough, anyway, to put the idea of writing about Marie Antoinette into his mind. Based on reading 'some children's books' and looking online, he completed his research – three days –and finished writing the play – four days.

At first, beyond a certain fascination with the figure at its heart, he did not understand why he was writing a play apparently so far out of his own experience until, 'I came to see in the middle of working on it that, "oh, these are my issues." I always want to write about these issues and explore these things. But … I knew it in some subterranean part of myself … I didn't understand it consciously until I had written it.'[46] As he explained in an interview with *Gay City*, 'The character of my Marie is fused with me … and people I know and the culture in 2006.' He saw his protagonist 'strung out and … neurotic, like a Jewish mother'.

They are his issues in so far as Marie Antoinette is an outsider, an Austrian princess required to fit into a French court which treats her with suspicion, she feeling isolated, vulnerable, and with problems focussing. She has difficulty making sense of her life in a system not designed for her. The reference to the culture of 2006 is to the figure of George W. Bush, 'the scion of a politically powerful family, put in this position he wasn't really equipped for and not knowing what was going on'.[47] Indeed describing the play, in 2011, he said that 'It's about Marie Antoinette topically, but it's really a play about America … I wrote it during the Bush years and unfortunately it's still enormously relevant.'[48]

It is the year 1776, seven years into her marriage with Louis who had become king in 1774 and who is portrayed as childlike, though Marie herself is only twenty-one having been fourteen at the time of her marriage. The French Revolution lies over a decade in the future though the American one already hints at a possible direction for affairs. There are public disturbances, though as yet not serious. For her part, Marie Antoinette's energy is deflected into questions of style. She is extravagant, seeing this as no more than her due given her status. In particular, her hair is piled high, ridiculously so at three feet in height. She takes pleasure in her role as a setter of fashions. That hair will be reduced in size and eventually cut off as she is stripped of power, as the real Marie had been required to strip naked in front of the court before being dressed as the French woman she was now required to be. Adjmi includes a production note on how this might be accomplished, insisting that 'In many ways this is a story about hair.'[49] Her splendid clothes, too, will be replaced by rags. Style is to be a measure of other transformations.

She is first seen having tea. Thus, when she says, 'let them eat cake' this is not a reference to the peasants but friendly advice about the need to indulge children. Adjmi's Marie, indeed, is not quite a figure from history. She has a liking for espressos. Her language, and that of those around her, is modern. She rejects accusations of profligacy as 'bullshit', (22) insisting that her brother's suggestion that she is barren is not his 'fucking business', (23) even as she dismisses her husband as being 'so quotidian'. (16)

For her part, she tries her hand at a fashionable pastoralism, wearing a shepherdess's clothes, her wig laid aside, a herd of sheep tastefully arranged in a fake environment, drinking from 'peasanty' cups modelled on her own breasts, albeit made of Sevres porcelain. However, the play, which Adjmi said he wanted to 'teeter on something lysergic and expressionistic',[50] has already taken a different turn, one of the sheep having appeared to her, though not to those around her, striking up a conversation in which he offers a warning of her growing unpopularity. The peasants who she celebrated without understanding the nature of their lives will become foot soldiers in the battle to come, the pastoral as artificial as her own life.

Where did the sheep come from? Adjei recalled seeing Michael Moore's *Fahrenheit 9/11* in which President George W Bush is seen reading *My Pet Goat* to children as he is told of the 9/11 attacks and for a while continues reading. It struck him then that here was a man who had no capacity to confront what was happening, that there was something childlike about him, as there was about Marie and Louis for whom the world is changing in ways they can neither understand nor respond to.

Ten years on, Marie is now more modestly dressed. She claims to have cut her expenditure but ever more destructive rumours about her are spreading. The action then swiftly moves to 1789, history speeding up. The Revolution is at hand. The king lacks the will to act. There is now an heir to the throne, but heir to what? The Bastille has been stormed. A series of titles appear indicating that a mob has attacked Versailles looking for Marie. The first act ends as a revolutionary appears, stripping Marie of her jewels and hairpiece along with her prestige and such dignity as she has managed to retain.

The second act is set in 1791, at the Tuileries to which the mob has insisted she and the king should be relegated. An attempt to escape comes to nothing and they are brought back, Marie's hair now white at thirty-seven, an accurate historical fact. She still thinks that things can turn out well, believing that armies will come to their rescue, while Louis remains impotent, even spat at by a revolutionary. Her son is taken away from her and in fact, though not in the play, is handed over to a representative of the Paris Commune and persuaded to become a witness against her, accusing her of committing incest. More titles are displayed indicating that they have been taken to the Assembly where a mob demands the deposition of the king, who is then killed.

The sheep now reappears, a projection, presumably, of her own anxieties except that he enters into a dialogue with her about Jacques Rousseau, Isaac Newton and Voltaire on the subject of whether there is a natural order to things, the sheep emerging as an advocate of democracy, unfortunate though his timing may be as the people are about to precipitate a period of terror. To him, America shows the way forward while for her it is 'a doomed experiment'. (87) Because she insists on the authority of the past, the sheep observes, she has become its victim and 'your own life lost to you', (83) even as he abandons his sheep's skin and becomes a wolf, attacking her, though a second later she has recovered herself and the sheep has gone. Her world becomes a mixture of fantasy and the real until she imagines her own death, an apotheosis which, ironically, will redeem her in that her name will now be part of history, she being reborn in the public memory, finally escaping the calumnies, except that history will not be so kind.

Adjmi leaves out the wider political realities which led France to declare war on Austria which did, indeed, support Marie, and whose intervention Marie looks for in his play. The king was executed as a result of a single vote majority in the Convention dominated by the Jacobins. She was executed in October 1793 and, not without relevance to Adjmi's play, was once again stripped of her clothes in front of her guards, the privacy which had always been denied her, denied again. Her hair was again cut. She was disposed of in an unmarked grave but in 1815 her body and that of her husband were exhumed and buried in the Basilica of St. Denisas, the burial place of French kings.

For Adjmi, the play was in part a drawing room drama with German tragic elements. It was an expressionist screwball tragedy, a combination evident elsewhere in his work, he being fascinated, in terms of character, by contradiction, and in terms of structure by swift changes of direction. As he has said, he is drawn to the Dionysian but there is a tension between that and the rational, hence the discussion between Antoinette and the revolutionary over Montesquieu and Diderot: 'they want to use *reason*: well guess what? I *can't* reason … I can't make sense of my *life*', (87) something that Adjmi himself confessed to feeling.

And what of his insistence that the play related to George W Bush? He saw a connection between his protagonist, out of place, out of her depth, buffeted by events, insecure, and a president equally bewildered, not, like Marie, functionally illiterate, but unable to articulate his views beyond identifying an abstract enemy and celebrating the virtues of democracy even while subverting them. The French Revolution was conducted in the name of equality, democracy, virtue without terror, even as terror is what followed. The revolutionaries declared freedom while arresting those assumed to threaten it. It was President Bush who, six days after 9/11, sent a memorandum to the National Security Council authorizing the establishment of secret prisons. What followed was a legal opinion, endorsed by the president, that torture was legal and, six weeks after the attack, the Patriot Act removed a number of key freedoms, the freedoms it supposedly existed to defend. Meanwhile, what became of the equality the revolutionaries declared implicit in democracy?

Asked how relevant the play remained in 2014, Adjmi replied,

I guess [it's] about … the question of democracy and equality and leadership, and what the right thing to do is … where do you find the ethical compass … the correct way to be in the world? We are all searching for it … Who am I supposed to be? What am I supposed to do in this world? … people everywhere are struggling with 'how can I be sovereign and how am I supposed to be myself and negotiate the needs of the cultures and communities that I am part of'.[51]

It was a question which could be applied both to the playwright himself and to all his plays. *Marie Antoinette* won three Connecticut Critics Circle Awards, including Best Play.

At the end of 2017 he had one play in development at Sundance while another, *The Stumble*, was scheduled for production at Lincoln Center in 2019. He had been self-supporting as a writer since 2006, regarding himself as 'insanely fortunate'[52] in that regard. It all began, though, with a fevered period of creation in that year when plays spilled out of him, his personal anxieties, his sense of a divided self, reflected in works which circled around issues of identity, and which bore the marks of those aware of a gulf between what they appeared and what they feared they might be. Stylistic shifts reflected an instability within and without, apocalypse not delayed but now. Humour may be a lure but somewhere it bends back on itself and becomes irony until things fall apart. His is not an art of consolation. He lacks the psychological or philosophical assurance for that. Rather he registers fault lines, divisions, uncertainties, the Sturm und Drang of personal and social life. For him, laughter and melodrama, rather than tragedy, characterize existence. Marie Antoinette says that she feels like a game that other people play without her. I suspect that David Adjmi feels something similar, his plays reflecting that fact as they explore the codes within which his characters only believe themselves to operate.

Charles Isherwood's response, in *The New York Times*, was to say, 'even in the play's sporadically insightful passages, it tends to be the playwright's voice we hear. Ms. Ireland has the problematic task of portraying Mr. Adjmi's ideas about Marie Antoinette more rather than a fully realized characterization,'[53] though he realized that characterization was not what Adjmi had in mind. He was responding to a production at Yale Rep. Julie Rattey, in *America*, responded differently praising 'the modern sensibility and rich themes of Adjmi's brisk and lively script, the larger-than-life mise-en-scène and the play's farcical and absurdist elements'.[54] *Variety*, too, responded to the play's 'delicate balance of comedy, tragedy and wild imaginings'.[55]

A year later, though, now at Soho Rep, with its seventy-three seats, the play had changed, Adjmi explaining that

> I hate to use the word 'Brechtian,' because it's so overused, but the play has taken on this quality ... It's almost like a chemical conversion. What does the play have inside of it when you take everything else away? ... Sure, there are these metonyms of opulence and glamour and lavishness ... but what we're leaning into now is the tension between all of that and this looming existential nightmare that was the Reign of Terror. The play is designed to let you forget that – until you can't.[56]

The New York Times, this time in a review by Ben Brantley, remained unconvinced, preferring Sophia Coppola's film. Jon Magaril, in *Slant*, however, while also invoking Coppola, found Adjmi's play 'affecting and erudite'.[57] The play would go on to be staged, sometimes with the original's sumptuous costuming, sometimes in cut down form. A sumptuous Houston production was seen as 'a triumph of writing, production and performance',[58] while in 2021, in a production which brought together several of those who had appeared in the original Yale Rep production, it was cut down still further when it was staged, without costumes, on Zoom in the middle of the pandemic.

Looking back, in 2020, in the memoir he had finally finished, whose title *Lot Six* was a reference to his homosexuality and something more, he noted:

> Without really knowing it, I'd fought some decades-long battle – and *won*. I knew I'd won because I no longer felt that terror, that queasy sense that I would always be an impostor in the world. I was able to accept some fundamental oddness in myself. I was a Lot Six – it was the unchanging part of me ... I was able to see how this queerness, this strangeness – which wasn't just about being gay, because my alterity was deeper and weirder than that – had actually *saved* me ... I would never fit in, because I was a Lot Six; it was my suffering and my redemption. It made me a writer. It gave me a play at Lincoln Center. It gave me a *life*.[59]

CHAPTER 2
JULIA CHO: LOVE, LOSS AND MEMORY

> For theater – or any art form – to thrive, I think it needs to reflect and engage with the society and culture it springs from. And making theater more inclusive, more diverse, definitely does just that. It has wakened me up in a really wonderful way.
>
> There are so many reasons not to write: it's arduous, it's possibly futile, it's ephemeral – and the list goes on. What keeps me going is the unshakable belief that telling stories is deeply meaningful and may even be the most meaningful thing that we humans do.[1]

The term 'Asian American' was coined in 1968 by Yuji Ichioka and Emma Gee when they founded the Asian American Political Alliance in Berkeley. Its virtue was that it united those coming from different backgrounds. It was simultaneously a declaration of political solidarity and a reaction against stereotypes which saw them as model citizens, with stable families, high achievers with particular skills, including a facility with mathematics. Its problem was that thereby it homogenized otherwise distinctive national identities. The Chinese experience was not the same as the Vietnamese, the Japanese, Cambodian and so on. There are currently 20 million Asian Americans from twenty different countries.

In October 2021, the Korean-American Jay Caspian Kang, confessing to his own anxiety about identity, published an article in *The New York Times Magazine*, adapted from his book *The Loneliest Americans*, entitled 'The Myth of Asian American Identity', in which he wrote that 'the confusion and the vagaries of "Asian American" result, in part, from necessity: What else could you possibly do with a group that includes everyone from well-educated Brahmin doctors from India to impoverished Hmong refugees? How could you tell a unifying story that makes all those immigrants feel as if they're part of some racial category?' 'Asian American', it seemed to him, is mainly a demographic descriptor

> that satisfies almost nobody outside the … upwardly mobile professionals who enter mostly white middle-class spaces and need a term to describe themselves and everyone who looks like them. I know many people whose families emigrated from Asia. I know almost no one invested in the idea of an 'Asian America.' And yet, while most Asian Americans may not feel any fealty toward the identification, that's the box they check whenever they're asked to check a box.[2]

His own family had moved up the social scale so that he was contemplating the fact that his young daughter might go to school in Brooklyn's St Ann's, the school attended by Anna Ziegler.

When it came to theatre, the East West Players were led by a Japanese-American, Makoto Matsu. The Asian American Theatre Workshop was founded by fifth-generation Chinese-American Frank Chin, himself opposed to the stereotypes which he saw as being embraced by fellow writers, including Amy Tan and David Henry Hwang. He was alarmed by the drive towards assimilation which he saw as destroying a unique culture, parents failing to pass on knowledge of the Chinese experience in America. The term, however, stuck with theatre groups and writers.

What to make, then, of a writer for whom an Asian identity was problematic, whose origins were clear enough but who felt detached from them, not least linguistically. Julia Cho was born in Los Angeles in 1975 to Korean parents, but does not speak Korean. She has said that she feels that loss acutely, that it is a source of shame and guilt. 'I felt there was no authentic Koreanness in me … I went to Korea at age 13, and it was a completely foreign place to me.'[3] Her parents regularly spoke to one another in Korean, so that she heard the language around her. Until *Aubergine*, though, none of her Korean characters speak in Korean even as she was reluctant that they should speak in broken English. In trying to explain, she recalled taking an immersion programme in French at Middlebury College in Vermont, where she was suddenly forced to use that language, having a dream of a teacher who spoke it fluently:

And in my dream I think to myself, Oh my gosh, her French is so good I can't even understand it! And I guess that's how Korean sounds to me. I'm not capable of it, and yet there's some subconscious part of me that understands it better than I consciously know. And to this day when someone speaks Korean to me, I really don't know a lot of what they are saying and yet it's totally familiar to me.[4]

There is a speech in her play *The Language Archive* which would seem to say something about her relationship to the language, and those in her family who were carriers of it.

I start thinking of my grandmother … I can still hear her voice with utter clarity. It tells me things in a tongue that is both as familiar to me as my own face and absolutely incomprehensible. This language, this cacophony, this gibberish, this … music. My grandmother kept it inside her like a recipe, like a riddle. And to me it made her strange … I separated myself from it and from her the very first chance I could. I've spent my whole life trying to make up for that. I guess I always will.[5]

Hers, though, was 'a very porous household', nor was she alone in hearing Korean in her family home while speaking English outside it. The same is true of the Korean novelist, Chang-rae Lee, whose first novel, *Native Speaker*, featured a Korean man and the struggle involved in assimilation. Separating yourself from an immigrant language offers freedom, access to a wider world, even as it severs a link that is personal no less than cultural.

Unsurprisingly, Cho has an interest in identity and language, which would surface in her plays (particularly, *The Language Archive*), language being shaped by identity and identity shaped by language, but she is suspicious of labels which she regards as a way of making the world 'convenient'. So, Korean characters appear in her plays, but they are not exclusive of other identities. 'For me to say that being of Korean origin influences my work is the same as saying being a woman or being American influences my writing.'[6] As to Asian-American theatre, this is, she has said, 'maybe a tainted vessel. It colours the way we see what's inside, but really, anything could go inside of it … Demographically, Asian American is changing. It's no longer APA (Asian Pacific American). It's Southeast Asian, South Asian, half-Asian, adopted. There's a generational shift, too.' Young Asian Americans 'grow up in a globalised world: they drink Boba tea, go karaoking and eat sushi at the mall. Their stories are different.'[7]

She wrote her first play in the eighth grade, about people trapped in a bomb shelter. It was seeing a production of John Guare's *Six Degrees of Separation*, however, that stirred her interest in theatre. She studied at Amhurst College writing poetry and prose but, in her final year, took playwriting classes with the playwright Constance Condon who was Playwright-in-Residence, a writer much admired by Tony Kushner. From there she went to New York University to take an MFA which led to a residency in the Julliard Playwrights programme. There she worked with Marsha Norman and Christopher Durang and took workshops with the theatre and television director Brian Mertes. Her parents, James and Sun Hui Cho, she has explained, were not well pleased when she decided to become a playwright but became converts, her first play, *99 Histories*, being dedicated to them. *99 Histories* and *BFE* were both written when she was at the Julliard.

Beyond everything, *99 Histories* is a deeply moving play which explores the relationship between the past and the present, remembering and forgetting, secrets held close in a desperate hope they will remain such. Most crucially it stages the relationship between a mother, Sah-Jin, and a daughter, Eunice, each looking to the other for consolation, linked by love but also a sense of guilt. The mother had left Korea for the possibilities of a golden California, carrying with her not only regrets but also a physical reminder in the form of her daughter. Cho explores the nature of love which can elevate but also give birth to regret. It is a play concerned with loss and the need to deal with it, with characters who tell themselves stories which are not always congruent with their lives.

99 Histories is set in a suburb of Los Angeles, though there are moments when the Korean past is retrieved, when we glimpse the characters as they were when young. Some of its scenes, Cho indicates, are memories or dreams, as others are 'everyday realities'. The play begins with a young girl playing the cello. This is Eunice, urged on by her mother who tells her that she can be anything she wants, that 'Words become reality,'[8] even as words, it turns out, can be deceptive, that other forces are at play. She never found the language to speak to her father while her conversations with her mother are fraught. She is at her most fluent when addressing someone who does not yet exist, the child she carries and who may never read what she writes in a series of letters to it. Beyond that, it is music which has a coherence and a harmony otherwise lacking from her life.

In the present, Eunice returns, pregnant, leaving behind the father, Joe, a white American man from whom she had already withdrawn. She plans on having her baby adopted, in a letter to the unborn child invoking Melville's 'Bartleby the Scrivener', who had himself withdrawn saying, to all approaches, 'I would prefer not to'. Her family, she writes, prefers not to talk about the past. As a child herself she had been asked to bring a family tree to school. Cho indicates that there should be a visual of a diagram with a few empty boxes where her forebears should be listed. While her friend had a hope chest (a chest containing linen and clothes in preparation for marriage), Eunice explains, 'I looked at it and thought to myself: I have no hope chest. I have no hope. I'm just saying, so what if you grew up not knowing where you were from? Maybe more than hair colour or eye shape, it's that feeling that proves you are mine.' (15) The past, then, is a blank, the future bleak, for this woman whose seemingly bright future as an accomplished cellist has stalled for reasons which only slowly become apparent.

Her mother tries to set her up with a man, Paul, a doctor, ignoring the fact that he is already engaged. As Eunice remarks, 'if you're Korean, with a pulse, you're good enough'. (18) Speaking to her mother, she invokes the figure of the Gentleman Caller in Tennessee Williams's *The Glass Menagerie* also already engaged when Amanda tries to set him up as a possible suitor for her daughter Laura. As it happens, Paul explains that what he feels for his fiancée is not conventional love but what is called chung, a feeling that theirs will be a good match, not quite the withdrawal that Eunice displays but a degree of detachment which she will learn also characterized her parents' marriage.

In her letter to her unborn child, Eunice explains that her own father had been shot dead in the convenience store he and her mother had run, though rather than elaborate she recalls that in school she had been shown the Zapruder film of Kennedy's assassination, a scene acted out by two figures dressed as Jacqueline and John F. Kennedy to the sound of whispering. The lights on them suddenly snap off and come on as we see the figure of Girl, the young Eunice, calling on her father to get up, to say something, do something. What Eunice does not write, and what she has not told her mother, is that she was present at her father's murder, running away before she is seen. This, though, is only one of the secrets, one glimpse of the past summoned up.

In a box kept by her mother she discovers a photograph of a young woman, as she does so the woman briefly appearing, along with a photograph of a young white American, Daniel, who also appears. Besides these is a book, Rainer Maria Rilke's *Letters to a Young Poet*, in which the nature of love is discussed at length along with a warning which has a relevance to *99 Histories*: 'if there is one thing more that I must say to you, it is this: Do not believe that he who seeks to comfort you lives untroubled among the simple and quiet words that sometimes do you good. His life has much difficulty and sadness and remains far behind yours.'[9] When Eunice declares 'I LOST EVERYTHING', her mother replies, 'and what do you think I have? I lost more. I lost MORE. Because at least you have yourself. I never had myself. I just had you.' (39) Daniel, it seems, was the man her mother had once loved, back in Korea. At this point the walls become white, opaque, a small piano appears, and Daniel and Woman (the Young Sah Jin) act out the beginnings of their relationship in Korea, a love affair, Eunice, for a moment, becoming her mother, only for Joe to appear as she becomes herself rejecting him as her mother had been abandoned.

Identities then blur as it becomes apparent that Eunice had abandoned her incipient career at the age of fifteen because of mental illness, even thinking of killing her mother before, as the Girl's playing of the cello becomes discordant, plunging the bow into her hand. Now, a suspicion grows. The photograph she had found in the box lacked the scar her mother carries from a childhood tracheotomy. Only now does Sah-Jin, after prevarication, confess that the photograph had actually been of her sister, revealing at last, what Eunice had begun to suspect, that she suffered the same mental disturbance. As Eunice says, 'Two parents who sacrifice everything for their child, who strive to give her only the best … And I don't inherit language or culture, hell, I don't even inherit your *hair* or your looks. I inherit a *disease*. That's my heirloom.' (40) Fearful that she will pass the gene onto her unborn child, still writing to him or her, she decides that rather than 'rotting you from the inside out' (41), she will have an abortion, this being an expression of love. As she says, speaking of her father planting a tree not realizing it was a lemon, 'I guess you never know what you've planted until it comes up', in this case 'bitter fruit'. (42)

Sah-Jin admits that her husband had not been the great love of her life realizing, instead, that Eunice was 'my great love. Because you are me, you are in me' (45) carrying more than a faulty gene, she having gone ahead with her birth in knowledge of the risks but already loving her daughter before she was born. And why did Sah-Jin choose a cello for her daughter to play? She did so because Daniel, the man she had truly loved, despite saying that she had never experienced a great love, was a cello player.

The play ends, or almost so, with what begins as a lament, but which allows space for the hope apparently abandoned and whose lyricism works against the despair to which Eunice had been drawn:

> We took pictures of the wrong things, and recorded the wrong events. We told the wrong stories, and we remembered the wrong memories. What has lasted is sadness; it will outlast flesh. What has lasted is forgetfulness; it wins over memories every time. But sometimes, in the blue hour, between midnight and dawn, I'll wake up and my hands will be alive, moving over an imaginary cello all by themselves … And then I feel such loss … but as Rilke would say 'You must not be frightened … if sadness rises up before you larger than any you have ever seen; if restiveness, like light and cloud-shadows, pass over your hands and over all you do. You must think that something is happening with you, that life has not forgotten you, that it holds you in its hand; it will not let you fall.
>
> (47)

Rilke's letters had all been dedicated to encouraging a poet looking for a way forward. For Sah-Jin it is the love of a mother for her daughter, and love has a memory, 'Memory plus time'. (48) The play finally ends with Eunice gathering her letters together and putting them in the Hope box as the Woman and girl (two ages of Sah-Jin) appear, past and present brought together, as Eunice for the moment plays her cello. To the sound of a Bach prelude, the Woman and Girl, along with Eunice, speak of goodness, memory, and a good day. Separate stories have become one.

Meanwhile, what will be the fate of the unborn child? Pressing her ear to her daughter's stomach, Sah-Jin says that she can hear what she declares will be a girl child, singing. If there is one thing which connects these characters, it is music. The mother is a pianist, the daughter a cellist who has not lost the skills she once abandoned. It is a bridge between them and, for Cho, more than an accompaniment to a drama in which it reflects the shifting moods and experiences of her characters. It is itself a hint at transcendence.

Sah-Jin is described as American-Korean, while Eunice and Paul are Korean-American. In *BFE* the characters are Asian-American. In *The Piano Teacher* two characters are, in turn, 'of any ethnicity' and 'of indeterminate ethnicity'. In *Aubergine* one character, born in Korea, is Korean-American, but so is one born in America. Identity, it seems, is not so easily defined, and, besides, Cho's approach to Korean characters would change after a hiatus in her career which saw her stop writing after a rich creative period in which several plays were staged in a few brief years. After *The Language Archive*, in 2010, she was, she explained, in some ways exhausted. There was, she said, 'this cavernous empty storeroom'. She moved out of New York and, in her words, was 'empty for a long while'.[10]

Cho's family moved to Arizona when she was twelve. She stayed there until sixteen, and Arizona is the setting for *BFE*, which stands for 'Bum Fuck, Egypt', in other words the back-of-beyond. Certainly, there is a sense in which the characters she assembles are emotionally stranded, even as they yearn for connection. Isabel, an Asian-American in her thirties, has been abandoned by her husband and is now agoraphobic, living in a house described as isolated, in a place that is 'hot' and 'lifeless'. She fails to register her own daughter's birthday. Her only connection is with a fantasy General MacArthur, who steps out of her TV screen, and a Pizza delivery man who she desperately tries to seduce, but who swiftly abandons her. Her brother, Lefty, who lives with her and his niece, retreats into painting Dungeon and Dragon figurines, like Laura with her glass animals in *The Glass Menagerie*, himself making a desperate bid for love with Evvie, an African American single mother who works in the department store where he is a security guard and is a reader of self-help books. They are of no use to Isabel with her commitment to plastic surgery as self-improvement. Asked what his hidden talent is, Lefty replies that his hands can be very still. The title of a Korean self-help book, not mentioned in the play, is *Stillness Is the Key*. Another is the best-selling *I Decided to Live as Me*, the question in *BFE* being who any of them are.

Evvie's date is her first in ten years. It doesn't work out. Lefty does remember his niece's birthday and buys her earrings but has failed to notice that her ears are not pierced. These are characters for whom human connections are problematic, adrift in a backwater. Isabel and Lefty, both adopted, know nothing of their past, except that they were abandoned and that the family that raised them left them feeling 'wrong'. Panny, fourteen, who attends what she describes as a middle of nowhere podunk school, whose father had abandoned her mother before she was born, connects with Hugo, a Mormon man in his twenties, over the telephone, lying about her age, a relationship which founders when he sees her face to face. At the same time, she conducts a one-sided conversation with a pen pal in Korea whose belief in everything America has to offer is at odds with the reality we have seen.

The play begins with Panny, addressing the audience assuring us that 'Things happen all the time out here', except that, at first, this seems no more than a friend thinking she had seen a UFO, keg parties and a man who carries a gun in case he encounters snakes, except that something has happened. Girls have been disappearing, the latest being the third most popular girl in the school, so that Panny ends by saying 'It's a very dangerous time.'[11]

The central character in *99 Histories* was played, in one production, by an actress with the same name as its author. It was an experience which sharpened her interest in mental health issues. In interview she commented on something that would also be relevant to *BFE* which among other things touches on the issue of body images, definitions of beauty. For Cho, the actress, it had a particular relevance when working in Hollywood but, she insisted,

> [the] pressures of having a 'perfect' body is put upon us, specifically girls and women, on a broader cultural/societal level ... I would be lying if I said I was completely immune to the images that bombard me from billboards, magazines, television and film screens. Fortunately, I was raised to believe that I was more than good enough and that I didn't have to look or act like anyone else. Everyone has their own path, and you go your own way ... I am forging my own path and I don't need to compare myself to others.[12]

In *BFE* Isabel's idea of an appropriate birthday gift for her daughter is the offer of plastic surgery having had it herself. 'I too was a plain little girl with big yearnings. A diamond in the rough,' she explains, 'all I did was polish it a little ... Everyone does it. Every celebrity over the age of thirty-five ... I mean, I watch TV, I know. Don't think of it as surgery. Think of it as a simple act of constructive self-improvement .... True beauty is not born. True beauty is an act of will.' (15–16) She suggests a little work on Panny's nose and eyes, evidently to make her a little less Korean American, she being conscious, from the age of five, that she was different, being called a Chink. 'I am a chink', she says to Lefty, 'you're a chink', as is Isabel. (17) 'I'm not beautiful', except that in a certain light, and for a brief moment, 'I wasn't me. I actually seemed beautiful.' (25) Panny's Korean pen pal is disappointed to learn that she is 'not full American', but 'just another Asian person', (21) despite the fact that she herself had plastic surgery to her eyes at the age of four, not least because 'all the movie and singing star also have surgery'. Besides, 'All my friend have eye surgery.' (22) It is Hugo, however, who recalls a French saying which translates as 'If you look in my eyes, you will find them beautiful.' (24) As the African American Evvie remarks, 'We don't know what we are, none of us.' (19)

All the time, there is a killer on the loose who eventually seizes Panny, except that she is not the blond-haired beauty he prefers, her Korean appearance ironically a protection. In recalling it for her pen pal, she fantasizes her successful resistance, except that in fact he had beaten and then abandoned her. Ironically, she now has an operation on her eyes which makes her look more like the preferred victims of the killer. He had had a blond wig to hand but nothing to disguise a Korean girl's eyes. 'It was my choice,' she explains to Hugo who arrives with a bunch of flowers. 'I wanted a change.' (52) The change, however, has left her with swollen eyes and red tears. The play ends as Lefty, Isabel and Panny watch television, and Hae-Yoon writes a letter in which she offers an untranslatable Korean joke, adding, 'cheering up, my friend. Remember, you are in America! How can life be bad,' (53) as the telephone rings, nobody picking it up.

If *BFE* clearly explores the nature of identity in the context of Korean characters, the world Cho creates, in which identity is insecure, contested, self-help books abound, plastic surgery is popular, the American dream problematic, the threat of violence a background noise, clearly transcends ethnic insecurities. Here is a vision of an America in which some tangible connection has been lost, in which meaning seems to evade those trying to locate themselves in terms of private needs and a promise of fulfilment. What is striking is Panny's detachment from her own life, which she narrates, and stages, retreating, finally, from a pain she can never fully address or understand. The phone rings, the television flickers, the man on whom she had built a fantasy leaves, as she sits beside two people whose own lives have lost all purpose and direction, in a place of no importance, Bum Fuck Egypt.

BFF was commissioned in 2002 but opened at the Long Wharf in 2005 after a series of staged readings, too many according to Marilyn Stasio writing in *Variety*. A *Curtain Up* review by Elyse Sommer praised Cho's 'fine ear for the nuances of dialogue and her knack of leavening sadness with humour',[13] while worrying about what struck her as an overstuffed plot, asking what landed the family in an Arizona wasteland and how could a security guard afford plastic surgery for his niece. Anita Gates, in *The New York Times*, hailed 'an insightful, beautifully structured drama' in which Cho gives 'the current culture an early warning that, like all life philosophies, even the useful idea that people make their own reality could be taken to extremes'.[14]

With her next play, *The Architecture of Loss*, Cho returned to the Arizona desert, on the outskirts of Tucson. At first there appear to be no Korean characters, though we learn that the mother of a central character was such, though she had died suddenly in a yard where everything was dead or dying. As the title implies, loss remains a predominant mood as it had been in *BFE*. It begins as Carmie, 25-year-old daughter to Catherine and her ex-husband Greg, addresses a tour group. It is a hundred and nineteen degrees and with no sign of rain. Not, she explains, that rain would be a relief in that it brings flash floods which had been known to kill people.

Catherine now lives with her father, Richard, a former drinker, his mind wandering, in a 'house alone in the wide desert … The sky … white with heat.'[15] The sun is so powerful that it bleaches the colour out of towels left out to dry as, it turns out, experience has bleached the life of those who live there. The city had once planned to expand into this arid land but decided against it, leaving it to its isolation and these characters trapped with one another and their memories of what had happened that drained them of hope. The architecture of their loss differs but has a common design having to do with abandonment, denial, guilt. Something is missing from their lives beyond a boy who once walked out of this house in an unrelenting desert, and never returned

Into this world intrudes Greg, Catherine's former husband, who had himself disappeared fourteen years earlier. He comes, he says, to make amends, now free of alcohol and a believer in God, as Catherine is not any longer since her son, David, has been missing for eight years. The story of that disappearance is then told to Greg, from Catherine's perspective, and we are back in time, eight years earlier, when her mother had died, and her father had lost his house through gambling. Greg had moved in with the family, a secret drinker, a hostile presence, defending himself against the accusation that he had been cruel to his wife recalling, to Catherine, that 'I didn't see you learning any Korean', (23) she not wishing people to know of her heritage. Following an argument, she tells him to leave only for her son to run out never, it turned out, to return. Some of her speeches are laid out in verse, laments for what is lost:

> And my son, who every day
> becomes more and more like a man,
> he is somewhere I can't go
> He is someplace I can't reach.
> We're taught that suffering is rewarded.
> Suffer now and someday you will have
> an equal share of happiness.
> Well, I think this is bullshit.
> I no longer believe in suffering
> Without reason or reward.
>
> (25)

Now it is Carmie's turn to recall events from eight years earlier. What she remembers is the time she was going to university and making a speech at her school. What she remembers is her male teacher kissing her, as she tells a tour group that rain will suddenly fill the desert with flowers, which have been waiting 'for the most simple thing; the chance to unfold. That's all they want, all anything wants, Just the chance to unfold,' (35) except that he goes back to his wife leaving her adrift, never to unfold. Looking to blot things out, she contacts a schoolmate for drugs who, asked what life is, replies, 'little by little, life takes away the things inside you. Till at the end of your life, you're nothing but an empty glove.'(38)

She had wanted to run away, she now explains to her father, as he had done, as her brother had done. But she stayed, university traded in for community college and a dead-end job. Did her father abuse her before he left? Was that, as he hints, why he left? If so, was it, as he suggests, an act of love? It is not something she can accept. But then we learn something of the trauma he experienced as a soldier, inadvertently shooting women and children, and later being laid off. We learn, too, that in a car crash he had killed a young hitchhiker he had picked up, a hustler, and who we glimpse throughout in brief scenes. He was the same age as David had been when he left. Greg has been in retreat from himself, hoping that in returning he can heal a wound, find redemption. If so, he has come to the wrong place, at the wrong time.

David never does come back, even as Catherine clings to the hope that he may. The play ends as the figure of a young man appears, raising his hand as if in greeting, as the sky opens, and it rains. So, what are we to make of that? Does he raise his hand only in greeting, or is it in farewell, or absolution? In her stage direction, Cho indicates the first, but the logic of the piece seems less certain. Is the rain an indication that something is about to unfold, desert seeds at last to bloom? That would seem a desperate throw of the dice.

Stories have their end. For Catherine, Carmie and Greg theirs do not. Hope, all but eroded, is clung to because what is the alternative? If what we have seen of their life is all they have then they can hardly be said to be living at all. Richard, trapped in dark memories, barely registering the present, marks out the limits of possibilities. Greg's God does not intervene, a thief who Richard sees as an angel, steals what he has. There are faint echoes here of Sam Shepard's *Buried Child* with its murdered child, as there are of Tracy Letts's *August, Osage County*, set on the Oklahoma plains, except that these are not like the characters in that play, or Albee's *Who's Afraid of Virginia Woolf?* Far from retreating into articulacy, they struggle to articulate feelings which have themselves been attenuated in this burned-over land. And if the son did return, after twenty-five years, what would he find?

Cho adds two epigraphs to the published text. One comes from a family survival guide for those who have lost their children. 'Hope', it says, 'is essential to your survival'. Pandora's Box contained pain and suffering. Once opened, these were released into the world. Only hope remained, locked inside. Was this, then, just one more source of suffering, and hence best secured, or a redemptive power nonetheless locked away? In *Waiting for Godot* hope breeds a comic irony. In Aeschylus's *Prometheus Bound*, Prometheus gifts men 'blind hope', which the Chorus greets as a great benefit. In *The Architecture of Loss* that last would seem to be an illusion. But then, there is the rain.

The other epigraph is from C.S. Lewis in which he speaks of the multiple meanings of a word which can be traced back to a common root, as in *The Architecture of Loss* we follow loss back through time, it meaning different things to all those who find themselves bound together even as, like the figures in O'Neill's *Long Day's Journey into Night*, they are simultaneously driven apart. And if love is a motor force it, too, takes different forms, born in hope but eroding into abandonment, except that there is a level at which, for better or worse, it is never quite extinguished, a level at which sacrifices are made, sheer survival necessitating them.

In reviewing the play in *Variety*, Marilyn Stasio objected that form and content went in different directions and that 'while expressive of the characters' alienation, 'the style is itself alienating because the language is too oblique and the action too evasive to sustain a dramatic scene',[16] though evasion is surely structured into the family's failure to communicate, obliqueness their defence.

John Simon, not always the most sympathetic of critics, writing in *New York*, found *The Architecture of Loss* 'the kind of play one wishes there were more of: totally unpretentious, of the utmost simplicity, and steadily close to the bone. It is, moreover, about real people (who sometimes speak a little too eloquently; but that, surely, is dramatic license or, in the occasional lyrical passage, poetic license).'[17] Margot Jefferson, in *The New York Times*, found it 'a touching new play' by a talented writer, which 'will stay with you'.[18]

On 13 May 2006, Cho opened *The Winchester House* at the ninety-nine-seat Boston House which, despite its name, is in Pasadena, California. It had only been open for three years, built on what had formerly been a car park. The play had been commissioned by Ralph Peña,

Artistic Director of the Ma-Yi Theater, whose mission was to develop and produce new and innovative plays by Asian Americans.

It is a play which on one level is about the seduction of a child by a man, and the consequences for all involved, but which also explores the nature of memory, love, secrets shared or withheld, loss. Characters are summoned to offer their own perspectives, changing over time. For one, echoes of a past event sound in the present, still with the power to disrupt an emotional life, peace of mind. For another, it is the one bright light in an otherwise disordered life. Rather as Paula Vogel chose, at some level, to withhold judgement in her portrait of Peck, who has an affair with a young girl in *How I Learned to Drive*, so here, the man involved is allowed to offer his version. And all the while one-time friends are disappearing, relationships fractured by divorce, parents succumbing to disease, witnesses to a life whose reality thereby thins.

Those to whom we are introduced can seem sealed in their own privacies, together and yet apart, each struggling with the business of living. There is a sense of the spaces between people, spaces which have opened up and with which people do or do not learn to live. And though the man involved is white and the girl, now woman, is Asian American, this is not a play in which that is of primary concern, though an immigrant woman finds it difficult to say certain things in an alien language. But then, all the characters freight their own language with meanings not always transitive, while there are other boundaries than those of language crossed. It is a play which at times is in verse, as the central character tries to shape experience into a song thereby asserting some control over a story whose incompletions are a primary source of a discontent deepening in the direction of despair. Can the past really exert its rights over the present? Can one seismic event leave aftershocks so long after it occurred?

It opens as Via, a thirty-year-old Asian woman, sings two verses of a song as she plays a guitar before addressing the audience, explaining that her immigrant father, a smoker suffering from cancer and a heart condition, had never made friends in the forty years he had lived in America. Before proceeding, however (in the text set out in free verse form), she asks the audience,

> maybe you could think a little about what brought you here tonight.
> Not just to this theater, but to this place, I mean, in your life.
> Maybe you could think a little about all the small decisions that brought you here.
>   To this city.
> To your job.
> Think of your age.
> Did you ever imagine this is what that age would feel like?
> Did you ever think this is where you'd be?
> Maybe you're satisfied with everything you've done
> and at night you can sleep the sleep of the good and the just.
> But I doubt it.
>
> If you are satisfied, then you have absolutely no need for anything I could possibly tell
>   you and really, you might as well leave.
>
> But if you are unsatisfied, stay.[19]

It is, she says, to be a play with three songs, and a half. Meanwhile, as her brother Ernest reminds her, she has difficulty with relationships, a tendency to have affairs, though there is, it seems, a reason for this, relating to a white man called John Bergin, a married professor in the Asian Art department of the local college, an incident in a barn when she was young. Certainly, she and her brother had stopped visiting, something that apparently baffles Helen Bergin, though Via and her brother's memories of the past differ and, if so, what is real?

Her own mother, who appears, had had difficulty even contemplating divorce, not because her husband had strayed but because he was wrapped up in his job as a physicist. Via becomes her confidante, her mother not speaking to her in English, a mother who she had not told about what had happened to her any more than she did her father, thinking to spare them, as she says to maintain their innocence. With her parents now dead, though, she feels free of any restraint. In a song, she sings of wanting a new story, with a new ending. She decides to confront the man who had seduced her, a man now dying of cancer, only to discover that he is divorced from Helen, she having never been the same 'since your brother rejected her', (25) presumably because he had accused her of complicity in her husband's affair with his sister. Husband and wife had then moved away.

When she meets Bergin, she recalls discovering that he had had affairs with other women before the relationship between the two of them when she was sixteen. For the dying man, it turns out, it is a moment he treasures, 'the only perfect and beautiful thing I have ever had in my entire life'. (45) Tears come to her eyes, though it is not clear whether they are prompted by memories, by pity, or regret.

Via now recalls a story which explains the play's title. The widow of the Winchester gun fortune had built a house, adding more and more rooms,

> convinced that the ghosts of all the people that Winchester rifles had killed were out to get her. She built room after room in an effort to hide from them. She never stopped adding on to the house for as long as she was alive. Staircases that went nowhere, windows that opened onto nothing, and to this day no one knows exactly how many rooms there are. Sometimes the inside of my head feels like that. All these halls and doors that go nowhere. There isn't light enough to see it all.
>
> (47)

The final stage direction, itself set out in verse, reads:

> *The song ends.*
> *The Barn.*
> *Via is sixteen.*
> *She smooths her hair.*
> *She smooths her clothes.*
> *She knocks on the door. Mr. Bergin opens it.*
> *She goes inside.*
> *He closes the door.*
> *The song ends.*

At the beginning of the play Via invited anyone to leave who felt they had nothing to learn from a play which asked people to consider what it was that had brought them to this point in their lives, whether they are satisfied with everything they have done, whether small decisions might have had a significant effect. For those who had paid for their tickets, those presumably remained open questions, as they do for Via. Fifteen years after this production, the play has yet to be published.

With *Durango*, her first play with only male characters, which opened at the Long Wharf Theatre on 20 September 2006, we are initially back in what Isaac, the twenty-one-year-old son of Boo-Seng Lee, calls 'Arizona's putrid warm … the armpit of the United States warm',[20] though much of the play takes place on a road trip to Durango on which the father takes his sons for reasons of his own. There are inevitable echoes of *Death of a Salesman* in that Boo-Seng Lee, at the age of fifty-six, is arbitrarily fired from his job with nothing but a watch to show for time with the company, pleading with his employer, even threatening him. He is, it seems, not well liked, lacking communication skills, keeping himself to himself. Like Willy Loman, he has the wrong dreams. He longs to go to Durango as for Willy Loman Alaska had been the place of regret. His two sons, meanwhile debate his firmness of mind, two sons who are themselves adrift, their seeming promise not realized. But there the echoes cease, or almost so.

Boo-Seng Lee is Korean born, his marriage an arranged one in which love seemed not to function. His wife, from a rich family, is dead from cancer so that loss is once again an intangible fact, though she, it appears, lacked any kind of agency deferring to her husband as Linda Loman did to hers. His sons, Isaac, twenty-one, and Jimmy, thirteen, are seemingly chasing an American dream, one returning from an interview in Hawaii where he was applying to be a doctor, the other a champion swimmer hoping that this will one day ease his way into university, except that Isaac never went for his interview and Jimmy has stepped away from swimming. All three characters are thus caught at a moment of crisis, unsure what and who they are, each having secrets they hold close.

The play begins as Isaac plays his guitar, singing a song whose lyrics only make sense later in the play as he sings of a neon girl about to dive in the dark, and of motels whose signs reading 'Vacancy' will have a resonance beyond their apparent meaning. If the guitar gives him a satisfaction that his studies do not, his brother is drawn to sketching a superhero, described as 'a beautiful, blond, young sun God', the Red Angel who, perhaps significantly, rescues his parents from a burning building. When Isaac points out the absence of Asian superheroes, Jimmy replies, 'My superhero's going to be normal. He's not going to be … like us … I just don't want to be limited'. 'Look in a mirror, Jimmy,' Isaac replies, 'What do you think you are?' (35) To Jimmy's lament, 'I wish I were a mutant,' Isaac replies, 'I think we kinda already are.' (37)

The boys have no interest in their father's stories about Korea, the privations he suffered. When younger, Isaac had been embarrassed by his father's accent, even as he and his brother had been picked on at school, their accomplishments being a defence. They may all have invested in the American dream but their access to it is problematic. That, though, is not the main thrust of the play. In the discussion of superheroes, Isaac explains his preference for Wolverine among the X-Men in what has its echoes from *The Architecture of Loss*. It is because, 'He was *made* to suffer. That's what his gift *is*. And because he suffers, because he feels pain, we see in him the truest expression of what we, as humans, experience. *That's* why he's the greatest X-Man. Not because he's the most powerful but because he's the most human.' (36) In *Durango* suffering takes different forms, a wife who failed to connect with her husband, a man alienated from his work and the boys in whom he has placed his hopes, two sons unable to come to terms with who they are.

For reasons he fails to reveal, Boo-Seng Lee decides that they should go on a family holiday, driving to Durango, Isaac, in particular, being resistant. Much of the rest of the play follows them on their journey, stopping off at a motel where Boo-Seng Lee confesses to a man he meets that he has always been bored out of his mind. Speaking of the job he has just lost, he asks, 'Why did I want so little? Where did I learn to want so little for myself?' (47) He is, a stage direction indicates, utterly lost no longer able to say what it is he wants. Greeted in Korean, he seems confused. 'Don't you speak your own language?' the man asks. (46) Does he then fall into the swimming pool, or did he perhaps want to end things? A neon sign now lights. It is in three parts and shows a girl diving down toward the water, the sign about which Isaac had sung at the beginning of the play.

There are moments when the missing mother is recalled, Isaac speaking as that mother in an imperfect English, recalling the love she had felt for him and her conviction that he had greatness in him. In Korea, she explains, she had been funny, but 'somehow in American I have lost all my humour'. As to her husband, he had suffered pain, sadness, disappointment, is fragile. His job is to 'love them and love *for* them when sometime they cannot'. (68–9)

The secrets are slowly revealed. Boo-Seng Lee had called in a favour to ensure that Isaac would secure a place in medical school while Jimmy is gay though not able to accept it. It seems likely that Bo-Seng's friend in Hawaii has not married because he too is gay, that their friendship had not been platonic, a source, perhaps, of the sadness and disappointment he feels. As he confesses to Isaac, when that friend had accused him of cowardice in not accepting who he was he had replied, 'You want to chose what you want to be, but that is not for our generation. You and me – we are just laying foundation. That's all.' (73)

When Boo-Seng recalls his wife, he speaks as her. A stage direction indicates that she is speaking in Korean 'but we understand her in English. There is no trace of an accent.' (78) Slightly drunk, he/she holds up a brochure, the one he kept years after her death. It is of Durango, the place he wished to go to because she understands that he will be seeing his male lover. Here, then, is the explanation of his desire, in the present, to go to the one place where he had known love. The play ends as they drive back, Jimmy throwing his sketches out of the window, arriving home exhausted, wordless. Finally, Isaac says that he will reschedule his interview in Hawaii as Jimmy says, 'Maybe I'll be a doctor,' (90) as Biff and Happy Loman had offered fantasies to their father. Jimmy says, 'I love you?' as Biff had embraced his father, in both cases too late. Boo-Seng listens to a message, in Korean, on his answer machine from his long-ago lover. Jimmy sits at his desk but does not draw, while Isaac, in his room, plays a few chords on his guitar, the beginning of the song heard earlier. Either the story becomes thereby a kind of myth, to be repeated, or a hint of pain now transmuted into art as the writer does with her play.

Julia Cho was not the first playwright to stage aspects of her play in a car. Paula Vogel's *How I Learned to Drive*, as its title suggests, also takes place, in part, in one. There is plainly more than one journey involved in both. In the case of *Durango*, it is the journey of an immigrant and his wife out of another world into an America in which, at some level, they remain strangers, never entirely masters of the language, in Boo-Seng's case never a master of himself. At one end there is a desert, literal and symbolic; at the other a world of dubious motels, lit by neon.

It is the journey of their sons towards a self-knowledge they are desperate to deny, having been burdened with compensating for their parents' personal and social failures, the Red Angel being an expression of Jimmy's feeling that he has to save his parents from themselves and what he senses is the hostility of those they find themselves amongst. Finally, the Angel disappears, now stripped of his wings. The play ends with stasis, the characters gathered, but not together.

Speaking of *How I Learned to Drive*, Paula Vogel said, 'it seems to me that one thing that gets left out when we're talking about trauma is the victim's responsibility to look the experience squarely in the eye and then to move on. That's the journey I wanted to craft.'[21] The figures in *Durango* each have a trauma of a different kind. The journey they go on begins the process of confronting its nature, but there is little sense that they will move on.

Variety's response was not encouraging: 'If the parts were as striking as the whole, the script might be remarkable. Yet even though she masters the big picture, Cho's individual scenes feel like first drafts.'[22] *Curtain Up*'s was not a full endorsement. While observing that it was an 'unremitting dour play', Elyse Sommer conceded that it was 'lit up by entertaining, touching, and even funny scenes', even though adding that 'the label "emerging playwright" still fits Ms. Cho in that she hasn't come up with a flawless play yet'. However, she added that 'she is nevertheless well on the way towards building an impressive body of contemporary, interesting dramas. These dramas involve a group of as yet not much written about Americans which provide actors with roles to dig into, and audiences with something to think about.'[23] Next, however, would come a play which received almost universal approval.

If *Durango* ends on a dying fall, a sense of exhausted possibilities, her next play was far darker. *The Piano Teacher*, developed and first produced by South Coast Repertory, in Costa Mesa California, on 11 March 2007, had its New York premiere at the *Vineyard* Theatre (which had staged the premiere of *How I Learned to Drive* and *Three Tall Women*) seven months later. The idea for it, she explained, came when

> I was in my early 20s. I got a phone call from one of my old piano teachers ... It was very surprising to me because the lessons were such a long time ago. She was just calling to see how I was doing, but at the time, it seemed odd. I didn't know what to say, and I remember there was a slight feeling of discomfort through the conversation. As time has gone on, I have the memory of that phone call, and it's so clear to me why she called. It seems so human to reach out and want to speak to your former students to see what kind of effect you had on them. And I felt sad, because my realization and understanding was coming so many years too late.[24]

In large part a monologue, it is something of a gothic tale, the story of a darkness slowly revealed. It begins as Mrs.K., an elderly woman, looks out at the audience with what the stage direction indicates, is 'a wonderful gaze,'[25] before handing out cookies to those in the front row as if inviting them to listen to her anodyne reminiscences. Eating, it turns out, along with television, is more than a habit. A talented piano player, not quite good enough to be a professional, she had worked as a piano tuner until an illness affecting her ears made her turn, instead, to teaching. Alone since her husband died, she is plainly lonely and it occurs to her to contact former pupils, succeeding in the case of Mary who drops by to see her.

The past, though, it turns out, had been best forgotten and it becomes evident that there is something she has put out of mind following her mother's advice that every marriage is 'built on a certain amount if lying'. So it is that, while insisting that her husband had been 'a very honest man', she acknowledges that he had 'lied to me', though she is 'sure it pained him to do so'. (106) But, then, back in the European country from which he came, he had witnessed rape and murder, assaults on children. She hoped that her normality would act as a balm, whereas, it becomes apparent, it had become a camouflage, a distraction, though for what only becomes apparent with time. She acknowledges that he could be unfriendly and unapproachable, but there is a suggestion that he had been shunned by neighbours.

Most of her memories are of her pupils, though she hints at one of them whose promise had been ended by something she forebears to recall or, recalling, understand. After all, he had been one of her husband's favourites. She also remembers a disastrous recital in which her pupils' playing had been so bad that they had ceased their lessons. When Mary visits her, she explains that she had stopped her lessons because Mr. K had made her 'uncomfortable', without specifying why, though it is clear that Mrs. K had her suspicions. Had he, perhaps, been molesting them? As Mary is about to leave, Mrs. K insists on playing a piece for her. At first it is beautiful but then it descends into cacophony, a reflection of the collapse of her apparent assurance.

Things finally come to a crisis when she has another visitor, Michael, the one whose indefinite offence she had obliquely acknowledged. Now, we learn that Mr. K. had entertained her pupils by telling them terrifying stories of death and torture, showing them drawings, pictures of crimes against children. Michael takes her back in time by playing the piano saying he has a perfect auditory memory. What he remembers, though, is more than a piece of music. It is the sound of voices which do not come from an idyllic past. What he recalls is the sound of Mr. K beating his wife. Equally clearly, it becomes apparent that Michael had been fascinated by those stories, stories he had absorbed, going on to be guilty of crimes himself, coming to feel that those guilty of such cruelty were, and are, 'People like us', (134) like, indeed, his parents. We live, he declares, 'among supermarkets and doilies and nice curtains on the window, simply because we have all agreed to hide our knives. For now'. (135) He says this in a living room which a stage direction is described as 'exactly like the living room of your oldest living relative'. (97)

Was Mr. K a victim or a perpetrator? And can the same be said of his wife, she who hands cookies to the audience and passes the time watching television? Certainly, she now confesses that she no longer sleeps well, dreaming that she is stepping into the kitchen as a child to be greeted by her husband. She recalls that one of his favourite plays was *Hamlet*, in which a king has poison poured into his ear, as he had poured poison into the ears of children. The play ends as Mrs. K chooses to put this out of mind, remembering that she had taught music and that one of her pupils might now be somewhere playing a song in a room that is 'beauti', a 'roo'. She is unable to complete the words, even as she declares that she will tell her story of a good man and she his dutiful wife, musician, player of beautiful music, teacher, 'to the end'.

There are secrets in her other plays but not quite as devastating as here. It is not only Mrs. K who puts the presence of extreme violence out of mind. The implication is that it is a fact of human experience, and not just an experience sealed off by time, a product of faraway places. Classical music, as we have all learned from accounts of the concentration camps, had been an accompaniment to genocide, the cruellest people responding to its harmonies. Mr. K does not import violence and cruelty. He just gives it a particular accent.

The part of Mrs. K was seized on by Elizabeth Franz who won the Lucille Lortel Award and a Drama League Award. For Charles Isherwood, in *The New York Times*, she had 'given many marvellous performances in her long career ... But the affable, sympathetic, piteously deceived Mrs. K must rank among her finest achievements,' in Cho's 'finely wrought play' which 'coolly and effectively imparts its own insights about the transmission of evil in a globalized world, where actions a continent away can spread their malign influence to the suburb next door.'[26] But is she piteously deceived or even self-deceiving? Joe Keller, in *All My Sons*, having sent men to their deaths, is happy to play cards with neighbours, while away mornings in the garden in a play which begins with an untroubled normality only, as in Cho's play, for the ground slowly to shift beneath his feet. America did not succumb to malign influences a continent away, believing itself the last best hope of earth, as President Lincoln declared on the brink of its cruellest war.

Not all reviews were as positive but *DC Theatre Scene*'s Jeffrey Walker welcomed a production in Columbia, Maryland, as 'a tightly constructed chiller of a play that leads you down dark paths only to reveal unexpected recesses where the truth is darker still', a play which 'carefully takes you by the hand through what seems to be a benign visit with a lonely widow', even as 'by the end, its grip is tight and it will leave a mark – just not the one you expect'.[27] *The New Yorker* found it a gothic work which triumphs in dramatizing the unknown.

Cho followed *The Piano Teacher* with a comedy, *The Language Archive*. She had spoken earlier of her guilt at not learning Korean, her sense of loss as a result. Now she wrote a play in which a lost, or nearly lost, language plays a significant part, though its immediate inspiration came from reading a newspaper article about the last speaker of a language dying, and, along with that individual, a culture. In the end, though, it became a play about the different languages we all deploy, the way in which language shapes behaviour, the gap between feeling and its articulation, the different meanings ascribed to the same word, misunderstandings, wilful and otherwise. If language is the bridge we cross to encounter others and the world, there are impediments along the way. Tom Stoppard had fun in *Professional Foul* in which a professor of linguistic philosophy demonstrates the different meanings of the same word.

It is a play in which the audience is addressed, implicitly invited to be privy to the unfolding stories of miscommunication, struggles to articulate needs, a sense of what is shared as well as what is not. And when a language is not helpfully translated the audience has a concrete example of the difficulty of crossing the language barrier.

At its heart is George, a professor of linguistics, reasonably fluent in a number of languages, including the invented language Esperanto, but not fluent when it comes to feelings, his own and that of others. Professionally, he is intent to record the last speakers of a language. At the same time, he has difficulty communicating with his own wife, Mary, who frequently, and seemingly unaccountably, cries and who, while denying it, has resorted to leaving cryptic messages for him scattered around in unlikely places, hoping he will understand, until his failure to do so makes her decide to leave him.

The two subjects of his research, Altar and Reston, duly arrive but when the recorders are turned on to capture them speaking in a soon-to-be-dead language, Ellowan, they conduct a spiteful argument in English, explaining that the beauty of their own language does not permit such exchanges, an echo, inadvertently, of George Steiner's assertion that Nazism was easily accommodated to the German language. Can a language be innocent, given that it is a carrier of history? Do some languages bend in the direction of poetry and others of a prosaic bluntness and worse?

The Language Archive is a play in which language itself is in some degree its subject given that feelings can be contradictory and their expression therefore problematic. At a railway station, where Mary has gone to catch a train to nowhere in particular, she encounters an old man who plans to commit suicide by jumping in front of a train. Anxious to prevent this, she says, 'sometimes you can feel so sad, it begins to feel like happiness. And you can feel so happy it begins to feel like grief … you can feel so dead that you start to feel alive.'[28]

Part of the reason Altar and Reston argue is that he affects to hate the food she cooks except that when he is suddenly hospitalized it turns out that it had been his illness which prevented his eating. Words, it seems, can fall short. Asked whether there are words in Ellowan which have no equivalent in English, she replies, 'Yeah, like whole thing! Whole thing have no equivalent,' offering a series of examples, including, 'There is a word for kind of woman who is beautiful when you see her from far away but not so beautiful when you see her up close. There is a word for man who act younger and younger as he gets older and older.' The sentiments may be the same, but they are not codified in the same words. Much the same would seem to be true when she explains that the words for 'I love you', in her language mean 'I never want to be left by you'. (200) which has a special relevance in that George's assistant, Emma, is in love with him but cannot allow the words to pass her lips. It is she who comments, that in Ubykh, 'You please me' translates literally to, 'You cut my heart', (203) which precisely reflects Emma's feelings for George. Incidentally, Cho claims to have done little research for the play but Ubykh, perhaps not incidentally, is a real, extinct, Caucasian language, the last fluent speaker of which died in 1992 at the age of eighty-eight. One of the linguists who captured their language was called George (Georges Dumézil).

The second act begins with George teaching the audience Esperanto, persuading them to repeat after him variations of phrases whose English translation is: 'I am being loved, I have been loved, I am about to be loved, I was loved, I had been loved, I was about to be loved.' (211–12). This is a prelude to a lesson in Esperanto taught by an instructor. The pupil is Emma. This time there are no translations, except that, asked, in Esperanto 'How much is the cake?' she replies, 'I love George.' (213)

Now on a high, determined to tell George of her love, she walks through the street and Cho requires that the theatre should be 'flooded, and I mean absolutely flooded, by the most amazing smell', (216) something of a challenge for directors, as is her requirement that Emma should enter a bakery that is 'so perfect, so beautiful that it looks like a movie set' while inside it is the most beautiful woman she has ever seen, challenges for the set designer director and actress, more especially since this woman now transmutes into Mary, she having taken over the bakery from the man she met on the station. Emma then tells George where he can find his wife, he now a man transformed, for the first time able to cry. The man whose project was with dying languages has come to understand that the language he and his wife shared is itself threatened with extinction.

Now it is Emma who stands on the railway platform which suddenly appears. On the train she meets L L Zamenhof, the creator of Esperanto, who died in 1917, the Zamenhof who spoke an array of languages, wrote the first grammar of Yiddish and was hostile to nationalism. To him, Esperanto was to bring people together in peace. His three children all died in the Holocaust. But then, whatever fragile element of realism there might have been now disappears. His advice to Emma is to fall out of love, the only condition really which will allow her to return to George who never recognizes her feelings towards him, though he does now appear on the train.

The train then transmutes into the lab where a letter from Alta and Resten suddenly appears, as do they narrating it before the actors appear as themselves describing the fate of the characters they have played. Altar and Resten, we are told, 'bickered lovingly' until their deaths. Mary continued in the bakery and, finally, listened to the tape given to her by George which says, 'I love you', in a variety of doomed languages. He recalls the moment when he and Emma had embraced, for him a reminder of something he has lost, even as he had not loved her while continuing to work beside her. For her, however, the embrace had been a moment of joy even as it had been a moment of grief as he realized his loss of Mary. The play ends as the tape plays, 'I love you' sounding out in an array of languages, some dead, some about to be.

A play in which a linguist struggles with language, in which words prove inadequate to feeling, translation constantly falling short of meaning, and in which no one is truly fluent in intimacy, *The Language Archive* is a series of often jolting scenes, in which seeming reality fractures and even the tangible world dissolves and re-forms. This is a place where languages go to die, only to be stored away as if they contain mysteries yet to be solved. For Noam Chomsky, there are certain structural rules applicable to all languages, independent of any experience, a universal grammar. For Cho, it is a universal experience which shapes language, the experience of love, the word which echoes through the play. Though its meaning may shift, from culture to culture, individual to individual, there is a commonality, hence the invoking of Esperanto designed to defy fragmentation, a place in which all people can meet.

The play won the Susan Smith Blackburn Prize, a prize for women playwrights. Charles Isherwood, in *The New York Times*, responding to the Roundabout Theatre's production, found it full of 'lovely writing' which nonetheless 'never dispels an air of contrivance', even as it contained 'some bewitchingly fine speeches on the manner in which words sometimes fail to convey the overwhelming nature of feeling and its capacity for flux.'[29] Writing in *DC Theatre Scene*, Tim Treanor, responding to Maryland production, found it a very fine if not perfect work, 'an elegant, graceful confection of a play, whose startling observations and sometimes loopy plot developments mask the tensile strength of Julia's Cho's theme.'[30] When it was staged at the Piven Theatre Workshop in Evanston in 2014, Chris Jones, writing in the *Chicago Tribune*, responded to a 'very stimulating play … quite a lovely piece of writing', a 'rather haunting little show' that 'leaves you feeling that not a moment of your time was wasted'.[31]

Something happened in the period after *The Language Archive*: Cho's father died. The question was whether she could allow that fact into her work. 'For a lot of the time', she explained,

> when I was not writing, when I thought about actually sitting down to write, it felt impossible. It felt like obviously I should write about some of the things that happened, but I really didn't want to. And I felt maybe it would even be horrible to use the experience …. there's a poet, Stephen Dunn, who wrote a poem where the first line goes, 'When Mother died/I thought: now I'll have a death poem./That was unforgiveable.' I think for a long time I knew that if I wrote at all, it would inevitably go in that direction … and so it felt better to not even write at all.[32]

It was a dilemma which confronted the Israeli writer David Grossman when his son was killed. He said that the immediate effect was to stun him into silence. At first, he confessed, the reaction is to be silent, or to shout, to cry out … Then, later, I realised that if I do not find words for what has happened the channels between me and this loss will be gradually closed, and I did not want them to close … like everything that happens to me in my life I understand it through writing.[33]

Much the same would seem to have been true of Julia Cho. She began writing again when she took up a residency at Princeton's McCarter theatre, and especially when she met Paula Vogel. When she explained that 'There's this big boulder in the way and while I don't want to write about how hard the years have been, I feel like I can't write about anything else either', Vogel offered advice, not about the difficulty of writing about loss and death, 'and trying to face and defeat it',[34] but about trying to articulate what it was that she wanted to write.

She was then asked to join a project, run by Berkeley Rep, in which writers were invited to come up with short plays about food. Given that no one was likely to see it (and, indeed, hers only had a reading), she began a play about food and memory, with a chef at its centre. Suddenly, she realized that her character had lost his father. It was, she said, 'all the stuff I wasn't going to write about or didn't know how to write about'.[35] What she did was write herself a contract in which she promised to write every day until she had a play. The result was *Aubergine*, which opened on 5 February 2016, after a gap of six years. It was, she said, a back door to the play she believed she could not write, a play not only with a dying man at its centre, but which describes the process of dying with a clinical detachment as if it was necessary to confront it in its details. It includes a man who had failed to tell his son of his mother's death, a failure to confront a central truth which does damage.

For a play in which dying and death lie at the centre, it makes its way not only towards acceptance but an understanding that death puts a back pressure on the living to grasp life. What, as a writer, and an individual who had tried to deal with the loss of her father, she had come to understand, was that this is a fact common to all and which, while seemingly experienced alone, is actually a bridge to cross over towards others. She has always been concerned with loss, but this was a particular one. However, the play is not simply to do with death and its destabilizing impact.

A sub-theme is the familiar Cho one to do with the difficulty of communication, that between father and son, between brothers, a man and his girlfriend, but also across languages and time. Connections are easily broken in a play in which the crossing of boundaries has left characters negotiating their memories as well as the meaning of experiences which seemed no more than the banalities of daily life, childhood relationships, family meals. Here food functions not simply in the Proustian sense of carrying characters back in time, a smell with the power to recreate a moment, a feeling, but as the place of conflict and an expression of love.

The play opens with a monologue by Diane, described as an American woman in her forties (as opposed to a number of the other characters who are immigrants). She recalls the passion for food which she shared with her husband, Mark, one memory triggering another as she remembers her father's making of pastrami sandwiches when she was young, preparing one for her the night before his surgery for cancer. He survived the surgery, she explains, but the chemo destroyed his taste buds before he died, a fact which also destroyed her own interest in food. The savour of life had gone.

What immediately follows, however, is not her story but that of a Korean American, Ray, whose father, born in Korea, is dying, at first in a hospital, then at home where he is treated by a hospice nurse, Lucien, a one-time refugee. Having, professionally, seen so many deaths he still thinks it strange that, given that death comes to all, people are still surprised by it, preferring to turn their heads away. In a monologue, he recalls his time in a refugee camp where the lack of food prompted memories of the food he had once enjoyed.

Seeking help, Ray turns to a former girlfriend, Cornelia, asking her to telephone his uncle in Korea, she, having been born in Korea, fluent in the language. What follows is a conversation, in Korean, English translations in the play only appearing as supertitles when indicated in the text, as they are not at this point, she explaining what is being said. Cho relied on someone else to undertake the translations, a reminder once again of her own linguistic limitation and perhaps her desire to pay retrospective penance for it. The uncle's response is to offer the recipe for a special soup, Ralph offering Lucien an aubergine which he has grown. He is, it turns out, a chef and, briefly, we are back in his kitchen when Cornelia had worked there and when his relationship with his father was not as close as impending death would make it not least because they are in contention over his overuse of his father's credit card.

Ray's uncle now arrives, speaking only Korean, though at first somehow Ray understands what he is saying, if only from his miming. Cho has confessed that there came a moment when a Korean knocked on the door in her script, she saying to herself, 'I'm sorry, but I cannot let you in! I do not know how to write you! Please go away! And I remember getting up from my desk and pacing. "What do I do? What do I do?" I kept thinking, "Are there ways in which I could have him speaking in English, but we would understand that he's speaking Korean?" Then I was like, "No, because you can't replicate the grammar." It wouldn't give you an honest sense of the actual language, how unlike English it really is. Until basically I just reached a point where I thought, 'I'm just gonna write it in English 'cause that's the gist of what he's saying.'[36] Stumped, she put an asterisk before all the uncle's lines with a note saying, 'Everything after this asterisk is in Korean.' There seemed no way forward until Sarah Ruhl recommended a translator.

There was, she said, a link between *Aubergine* and *The Language Archive* because that play had been about '"Why don't I speak Korean?" How is it possible to be around a language all your life and not pick it up? It boggled my mind. *Language Archive* poses the question, "Why? Why don't we speak the tongues of our relatives?" *Aubergine* explores the consequences of that in a more immediate way.'[37]

The uncle's first gesture is to prepare ingredients for turtle soup, for which he has arrived with a live turtle. There follows an extensive interchange between Ray and his uncle, Cornelia translating into Korean. This time there are supertitles. For Ray there is no point in a soup his father cannot eat, a father who had never shown any interest in food except that before leaving for America his mother had prepared a soup which reduced him to tears.

Part Two begins with a monologue by Cornelia. Her mother, she explains, had been obsessed with food, originally a bond between mother and daughter until the time came when she rebelled and subsisted on peanut butter and crackers. When she met Ray, however, he won her with the simple food he offered, a bowl of mulberries. 'That's how I fell in love,' she confesses.[38]

Ray now cooks the soup but his father turns away, anyway never having appreciated his son's cooking even when, proud of his new skills, Ray had cooked him an elaborate meal, instead preferring ramen, a Japanese noodle soup costing almost nothing. His father now dies, but in the following scene has his own monologue even as he is aware that he is dead.

At the funeral, Ray recalls his father beginning a story about looking at himself in a full-length mirror and suddenly seeing something. What he saw, Ray now realizes, as he had looked at a similar mirror before coming to the funeral, is his own death, 'And I saw how, even though we are alive, we are in some respects dead. Even in the daily movements of life, we are already in our graves. That's what my father was trying to tell me. You are always already dead. So why not live?' (331)

In the penultimate scene, following the burial, Ray sits at a table opposite a mirror in which he sees his father, a father who duly appears. They begin to eat, Ray seeing his own future. In an epilogue, Diane appears for the first time since the opening scene. She is a customer in the restaurant on the evening of its opening, a place where Cornelia is a waitress and Ray the chef. As she sits there so she is brought 'a perfect sandwich … a pastrami sandwich' of the kind her father had once made. As she eats, so Ray and Cornelia watch, her hand on his. 'They smile.' (341)

Whatever they have been severally searching for they seem to have found. A certain grace has been granted. Relationships have been re-established. In an aquarium in the restaurant a turtle is swimming, reprieved from the moment it was seen as no more than an ingredient for turtle soup. These are all survivors who have come out the other side of something that had seemed an ending.

Writing in the *Los Angeles Times*, Charles McNulty welcomed 'a moving new play' which he saw as 'a rare form of entertainment, closer perhaps to enlightenment than we are accustomed to in these days of superficial distraction'.[39] Charles Isherwood, in *The New York Times*, found it a 'sensitive but sometimes sluggish drama', while observing that 'Although each of Ms. Cho's plays is markedly different, "Aubergine" … shares with earlier work like "The Language Archive" and "The Piano Teacher" a perceptive sense of the invisible barriers that mysteriously spring up between people, and the equally mysterious impulses that bind them together.'[40]

Her next play, *Office Hour*, was commissioned, developed and produced by South Coast Repertory, opening on 15 April 2016, its New York premiere, at the Public Theatre, following in December 2017. A Long Wharf production opened in January 2018. Berkeley Rep staged it a month later.

To the general bafflement of those outside the United States, and many within, America's Second Amendment puts guns into the hands of those happy to use them against themselves and their fellow citizens, not simply in the process of robberies, gang violence, racist assaults, drunken arguments, revenge attacks, marital strife, suicide, but in seemingly unfathomable moments of anarchistic slaughter of those who have become the focus of their dark imaginings. Sometimes they hear God whisper in their ears. More usually, what they hear is the echo chamber of their own resentments, loners by choice or, as they feel, as a consequence of exclusions. Most bewildering of all, however, is when the shooter walks onto a campus or into a school and kills those once their fellow students and pupils.

In April 2007, someone with Julia Cho's last name shot and killed twenty-seven students and five members of faculty at Virginia Tech. Seung-Hui Cho, who then killed himself, was an immigrant from South Korea and had suffered mental problems. Ordered to have treatment, he failed to turn up for appointments. He had always had difficulty communicating. He was often silent and hated to be touched. At school he wrote a report in which he said he wished to repeat the Columbine shootings where twelve students and one teacher were murdered. The two shooters, Eric Harris and Dylan Klebold, laced their creative writing projects with violence. Three years before *Office Hour* Adam Lanza, himself fascinated by Columbine, shot and killed twenty-seven people at Sandy Hook Elementary School in Connecticut before shooting himself. He hardly interacted with fellow pupils, feeling and being isolated, and wrote about violence. He had mental health problems.

At Virginia Tech, Cho switched from majoring in business information systems to English and wrote a novel which was rejected. What he wrote was often violent and fellow students were afraid of him. He had an altercation with a professor, writing letters of complaint, and purchased guns frequenting a shooting range.

It was this event which prompted Julia Cho to explore a character who shared many of the characteristics of the Virginia Tech shooter, and, indeed, those at Columbine and Sandy Hook, but the play goes beyond that, enquiring into those around a young man whose behaviour is, indeed, alarming, but who is not unique in his sense of alienation, of a world which does not come into alignment with dreams of perfection and right action. The printed text includes an epigraph from the Swedish novelist and playwright Hjalmar Söderberg: 'People want to be loved; failing that admired; failing that feared; failing that hated and despised. They want to evoke some kind of sentiment. The soul shudders before oblivion and seeks connection at any price.' Just how do you convince yourself that you exist in the world, that you are not invisible to yourself no less than to others? What are the terms on which existence could be said to have meaning, that you have registered on the consciousness of others?

The setting is a university campus. Instructors discuss a student, Dennis, who refuses to respond to questions and submits work in his creative writing class, and then a theatre class, which is violent and sexually perverse. He alienates, indeed frightens, his fellow students. His refusal to speak, along with the violence of his writing, suggests that he might fit the profile of a shooter. He wears a cap pulled down and dark glasses. Attempts to report him come to nothing. The suggestion that he should seek therapy comes to nothing since he would have to refer himself voluntarily. After all, he is a would-be writer and as such is encouraged to write as he will. One teacher's response is to fail him, only for negative ratings of his teaching to appear on web sites, along with anonymous letters to the dean. Only one of the tutors is less sure, Gina, whose class he has just joined.

It is she who begins to open him up as he comes for a required meeting. At first, he remains silent until he suddenly reaches into his backpack, removes a gun and shoots her, except that, following a brief blackout, the scene continues, nothing having actually happened. It is she who now begins speaking, recalling that, when young, she had also spent a period being silent. Though she had set out to learn about him and his background it is her life that is slowly revealed. She is only an adjunct, with no hope of tenure. She suffers from insomnia, confesses to the problems of being a writer, tempted to feel as if writing were 'some kind of shadow we cast' wanting 'to throw the biggest shadow possible',[41] as Arthur Miller once wrote of Willy Loman trying to write his name on a block of ice on a summer's day.

She slowly lures him out of his isolation, trading information about herself. She is getting divorced, has no children, is herself, it seems, the daughter of an immigrant who had experienced rejection, her marriage enabling her to be treated as an American. It is a tactic to draw the student out, but, at the same time, a sleight of hand by Cho as Gina becomes as much a subject as Dennis.

Gina suggests that she understands his rage. Her own father had been so depressed that 'he wouldn't move or talk for days, weeks', now realizing that this had been about power: 'the quieter he was, the more he controlled us. All we could do was talk about him, wonder about him', (375) as Dennis's teachers do about him. Her father, she confesses, does not talk to her, since she had raised her voice when he was about to attack her mother, a father who was 'troubled and sad and angry'. (390) She, herself, has been in therapy. She needs to be liked which he, it seems, does not. Her mother, she confesses, did not want her to be a writer, and still does not.

Conscious of his pain, she puts a reassuring hand on his shoulder, only for him to kiss her. She pushes him away, another rejection. But then she discovers he owns a gun and, indeed, is carrying more than one. She then shoots him, except that, once again, after a blackout, it is apparent that this is not real, simply a projection of fears, her own and that of society because, as she says, 'all of us have guns'. (390)

They are interrupted by David, an instructor, himself angry at the anonymous abuse he has been receiving. A 'cacophony of many different versions' is played out, David shooting Dennis, Gina shooting herself, David shooting Gina, Dennis shooting out the window and David shooting Gina, a man in black appearing in the doorway and shooting them all. The doors of the theatre open. There are men in the doorway as if the audience is about to experience an attack, except that, once again, this is unreal. Following a blackout, the previous scene resumes.

It is now, Gina says, David who makes her feel unsafe while advising Dennis to go to student services for therapy. Dennis is then seen alone, at four in the morning thinking about something he has read about garbage in the Pacific, that is 'so far away. We know it is there but we don't see it. And because we can't see it, we don't think about it. So it just sits there. Getting bigger day by day by day by day', (397) just as the spasm of violence in the country is accommodated to a supposed norm.

The fantasy moments in which the characters shoot one another are precisely an expression of what is there but not acknowledged, seemingly remote from daily experiences but an ever-present fact. Every day twenty-two children and teens are shot in America. Ninety people a day are shot unintentionally. Over 40,000 Americans are killed each year by gun violence. *Office Hour*, though, is not a rallying cry against the gun lobby, even as a student carrying two guns on a campus disturbs more than the supposed equanimity of what is sometimes thought of as an ivory tower, along with the equanimity of the audience. Dennis clearly does have the potential to turn fantasy into reality, but he is not the only one who has experienced rejection, alienation, depression. Gina, like 60 million Americans, has been in therapy. Her marriage has collapsed. She is insecure in her job, has seen violence at first hand in her family, has witnessed the problems of immigrants and what it is to be the daughter of an immigrant. The Virginia Tech shootings may have provided a model for a young man with the potential for violence but, beyond probing into his psyche, Cho is interested in the woman who seeks to understand him and, in the process, reveals aspects of her own life.

Reviewers were uneasy about the alternative reality summoned up and the use of guns. 'Why', Jesse Green asked in *The New York Times*, 'in lamenting the terror that our gun culture has unleashed, should a play take up the weapons of its enemies?' but, then, he confesses that 'triggers are my trigger. The firing of guns in plays upsets me in ways that can overwhelm whatever other response I might have.'[42] In a play which laments the fact that people put the reality of gun violence out of mind, confrontation with it would seem to be part of the point.

Michael Feingold, writing in the now-defunct *Village Voice*, responded positively to the play while suggesting that,

> For all its focus on gunfire, it doesn't really deal with school shootings and what makes someone a shooter. It's more concerned with emotional comprehension and issues of

creative expression – matters that dominate earlier Cho plays like the bittersweet idyll *Durango* (2006) and the tenderly sardonic comedy *The Language Archive* (2007). Though Cho has carefully constructed Dennis to convey the outward image of a mass killer, we see little of the mental disturbance that runs deep inside all the known cases.

He concludes, 'Making sense of violence isn't easy; striving to make sense in a play that struggles to comprehend such violence must surely be a fearsome task.'[43] In his review he describes Dennis as Asian American, and he was indeed played by the South Korean Ki Hong Lee in the Public Theatre production, but in both the South Coast Repertory and the Long Wharf productions he was a white American, as were the shooters who provided the models. Nothing in the text suggests otherwise.

Reviewing the New Haven production, Donald Brown put his emphasis elsewhere.

Perhaps we used to assume that homicidal sociopaths don't sign up for writing courses or maintain a GPA in college. These days, there are no such certainties, but what Gina and Dennis also face in Julia Cho's aware play is the great uncertainties that have always faced the writer: is anyone listening, does anyone care, and does anyone see things the way I do?[44]

Struck by the tone of many of the reviewers, Paula Vogel wrote,

I thought of MARAT/SADE as I left the Public theatre, having seen Julia Cho's OFFICE HOUR. Of course, by the time I saw the play, some of the almost hysteric reviews worked as effectively as the trigger warnings (note: because of the origins of the word hysteric I only use that word when men are in the mix). I expected the stage effects, and therefore I was braced for the impact on my heart. But it did have an impact; how could it not? It had the impact on my heart that the news of successive massacres no longer have as I read the papers and watch the news. Repetition deadens the impact.[45]

She was drawn to recall Artaud's theatre of cruelty. It is not hard to see why she invoked Artaud, who wished to abolish the line between stage and auditorium, as Cho does in having that auditorium not only invaded by sound, physically affected by it, but also by actors, except that Artaud had a suspicion of language. He looked for a poetry in space rather than what he called a poetry in language, asking 'whoever said the theatre was created to analyse a character, to resolve the conflicts of love and duty, to wrestle with all the problems of a topical and psychological nature'.[46] He reacted against the idea of a performed text. So, while Vogel focussed on the physical activity, the swirl of action, this was in the context of a play in which language is central and that did concern itself with love, duty and problems of a topical and psychological nature. Cho also has nothing of Artaud's mysticism which would so appeal to the Living Theatre.

Speaking in particular of *Aubergine*, she has said that while there is one way in which a story exists with a beginning, a middle and an end, it is not the only kind of story. During her career she has experimented with different ways of telling stories, breaking into the action, having characters address the audience or themselves, including moments of fantasy. Her interest in questions of identity has led her to be fascinated with language, her own prose sometimes lyrical, sometimes elliptical, sometimes brutally direct. She is interested in the small change of life which in the end proves of greater significance than it seems. She charts the ambiguities of love, characters who feel the need for connection even as that can seem impossible.

When she was thirty-four, and her daughter twenty-one months old, her husband died suddenly, drowned in a Swiss lake. There is a reason, then, why she has identified her themes as love, loss and memory, why, indeed, she is writing a memoir, though those themes were already evident as she wrote about the loss of a culture, of intimate relationships, of a sense of self in a society with its own imperatives. There are few of her plays not touched by humour. Along the way, from staged readings, development, the smallest of small theatres, to major stages, she has won a series of awards and has also turned her talents to television as a writer, story editor and producer. She has established herself as a unique voice in the American theatre, never predictable.

Speaking in 2007, at the beginning of her career, she said something which I suspect she would still say today, despite many plays and much success:

> I'm grateful to be where I am. I know how difficult it is to get produced, and I feel enormously lucky to have worked at such amazing theatres. But I think there is also always a kind of dissatisfaction with my own writing. I want to be better – not just as a writer but as a person I want to know more, feel more, imagine more ... I continuously feel like a beginner. With each new play I sit down, and I have no idea how to write it. It always feels like there is so much to learn; it's endless. It's the work of a lifetime.[47]

CHAPTER 3
JACKIE SIBBLIES DRURY: STAGING RACE

> People feel the need to ask the artist to explain what the play meant, and that seems very destructive to [the] idea of asking people to try to take their own meanings from this show. (Jackie Sibblies Drury on *Fairview*).[1]

Jackie Sibblies Drury's parents were, she has pointed out, not members of a minority in Jamaica. It took America to make them that, a fact which shocked her mother: 'I think moving near Newark in the early '70s, when there were race riots happening, it was like America is racist and terrifying. But I think that she didn't think about race that much before coming to America.' In Jamaica, though, there had been another problem:

> For West Indian people, generally, colourism is a huge issue. I feel that my mom was more sensitive to that than she was to race in some ways ... A lot of her sense of fairness and equality is shade-oriented rather than race-oriented. And in some ways that was really helpful for me growing up in terms of feeling kinship with lots of different minorities. I feel like my mom was like, 'Americans are racist. You have to be careful.' And she'd be like, 'Jamaicans are sexist. So you have to be careful.' Not wrong. I just think it's more complicated

how much so being evident in her plays. If Drury was interested in the nature and impact of racism, she would also be concerned with the position of women, in and beyond the theatre.

She was raised by her Black mother (Sibblies being her maiden name) and white grandmother, and so grew up in a largely female space, her father leaving following divorce. Unlike Martyna Majok, she did not experience poverty but was sent to a private school which, though multi-cultural, nonetheless could sometimes see pupils align themselves along racial and class lines, 'segregation even in a harmonious community'.[2] It was her introduction to the idea of entitlement, some of her fellow pupils being members of country clubs. Her mother, however, became a successful business woman, working for a major supermarket, a job with its perks, enabling them to have free tickets to the theatre, and she became a regular theatre-goer, though often finding herself the only person of colour in the audience, a fact which would later play its part in her interest in the audience as part of the dramatic experience. In contrast to her mother's Jamaican experience, she did grow up thinking of herself as part of a minority, but she would say that while 'Race is involved in the way I go through the world ... it's only one aspect of what makes up a person.'[3]

She was in her mid-teens when she bought a copy of Ntozake Shange's *For Colored Girls Who Have Considered Suicide/ When the Rainbow Is Enuf*. It was, she would say, one of the first plays she had bought with a Black woman on the cover, though she thought of it as a series of poems rather than a play given that it departed from what she assumed was the normal form.

Years later, with her first play, she would herself experiment with form in a work whose title would be twice as long as Shange's, though the same length as Peter Weiss's *The Persecution and Assassination of Jean-Paul Marat as Performed by the Inmates of the Asylum of Charenton under the Direction of the Marquis de Sade*.

When she attended Yale University, she encountered people who were 'very, very, very entitled, expected everything from the world and expected the world would greet them with open arms and give them whatever they wanted'. In retrospect, though, she felt that 'if I hadn't been completely drowned in that kind of psychotic self-interest ... I don't think that I would be thinking that I could write things that other people would find interesting.'[4] She found her place, however, among those studying and making theatre.

At first she thought of herself as an actor, though confessed to not being particularly good at it. Her first attempt at play writing came in a class taught by the performance artist and playwright Deb Margolin, co-founder of the Split Britches company, a class which she has described as life-altering for those who took it. It was a solo performance class in which students were asked to write pieces about their lives and then perform them.

From Yale, she went to Brown University where she studied with the playwright Mia Chung, daughter of South Korean parents, and Mallory Avidon, writer and dramaturg in a programme headed by Obie Award-winner and Pulitzer finalist Lisa D'Amour and the experimental playwright Erik Ehn, whose *Maria Kizito* was based on the Rwandan massacre. Maria Kizito was a Rwandan Benedictine nun sentenced to twelve years in prison for her role in the deaths of hundreds of people taking refuge in their convent, the Mother Superior receiving a fifteen-year sentence. Together, not only did they direct death squads to the convent, they provided fuel to burn it down with their victims inside.

All her teachers had different approaches to writing which meant that those studying felt free to develop without conforming to any template. What Brown gave her was time and being taken seriously as a writer. It was while she was there that, as her thesis, she began work on *We Are Proud to Present a Presentation about the Herero of Namibia, Formerly Known as Southwest Africa from the German Sudwestafrika, between the Years 1884–1915*. It came, she has said, out of a class she took on historiography. 'The students who were white felt the immediate need to apologise for their privilege ... They looked to the ethnic people in the class as experts and felt they had nothing to add to the conversation.'[5]

The subject, which she stumbled on when researching another possible idea, was the massacre of the Herero people by Germany before the First World War, in what was then German Southwest Africa (today, Namibia). It followed a rebellion against German colonial rule. On 2 October 1904, General von Trotha, describing himself as the great General of German troops, issued a proclamation offering bounties on the leaders of the rebellion and requiring the Herero, a pastoral people, to leave the land. Anyone failing to do so would be shot, including women and children. Ethnic cleansing would be a polite description. What he wished to do was annihilate, his word, the Herero, this in what turned out to be a century of genocides including the Rwandan genocide of 1994 (the subject of J.T. Rogers' *The Overwhelming* as well as Ehn's play), and that in Srebrenica (dramatized by Nicolas Kent in *Srebrenica*) the following year. Perhaps oddly, there are, as far as I am aware, no references in her interviews to any of these genocides, despite studying with Ehn and exploring an African genocide which took place over a century earlier. On the other hand, the resonances are hard to ignore.

This was the first draft and had a workshop in the middle of the semester. It was, she has remarked, 'really terrible'. It had a different ending every day. She came to realize that the problem lay in trying to write directly about the genocide, her failure to do so eventually opening up possibilities as she wrote a play, as she explained in a conversation with Ehn, in which actors would themselves fail to make the same play she had failed to make. She subsequently submitted it to the Ignition Festival in Chicago, designed for emerging writers of colour under the age of forty. It was chosen for production following further workshops. Later, as part of the SOHO Rep writers group, a different version of the play was produced. When she wrote it she had no expectation of a production, otherwise, she has said, she would never have given it such a long title.

She has noted that 'the way that we talk about race now, and the way that we deal with racism, is by not talking about it and not dealing with it, or feeling that we have already dealt with it, and I think that that can be really damaging'.[6] Hence a play that would do so, focussing on an event about which she had originally known nothing and of which she was reasonably certain audiences would also be ignorant. The question was how to approach it, to inform without resolving into a graceless download of information, except that that would itself, in turn, prove the solution.

J.T. Rogers's approach was to introduce the genocide through two naïve American characters. Drury's differed. Along the way she 'introduced this meta-theatrical element' which allowed the actors to 'struggle with a similar thing that I felt I was struggling with – in trying to capture this story'. The solution was to begin with actors trying to produce a lecture. However, she continued to have problems with the ending, slowly working her way towards it, trying to avoid an easy resolution that would do an injustice to the subject and leave audiences free to say '"Racism is sad. Genocide is Sad. I feel Sad. I can leave, and go get a sandwich …. I wanted to free the audience and the performers of that need to make everything OK, because it's just not OK. Allowing that was really important to me."'[7]

Along the way, though, the play would be less about the Herero people than a story about America and race. As she confessed,

> I was hyper aware of the fact that in some ways I was just using their story to tell a different story. It could be seen as incredibly offensive to boil … this huge atrocity down to an example of something, and point at it and not investigate it … I just felt completely incapable of creating a piece of theatre that would somehow speak for these people … I did feel I was equipped to tell a story about America and contemporary race dynamics …. I take solace in the fact that even though the play is ultimately not about Africa or about Namibia or about the Herero, specifically, it is at least exposing people to that history.'[8]

The theorist Saidiya Hartman has said,

One of the things I think is true, which is a way of thinking about the afterlife of slavery in regard to how we inhabit historical time, is the sense of temporal entanglement, where the past, the present and the future, are not discrete and cut off from one another, but rather that we live the simultaneity of that entanglement. This is almost common sense for black folk. How does one narrate that?[9]

Jeremy O. Harris would find one way, in *Slave Play* (2018), eliding the slave plantation with the contemporary. Drury takes a different path, linking colonial Africa to a modern experience.

When the play was staged at the Bush Theatre in London, in 2014 (in a slightly modified version, the characters being British), and published by Bloomsbury Methuen Drama, it was accompanied by a somewhat elliptical note by the author entitled 'Empathy by Another Name'. It began by invoking a number of what she called cop shows, police procedurals, recalling the theory that they are so popular because 'everyone wants to believe that someone is going to care about them after they're gone', that someone will shout out, 'She was a human being, dammit! She matters! ... She Mattered.' To her, theatre was an expression of this, the need for, and a means to express, empathy which was why, she explained, she was 'drawn to history, to remembering, to study how people have been remembered by other people, to remember how people would like to be remembered'.

But to study history is to study death, or deaths, which can so easily be 'elided as history is canonised',[10] in other words care for the individual can be lost in the broad sweep of that history. Genocide is about the silencing of a race; it is also the silencing of the individual, care for whom is the essence of humanity, the past to be re-imagined in so far as the trace of that individual is to be identified. Theatre can place at centre stage those who history, and forgetfulness, has displaced from the public mind, its very processes requiring empathy on the part of actors and audiences alike, its communal nature proposing a model of shared experience.

Hers might seem a somewhat misleading introduction to a play which begins with what appear to be barely competent actors trying to find a way of approaching a serious subject, unsure quite how to handle it, in the process creating a humour seemingly at odds with the task. On the other hand, it is a play about remembering, about a past to be retrieved even if things don't quite go as planned, even as the ostensible subject moves in unexpected directions, apparently unexpected by the actors as by the audience which also has its part to play. As in her subsequent work, Drury is interested in disorienting audiences, defying expectations, shifting her ground. Genocide would hardly seem to lend itself to farce and yet that is how the play begins as an amateur cast struggle to understand their roles, relate to the subject, distracted by actorly problems. The very form of the play, lurching from an earnest presentation of facts to comic set pieces, from performance to rehearsal, the one acknowledging the presence of the audience, the other not, is designed to be unsettling while all the time the subject is supposedly mass murder. Is it permissible, then, to laugh, or is that to become complicit? In the title there is no mention of genocide, merely of a presentation of information about an obscure people in a remote country at a distant period, as if this were to be no more than a lesson in anthropology. And what to make of the proposed connection between events in Africa and the world closer to hand, to make sense, finally, of the ending?

As she has said, 'audiences were pretty polarized, but I don't think that was surprising to me. There was some reaction where people didn't know what to do with that openness and felt unguided or uncared for and didn't think that it was a dramatic work.' That, however, she found 'exciting to think about: getting the chance to expose people to a different way of telling a story or a different way of interacting with a play'. For her, the worst way to do the play

> is to explain all the connections. To me the play ... combines two different events, or two different forms of discrimination. And I don't think that it equates them, but I do think that it puts them next to each other on the same plate. And the actors get confused

about it, and I hope that the audience gets confused about it too because I certainly feel confused about it! ... I think that was all very cryptic and vague and maybe slightly pretentious.[11]

The play, whose London production differed somewhat from the American one, features three Black and three white actors, only one identified by name, who are rehearsing their parts, sometimes aware of an audience, sometimes not as they make their way towards a final version. Part of the time, they are stumbling to recall what they have agreed in the way of a text, conscious that they addressing an audience ignorant of the subject matter and of what their approach will be. Part of the time they are rehearsing as though without an audience, the whole adding up to the various stages of a production, so that in some sense theatre itself becomes a subject, the problem of communicating a truth through simulation, discovering a style, acknowledging, indeed, that this is a performance, that actors have another existence. I once did a platform performance at Britain's National Theatre with Alun Armstrong. At one moment he stepped forward and played a particularly moving speech as Willy Loman in *Death of a Salesman*. As he did so, however, he turned to me, upstage, and winked, simultaneously Willy Loman and Alun Armstrong. The relationship between performer and role is not a simple one, the artifice of theatre being evident in all aspects of a performance, from the moment of entering the auditorium, to the programme notes, the curtain, the lighting, costumes, set design.

In the 1960s it was a commonplace for some theatre companies to foreground that artifice, for actors to announce their real names, physically interact with the audience, deconstruct texts in favour of improvisation, suspicious of the authority of writers, language's power to deceive. Drury draws on some of those techniques in a search for an entry point into her apparent subject, mixing humour, slapstick, seeming improvisation, elements of documentary theatre, even while parodying it, rushing through history as a series of bullet points presented in a casual colloquial style until 'big finish' as all the actors join together to announce the play's title.

On one level, then, the play is a satire on the acting profession, actors seemingly in search of truth but meanwhile negotiating their primacy in a competitive environment even as they celebrate being part of an ensemble. A character, trying to express sadness, thinks of her cat in an exercise in affective memory, underscoring the ironic discrepancy between the painfully real and the potentially banal. Actor 6, the 'sort of' artistic director, asks Actor 5 'to think of your cat as though it were still alive today', adding that 'the saddest thing that I have ever seen was a really old cat', (32) a story which is then elaborated to the point of absurdity and which a note indicates 'is probably a lie'.

Her characters are in their twenties and should 'seem open, skilled, playful and, perhaps, at times, a little foolish'. In notes, she suggests ways in which violence can be presented, calling for 'real contact', a slap on the shoulder and a loose rope around the neck feeling more dangerous than theatrical devices.

The play begins as the actors enter, one, a Black woman, acknowledging the audience and clearly not fully prepared, beginning with special announcements relating to the theatre or a nearby bar, crossing off a to-do list on a stack of note cards and explaining what they plan, a 'sort of' lecture and a 'kind of' overview 'before the lecture, which is before the presentation', all of which is to be 'Super fun', (6) this in a play apparently about a genocide, even as the word is not signalled in the title. She, who describes herself as 'kind of' the artistic director of the 'ensemble', then introduces the actors, each of whom identities himself or herself as, indeed, performers. She will, she explains, be playing the part of Black Woman even as she is 'also Black in real life', which she confesses might be confusing, as is the fact that the man playing White Man is also white.

They then begin a lecture, offering details of the languages spoken in Namibia, including English and Afrikaans (by virtue of colonization), quickly outlining historical details and dates in a manner which Drury indicates should be 'fast-paced', 'cartoonish', frantic, each brief note marked by the ding of a bell and 'a brief comic tableau' which 'sums up what was said about the previous year'. Then, 'bam: we're in the rehearsal room', (16) with a whirl of activity, disagreements over staging. 'It's theatre, you know?/ You don't just stand there.' (18)

Particularly at stake is the question of the reading of letters ostensibly sent home by German soldiers, if, indeed, they are to be used at all, though in fact all of these were written by the author, she not even being sure there were any, simply presuming there must have been. Apart from anything else, the question of authenticity is plainly central. Who is telling whose story? Is it the Germans, the playwright, the actors? And what is the story?

Unable to make out, or pronounce, the names of the recipients of the letters, the actors decide that they should all have been addressed to someone called Sarah, hence the one named person in the dramatis personae. The rehearsal is familiar to those who have taken part in, or observed them, in that it consists of discussions/ debate/arguments about meaning, possible back stories, the use, or not of accents, Actor 3 announcing that he can do 'several regional accents in German', another claiming that he can do a great Edelweiss as if this were *The Sound of Music* and, indeed, he proves it by singing. Actor 2 announces that he 'can do an African accent while speaking German: Ich bin ein Berliner', (28–9) John F. Kennedy's famous remark in his 1963 speech in West Berlin. Interlaced with this, as suggested by that claim, are professional rivalries, Actor 5 (Sarah) saying 'I'm trying to be sad but he's not giving me anything to work with', (30) Drury's one-time ambition to be an actor showing through.

From the rehearsal, the play briefly moves into performance and, in truth, an exchange of stunning banality which does not bode well for the finished drama, before we are back in rehearsal and a parody of actor insecurity as Actor 5 complains that she doesn't know what her character is supposed to be doing, what her perspective or motivation is, desperately inventing an ever more elaborate back story in order to enter the character, deploying an unconvincing German accent as one of the other actors hums Edelweiss. For a moment they are all enrolled in this back story as she invents two children, one called Leipzig, this evidently being a word which comes into her head, a boy who is bullied at school, she advising 'Find ze grossest boy and give him ein shtomp'. (37) None of them can go much beyond cod German and fake accents.

In performance, though, they reveal a new, and surprising, competence even as the style shifts again, Sarah singing a folksong which devolves into a dance, even sampling a popular song before White Man raps a letter while Black Man beat boxes before we are once more back in rehearsal as the actors again try to develop more of a back story for the letter we have just heard. What Drury calls Presentation, the actual performance, now moves on in time with what is a love letter between a German soldier and the woman he has left behind, only for those in rehearsal to ask why they are acting a scene in which a white person is writing home rather than discovering Black people which, by this time, with the play approaching its halfway point, audiences might themselves have begun to wonder, Actor 2 objecting, 'This is some Out-of-Africa-African-Queen-bullshit … If we are in Africa, I want to see some black people', (45) even as the Africa they envisage consists of trees dripping with fruit, monkeys, elephants and giant snakes, the Black actors adopting fake 'African' accents, fantasizing scenes in which they ululate, dance, kill and eat tigers (of which there are none in Africa).

This, however, is a key, if ironic, moment because Actor 2 (Black Man) now insists that the point of the play is that 'Black people can understand what black people went through', as Actor 6 (Black Woman) explains that for her the idea for the play began when she realized there was a connection between her family and a distant tribe that had nearly been destroyed, 'It was like I was having a conversation with my grandmother'. (49) That, of course, was, in a sense, the starting point for Drury's play, in that she was concerned to establish a pre-history to the American experience. When she had been researching it she had come across traumatic pictures of a Herero man hanging from a tree, 'and it was so difficult for me not to associate that with lynchings in the South'. Though different in time and context, it was, she said, a palimpsest, in other words the later image over-writing the earlier one, as pentimento is a painting which obscures and replaces the original. An event which she had stumbled on when researching a different subject had thus become more than an interesting historical footnote. The problem was how to establish a nexus between the two experiences, and how to find a form which could forge that link.

What, though, is the role of Actor 3 (Another White Man) who, while assuming the role of Actor 6's Black grandmother, says 'You can't take no walk in somebody else's shoes and know anything. You ain't bought those shoes, you ain't laced those shoes up, you ain't put those shoes on day after day … You can go ahead and steal somebody else's shoes and guess what? They ain't your shoes', (54–5) even as that is what, at that moment, he is doing, even as that is, in part, what the theatre, the novel, art, is about. If empathy is what is required are campaigns against cultural appropriation adequate to the task? Here, after all, are Black actors presenting themselves as white Germans and as Africans of whom they confessedly know nothing they have not discovered on Wikipedia. Drury deliberately lays a trail of breadcrumbs with no indication of where they should lead.

The problem is that for the Germans, whose letters they read, Africans are disposable, invisible, not a subject for letters home. Thus, more than halfway through a play whose title had promised to be 'about the Herero', they have barely had a mention. The actors accordingly consider improvising, though Actor 1 (White Man) objects that 'we shouldn't be making things up, we shouldn't be doing anything other than what's real', (57) even as that is what Drury herself is doing, the letters themselves being invented and, indeed, the actors now invent their own letter play as if to underscore that fact.

The play clearly has other issues beyond race, the need to recuperate history. Throughout, it is also a debate about authenticity, legitimacy, the ability, or otherwise, of theatre to arrive at the truth through lies. It was Maya Angelou who observed that truth and fact may not be the same thing, that facts can obscure the truth even as, here, Actor 1 declares, 'there's facts, there's truth', (61) while confessing to the problem of accessing either. It was Arthur Miller, in his Thomas Jefferson Lecture, who quoted Harold Clurman as speaking of the theatre as lies like truth, himself confessing that the theatre does, indeed, lie, that the actor lies, from 'his calculated laughter to his nightly flood of tears' while insisting that this may nevertheless 'fabricate a vision of some important truth about the human condition that opens us to a new understanding of ourselves',[12] the more important at a time when politicians become actors, mostly bad ones, fabricating themselves, when truth is not simply up for debate but a casualty of political polemics.

Throughout her play, Drury stages not only a remote event, with contemporary significance, but an exploration of both the problematics of theatre, potentially compromised by its very status as a fabrication, and its capacity to arrive at revelation, telling the truth but, in the words of Emily Dickinson, telling it slant. The presentation of rehearsals, alongside the finished production, is a reminder that the play is itself a construction, a text to be interpreted by the director, actors, designers, composers, something she was happy to encourage, looking for them to put their own stamp on it before audiences brought their own experiences to bear, offered their own interpretations, her technique of pulling the rug from under their feet destabilizing any certainty they may have arrived at.

One evidence for that destabilizing comes when one of the actors relates the Herero genocide to the Holocaust which reference did, apparently, shock not simply because of the difference in scale but because for some, at least, the Holocaust has a unique status. It is as though she were dropping a stone in the water leaving the ripples to spread out even as the action moves on, the actors now imagining the relationship between a German soldier and his wife, bringing to bear a passion and even poetic sensibility in contrast to the events they are supposedly committed to staging.

Finally, they return, briefly, to 1892, recalling their supposed subject, before they rehearse a scene set two years later in which the actors demand a break. Then, the pace picks up as, in 1905, the General's edict dispossessing the Herero of their land is elaborated and the actors begin an improvisation which is 'a great improv', (77) in which one of the Herero, wishing to return to his home, is shot. For the first time now, a link is established with America through a story told by Actor 3 (Another White Man) in which his white great-grandfather had shot a Black fellow soldier in the Union Army to save himself from Confederate soldiers angered that the Union was using Black soldiers. For Actor 2 (Black Man), however, this is simply one more example of a white man's version of the past, insisting that 'It doesn't matter if it's true or not.' (87)

What follows is a confrontation between the German soldiers and a Herero man in which he is told 'run, nigger', Black Man running, as the Ensemble chants, the whites mocking him until 'words become chants or song' and then dance, a counterpoint set-up between Black and white characters, racist jokes interspersed with Black Man insisting on his racial identity as a noose is put around his neck and the rope thrown over a beam, this jolting the actor out of his role.

The nature of the ending is described in an elaborate stage direction which calls on the actors to 'process what just happened … Discomfort, Frustration. Awkwardness. Nerves. Adrenaline. Uncertainty. Buzzing. Embarrassment. Guilt. Shame. Anger. Excitement. Something … Which might lead to a smile. Which might lead to laughter', quite a demand. They might 'laugh and cry, laugh and scream, they might laugh and be silent, they might laugh and rip things apart. They might laugh and break … the play might lose control, but the performers cannot stop until there is laughter, and it is genuine. The performers say and do whatever is in their minds.' The actors then clean the stage placing the noose in a box of letters. Actor 5 looks at the audience, tries to speak, but fails. (101–2)

The jumble of responses, the contradictory impulses, shifting tone, the final surrender of control by the author, reflect both the play in which they have struggled to find an approach, and the likely response of audiences who have been asked to adjust to a shifting dramatic strategy and to offensive humour even as they are confronted with disturbing images, audiences aware of the responses of other members of the audience. Drury throws the pieces in the air seemingly content for them to fall where they may, distrustful of an ending which assumes that the bridge between then and now can be easily crossed, that there can be a neat resolution, the gift of a mystery resolved, a catharsis finally realized, concerned, as she is, to start rather than end a conversation. The code of racism is not broken, only inhabited. The paradox of genocide by those who see themselves not only as civilized but also humane is not resolved. The link between the Black experience in Africa and America is simultaneously real and too easily homogenized. There is no absolution, not only for those who perpetrated genocide or racial violence, but for those tempted to feel themselves immune, free to watch the play as though observing alien impulses, protected by the passage of time, history as analgesic, memory cauterized. It is a play in which Black and white are not binary opposites, culpability and a potential for empathy disturbingly co-existing.

Asked to describe her play in five words she said that it was about history, irony, race, performance and well-meaningness, the last an awkward word and still more an awkward concept in a play in which the German soldiers, as represented, show none of it even while the actors do as they struggle to engage with a subject for much of the time beyond them, perhaps past all understanding.

At the beginning of her career, there is a sense that Drury was herself improvising, feeling her way towards a form adequate to a subject which itself pulled her in different directions, forging connections along the way, anxious not to be constrained. Her next play would move her in an unexpected direction as she moved from the long dead to the undead.

In a largely positive, and extensive, review of the Soho Rep production, Charles Isherwood, in *The New York Times*, thought that while Drury was 'Pushing hard to be provocative' overplaying 'her hand in a raucous finale', she nonetheless 'navigates the tricky boundaries that separate art and life, the haunted present and the haunting historical past'.[13] For *Time Out, New York*, it was an extraordinary work, funny and with a convincing metatheatricality.

Reviewing the London production, two years later, Michael Billington, in *The Guardian*, felt that 'while witty and ingenious' it 'tells us rather to much about the theatrical process and too little about the actual historic event', calling for 'more matter with less art'.[14] *Time Out, London*, found it 'a smart piece of self-reflexive theatre, constantly questioning the appropriation of characters, narratives and cultures that are commonplace elements of "storytelling"', while feeling that 'Drury's script … overplays its hand in the harrowing conclusion, as the deft strokes of the earlier scenes are obscured by a sledgehammer crash … but it's still a bold and distinguished work, particularly in its suggestion that theatre itself can be an act of colonialism.'[15]

Social Creatures, which opened at Trinity Rep in Providence in March 2013, was something of a jeu d'esprit, albeit disturbingly, if inadvertently, prescient, an absurdist comedy. It features a group of people hiding away from zombies, though the word is not uttered. She told Brown University alumni magazine that she had felt something disturbing walking through the local Providence cemetery where the horror writer H.P. Lovecraft is buried, his gravestone, I note, carrying the ambiguous inscription 'I AM PROVIDENCE'. Online, she discovered the case of a Rhode Island man who, in the 1890s, had believed that vampires had given his family tuberculosis, the cure for which was feeding his son the heart of a disinterred corpse. For her, though, it was less vampires that attracted than zombies while the play was 'about how we become scared of anything outside your own group, however you define it', she feeling that in America, 'we're divided and suspicious of each other. People are terrified of everyone that they don't know.'[16]

With the exception of a single Black man, all the characters are white or Asian American even if, for some, their heritage is somewhat more complicated than that, one of the white characters having an African American maternal grandmother. The action, she explains in a lengthy direction, takes place over a two-week period a few years after an international pandemic has turned people into flesh-eating creatures (this, of course, being before an actual pandemic sent people, like her characters, hiding indoors, divided and suspicious of one another). Those gathered together do not know, or even particularly like, each other, but have come together, laying in supplies in the hope of surviving. It is not altogether clear that the threat is entirely external.

As with her first play, this takes place in a theatre, the characters retreating there having been forced from other supposedly safe places. George Romero's zombie apocalypse film, *Dawn of the Dead* (2004), had been set in a shopping mall, in part a comment on consumerism, literal as far as the zombies are concerned. *Zombies vs Strippers* (2012), as its title suggests, takes place in a strip club whose patrons are the living dead, the patrons of actual clubs being scarcely different. The British comedy *Shaun of the Dead* (2004) ends up, where else, being British, than in a pub, though comedy is never far away when it comes to zombies. The theatre, a space apart from the world outside, even as it comments on it, in which actors transform themselves, is perhaps an apt place for a play in which zombies fail to make an appearance but those sheltering from them are closer kin than they like to believe, themselves playing roles. Besides, for Drury the theatre is not a safe place. When she was writing *Social Creatures*, the television series *The Walking Dead*, in which an external threat would expose human nature in its darker form, had already begun what, by 2021, would be its final eleventh year. As the lead characters say, 'We're all infected.' Trust is in short supply as it is in *Social Creatures*.

As the action begins a couple, the Joneses (all the characters have common names), with a habit of addressing each either formally, consult a manual by flashlight, their generator having failed. It is his fourth marriage and there is a tension between them, as there is between all of them, monitoring one another's use of food, looking out for symptoms, and when one of them, Mr. Smith, leaves the building the tension builds even more, though zombies are not their only source of anxiety. Fear of thieves, rats, food supplies, one another, is closer to hand, especially when a man enters, the only Black man they have seen, a man Mrs. Jones calls Brown explaining that it is because it is a common, easy-to-remember name, quite as if her own were not. They immediately box him in, contain him, as they had cornered a rat.

At this point Mrs. Smith enters a booth to watch what Drury calls a catalogue, explaining, in an elaborate note, that these should take place in a separate, private space:

> A close-up of the performer's face is projected for the audience and their voice is amplified, so it feels close to us. The Catalogues happen out of time – or rather in between time; they do not need to be thought of as occurring precisely when they fall in the play, but they shouldn't happen in isolation. As each Catalogue is filmed, there should be a live event unfolding on stage – a counterpoint, or gesture that might otherwise go unnoticed in the course of the scenes. I'd like to think of this as a place where an ordinarily non-theatrical event (or series of events) can be 'choreographed' to the 'music' of the stutters, pauses, assertions and non-sequiturs that create each Catalogue.[17]

As Mr. Brown, who is not sure that he wants to join these people, zombies presumably having the edge over those capable of creating their own life-sapping world, resists, so Mr. Smith appears in what is seemingly a recording. Certainly, his wife fast-forwards and then re-winds his speech about his schooldays. Sometimes Drury can seem somewhat whimsical in her stage directions. So, we are told that Mr. Jones and Mr. Johnson are 'engaged in an activity elsewhere in the space (best stage direction ever, ur welcome)', (46) something, though, involving sharp blades, threats accumulating. Nor are they all a product of the pandemic. Things were dying before that, animals, the environment.

Mrs Jones is suspicious of the interloper, as the others rally around him even as Mrs Smith hears her missing husband, seeing him as the others cannot. In another gnomic direction we are told that we 'are in an in between space – is it a catalogue? A memory? A hallucination? Is it on video? In the space? Both? I'm not sure – but it's charged. It has the feeling of a couple who has gotten into a huge fight, and now they want to forgive each other but are still so hurt.' (60) The others grow suspicious that she might have been infected and, accordingly, wrap her in plastic to avoid contamination, she gasping for breath. Again, in the 2020s, this would have a disturbing relevance as people shrouded themselves in plastic PPE's, wearing masks, maintaining social distance from one another from fear, breathing with difficulty, trying, as here, to isolate the virus, this after Steven Soderbergh's 2011 film about a pandemic, *Contagion*.

For Mr. Johnson, there is not much difference between the zombies and supposedly normal people, since 'Everybody's terrible once you get to know them.' For his part, the only Black character, Mr. Brown, evidently also sees little difference between his current plight and the life he has lived: 'You do what you can. You're tired. Burned out. Nerves is raw. You ain't got nothing extra. Can't save nothing. It's not enough. Nobody wants to help you, nobody thinks you're worth anything. You're on your own. You get sick, you die. What's extreme about that?' (77)

It is not, though, that his function in the play is as the threatening, or threatened, outsider. He suggests that rather than there being a virus it is 'just white people going crazy', (73) desperate to consume everything. 'That's what I heard.' During the actual epidemic of the early 2020s, a rumour spread that the vaccines on offer turned people into zombies, quoting the film *I Am Legend*, which led *The New York Times* to point out that it was a re-programmed virus and not the vaccine which brought about the transformation while its screen writer Akiva Goldsman felt the need to say, 'It's a movie. I made that up. Its. Not. Real.'

Mr. Smith now goes into the 'booth', where a stage direction indicates that he should sing a song, loudly and off key, while dancing, with 'a lack of inhibition'. The effect is to be funny and uncomfortable in turn. While this is going on, Mrs. Smith is partly suffocated before recovering at which she rips Mr. Johnson apart, blood splattering everywhere as the others scream. As Mr. Brown sings, so she also rips him apart, the others subsequently taking this in their stride except that Mr. Jones smothers his wife. The play ends in general bedlam as the zombified Mrs Smith escapes, Mr. Jones shows every sign of being infected, and the outside door is open.

In the play, Drury said that she wanted 'to talk about current politics in a different circumstance, "right now".[18] The 'right now', in 2012, however, saw President Obama begin his second term, though it did also see the shooting of Trayvon Martin, essentially for being Black in the wrong place, while twelve people died when shot in a movie theatre in Colorado and six were killed and wounded by a white supremacist in Wisconsin, an American tradition carried forward to subsequent years. It plainly did not need zombies to establish the presence of a threat nor of social and racial divisions. *Social Creatures* is an ironic title.

There is more than a whiff of Joe Orton about it, a faint echo of Pinter, a menace and violence laced through with the surreal. Plot and character defer to broad gestures, the vapidity of conversation freighted with insecurities and aggression, liable to careen off in unexpected directions. Characters suddenly sing and dance, offer their curricula vitae, asphyxiate one another, casually wipe fresh blood from polythene sheeting, advising one another on the proper way of doing so, accommodating themselves to the violence around them as, surely, Drury seems to imply, do Americans for whom it is a fact of life not often encountered but somehow part of their consciousness.

This is the play of someone flexing her theatrical muscles, testing the boundaries, bending conventions, still developing a distinctive voice, not quite crushing and hypnotizing the sensibility of the audience, as Artaud had set out to do, but happy to disrupt it, discommode it, surprise and discomfort it in a space she clearly delights in insisting not to be regarded as safe.

Her next play, *Really*, staged at Abrons Arts Center in New York City, on the Lower East Side, a programme of the Henry Street Settlement, in March 2016, could not have been more different. It was directed by the playwright and experimental director Richard Maxwell, in a space which allowed entry to only thirty members of the audience, the action turning out to be inside a camera obscura, though that was not a requirement of the text. It began with a fascination with photography and her reading of Roland Barthes' *Camera Lucida*, a book essentially about love and grief which stemmed from the loss of his mother, a book, incidentally, invoked by my friend and colleague W.G. Sebald who, in *Austerlitz*, his last book, wrote of his protagonist's search for an image of his lost mother. Among the epigraphs to the text of *Really* is a quotation from *Camera Lucida*, the original French edition of which, and tellingly in terms of the play, being entitled *La Chambre Claire* (the light room).

The quotation she chooses emphasizes the degree to which a photograph is not simply a memorial but an intimation of mortality: 'I read at the same time. This will be and this has been ... The photograph tells me death in the future ... Whether or not the subject is already dead, every photograph is a catastrophe',[19] a word echoed by a character in *Really*. It was Sebald who observed that to look at photographs is as if the dead were coming back, or as if we were on the point of joining them. For Drury, it was the link between photography and loss which prompted the play.

A quotation from Susan Sontag's book *On Photography* stresses the fact that, to her, 'Photographs alter and enlarge our notions of what is worth looking at and what we have a right to observe.' Again, a character in the play, a photographer, echoes an element of this quotation that photography is making something worth looking at. A third quotation is from the philosopher Vilém Flusser's *Towards a Philosophy of Photography* in which he had argued that the camera shapes the meaning of what is seen, though the quotation she uses stresses the magical world of the image, with its own space and time. (4–5) Photographs, of course, can be like ghosts from the past, haunting the present, and so they are in *Really*.

The play, she insisted, should not aim at photo-realism but lend itself to shifts in time and perspective, meanings being imminent rather than always expressed. There came a moment when Alberto Giacometti came to feel that his vision of the world had been 'photographic' while his view of reality diverged from 'the supposed objectivity' of a photograph. When Ezra

Pound objected to what seemed to him to be the realism of part of T.S. Eliot's *The Wasteland* he scrawled the word 'photography' on the typescript, as Robert Lowell saw the photograph as 'paralysed by fact', implying a Gradgrindian quality, both the latter objecting to an absent dimension as though it had a purely documentary quality. For Drury, the truths told in photographs go beyond the immediate surface, as they do with people not always revealing truths to others or themselves.

As with the ambiguously titled *Social Creatures*, she revelled in the plasticity of language explaining that,

> I feel ... Really is a funny word that we use in so many different ways; it's meaning depends on what's around it ... It can be used to describe reality, or the literal world around us, but more often it's used to indicate emphasis, or incredulity, or veracity, or authenticity, or excitement, or disappointment, or or or ... I wanted to have the world of the play, the relationships between the characters, their ways of thinking about the past and thinking about each other – all of it to be as slippery and variable as the word really can be.[20]

Her descriptions of the characters, in a three-character play, are elaborate, providing extensive back stories of the kind she had satirized in her first play, though here offered as templates for the actors, short-circuiting the questions often asked in rehearsal, even as elements of these stories exist in the dialogue. The Mother, a white Anglo-Saxon Protestant, is 'charming, witty, attractive ... who identifies herself as someone who can get along with anyone'. She attended a Seven Sisters college, majoring in art history, moved to a city, married, left the city to start a family and has never worried about money.

Girlfriend, in her twenties, is brown, never passing as white or wishing to do so, being of Caribbean, East or West African, Asian, south Asian or multi-ethnic background. She is attractive, serious, shy, a 'first-generation-ish American', who grew up in an aspiring middle-class household on the East or West coast, living 'a liberal urban way of life and with artistic aspirations'.

The third character, Calvin, is white, an artist, confident in himself and his talent, a man who had been 'a star of his art-school cohort', at the top, or on the rise, neither personally warm nor intentionally cruel, raised to be adored, and demanding adoration. He, too, has never worried about money. Two of the characters are thus defined in terms of their relationship to the third, suggesting where the focus will be.

She also offers notes, sometimes of a Pinteresque kind. Hence, 'a silence is much longer than a pause; a pause is longer than a space between lines', while 'The Silences, Pauses, Unfinished Sentences, Interruptions, and the Sound of Pictures Being Taken are key components to the structural integrity of the pieces', (4) the capital letters suggesting the significance of what, in the play, can seem at times like musical notations. And, indeed, the silences, etc. do flood with meaning, what is not spoken often, paradoxically, speaking clearly.

The play is set in Calvin and Girlfriend's apartment, a workplace with boxes of photographs, and begins as Mother sits for a photographic portrait to be taken by Girlfriend. The Mother has come to see Girlfriend after a gap in time, anxious, it seems, to assure herself that she is not in a relationship as it becomes apparent that Calvin has died, a subject which at first she addresses only obliquely except that he is what she wishes to talk about, his very absence making her recall his image, his life, now lost. Her husband has also died, but that, it becomes clear, is not who she wishes to bring to mind, they, it seems, not sharing a sensibility.

The conversation is one-sided, a spill of words to wall her up against feeling, to distract from her real subject, her fear, in particular, that if Calvin's girlfriend established a new relationship, she will lose one connection with her son, even offering a vague threat since, she reminds Girlfriend that some of the things in the apartment are hers. She becomes more insistent at the thought that someone may already have replaced her son, suddenly declaring, 'I'm not crazy', a stage direction indicating that she laughs, 'louder than we'd think'. She is, she confesses, after a silence, 'all alone'. (14)

In the second scene Calvin, Girlfriend and Mother are together, their conversation interrupted by the sound of a camera's shutter, like a punctuation mark, the mother side-lined, her only words being 'thank you', this in contrast to her spill of language when alone with Girlfriend. Here Calvin is in charge. In the next scene he runs his finger round the rim of a glass as his mother talks about her loneliness, except he is not there, beyond existing in her mind, as subsequently a bass note sounds out and his girlfriend warms to his attention. Though we are apparently in the present, when Calvin is a memory and, perhaps, a reproach, he still haunts the scene, not as a ghost but a presence, a word spoken by him echoed by his mother, even as she does not see him.

It slowly becomes evident that not all was well between Calvin and his girlfriend or, indeed, him and the mother who affects to be devastated by his loss. He had apparently burned his girlfriend's books accusing her of being pretentious, only for his mother to fly to his defence.

Girlfriend takes photographs but is also a model. Challenged by Mother, who asks whether she can stand seeing herself all the time, she replies by asking whether she did not think about what she looked like to other people. It was Barthes, in *Camera Lucida*, who remarked that in front of the lens a person is simultaneously who they think they are, who they think other people think they are, and the one the photographer thinks his or her subject is. A similar slippage lies at the heart of *Really*, one meaning of which is underlined when Girlfriend says that she does not recognize herself, as Barthes, in looking for a picture of his mother failed to find one he recognized until he came upon one of her at age five. Girlfriend objects that each photograph leaves little room for her.

Talking to me in 1999, the British playwright Michael Frayn said,

> If someone takes a photograph of you, you can't help but feel that it has caught very little about you. What we all feel about ourselves is that we have a great range of possibilities. We have got a past, we have got memories, we have got hopes and fears for the future. We have got many different moods, many different ways of being, we have probably got more than one suit of clothes, but in a snapshot, in a photograph, there you are with no past, no future, no expression on your face except the one you happened to have when the camera clicked, and just one suit of clothes. We all feel diminished by that ... But then how do we get hold of anything in life either in terms of words or pictures, or even in mathematical formulae, if we don't diminish it, if we don't reduce it?[21]

'Simplify, simplify' Thoreau suggested in *Walden*, intent to shrink life to its essentials, but who knows whether those essentials may not have inhered in what is discarded, in what exists beyond the frame of immediate attention. *Really* is not only concerned with grief and loss, a desire for proprietary ownership of memory, an exclusivity when it comes to relationships in the present or past, but with the image we have of ourselves and one another, photography being a metaphor.

As to the shuttling around in time in her plays, Frain had something to say about that:

> I don't think people in the audience sit there worrying about where we are in the time zones because this is the way we live all the time. We do live in different times. We are here in the present and even as we are here and I am talking to you, you are listening to me, but you are also thinking about what you did last week and remembering some painful memory twenty years ago … It's a bit like quantum mechanics where the modern view is that all different possibilities coexist simultaneously … either as different universes or different narratives, different histories.[22]

Her characters in *Really* do exist in different narratives, have different histories. Because people coexist does not mean that they inhabit the same story. For Girlfriend, memories become literal, as they did for Willy Loman, it being the nature of memories that they exist in two different times, presently experienced even as they summon the past. In what time do photographs exist, freezing the moment, capturing what may be false in so far as an inner truth is not available, being constructed in the moment? Through much of the play the sound of the camera shutter clicking beats out time, the moment an image is preserved which will capture nothing more than what light reflects back from the subject of momentary attention.

As the play progresses the tension between Mother and Girlfriend intensifies and, slowly, a portrait of Calvin emerges, a man seen differently by them. In a scene between him and his girlfriend it is evident that though together they feel apart, he even saying 'I don't know who you are', or it would be evident but for a curious stage direction: 'The lines are whispered into each other's ears. They are inaudible to us.' (30) So, the actors presumably rely on proxemics to convey their simultaneous intimacy and detachment as the audience has to read what to them is non-verbal, themselves relying on the image they see.

That is even more true in the subsequent scene in which, as Mother looks at one of Calvin's photographs, 'two tones enter the room, slowly: as base and a treble. We iris in on Mother as the tones enter. The bass grows louder. And louder. And fuller. And louder. We can feel it in our chests.' The 'iris in' turns the audience into a camera, the Mother now herself making a noise 'in tune with what is heard'. It is, the note explains, 'the sound of screaming silently in one's own mind'. The audience does not see the image on the photograph, only the blank white of its back. The photograph triggers a response for which language is not adequate, though whether this is the anguished sound of grief, or something else is not yet evident, given that she and the son she mourns were evidently estranged, that she is in some way, not yet evident, more than complicit, the sound the wail of a Medea. It is enough, though, to send her back to a moment with her son in which she poses for him, but they fail to communicate. 'Can you listen?' he asks, 'I'm talking, you aren't listening.' To which she replies, 'You don't talk to me anymore.' (32–3)

Girlfriend has launched on a project to document her life which will involve documenting Calvin's work which Mother sees as an act of appropriation insisting 'You have no idea who he is', (36) the tense instructive, involving, as it does, a level of denial. 'There's something unforgivable here', she insists, though it is not clear who might be in need of forgiveness despite her conviction that his life might have taken a different direction had he not met Girlfriend.

Calvin now returns as a young boy, rising up 'somewhere high', to the accompaniment of a 'tiny treble tone', as if that were a reflection of his youth, though what follows is a tumble of language from him as he climbs, or falls down, wiping away his mother's kiss as she, in turn, in 'a rush of words', recalls her fears for his safety.

For her part, Girlfriend's worries are more profound as she contemplates the decline of civilization, after a century of wars, violence of all kinds, Calvin dismissing such thoughts as naive and destructive of her art. He wants her to be 'what I can see you are'. (43) They physically wrestle one another to a standstill before we are back with Calvin and Mother, he, apparently a child again except that when he turns to leave, she tries to stop him, time, as a stage direction indicates, having itself stopped. Her anxieties about his safety as a child have transformed into terror that he will leave, has already left, sensing that she had been responsible. If he stayed, she says, 'I would love you in the right way', (44) as if confessing the suspect nature of her love. Calvin leaves.

Mother is alone, missing her son more with the passage of time, as Girlfriend's art is impacted, even as she says, 'I don't know how to make what I want to see.' (47) In the final scene, she teaches Mother how to take a photograph, while herself not only asking how she can live without Calvin, whose work, she confesses, was better than her own, but convinced that 'for most of the people that have ever lived, the lives that they lived were horrible'. (50) For herself, she is faced with loneliness and a feeling of failure.

A stage direction now indicates that 'this could be the end of the play. Or. There could be final scene that is Now. Really now.' (52) Alternatively, there could be a show of sorts in which photographs of Calvin are on display, along with pictures of 'things they did, And things they thought, And things they felt'. Or 'things we think they did, doing things we think they didn't do', something surely difficult to accomplish. The audience is invited to join the actors or 'just leave'. (52)

So, what is *Really* really about? It is certainly as slippery and variable as she suggested, exploring how the characters feel about themselves and the past, how memory operates, what access photographs offer to the past or present. Photography purports to register reality, but what is that reality caught in the moment? Does it amount to subjects being posed, serving an aesthetic rather than literal truth, and if so what kind of truth is that? And what of the wider society beyond the frame of portraits which themselves convey a suspect truth? There is an ambiguity to the phrase 'still lives', as if lives were frozen or a guarantee that, at least in a photograph, they continue. The two women mourn separately, both damaged, even as there is a question of whether the man they have lost was himself worthy of their love or even whether that is relevant. And why did Calvin die? Is Girlfriend's race significant for all it is not directly referenced? And what trace will they leave as photographs seem to fix something against an unimagined future? These question marks are of the essence in a play in which motives, judgements, feelings, the capacity to recuperate them, lie at the centre of what seems no more than the conflict between a mother and the woman who threatened to take her son away from her, as he has been taken away from them both.

For Ben Brantley, in *The New York Times*, was a stylishly contemplative play 'that focuses on fixed images culled from life's flux … highly cerebral [which] deftly uses the self-consciousness of its characters to create a more pervasive, self-examining consciousness about the artistic process … "Really" is unusually clearsighted about the ambiguities of its subject.'[23] Reviewing a Philadelphia production in 2018, Deb Miller, in *DC Metro*, noted, 'Employing the metaphor of photography to explore the concept of what is real, the work raises many profound questions about the mysteries of our existence and legacy that remain unanswered, and unanswerable.' It was 'an affecting work that will leave you shaken and disturbed'.[24]

In 2021, Britain's National Gallery staged a show of the work of the Nigerian-American artist Kehinde Wiley, best known for his portrait of Barack Obama seen against a William Morris-inspired background. In this exhibition not only did he insinuate Black figures into classic works but projected a film in which he had taken Black Londoners to Norway, filming them against the white of snow, a comment on Black lives lived in a white context. 'The work that I ultimately made,' he has said, 'was informed by a type of empathy that comes from an outsider's sensibility.'[25] He denied that his work was primarily political but at the same time was making a comment on the context in which Black lives have been lived. Those visiting galleries, for the most part, have looked at art which captures a world seen through the eyes of white artists. He is himself an admirer of such work, but seeks to reimagine, re-present, infiltrate a white space.

In an earlier exhibition he celebrated ordinary Black Londoners. It was entitled, 'The Yellow Wallpaper', a reference to the short story by the nineteenth-century feminist Charlotte Perkins Gilman, a friend to William Morris's daughter, and Morris-like designs form the background. The story concerns a woman whose mental stability is disturbed. Gilman was white but what interested Wiley, he told *Guardian* journalist Claire Wrathall, was

> the correlations, for me at least, between the sense of powerlessness and the sense of invention that happens in a person who's not seen, who's not respected and whose sense of autonomy is in question ... These same issues can be seen in conversations concerning race and class. In Perkins Gilman's case it was to do with gender, but it made me want to explore the [effects of] different types of confinement. And the story provides the perfect foil for that.[26]

Toni Morrison wrote of an awareness of a little white man sitting on your shoulder checking everything you say, and of the need to knock him off in order to be free. The white gaze is not only relevant to art. For all the history of plays by Black authors, the American theatre has, at least until recently, been resolutely white, in all its aspects, from writers, to directors, actors, reviewers and, most crucially, audiences. This is no less true of those who run theatres and are thus in a position to curate what is seen, from regional venues to Broadway. Of course, in the general population Black Americans represent only some 13 per cent, while theatregoing is not so embedded, precisely because it has not always been a welcoming space, somewhere offering a reflection of their own lived experiences. In recent years there have been attempts to redress the balance, an increasing interest in the work of those whose identities have been forged out of a tension between the pull of a supposed homogeneous national norm and lives lived at odds with it. The fact remains, though, that because of the composition of the audience their work is liable to be looked at from the outside, observed rather than lived. When it comes to race, in a country with a legacy stretching back to slavery and on through its social, psychological, political, moral consequences, audience responses may be inclined to be shaped by an awareness, conscious or otherwise, of that history and its living residue.

Theatre can offer a reassuring hermeticism, a comfortable and comforting environment, apart from the everyday traffic of life, offering completed actions, resolutions. When actors step forward to take their bow it can seem an assurance that performance exists in a different sphere, the dead arising, the tragic hero no more than a man who will now go out for a late-night meal and a taxi ride home. It is not, of course, that it lacks the power to move, to stay in the memory, even, perhaps, to prompt a shift in attitudes, Naomi Wallace speaking of theatre's power to educate the imagination, perhaps, in part, Drury's objective.

While in the theatre we are collaborators, actors responding to audience reactions, as the audience to the actors' words and gestures, for all its immediacy, its present tense communality, there is still a line between those on stage and those who sit in the darkness and watch. We are observers, maybe even voyeurs, bringing to the moment our own values, our own sense of the way things are and perhaps should be, often seeking out the kind of play we think will be in tune with our sense of a good night in the theatre, by which we may mean a place where we can relax and be entertained, not an unworthy objective, indeed a necessary one. But what happens if such assurances are disturbed, if what we see disrupts our sense of propriety, good taste, an assumed order, if the style morphs, the characters are subverted? What if the actors do not take a bow, smiling, pleased with their performances, the audience even rising to its feet, as for some reason America audiences regularly seem to wish to do rather than to mark a special level of achievement? What if our security as an audience is challenged, if we are invited ourselves to be performers, to step up onto the stage, leave the apparent security of the auditorium? It was such thoughts, such an approach, which interested Drury and with which she would now engage.

The initial audience going to see her next play, *Fairview*, which opened at the Soho Rep in June 2018, will have been surprised, surprised by the fact that there was, apparently, no surprise from a writer committed to experiment, to shifting perspectives, games played with time, a fascination with the implications of theatre and performance. Here, it seemed, was a conventional comic family drama of the kind she had previously shunned. When the text was published, there were no epigraphs (well, one quote), no elaborate accounts of who the characters were, their pre-history, temperaments, and, crucially, their colour even as, at first, that seemed obvious. Beneath the surface, though, in the depths, was a deceptive current which would indeed surprise, disturb, divide audiences taken unawares.

It was a change of direction which, she has confessed, was not part of her original plan, emerging from discussions she had with the director, Sarah Benson. It was to have been a play about surveillance, the effect of observing others, in particular the effect of white people watching, and making judgements on, Black people. There is, of course, a history of white people watching Black people on stage, which would include minstrelsy and Black face entertainment. The so-called Negro Unit of the Federal Theatre was directed by two white men, Orson Welles and John Houseman. Alice Childress's 1955 play *Trouble in Mind* was about a Black actress who appears in an anti-lynching play written and directed by two white men. *Trouble in Mind* did not make its way to Broadway then but did in 2021, interestingly one of five plays by Black authors to be staged on Broadway in 2021–2. In Childress's play, itself seemingly a comedy, though undercut by the apparent seriousness of its subject, power lies with the white actors. In other words, there is a politics, a psychology, to such an interaction. Drury's two-act play, however, became a three-act play when a more radical idea emerged.

The first stage direction is itself interesting as it indicates 'Light up on a negro'. What's in a name? Martha Jones, a professor at Johns Hopkins University, has rightly said that the language of race has always been a moving target. More than a century ago, coloured was the common term, followed, in the late nineteenth century, by negro with a lower-case n. W.E. Dubois argued in its favour. Then, in 1930, the *New York Times* announced that it would capitalize it saying that it was an expression of respect. In the 1960s, though, Black was preferred. In the late 1980s, there was a move to replace Black with African American, Jesse Jackson being a proponent of it. Others preferred Afro American. Later, people of colour (with its echo of coloured people) would begin the process of generalizing, which continues with BAME (Black, Asian, Minority Ethnic). Denomination is a reflection of social and political values. It is also intimately involved in power, or its lack. When Kamala Harris was elected Vice President, she was described as the first woman, first Black American woman, first woman of South Asian heritage to hold the office, people careful to list all the component elements of her identity as if they were severally definitional and to be acknowledged as such. Interestingly, in interview Drury herself referred to 'people of colour'.

So, why does she choose 'negro', and with a lower case n? The answer lies in the one quote which precedes the text. It comes from *Black Skin, White Masks* by Franz Fanon '"Dirty nigger!" Or simply "Look! A Negro."' As she says, 'This, reversed, is the play, in a way.'[27]

The first act is unthreatening. The family at its heart seems familiar from other comedies featuring Black characters, *The Jeffersons*, *The Fresh Prince of Bel-Air*, *The Cosby Show*. One of the characters, Jasmine, indeed, likens the action to 'one of those movies ... a good old family drama ... just watching real stories about real people', (22–3) while her sister, Beverly, objects that 'We are nothing like the people in those movies', (23) the suggestion being that they are.

The audience, liable to be substantially white, middle-aged and female, was thus, it seemed, to be offered an amusing evening watching a reasonably well-off Black (negro) family's minor trials and tribulations in a set which is to be like 'a nice living/dining room', in a 'nice house in a nice neighbourhood', (7) the word nice itself being disarmingly bland as is her description of the relationship between Beverly and her husband, Dayton, which she describes as 'sweet', family being 'everything'. So, very American, very reassuring.

Beverly is seen peeling 'real carrots', ironically underlining the apparent realism of a play in which Jasmine looks in 'a pretend mirror hung on the fourth wall', commenting that 'it's a very normal thing to have happen in a play'. So, not so realistic. When her husband surprises her, Beverly 'feels herself being looked at' and says, 'you don't just watch a person and they don't know you're there', (8) even as she complains of Dayton that 'he doesn't care what we look like to people', (11) this foreshadowing what will be both a theme and a device later in the play.

The occasion is her mother's birthday. When Keisha, Beverly's daughter, appears 'she just does Everything That Teenagers Do', the capitalization, and the note, underscoring the sense that this is to be a conventional play in which the characters play conventional roles, as Keisha does, speaking the 'run-on sentence', of a teenager. (18) There comes a moment, however, when she looks towards the audience delivering a soliloquy.

The only drama appears to be a burnt cake, except that Beverly collapses as the act ends before the second act reprises the first but instead of hearing them we hear a group of white people reacting to the play, in a conversation, with 'overlapping text and ad-libbed reactions, stutters, and sounds', (32) which, the author has said, they would never have had in the presence of people of colour. The Black characters are muted so that, to Drury, it becomes a 25-minute-long theatre dance, the muting having a significance beyond a theatrical device.

Prompted by what they are watching, the off-stage characters discuss what, should they be able to change it, their preferred race would be, whether race is a construct, even as they construct their version of Black lives or, indeed, the lives of any unlike themselves. The answer for one of them, Jimbo, is that he would be Asian, partly based on his experience with girls he has dated, but not, he insists, the traditional Asian, pressured to conform, even as Suze attacks him for making generalizations about race, he, in turn, denouncing what he sees as her vacuous liberalism.

For this group of people race is an academic issue, a subject of debate, even game playing, seeing it as no more than a function of identity politics. So, another character, Mack, wishing to opt for an identity in line with his sense of himself as 'fiery', would choose to be Latinx, careful to use a gender-neutral term, more anxious to avoid the implied sexism of the words Latino or Latina, to be up to date with shifting linguistic sensitivities than with any conception of other cultures or races. Unfortunately, he cannot speak Spanish having no one to practise with, in other words having no contact with the some people he affects to admire for the qualities he ascribes to them.

Another character, Bets, while thinking Americans obsessed with race, (herself clearly an immigrant, speaking imperfect English), would prefer to be a Slav because the countries from which they come have flat landscapes, marked by 'a boulder with a little snow. That is all there is there', this despite the fact that Slavic countries are known for their mountains and the cluster of different languages spoken. In other words, below the intellectual chatter is a level of genuine ignorance. There is also the sense that non-whites tend to be classed together, the word 'minority' having more than numerical implications. To Drury, this can be traced back to slavery while immigrants, in turn, are easily accommodated to existing notions of social exclusion: 'this white and this other ... America ... makes everyone else ... in this shunted off pile'.[78]

A further twist comes when Suze says that she would like to be African American because the person she loved when growing up was a Black maid/cook/substitute mother (at this moment Dayton, until then like the others from the first act, mute, says 'Ta-da!' as though commenting). They then discuss the difference between being Black and poor and Black and rich retrieving the names of such Black actors and athletes as they can, one being O.J. Simpson, Jumbo objecting that to want to be a rich Black person would not be authentic: 'if you want to be a real black person, then you have to be a poor black person'. (56)

In between these conversations they watch the unfolding action of the first act, affecting to discover confirmation of their remarks. Indeed, from this point the two intersect, Drury indicating that 'This text tethers directly with the text that was/is being delivered by the family onstage. For the most part: Suze tethers with Keisha ... Jimbo tethers with Jasmin ... Mack tethers with Beverly.' (57) She identifies the lines on which this fusing is to begin, what amounts to an intricate weaving together of the two texts, a series of counterpoints, the palimpsest she had referred to talking about her first play, the initial production of which had seen the audience distributed around the side of the room and hence visible to one another. It was not, she insisted, an accident, as a young theatre-goer having herself been aware that, as frequently the only Black person in the audience, she was observed. As she has said,

> I am a little bit obsessed with watching whiteness and blackness ... I feel like watching white audiences watch the work of people that I love and admire who are people of

colour ... seeing how the audience changes the work, I feel is a big part. Just acknowledging the inherent power dynamic in that and how that feels connected to power dynamics in society. It just felt like this weird, dense metaphor.[29]

The play, to her, was in origin to have been about the pressure that people of colour are under as they are watched and judged through no fault of their own.

As they struggle to identify what they see as the distinguishing marks of Black women, and Suze recalls the barriers which prevented her from offering love to the one black woman who she believed loved her, so a note indicates that 'The tethering gets even closer now, almost syllable for syllable'. (59) As at the end of the first act, Mama faints, while those watching discuss the play, condescending, interpreting, offering alternative lines, riffing on their own concerns. When Jasmine takes cheese from the table, Bets remarks that, as a character 'she wrings the most from this little life she has', as Mack says that 'She is not made for housework', while the grandmother 'is the heart and soul of the whole family [in the African-American tradition]', the bracketed text, Drury indicated, being optional. (65–6) They debate whether their reference to a cakewalk (inspired by the play's reference to a burnt cake) is, or is not racist, whether or not they are themselves, less a real question than a debating point in what increasingly seems a narcissistic group. Jimbo, in particular, as the Black family dance and set the table, launches on a four-and-a-half-page rant announcing, 'I'm smarter and richer and I fucking dominate/that's who the fuck I am.' (72)

Meanwhile, the action continues after Beverly's faint, Drury offering a three-and-a-half-page summary of the action, suggesting, but not insisting on, the precise nature of a monologue by Dayton. Indeed, all the dialogue she proposes is no more than an indication. So, Jasmine 'says something about their mother'. (76) They dance, though 'with lots of other things happening', (77) a dance which includes fake foods which 'get stranger and stranger'. (78)

It gets even stranger, though, as, in the third act, the white Suzie appears in the role of Mama, at one stage attempting 'a beleaguered mamma/maid voice' (93), as Jimbo is now Jasmine's uncle, a rapper, complete, Drury suggests, with a gold chain and a 'bad-ass pose', (84) watchers becoming grotesque parodies of the characters they have been watching, enacting racist tropes. The Austrian playwright Peter Handke wrote *Offending the Audience*, which might have been an alternative title to *Fairview* which swiftly escalates offence. Thus, Mack appears, 'dressed like a drag version of a black teenage girl. Think glitter. Think sequins. Think confetti.' He lip-synchs before holding a pose for the audience, turning to his fellow whites asking, 'Was that too much?' (86)

They slowly subvert the original text bringing it more into line with their own preconceptions. So, the teenage Keisha, increasingly bewildered by what is happening, is to be pregnant and not able to go to college because they have lost their money, Jimbo flourishing eviction notices, an intervention which shocks all the characters, Black and white, Jimbo now recklessly improvising. Grandma, played by Bets, appears as an over-the-top vamp, with a golden turban, smoking a cigarette, declaring herself to be 'too much'. (91)

The Black characters partly resist and partly accept the new narrative they are offered, even as they struggle to keep up with the accusations levelled at them. Drayton, apparently suffering from syphilis, and having committed adultery, has supposedly lost his money through gambling or, Bets suggests, drugs, insisting 'It's a common story', (98) while Suze, as Mama, claims to have worked as a maid. By degrees, what had been a comfortably off family is re-made to fit what, from the point of view of the white characters, is closer to the model they prefer. What follows is a food fight in which the white characters are the aggressors and 'Surprising things happen'. Some of it, a note indicates, 'silly', even as this gives way to violence.

Finally, Keisha, whose story has been manipulated, challenges Suze, in doing so focussing precisely on what lies behind the play: 'I need to ask you to leave/so that I can have some space to think/ I can't think/ in the face of you telling me who you think I am … I want to know what that space is./ What that space would be like./ For me./ Without … you.' (100) That, however, leads to a more radical proposal, that white members of the audience should come onto the stage, as she steps through the fourth wall to join the audience. 'Could I say,' she asks, 'See, there's Terri./ She's our stage manager./ She's amazing. /She's white. /She's coming up here.' She invites them to leave their coats and bags, not worry about them but 'worry about … what you can do to make space for someone else'. (103) Terri (K. Kohler), incidentally, was the stage manager of the Soho Rep production.

The audience are told they can sit on the chairs, touch the fake food, look into the stage lights, while she should be joined by any 'people of colour', because she wants to tell 'a story about us, by us, for us, only us', confessing, though, that 'that's not telling the story'. (106) There are, in fact, many stories, even as she feels that the central one is understanding that they are what they have made of themselves, that only that is fair, hence the play's title. What she wants is for the white audience 'to make space for us', asking, 'Do I really have to tell them that?' The gesture of inviting white members of the audience onto the stage was designed to make them physically clear space for non-whites in the audience who themselves thus become observers, the whites being the object of their gaze.

The play, then, focuses on conscious and unconscious racism, the gap between lived and observed experience, the persistence of stereotypes, cultural appropriation. Its humour is by turns seductive and caustic, likewise the music and dance which are energizing or ironic. Her breaking of theatrical conventions is scarcely new, even to her, but here is in the service of forcing a change in perspective, a reminder that audiences bring their own history, assumptions, biases with them only to find their expectations at odds with a play whose stylistic shifts, sudden inversions, disorient. Her armoury consists of her ability to shock, affront, anger, embarrass, provoke, a paradigm shift being only possible once the existing paradigm is acknowledged.

Beyond that, surveillance is not only a factor of Black lives; it has increasingly become a fact of social media, of every online purchase we make, political campaigners increasingly able to predict and shape how we will vote, to invade what we naively believe to be our privacy. *Fairview* may be centrally concerned with the surveillance of Black Americans, inspired in part by Simone Brown's *Dark Matters* which explores that over time. On the other hand, as the last line of Ralph Ellison's *Invisible Man* observes, 'Who knows but that on the lower frequencies, I speak for you.'

It was something Arthur Miller explored in *The Archbishop's Ceiling* in which a group of writers talk in a building whose ceiling may or may not conceal hidden microphones. The effect is to turn those surveilled into actors, the degree to which the pressure of the observer exerts an influence on the observed. Incidentally, almost all Black writers in America, from Richard Wright to Lorraine Hansberry, were the subject of surveillance by the FBI as, of course, were Stokely Carmichael and Martin Luther King. Surveillance is power.

The reaction of audiences varied. Asked what she wanted white members of the audience to feel, Drury replied,

> I didn't think of shame, or lecturing, or scolding ... In conversations that I have been having with some people, white guilt is a real thing. People feel so overwhelmed or shut down by identity politics in general. Some white people can get defeatist really quickly. It was a hopeful gesture, at least initially. Even in this small way, in this fictional space, this moment offers something the white audience can do. It's an active, positive, uncomfortable but possible thing.[30]

She is aware, though, of the irony that a play with which she wished to 'decentre' whiteness relies on there being white people in the audience in order to function.

People did take offence, even leaving, though not so much after it was awarded the Pulitzer Prize, even as there was a sense in which this intensified the feeling of disorientation she was after. As she remarked, 'I feel some people are going to come in and be like, "Oh, this has won a fancy award. This must be a fancy experience." And they're going to come and be like, "What?"'[31]

Some people, she has said,

> feel really offended and hurt at being categorised in a way that they don't categorise themselves. Some people feel ... a sort of catharsis at the end of the show. Some audience members cry. Some audience members storm off and are really uncomfortable and angry ... that's part of why I love theatre, that ... one event is able to splinter off into so many different experiences that you are able to see and participate in at the same time.[32]

The poet, playwright, essayist Claudia Rankin attended the play. It certainly provoked a response, from her and a white friend, worth quoting at length to acknowledge both Drury's success in stirring the waters and the conflicting anxieties of those who, while enjoying the play, had contrasting responses which did reflect a racial divide, but which also raised questions about the legitimacy of Drury's approach. She may not have wished to provoke feelings of shame or scolding but could, indeed, lead some members of the audience to shut down:

> The playwright might be waiting for a black person to get on the stage with white people. None do. The playwright might want me to think her request is divisive and walk out of the theatre: not a black stage, nor a white stage, but a 'United Stage.' The playwright might have calculated what percentage of the audience, 'white members of the audience,' would not comply ... The playwright might think, Why are they listening to me? as more and more white audience members fill up the stage and people of color stay seated.[33]

What really bothered Rankine, however, was not that people of colour stayed seated but that a white friend did so.

> Why won't she do what was asked? ... Why can't she see it matters? Does it matter? In the sense that race matters, her refusal feels like an insistence on full ownership of the

entire theatre … I say to my confounding friend, I didn't know you were black … She must understand the play's request is made in response to a world where black people's requests don't matter … Is she telling the black audience, you all don't get to look at me. You don't get to see me as a white specimen … Or, is this simply, I don't have to do what a black woman tells me to do. I am white. Can't you see that?

(197–203)

Confronted, her white friend explained that she felt harangued by the play – 'I didn't want to be in this' – even as she thought the play brilliant and would not change it. After a while she wrote an explanation for her response noting,

I shrink, sometimes a lot, sometimes a little, from scenes where I'm asked, personally or generally, to feel bad as a white person – where, whatever else is being asked, I'm also being asked to feel shame, guilt, to do penance, to stand corrected, to sit down chastised … I react with a kind of nausea when I smell, as Darryl Pinckney put it, 'White audiences [who] confuse having been chastised with learning.'

(209)

The Pulitzer Prize aside, the play received positive reviews, even as they conspired in suppressing details of its methodology and denouement. Ben Brantley, in *The New York Times*, found it 'dazzling' and 'ruthless', perhaps ironically suggesting that it displayed 'a very American ingenuity', when it came to its construction, 'a galvanising addition' to plays about race and a 'glorious, scary reminder of the unmatched power of live theatre to rattle, roil and shake us wide awake'.[34] The *LA Times*, reviewing the Berkeley Rep production, described it as 'blazingly inventive' with a 'hurtling energy', Charles McNulty adding, 'It is rare these days to encounter a dramatic performance that unfolds like a work of conceptual art. But Drury wrestles with theatrical structures to give us a fairer view of a society that for too long has been practicing another form of mass-incarceration – this one through stereotypes.'[35]

In London, *Time Out* responded to a dizzyingly inventive satire, a fantastically original and probing piece of theatre. *The Stage* praised its shattering ingenuity and ambition. The *Evening Standard* found it absurdly brilliant, a seminal work that would be discussed for years to come. In the *Guardian*, though, Michael Billington remarked that 'while I loved its intellectual cleverness and theatrical daring, I found myself wanting to argue with it'.[36] His reservation had to do with the fact that, to his mind, it failed to take account of shifts in contemporary culture, invoking the success of *Hamilton* in reinventing a white narrative. He nonetheless insisted that it was a play to see and argue with, which was, of course, her intention.

In 2011, in Brooklyn's St. Francis College, as part of Women's History Month, a tribute was held for Mary Seacole, not a name which resonates over much in America, though the occasion did merit a mention in the *New Yorker*. As it happens, the evening was largely dedicated to discussions of nursing. Elsewhere, though, and for good reason, she evidently meant more.

On 23 November 2021, a painting of Mary Seacole was given, on loan, to Guys and St. Thomas's hospital in London on what would have been her 216th birthday. It depicted its subject at her 1857 home in Soho Square. It would later be permanently housed at the planned Mary Seacole Memorial Park. This was five years after a statue of her was erected at St. Thomas's, believed to be the first statue in the UK dedicated to a named Black woman, a gesture attacked by the right-wing *Salisbury Review* on the grounds that she had never been a nurse in the Crimea while Florence Nightingale was. The 23 November had previously been named Mary Seacole Day in Jamaica, she being of Jamaican-Scottish background. Another portrait is in Britain's National Portrait Gallery. She even appears on Britain's National Curriculum, being taught in primary schools. Why this belated interest in her?

She had set up a hotel in the Crimea where Britain was waging its disastrous Crimean War, becoming famous and mixing with royalty before being largely forgotten, even the site of her grave being lost until 1973, a renewed interest only occurring in the 1980s and thereafter, Salman Rushdie invoking her in *The Satanic Verses*. The NHS Mary Seacole Centre opened in 2020. Plainly a new consciousness was at play, the past being re-explored in order to retrieve those who had been forgotten because of their gender or race.

It was Seacole's autobiography which led Drury to begin thinking about her next play. It took her some time, however, to work out how she could use it dramatically given that it only offered a single voice and that she had no interest in offering an historical monologue. Despite its name, *Marys Seacole* seemingly features only one Mary, even as the other characters all have names beginning with M. Mary herself, though, was many things, and appears as such. It was only when Drury decided to introduce contemporary material, however, that she found her way to the final work.

In the text Drury begins with a note: 'Mary Seacole stands before us. If you don't know who, well, look her the fuck up.'[37] Mary reads from a leather-bound volume announcing the first act. A note asks, 'Are we impressed? Who cares. Fuck us'. (3) Certainly, Mary announces herself with a measured authority noting that her birth was an important event, a fact confirmed by a note, one of many, offering a running commentary – 'It was. This is the world we are in right now, where the birth of Mary Seacole is important.' She declares that she is Creole, daughter of a Scottish soldier, the note indicating, 'Obviously I am not as black', she prioritizing her Scottish roots over her mother's, though it is to that mother, Duppy Mary, who now enters, that she owes her interest in medicine.

The next note suggests a new direction: 'And then a shift we don't yet understand. She's been talking to us, of course, but now MARY Talks To Us. She is half Mary and half Mary Seacole and half something … else.' (6) For a moment, then, she acknowledges the audience, declaring 'I see you', as she hints at her various lives before reverting to herself except that Duppy Mary appears and places a Bluetooth earpiece in her ear, only, like Mary's white patroness, to die. The bridge between then and now, however, goes beyond the Bluetooth earpiece as she transforms into a contemporary nurse even as she details her experience in treating cholera in Jamaica in 1850 before she had moved to the Crimea.

The actual Mary Seacole herself moved through time and space. The play does likewise, the bridge being those, like Seacole, involved in offering care, responding not only to illness, to the consequences of violence, but to the need of those looking for support. So it is that the characters in one time period meld into those in another, their roles not so different. As Drury explained, 'I was trying to write about care and how it's a really difficult thing to do. Also, I think that because we are so used to seeing black women doing that kind of work it becomes invisible. It's hard to care for someone else, or care about someone else in the way that actually helps anyone else.' Almost as if she were Martyna Majok, she has said, 'I tried to think about all of the different traumatic relationships that could exist between caregiver and caretaker, or even thinking about the person that receives care as not a passive [thing] but as a demand. That makes it seem more dramatic. I tried to think of all the different permutations of that and see which ones resonated. It is difficult to try to depict someone that demands care being taken of them.'[38]

The telephone rings and she is in a nursing home, where May, white, is talking to her mother, Merry, while anxious to escape from a place which a note tells us smells of urine and bleach. Mary, played by the same actress, is now a nurse. The mud of the Crimea and the shit of a woman in a nursing home are not so different when it comes to the need for care and part of Drury's concern in the play is with caregivers, a role traditionally performed by women and those of colour, people who pay a price, care given to others often at the cost of care withheld from their own.

Mary, as Mary Seacole, declares, in a Jamaican patois, 'me nah stand anywhere but mew own land me dig in me own space me built with me own two hand, and me own sharp mind'. (33) She insists that she, who built her own hotel in the Crimea, also built her own identity.

The time switches to the present and a city park as May walks in talking on a cell phone securing medical supplies even as Mamie receives a WhatsApp photograph of her daughter, like Mary raised by a white woman for whom she cleaned and cooked, her own daughter, meanwhile, back in Jamaica, a Jamaica which for the white Miriam is a holiday destination. It is on her cell phone that Mary learns that her offer of help in the Crimea has been rejected, time evidently being permeable.

Now again narrating her life, Mary recounts being rebuffed by Florence Nightingale before the scene moves to what seems to be a nursing school in the Crimea, though it is less anticipating war wounded than the victims of mass shootings, a scene inspired by Drury's witnessing drama students simulating wounds for medical students, and these are evidently such, volunteers required to sign liability waivers, one working for extra credit, in a scene which is increasingly funny as the would-be actors are less concerned with the exercise than inhabiting their roles. Nor are the students unaware of being actors, May declaring that she is 'wonderful with flesh wounds'. (85)

In an era in which liability and sensitivity warnings have become standard, the possibility of litigation is always in mind: 'Please be aware that the scenario is intended to replicate a real mass casualty situation, and therefore can be triggering to individuals with PTSD or who have lived through other traumatic circumstances such as mass shootings or other terrorist attacks, active battlefields, natural disasters, etcetera. If you have been a victim or a survivor of any of these situations, or any other violent or traumatic situation, we strongly suggest you carefully consider your participation in the scenario,' (80–1) a reminder of the status of *Marys Seacole* as itself a piece of theatre and, perhaps, of Seacole's own capacity to stage herself, she commenting on, 'The Continuing Glory of Mary Seacole'. (106) The scene ends with a mock birth, a supposedly fourteen-year-old pregnant girl with a chest wound, who rather than deliver a baby produces something 'like a bloodied hillside', a link to the Crimea where 'real' bodies and body parts are lying around and May becomes Florence Nightingale.

The second act begins on the Crimean battlefield which 'becomes everywhere else and every-when else we have been', (106) the Jamaica Mary left and the America with its promises and threats. It is Duppy Mary who sounds a warning:

> You go there and they will kill you. You go there and they will shoot you in your back shoot your children in them back and not even say boo. You go there and they will rape

you and take your money and your dignity and then your life. You go there and they will make you work and mock you while you do it.

(119)

In the end, this is a comment on America seen through the lens of a nineteenth-century Jamaican woman. In a play which moves through time, it is a link between the distant past and a modern world in which injustices have not faded and in which the relationship of children to parents, the need for, and provision of, care remain a constant. Those who had been subservient, or treated as such, still negotiate their private lives with their competing necessities and even loyalties.

Mary Seacole, in her various guises, journeys not only from country to county but to possession of herself, a meld of Jamaican spirit and Scottish resilience. She emerges as a woman confident in herself, her arrogance being a factor of her assurance, her refusal to accept the given as defining the limits of her actions. Drury's pluralizing of her is an assertion that she is more than one person, a daughter, to be sure, passed to a white woman to serve and educate, but also a mother not to children of her own but those who she treated as such, recognizing need when she saw it. She exists in more than one time because, despite her singular gifts, and historic role, she has her counterparts in a world for which she herself would for long be a mystery, she often existing in the shadow of Florence Nightingale.

This is a play in which the only way a man could win a place on stage would be as a dead body. It concentrates on women not simply because there is a woman at its heart, but because Drury is interested in their role as caregivers, within and without the family, the sacrifices they make out of love or necessity, the two not being so different. For many, they were and are if not invisible then relegated to the margin. Not so, Mary Seacole. She, of course, told her own story, determined not to be marginalized. In its opening speeches she uses the word 'My' four times, followed by 'I' and 'Me'. The play ends as the women come together and declare, 'I am Mary Fucking Seacole!' followed by the word 'My' seventeen times followed by 'I'. She made her world and declares, 'I. Me make up myself, me alone, me dream up myself, me alone. Me give power to myself. You hear me?' (127)

The actual Mary Seacole often dressed flamboyantly, never hesitated to challenge those with power, and if they did not respond, simply drove forward regardless. As it happened, she had much support from men of all ranks, because of her work in Crimea. When she went bankrupt, they rallied to her support. She did not set herself up against men. Indeed, in war it was to those she tended. And when she faded from view another woman did not, Florence Nightingale. She, however, was white, far easier to fit into a story of national heroism. She was served better in Jamaica. On the other hand, she did not identify herself as Black. Drury, though, is not interested in reprising the details of her life, celebrating the myth or reality of that life, but in creating a play which would see her as a means to explore what it is to be a woman who spent much of her life caring for others but who refused to see that as requiring subordination, a respectful silence, the surrender of her very self. In her book *Just Us: An American Conversation*, Claudia Rankine notes, 'all the narratives end up naming blacks with words that begin with the letter "N." Nurse could be one. Nanny another. No one, could be yet another.'[39] For a considerable time, Seacole, fading from memory, threatened to be no one until retrieved to become once again the protagonist of her own life as well as a figure transcending the moment.

Ben Brantley, in *The New York Times*, found that 'Ms Drury gloriously confirms her status as a playwright for whom the long view is disturbingly, divertingly and endlessly kaleidoscopic', saying that for him, 'World history starts to feel like one big funhouse.'[40] In the *New York Theatre Guide* Tullis McCall described it as 'a majestic piece of work that takes no prisoners. Pay attention or get left behind. This is the style of the play and the lasting echo that follows you out the door.'[41] The *New York Stage Review* was less certain, Michael Sommers who, after welcoming 'the latest – and dizzyingly adventurous – drama from Jackie Sibblies Drury, the up-and-coming playwright', found it 'challenging to follow as it becomes increasingly expressionistic in style', feeling that Drury 'does not fully control and articulate the themes of her ambitious, sprawling play',[42] *The Hollywood Reporter* was equally sceptical, Frank Scheck, while acknowledging, 'a thematically ambitious, experimental work', thought that it 'squanders its fascinating central character by reducing her story to post-modern tropes'. Conceding that it had 'powerful moments', he found these 'too often buried in the theatrical cacophony'.[43]

Clearly the words 'expressionistic' and 'post-modern tropes' here carry negative connotations, evidence of discomfort with a play which resists realism and, presumably, 'realist tropes'. It is a point of view. Throughout her career, though, Jackie Siblies Drury has been concerned to discomfort audiences and critics alike, thereby making demands not merely on attention and, perhaps, patience, but on the need to link together apparently disparate elements, times, places, experiences while, at moments, introducing less cacophony than a pluralism of sounds, a sudden flux, music, the resources of theatre which, to her, is indeed a kaleidoscope in which patterns form and dissolve, in which, often, she allows, and welcomes, the contribution of directors and actors, adjusting accordingly.

Marys Seacole is not a biodrama taking audiences through the details of a life, Seacole herself having done that in her autobiography. It is an attempt to stage not one woman's life but the lives of many as there were many facets to her own existence. Seacole never saw herself as a Black icon, and is not so represented here, even as race is a factor. After all, there is a reason Florence Nightingale was celebrated long after her death as Seacole was not. She was not a trained nurse. Her idea of offering comfort could be more to do with sustaining the spirit rather than the body. But that would seem to be true of those other caregivers Drury features looking after others even at a cost to themselves. From her first play, she has a habit of approaching history in part to see what it can offer by way of understanding the present, fracturing surfaces, displaying theatre's legerdemain, as a magician may purport to show how a trick is done and yet command our belief.

She has little interest in leaving audiences in an equable state of mind believing that incompletions, contrarieties, unresolved tensions, surprising shifts can contribute to understanding. She is not experimental in the sense of being a signed-up member of the avant garde. She does not set out to épater la bourgeoisie, even as, in truth, they represent the majority of theatre audiences. She is, though, dedicated to shifting the ground beneath their feet, hoping that the aftershocks may last beyond the doors of a space which, historically, has had its own social ecology. Peter Hanke said of *Offending the Audience* that he wished to make audiences see plays more consciously and with a different consciousness. That is equally true of Jackie Sibblies Drury.

CHAPTER 4
WILL ENO: A TOUCH OF BECKETT

… in writing plays, you can pretend Beckett does not exist, but you do so at your great peril, and you're probably not really writing plays. Shakespeare, Thornton Wilder. You have to recognize these people, adjust yourself to them, as you do with the lines on a tennis court, and find some room for yourself that isn't occupied. A lot of people write plays that, very essentially, have already been written. They do not take care to at least try … to make themselves necessary somehow.[1]

Will Eno, son of a lawyer, whose name has a French-Canadian origin, was raised in several different small towns in Massachusetts (Billerica, Carlisle and Westford), attending a series of public schools including the Concord-Carlisle High School in Concord. He has confessed to being fairly quiet as a child, suggesting that there might be a connection between that and his interest, as a writer, in monologues as if they were, in a sense, conversations with himself.

He could not recall ever being asked a question as he grew up, not even how his day at school had been:

On the one hand my dad was … a silent dark cloud; on the other, my mum … was a very sunny but distant figure, never loved talking about feelings. In fact, she does love talking about the weather. I was trying to figure out the purpose of people talking, really. It all seemed like a secret, secret code. It gave me some distance from it but also some deep desire to figure it out.[2]

I think I never really thought I existed when I was little. I somehow got the feeling that it was best to keep myself to myself and as that misunderstanding hardened into my personality, it got harder and harder for me to talk, and I felt like I was starting to disappear. But I knew, somehow, that a person's identity, and I guess, therefore, their existence, depended on and arose from what they said, out loud, to people. So, if you have this sense that all you are and ever will be is what comes out of your mouth, I guess you'd get pretty interested and even a little anxious about what to say and how to say it.[3]

In a discussion of existentialism, he related it less to angst-ridden intellectuals than a seven-year-old wondering if anyone saw him. In a conversation with Edward Albee, he suggested that what the two had in common was a concern with identity, an uncertainty about the self, along with a fascination with language, and in both cases that could be traced back to their childhood.

The idea of writing did occur to him, but he hesitated to give it a try, describing it as a secret he kept from himself. He even went so far, in the fourth grade, as to steal pencils from school and had accumulated, he thought, some five hundred before his brother informed on him. The writing never got done.

He went to the University of Massachusetts Amherst but dropped out after three and a half years, in a four-year degree something of a perversity. His ambition, at twelve, had not been to be a playwright but a cyclist and he went on to train in the Olympic training centre in Colorado, winning a medal in the national championship, coming second and even racing in Italy. He gave up at twenty-three aware that however good he was he was not good enough to move on. Meanwhile he made money painting houses (something he would continue to do when money was short) and working in construction, before starting as a trainee broker in New York, if that adequately describes someone who cold calls people, as he was to say, selling them what they did not need. He earned $6 an hour for a ten-and-a-half-hour day.

Perhaps not altogether surprisingly, he felt lonely and, as he has said, sidled up to the idea of being a writer. There is a line in his first play which, despite the fact that it occurs in the context of what seems a satire, has the feeling of truth about it, if also an echo of Tennessee Williams: 'we speak to keep at bay the bloodied wolf of loneliness.'[4] In *The Realistic Joneses* a character speaks of he and his wife 'throwing words at each other,'[5] and that is what his characters often do in conversations which are not always transitive. Eno has a fascination with words, with jokes, double meanings, sentences which bend back on themselves, breaking that solitariness by virtue of sharing space and time, the grounding fact of theatre.

Out of hours he wrote stories and plays, inspired by the work of Beckett who would remain an influence before, at the turn of the century, watching the actor Conor Lovett performing selections from *Malloy* at the Irish Arts Centre, later workshopping one of his plays with him in France where the Gare St. Lazare Players, founded in Ireland, and whose director was Judy Hegarty Lovett, now performed Beckett's plays. Conor would later appear in, and Judy Lovett direct, *Title and Deed*. Looking back to that time when he returned from the stockbroker's office, where the only currency was anything but human, 'I wrote,' he has said, 'a lot of clean sentences with not a lot of adjectives or adverbs. I was too exhausted to maintain the front of prancing around on the page with the pen,' adding, 'In some ways that year-and-three-quarters on Wall Street – you can tell how joyful it was, that I mark the three-quarters – was almost an exercise in putting as little personality on the page as possible and seeing what was still left.'[6]

He studied for a while in New York with the writer and editor Gordon Lish who, as fiction editor at *Esquire*, had published Raymond Carver (savagely editing him, but thereby influencing his style), and Richard Ford, subsequently becoming a senior editor at Alfred A. Knopf where again he introduced new fiction. Asked later for book recommendations, Eno listed Lash's *Epigraph*. Lish could be peremptory in his judgement of major figures, casually dismissing Bellow and Roth, but Eno was not alone in acknowledging his help. Under Lish's tutelage, as he explained to Alexis Soloski in *The New York Times*,[7] he moved from writing fiction to plays, his first entitled *A Canadian Lies Dying on American Ice*, set during a hockey match. He was inspired to turn to drama on reading a one-page play by Don DeLillo, *The Athlete in Rapture is Assumed into Heaven*, about a tennis player who achieves his greatest triumph on the last day of his life, subsequently expanded and made into a film. 'It's just a one-page play about somebody winning a tennis match. This announcer comes out and says all these great things. I was … amazed at how complete an experience it was. It has to do with the mysterious thing about human bodies and light and sound and people saying things in the general dark: that just instantly seemed like a very strange thing to me. Also, you end up doing the thing you feel least bad at, and I can safely say that I am least bad as a playwright.'[8]

In 1996, Eno attended Edward Albee's Foundation at Montauk, where Albee lived, set up with the profits from *Who's Afraid of Virginia Woolf?* Here he worked on his fiction and Albee became a mentor. It was while he was there, though, that he also worked on a few monologues, himself reading one in the storefront theatre at Montauk. Albee described him as James Agee with a sense of humour, Agee not only being the man who rushed news back from the front line of human and political dereliction, in *Let Us All Now Praise Famous Men*, but also a stylist with a fascination with language and, as it happens, Albee notwithstanding, considerable wit.

Eno was struck by the fact that Albee had suffered disregard in America for two decades while being respected in Europe (he might have added Arthur Miller who suffered similarly). That, in itself, was a lesson in persistence, in retaining confidence in one's work and, as with Christopher Shinn, and David Adjmi, it would be Europe, more particularly England, that would, when he was thirty-five, give him his breakthrough. He had been working as a proofreader of psychology textbooks, which handily gave him access to a Xerox machine so that he could copy his plays. He then distributed these around New York theatres before boarding a cheap flight to London. Where Shinn would leave his at the Royal Court Theatre, Eno left *Tragedy: A Tragedy* at the stage door of the National Theatre. As he has said,

> It was an amazing thing. I just dropped off a play at the stage door of the National Theatre with some crazy note saying, 'Written with my left hand,' and within a couple of weeks Jack Bradley, who's the literary manager at the National, called up and said he wanted to do a reading at the Studio Theatre, and then a BBC production ... It's ... an amazing thing that the National Theatre in London ... will get back to you, but you can send something to Theatre Under the Stairs in Baltimore, Maryland, and never hear back.[9]

Tragedy: A Tragedy, which, when published in a volume of other Eno plays, carried a dedication to Gordon Lish, had a reading at the National Theatre Studio in June 2000. Its premiere followed in April the following year, at the Gate Theatre, a 75-seat theatre above the Prince Albert pub in Islington. It would be another seven years before it reached America where it opened at Berkeley Rep.

Henry David Thoreau, in *Walden*, observed:

> Hardly a man takes a half-hour's nap after dinner, but when he wakes he holds up his head and asks, 'What's the news?' as if the rest of mankind had stood his sentinels ... After a night's sleep the news is as indispensable as the breakfast. 'Pray tell me anything new that has happened to a man anywhere on this globe' – and he reads it over his coffee and rolls, that a man has had his eyes gouged out this morning on the Wachito River; never dreaming the while that he lives in the dark unfathomed mammoth cave of this world and has but the rudiment of an eye himself.[10]

There is a sense in which much the same thought lies behind *Tragedy: A Tragedy*, beyond its satirical take on a modern version of our willingness to be distracted from distraction by distraction, our belief that what we see of the world, reflected through a glass darkly (television or computer screen), selected for its inherent appeal, bears on who we are and what we might truly need.

Television news in America, especially local news, is an odd mix of show biz and faux seriousness, the carefully modulated tones of reporters designed to be appropriate to the occasion, conversations between those in the field and the presenter back in the studio simultaneously suggesting professional detachment and intimacy, an intimacy to be shared with viewers who want information and entertainment as they watch news of violence and disasters, these being the staples of what is itself a form of theatre. All stories, no matter how trivial, must be delivered with dramatic intensity, their significance implied by the fact of their coverage.

Tragedy: A Tragedy, despite its title a comedy, a satire, features a live newscast and takes place in the studio and other locations as news comes in of an apparent disaster. As Eno's preface indicates, 'Something is on the television, relentlessly. A plane crash, probably ... or it is one of those new little wars. A scene of an empty street where something important recently happened.' Meanwhile, 'Before it all, whatever it is, stands a dashing reporter, talking. Perfectly groomed, dressed in appropriate clothing, properly grave as the moment demands. His teeth are amazing. He shouldn't be there.' Why not? Because he could be acting in a different sense, involved as, of course, could his audience. Yet he is there to define what is real, showing us 'Real life, on earth, on television',[11] somehow a contradiction in terms.

The play deploys the self-consuming language of television reporting, with its familiar linguistic tropes here oddly distorted, the banal invested with significance, words turned against themselves, clichés elevated to the status of truth. One reporter specializes not so much in winsome details, sentimentalities, though she deploys them like an Edna St Vincent Millay manqué, as a desire for reality to conform to her saccharine view of it. A generic, if unfocussed, tragedy has indeed occurred except that this, at first, seems no more significant than the setting of the sun. Nonetheless, it attracts that admixture of breathless delivery, vapid observation, down-home sentimentality, ersatz seriousness which are the accepted commonplaces of reporting as nothing much happening must continue not happening because those involved in news require it to. As Michael, a legal advisor, reporting from the steps of the capitol building, remarks, 'I've just gotten word that we don't know anything more.'[12] John, interviewing a man who may have witnessed the sun setting, asks whether he had seen any 'sign to foreshadow the coming dark, anything to indicate that tonight might be unlike any other in the star-spangled history of night? Some omen? The famous branch against the window or some infamous wild animal howl ... a piercing scream, a change in the air, a lack of change? Did you sense any signs like that?' To which the man replies, 'No.' (82)

News, it seems, rolls with a momentum of its own, a perpetual motion machine, a commodity to be consumed by those who thereby feel themselves real by virtue of being enrolled in the process. For a medium concerned with communication, television news can seem like an Escher drawing, a closed system, with its own codes, even as it purports to offer a window on the world. In that sense the audience exists in that same space, television news requiring the complicity of its viewers as it assembles a reality from fragments, affecting to discover meaning in events trivial or otherwise. In a production by Red Tape Theatre in Chicago, the audience was divided into separate rooms, as though they were watching it in their familiar domestic environment, even as they could hear others responding, a reminder, in a play with references to other plays, that this may in some degrees be a work about theatre, and Eno has spoken of his anxiety about the confected nature of theatre, its contrivance with formulas on top of formulas.

As the play continues, so the mood, along with the sky, grows darker as it becomes apparent that something is indeed happening and that the sun may have died, whereupon the Governor issues a statement which falls some way short of reassurance, not least because he subsequently runs away: 'Quit asking why it's so dark, and start remembering how great it was that it ever got light. Believe me, if we stay stuck in this fucking darkness, you won't see me crying. So, I say let the looting begin ... keep in touch. Be sweet to yourselves. I'm a ghost.' (89) From the studio, Frank adds his version of the seven ages of man: 'Let us not forget that life used to consist of being born, being scared, sleeping on the ground, getting a stick to protect yourself, shaking through the night, catching a cold, and then dying.' (89–90) By degrees they all slip into ever greater incoherence, the Governor leaving a last message: 'Thank you for your confidence, which I will now betray.' (96)

The fact that the English theatre obliged by staging his first play did not mean that English critics would prove hospitable. Lyn Gardner, in the *Guardian*, declared that for much of its sixty-five minutes it had bored the pants off her telling audiences nothing they did not already know about how news agendas are set, and the way disasters are covered. However, she added, 'Eno's play is clever, and you don't doubt for a moment he can write. And while I didn't like this play very much, his is such a quirky talent that I'd be prepared to travel quite some way to see his next one.'[13] It fared better in *Time Out*'s review of the Red Tape Theatre's production in which Kris Vire praised his delicious facility with language.[14]

His next play, *The Flu Season* (2003), a title which picks up a line from his first, also opened at the Gate Theatre in London. Its text comes with three pages of notes about casting, staging, acting. It is, he explains, an experimental play but should not be experimental for the sake of being such, and should not be staged accordingly. What he is after is 'an effect that is brave and new and moving and meaningful', (54) admittedly a more than somewhat vapid requirement but in fact it is simultaneously witty, linguistically inventive, ironic, playful and soulful, by turns lyrical and dark, while evidencing what in Sam Shepard's *A Lie of the Mind* a character calls fire in the snow, a flicker of possibility.

The setting is a mental health institution. There are two narrators, one of whom delivers a prologue, the other an epilogue. The characters, as described in the dramatis personae, have a certain equivocal, imprecise nature. Thus, Man is 'Intelligent, somewhat scrappy, late twenties or so'; while Woman is 'Intelligent, somewhat scrappy, late twenties or so.' Doctor is 'doctoral, dignified though somewhat distracted, fifties or so'. Nurse is 'maternal, also dignified though somewhat distracted, early fifties or so'. (3)

Tragedy: A Tragedy ended in darkness. *The Flu Season* begins in such as the Prologue enters, summoning the lights as he welcomes the audience to a play entitled *The Snow Romance*, set as winter approaches, explaining that it is to be 'a chronicle of love and no love, of interiors and exteriors, of weather, change, entry-level psychology'. (5) He is followed by Epilogue who announces that the title has been changed to *The Flu Season*, following a number of drafts, and that it still needs work. He could, he points out, have been given a name but 'names don't matter'. The Prologue, he indicates, can neither see nor hear him adding 'Strange. Theater. This. Certain things we have to live with. Little rules and lies.' (6)

The Doctor's first comment to Man could equally apply to those who sit in the dark and watch the play unfold: 'All alone in the dark, are we? Sitting in the twilight of the exit light, dreaming of some great difference, some healing hand ... Or just sitting there.' (7) Likewise, when Nurse opens a conversation with Woman saying, 'I think that would be fine,' she replies,

'What would? No one said anything. You're just going to start talking to me, totally out of the blue?' much as plays begin with actions already underway though, as Nurse remarks, 'That's just how life goes.' (9)

A portrait begins to emerge of two people, each adrift, disconnected, certainly from one another but also from the world beyond, the families that had betrayed them or perhaps offered solace, abandonment being something the Nurse, too, had experienced being rejected by a lover. Man stands by a telephone awaiting a call that will never come as Woman waits to make a call, to connect with someone, though who is not clear. Neither connects either then or later. No one visits. At this moment, though, Epilogue intervenes to explain that in 'a little while, we begin to depart from an earlier reality, from the original mess of real life we built our play on', (12) as if a never-established realism is to be abandoned.

What follows are effectively monologues as Doctor and Nurse recall the loss of youth and of others. The truth, as Epilogue suggests, is that the 'wonderful world falls apart round the clock', (16) happiness and sadness alternating with no evident logic, though in the next scene we hear a television report speak of a drowned family, one with an echo of *Tragedy: A Tragedy* as a description of their death ends with the observation that 'One bright spot. They leave no family behind' and an invitation to 'Stay tuned for some holiday gift ideas and tips on ways to keep your car battery from freezing.' (17)

Man and Woman converse, though elliptically, raising the possibility of some relationship, neither being married though bizarrely he wishes that he might have been so that he could be divorced. Such a possibility, however, prompts an intervention from Prologue who anticipates what might be going through the mind of an audience anxious to make sense of what they are seeing, and perhaps anticipate a resolution to what might seem a plotless plot. 'Do things seem aimless?' he asks of the audience, replying, 'Maybe that's how things are. Do you think anyone has a future? An aim? The man and woman? The nurse and the doctor? Are you an optimist? Do you see a love scene on the sunless horizon?' (18)

In response, Doctor echoes the seven ages of man speech from *Tragedy: A Tragedy* except these are now collapsed into four: 'You're a smiling baby, a reckless teen, a tax-paying adult, a corpse … You're just getting the hang of the toilet and, suddenly, time to pick out a coffin', (20) an echo of Pozzo's line in *Waiting for Godot*: 'They give birth astride of a grave, the light gleams an instant, then it's night once more.'[15] As Beckett remarks, when speaking of Proust,

> There is no escape from the hours and the days … There is no escape from yesterday because yesterday has deformed us, or been deformed by us … We are not merely more weary because of yesterday, we are other, no longer what we were before the calamity of yesterday … The immediate joys and sorrows of the body and the intelligence are so many superfoetations [the simultaneous occurrence of more than one stage of developing offspring in the same animal]. Such as it was, it has been assimilated to the only world that has reality and significance, the world of our own latent consciousness.[16]

The Prologue declares, 'The weeks change … Then … here comes more time, giving us life, rushing past, taking it away', Epilogue adding, 'In other words: tick-tock, tick-tock … Time is important here, to us … Slow and deadly, it just goes by', even as he addresses the audience 'sitting there in the dark. Strangers, forever, on either side of you', expecting, but clearly not getting, 'Real American realism', (21–2) hoping for a surprise in the face of the determinism seemingly on offer. And perhaps there is one as we are told that the Woman falls in love with the man, even as the Epilogue declares that the 'history of plays and the history of the world is a set of the same conversations being had by different people ... "You are the only one, forever," we swear, having sworn it twice, or more. People are liars.' (25)

The Epilogue announces an intermission of fifteen minutes, thereafter welcoming the audience back to a play of which Prologue confesses he can make no sense. At one stage Woman walks downstage and stares at the audience, a stage direction, difficult to act, indicating that 'Perhaps she is thinking and feeling, "It is your need for plays that is causing all this to happen, that is causing me all this pain. Are you happy now?" (41) She has an abortion asking, "Will this be going into your play?"' (44) 'What flowers could grow out of this rocky garbage?' asks the Prologue, 'A gross of broken statues and a pile of overdue library books', a reference to T.S. Eliot's *The Wasteland* with its reference to branches growing out of stony rubbish, and Ezra Pound's *Hugh Selwyn Mauberley* Part 4, with its reference to lives laid down pointlessly for a botched civilization, to broken statues and battered books.

The woman commits suicide, confirmation, perhaps, of Eno's remark, in his production notes, that the general effect of the play, and of the characters, should be like watching a pane of glass slowly break. 'Stop crying', Epilogue gently instructs the audience, 'Practice holding and kissing your pillow, for when the day comes you really need to hold and kiss it', (46) art rehearsing loss until loss itself becomes the experience of all. 'Life', he declares, 'is a word game. I don't know what else ... Everything is worse, including our desire for improvement. Of a life, a life story, a play. All are awful, worse, the same, but, in the end to be lived with. Life is fine. It's spring,' (46) April, of course, being the cruellest month. The play concludes as the Epilogue reminds the audience that the characters were no more than that, nor did anything truly happen, remarking of the play and, beyond that, existence, 'Life. Try again some other year. This was a mess. The wrong words too late', (50) as Beckett, in *Worstward Ho*, had said, 'Ever tried. Ever failed. No matter. Try again. Fail again. Fail better.'[17] The play ends as the audience are thanked for coming.

The Flu Season can seem challenging, but reviewers warmed to it. Lyn Gardner, who had complained that *Tragedy: The Tragedy* bored her, while still finding moments of ennui, declared that it was 'not a play that you can lose patience with, because Eno has a good theatrical brain and a quite startling theatrical voice. His smart-alec games with form and style are very witty, youthful and enormously engaging.'[18] When it reached New York, the following year, produced by the Rude Mechanicals Theater Company at the Blue Heron Arts Center on 24th Street (which closed in 2005), Margo Jefferson, in *The New York Times*, found it 'alive and unpredictable', calling on audiences to 'Look for a love of language ... Look for intimations of a larger world.'[19] It went on to win the George Oppenheimer Award, for the best New York debut by an American playwright, and the first Marian Seldes/ Garson Kanin Fellowship.

That same year, though, 2004, saw another production, first in Edinburgh and then at the Soho Theatre in London, before reaching America the following year at the DR2 Theatre on East 15th Street in New York. *Thom Pain (based on nothing)* is an hour-long monologue in which he rides language, sometimes like a stylish equestrian and sometimes like a rough rider, slowing down, speeding up, a musician changing key seemingly on a whim. Sometimes he is a lyrical poet caressing words, sometimes inhabiting a curt prose firing words with an abrupt randomness, scatological, deliberately provocative. There are moments when this seems like stand-up in a morgue, mortality a joke; there are others when words are shaped to offer a kind of redemption, the everyday charged, for a moment, with a bruised beauty.

At times the figure of Thom Pain (not Thom Paine, revolutionary writer, spelt with an e, the figure with which Eno had begun before abandoning him with an alphabetical scalpel) seems like a Brechtian cabaret performer, sardonic, addressing an audience to be shocked, yet in on the joke. At other times he is a figure from Beckett, the audience an extension of his own inner conversation as he free-associates about lack of freedom presented as a fate, cod philosophy mixing with strained truths, jokes echoes of a larger joke which is ultimately on him, though not him alone. There are moments when words pile up before collapsing of their own weight, subjects change in a moment, statements breed contradictions, propositions are offered only to be retracted in a play about things falling apart.

Eno has always acknowledged the importance of Becket to him while equally anxious to insist that he is not simply Beckett with an American accent. Nor is he, but Beckett is a felt presence in this play. Pain asks,

> Someday, some minute, you'll have thirty seconds to live … What if you only had one day to live? … What if you only had forty years? What would you do? If you're like me, and – no offense, but – you probably are, you wouldn't do anything. It's sad, isn't it? The dead horse of a life we beat, all the wilder, all the harder the deader it gets.
>
> (19–20)

In Beckett's *A Piece of Monologue*, a play which he wrote in response to a request for one about death, Speaker calculates the length of his life bringing together memories of his youth and of funerals. He describes the attempt to light a lamp with three matches, as Pain struggles to light a cigarette with two.

At the same time, Beckett's world is contained. The characters in *Waiting for Godot* may be vaudevillians but they do not venture into the audience, though they do make references to its existence ('I've been better entertained', says Estragon;[20] 'It's worse than being in the theatre', remarks Vladimir[21]). Eno's Pain addresses it (like John Osborne's Archie Rice), comments on it, plays with it, chats to it, asking its members if they have kept their non-existent raffle tickets. He steps down from the stage, like the conjurer he promises but fails to be. Though a monologue, this is not really a one-man show. It is a play in which all are required to participate, precipitating that sense of vulnerability which ensues when the boundary between performer and audience is breached.

He tells jokes which have lost their punch line, or which sidestep into acidity: 'So, a horse walks into a bar. The bartender says, "Why the long face?" And the horse says, "I'm dying of AIDS. And I guess I feel a little sorry for myself." In response, the bartender says, "My God, that's awful. I'm so sorry."' (20) Does the audience laugh at the misdirection, and if they do have they been betrayed into laughing at a subject not inviting humour? The Israeli novelist David Grossman would later take a mordant stand-up comic, whose sometimes lugubrious jokes reflect his own life and those of his audience, as a protagonist in his novel *A Horse Walks into a Bar* (2017).

The play begins in darkness, the darkness which had been charged with significance in his earlier plays, but also that of a theatre before the lights come up. It is a play which requires the ear to attune to its particular music, to accept a seemingly plotless play reflecting a seemingly plotless life, and Eno has a man leave abruptly when the play is barely underway, his departure a blank refusal to engage but also the occasion for a further riff on being and existence: '*Au revoir*, cunt ... I'm like him. I strike people as a person who has left. But, our little performance, our little turn, on the themes of fear, boyhood, nature, hate, the nature of performance and vice versa, the heart of man, of woman, et cetera.' The sentence never concludes, one thought ceding territory to the next. 'You know,' he says, 'you might be better off if you had gone with your heart and left, like our friend, now departed, who just left with his heart.'[22]

He recounts the death of a boy's dog in bizarre circumstances, a first introduction to the pain of loss, the first intimation that there is a limit to existence. The boy, he says, lived through this, carrying the wound of a new knowledge though not a knowledge to be celebrated. 'What a happy life,' he says, 'What a good game,' while asking 'Who can stand the most, the most life, and still smile, still grin into the coming night saying more, more, encore, encore, you fuckers, you fates, just give us more of the bloody bloody same.' (17–18) 'Oh, the varieties of experience', he declares, 'Religious ecstasy', (18) surely an ironic reference to William James for whom American optimism managed to ignore the fact of pain and suffering even as he embraced religion as an antidote. Not here, though. Nor for Pain.

He is, he explains, 'like you, in terrible pain, trying to make sense of my life', in a universe of a billion galaxies. 'And you think you're pretty special. Math. There's a lot of zeroes out there.' (22) Nonetheless, he is trying, 'Poor Thom's a trying. Poor Thom is fucking cold', (23) though Shakespeare's Poor Tom, Edgar in disguise, who also complains of the cold, is less trying than escaping from the cruelty of the world, his assumed madness a kind of truth.

The essence of a monologue is that it has two audiences: the mind of the narrator restlessly shuffling memories, rummaging through life or inspecting it as if it were a kind of Rorschach test, and those who watch and listen trying to make their own sense of the flow of words as though truth could in some way be assembled from the fragmentary stories, confessional admissions, seemingly irrelevant details, the admixture of truths and lies. Indeed, Thom Pain mocks that very process. 'Why is a fat girl like a tiny motorcycle,' he asks, only to say, 'Well, of course, she isn't, she isn't at all. You should be disgusted with yourself for even for a second trying to think of how she might be.' (8) Beauty exists, feelings of contentment and more, but they co-exist with their opposite, a dog lapping water is electrocuted, a boy is stung by bees, love withers on the vine: 'Love cankers all', (29) he declares, proud of his pun, albeit a pun with a truth at its heart, if it is true that he abandoned the woman who had breathed new life into him.

He wanders back and forth through his life, like Krapp in *Krapp's Last Tape*, though without the technology. 'Where are we supposed to learn about things?' he asks, 'What happens in this little spurt? In the little time we are, I guess, given?' He takes a letter from his pocket saying, 'Maybe this'll explain.' Having read it, though, he says 'Nope.' (34) As Pinter had declared, the desire for verification is understandable but cannot always be satisfied.

As the play ends, Pain brings a member of the audience on stage for what he calls the disappearing act, but the disappearance will be of himself as all the broken threads of his life are invoked and he offers the audience the only advice he can, 'Keep in mind how little time there is, how little time there always was. Then try to be brave. Try to be someone else. Someone better ... I know this wasn't much, but let it be enough ... Isn't it great to be alive?' (37) Given his account, his cataloguing of pain and the breakages of his life, hardly.

Eno has said that he had always disliked one-person shows, finding them dull while taking the audience for granted. What he wanted to do was break the fourth wall not only to allow the consciousness of the performer to penetrate the audience but equally the other way around. So, he made his peace with the form explaining that,

> In some way I'm probably drawn to the monologue … because I was a pretty quiet kid, as there wasn't a lot of emphasis on talking in the house I grew up in, and so a lot of the conversations I had were in my head or to rocks and dogs. That said, I've always found it to be a form that, potentially, has a great amount of theatrical energy in it. The total effect and meaning of a play probably always has to include the audience's private responses and conjurings, and if the thoughts and feelings of the play can ping back and forth between audience and performer, a large and meaningful amount of area can be covered. The monologue strikes me as an elegant and economical way to accomplish that pinging.[23]

Beyond that, he has said that he likes writing monologues because he is more interested in one consciousness coming apart rather than a couple of consciousnesses.

Thom Pain (based on nothing) was potentially a challenge to audiences and critics alike. *Godot* had been turned down by a raft of directors, baffling 24-year-old Peter Hall who directed it, provoking audiences and reviewers alike. Harold Pinter's *A Birthday Party* closed in London after eight performances. In both cases, however, a significant reviewer championed them. *Thom Pain*, though, a monologue, not itself a form which always attracts, prompted reviews that were more than positive, beginning with its production at the Edinburgh Festival which had *The Guardian*'s Lyn Gardner, observe that 'It is vicious stuff, written in a language so deceptively innocent, so full of platitudes, that you don't realise it has cut you deep until you feel the warm seep of bloody despair. James Urbaniak's astonishing performance makes it hard to watch and even harder not to. There are two people on this stage: him and us.'[24] David Gritten, in The *Daily Telegraph*, observed, 'It's hard to imagine more dazzling writing on any stage in Edinburgh this year,' Eno having created 'a true paradox, with this utterly forgettable man who lingers in the memory.'[25]

The New York production provoked not so much a review as an encomium from Charles Isherwood in *The New York Times* who found it 'astonishing in its impact … one of those treasured nights in the theatre … that can leave you both breathless with exhilaration and … in a puddle of tears. And also in stitches here and there.' It 'invites embarrassingly vague panegyrics of the kind critics like to think they're above. Are above. Except for this one occasion.'[26] It ran for a year and a half.

Isherwood was not alone. In Edinburgh it won the First Fringe Award. In America, it was shortlisted for a Pulitzer Prize. In four years, he had moved from a production in a 75-seat theatre above a pub in London to coming close to winning America's premiere theatre award. It was a play that would go on to have performances across America and be translated into multiple languages.

He would, however, be back to a small theatre in 2007 when he presented a group of six one-act plays under the title *Oh, the Humanity and Other Good Intentions* at the 74-seat Flea Theater in the TriBeCa area of New York. *Oh, the Humanity* is a reference to the words spoken by the radio reporter who watched as the Hindenburg airship fell to the ground in flames, and several of the plays circle around the attempt to explain disasters as they do around the issues surfacing in *Thom Pain (based on nothing)*.

The first of these, a monologue titled *Behold the Coach, in a Blazer, Uninsured*, features an unlikely press conference presided over by a coach trying to explain the poor performance of his minor league baseball team, which devolves into an existential confession of despair in which he pleads for someone to help 'clean up the spill that is my life on this earth', to 'help me through this punishing crushing nauseating sorrow',[27] a sorrow which is not simply a consequence of a disastrous season but of the loss of the love of his life.

Spokeswoman for Country Air, also a monologue, features another press conference following an air crash. In a show of human understanding, falling somewhat short of empathy, a woman announces that the planned picnic will be cancelled on the grounds that no one 'wants to see … us enjoying life, drinking too much and driving home drunk with someone from personnel, with a temporary tattoo and a sunburn', recalling that she, too, had lost someone, her father, though admittedly 'not in a plane in flames, screaming downward at the speed of sound'. (89) The cause of the accident was perhaps, she speculates, gravity, while suggesting that those on the crashing plane shared a fate with all since everyone is dying whether in the air or 'just sitting there being human … The body is its own disaster area. The human face is a call for help', (90–1) meanwhile taking consolation in the miracle that the plane had managed to get in the air at all.

In, *Oh, the Humanity* a couple are on their way either to a christening or a funeral, two events being so close given time's velocity (not merely a Beckettian gesture since Eno's own father died and his daughter was born within twenty-four hours of one another), the woman quickly offering a litany of the events, large and small, which fill the gap between them. They are sitting in a car indicated by two chairs, except that when the man tries to check the battery all he can find is the chair, theatre and life intersecting. A second man appears declaring that he represents the beauty of things, insisting that 'we are loved, that people love us, that God exists and loves us, that people exist', (121) even as the couple try to make sense of their situation.

In *Ladies and Gentlemen, the Rain* a man and a woman separately record videos for a dating website at first explaining their qualities, likes and dislikes, except that these monologues, designed for an invisible audience while performed in front of a real one, quickly devolve into ever odder statements, he having a liking for cholesterol and confessing that bugs have a tendency to fly in his mouth, while she dislikes nerve damage, heart disease and death even as she wishes to celebrate life aware, nonetheless, that 'the world moves on, destroying things', (81) she herself suffering from cervical cancer. The juxtapositions define the parameters, the contradictions and paradoxes. 'I picture us in a cemetery', he says, as she remarks 'What a beautiful day.' (83) They end, each solitary, longing not to be.

The Bully Composition features a photographer and his assistant. He sets up a camera which faces the audience and they each speak mainly to that audience, the supposed subject of the photographs. The idea is to re-enact an historical photograph from the Spanish-American War. The photographer now goes into a reverie, speaking as Private Thomas who recalls the brutality of that war, before apparently photographing the audience asking them to pose and questioning whether they are 'afraid of dying or happy to be alive … Show us you, trying to be better, mortally afraid … more tragic. More forgiving. More unknowing. More mortal. Try to be mortal. As much as you can stand.' (107–8)

Taken together, these plays circle around the same empty space, suggest the same possible transcendence, no sooner invoked than denied. Their characters are half aware of themselves as performers, life as a form of theatre in which people struggle to understand their roles, a world of losers unsure what winning might look like, yet somehow still trying to make sense of their feelings of abandonment, the fate accelerating towards them.

Monologues have a way of intensifying the sense of solitariness which the characters seek to transcend, reaching out to the audience in an attempt to establish a connection, break out of a self-reflexiveness which seems the condition of their being, theatre, of course, offering the sense of community which they seek even if what they communicate is the fact of a shared and irremediable fate. Eno is very like Beckett in staging existential dramas in which humour is a tactic even as the final joke is on characters who sense their plight but devise ways of addressing it without submitting. There are few actions in these plays because the characters are in a conversation with themselves or those they sense may be out there in the dark, willing them the grace they seek, resisting the logic presented to them in these dark arias.

Alan Schneider, Beckett's American director (and also, incidentally, Edward Albee's and Pinter's), recalled the advertisement for *Waiting for Godot* on its Florida premiere, a production which closed after two weeks. It read: 'Waiting for Godot, the Laugh Sensation of Two Continents.' He thought that might have been the cause of its failure though maybe it was more accurate than he was willing to concede. Eno's plays, if not quite the laugh sensations of two continents, work as well as they do in part because of their humour. As to the arbitrariness of life, the closeness of life and death which fascinated Beckett and does Eno, Schneider, crossing the road in London to post a letter to Beckett, was killed by a motorcycle. He looked the wrong way.

In November 2010, *Middletown* opened at the Vineyard Theatre in New York before a production the following year at the Steppenwolf Theatre in Chicago. The play is named for its setting, but there is a plethora of Middletowns across America, this one perhaps standing for them in the way that Thornton Wilder's Grover's Corners in *Our Town* does. And though Eno disavowed the connection, there are points of contact as we are inducted into Middletown's daily doings through direct addresses to the audience in a play which explores the nature of human relationships, the hopes, losses, lives and deaths of those who live here.

Its first scene is set on an 'average evening' in what seems an average town with its town square, library, houses through whose windows we can glimpse those going about their regular lives, though a Cop looking into those windows senses a loneliness in himself and those he sees: 'Along with the whole world, the lonely billions.'[28] There is a darkness here if also one in which, in the second act, a certain light falls as Eno comes close to a resolution resting on the acceptance of a continuing tension.

The Prologue, by a Public Speaker, is a virtual parody of inclusiveness as all are welcomed, not merely ladies and gentlemen and esteemed colleagues but 'those whose eyes are tired from trying to read something into everything, those at the crossroads, in a crisis, in a quandary, a velvety chair, the dirty, the hungry, yes, we the cranky ... the majority of us silent, stifled, delinquent, in the background, barely hanging in, running out of time, hope, air'. (11) It is a prose poem which sets the tone for what follows, conversations in the play seeming naturalistic until they veer into strange territory, sentences changing direction, the ordinary suddenly not so. The address, however, ends, in a meta-theatrical gesture, with him pointing out the exits as we are ushered into the first scene.

Nor is he the only character to address the audience, the Cop offering details, as the Stage Manager does in Wilder's play, though in a way that disturbingly strays away from familiar platitudes: 'welcome to the little town of Middletown. Ordinary place, ordinary time. But aren't they all? No. They are not, all … Anyway, Middletown. Population: stable; elevation: same. The main street is called Main Street … Things are fairly predictable. People come, people go. Crying, by the way, in both directions.' (13)

Into this town comes Mrs. Swanson and her husband (though as he is a salesman, she rarely sees him), anxious to get to know this seemingly reassuring place, wanting, too, to start a family. 'Good for you,' says the local librarian, 'The world needs another person.' (16) This is somewhere, the librarian tells her, that people come to raise families or retire, 'drawn', she says oddly, 'by the excellent clouds', (15) but then, conversations in Middletown tend to take oblique turns. She welcomes the idea that someone would wish to have a library card when 'a lot of people figure, "Why bother? I'm just going to die, anyway"'. (14)

The town itself, she explains, was built on the ruins of an older one, long gone, and is in an area whose Indian tribe, which had 'a highly developed culture', has disappeared. A planned glass museum never happened. Beneath the reassurance is a whisper of fragility not least when another character, Mechanic, addressing the audience, explains that he had once thought of killing people in a car by dropping a rock on them, but had changed his mind, 'So now some family's driving around, not knowing how lucky they are … If I had more self-esteem, more stick-to-itiveness, I might have been a murderer.' (19–20)

There is a touch of the gothic about Middletown. A tourist explains of herself and her husband that 'there's a long history of death in both our families', (24) as the tour guide points to the ground saying, 'It's people strewn all the way through … most of the rest is dead human skin.' (25) The librarian, meanwhile, reads from a book, describing the notes written in its margin by a child: 'anxiety, sickness, death, spiritual'. (31)

The other principal character is John Dodge, forgetful, subject to panic attacks and claustrophobia, dark nights and dark days, a man liable to sudden corrections, warning against marriage and equally against divorce. He has lived in the town for ten years, quickly correcting himself to fifteen and then twenty, along with two nieces, which he corrects to one. He is uncertain which day it is. Words somehow get ahead of thoughts: 'Sometimes you get used to the words for things, and then you suddenly remember the things.' (29). He does odd jobs from time to time but meanwhile is taking a course on watercolour painting, only to confess, 'It's not really a course.' (28) This is a man who thinks of slitting his wrist. Mrs Swanson's bright if strained optimism – 'When you think of all the miracles it takes just sit in a chair'– is balanced, in the same conversation, by her own anxieties and by John Dodge's confession that he is afraid of dying, explaining that 'I've wanted a lot out of life. First air, then milk, and then it just kept going.' (36)

Then, suddenly, we are in a space capsule, the town having produced an astronaut who rhapsodizes over the earth, 'a fragile thing', (33) fragility evident everywhere. His conversation with ground control, though, is not without its strangeness as he confesses that he had never realized how round the earth was and recalls a man who had once discovered an ordinary rock thinking it to be a meteorite, though less concerned with the fact than with, 'The words he used to refer to it, the breath it took to make the words.' (33)

The first act ends with an 'audience', consisting of a young woman with a mild mental disability, her aunt, a couple, and a freelance writer, assembled on stage as recorded applause plays. In part they ignore the play, chatting among themselves even as they pick up fragments trying to work out the meaning of what they have seen, as the real audience will do as the actual intermission begins.

The second act marks a stylistic transformation, and a change of atmosphere. Mrs. Swanson, pregnant, is in hospital for the delivery, her doctor speaking of love and forgiveness, at the same time as Dodge is treated following a suicide attempt only to die of an infection. A man dies, a child is born, given the name of John. The circle is closed, or the circle turns, not so much an epiphany as simple continuity, acceptance. Irony drains away. The Cop's mother has also died, but the mood has altered. Characters now tend to be addressed by their first names. Those who were separate come together.

Eno created the play, he has said, because he wanted to write something about how life felt to him, insisting that it is a brilliant thing to be a human being.[29] In the end *Middletown* works its way past the loneliness, despair and pain which are equally part of life on earth, in this place where civilizations have faded and which seems to have nothing distinctive about it, until this no place becomes a place. Yet the irony persists. *Middletown* is like a conversation between Thornton Wilder and Samuel Beckett as characters talk of love and time's consolations, or of the ironies of both. 'I think we're born with questions and the world is the answer,' says the Librarian; 'it's very lucky to be a person, just a regular person,' (60) observes a doctor. Then Wilder becomes Beckett: 'Whhhshhhhhhh,' says another character, explaining that 'That's my impression of a cell dividing – or, I don't know, metastasizing. Same thing probably, for a while – until it isn't.' (46)

Outside the plays, in interview, Eno tends to be hesitant, tentative, diffident, even uncomfortable, if also ironic and humorous, engaging but wary of self-exposure (something happened to him when he was twenty-seven, he has said, without specifying what it was), his seeming modesty perhaps an aspect of that. In speaking, his phrases tend to be separated by silences. He is willing to talk about his work but with a preference for periphrases, guarded as if explication might diminish it. He tends to make several approaches to a thought, circling around a meaning he is not quite prepared to expose. Meanwhile, there is a rhythm to his work but equally a willingness to disrupt it, an interest in discontinuities if also in an underlying continuity. There is, in other words, an element of John Dodge about him. His fascination with language extends to the need for precision, even as he is aware of its failure fully to express what it effects to capture, a gap between experience and the attempt to express it. And that, too, is evident in *Middletown*.

For Charles Isherwood, in *The New York Times*, it was a play which 'provides a steady stream of quiet pleasures. "Middletown" glimmers from start to finish with tart, funny, gorgeous little comments on big things: the need for love and forgiveness, the search for meaning in life, the long, lonely ache of disappointment.'[30] For Chris Jones, reviewing the Steppenwolf production in the *Chicago Tribune*, it was 'a wonderful … play … profoundly wise', with dialogue that was 'uncommonly rich and poetic'.[31]

Middletown was followed, in 2012, by *Title and Deed*, originally written for Conor Lovett, indeed in part prompted by Eno seeing him in performance. As it happened, and not accidentally, the fact that Lovett is Irish, and that he had performed outside his country, was not without its significance to the play. It opened at the Edinburgh Festival to enthusiastic reviews, receiving a similar response when it moved to London and New York where it was staged as the first of three plays he would write for Signature Theatre's Residency Five which guaranteed a writer production of three plays over a five-year period.

A monologue, its setting is 'the theatre, a room, the present', while the narrator/conversationalist is, as he declares, 'not from here'.[32] As a result, he sees things from an outsider's perspective. And that seems to apply equally to language which describes different realities, not everything translating easily, including humour. Indeed, there are moments when it is not clear how sensitive he is to the nuances of words. When he says that love is 'a many splintered thing' (20), however, he is doing more than playing with words. After all, when he remarks that his country's principal exports are 'sarcasm and uric acid', (16) the joke turns on a level of linguistic competence. If he is an outsider, though, this carries other connotations, existential, he not alone in being 'away from home, not at home'. (31)

Eno is interested in the question of identity, its dismantling and reconstruction, fascinated by the notion of contending selves, with loneliness and connection, contradictions. 'Life', the significantly titled MAN declares, Beckett-like, 'was essentially a parade and it would only stop to let the ambulance through'. (30) In a familiar Eno reversal, his character declares, 'I like to think I'm a good person. I mean, not deep down', (25) 'I wouldn't trade them for anything, words. No, actually I would.' (29) 'I once was ... I probably never was', the thought never completed. Life, as he recalls it, remembers, misremembers, somehow seems to exist between contending terms, opposing feelings, contradictory interpretations.

He has gone on a journey, a journey 'with no maps, compass', (31) which mirrors the greater one which is a life to be contained between 'the human-cannonball feel at the beginning' and 'the sickening thump at the end', (28) a stranger in the world with the single obligation to 'keep breathing. In and out, for as long as we could ... All of us marching out of the ocean, breathing and breathing and breathing, and then dropping dead on land, on some land we like mistakenly to think of as ours', (33, 35) he and the audience alike part of the 'great swarm, the living billions', all trying 'to get our footing, place ourselves in some continuum, before the lights go out and the thing discontinues ... Now you see us ... now you don't ... The whole fucking swill-hole is just a long line of informative and beautiful funerals.' (42–3)

It is words, he suggests, which give such an arbitrary process shape, a function of theatre, where this monologue takes place, of this dialogue with those who sit in the dark and watch and listen. 'We should', he says, 'thank our stars ... for the listeners of the world', (44) addressing the audience who conspire, for the moment, in creating a longed-for meaning, no matter how contingent, how transitory, how deceptive.

The past which he recounts is not necessarily secure even as it is described, consisting, as it does, of random moments, arbitrary thoughts expected to cohere into a life. The present is what is shared with the audience in the knowledge that some things are never shared, merely experienced severally. 'Time, place, happiness', he says, 'A person should be able to figure it out. It's only three things.' (52) Religion and philosophy, he suggests, have both failed to make sense of the drift of existence which seems to consist of accumulating losses. The light begins to fade. 'It's a funny thing', he says, 'Being a person. All the needs, the feelings, all the different things arising, thoughts ... The earth.' (60–1)

It is hard to know whether we have been watching the assembly or disassembly of a person except that here is a character looking within and without to explain if not justify. Language is a compromised tool even as it is the only resource, with the power to step out of the self, express hope and despair within a single sentence, within a single life. Here and elsewhere Eno speaks of loving life and hoping that people will take away from his plays a sense, as here, that 'life and the world were bigger and scarier and stranger and more beautiful, and maybe more lonely but in all those bad things that you would feel there was a whole world of people who were feeling similar things'. He trusted that audiences would feel 'challenged, encouraged and excited about being alive'.[33] Perhaps, though there seems more than an echo here of Eugene O'Neill's hopeless hope.

For Lyn Gardner, in *The Guardian*, he had torn 'into our loneliness' and exposed 'it like a huntsman pulling a bleeding heart from a terrified deer', the artifice of the theatre reflecting 'the self-consciousness of this eternally wandering everyman'.[34] For the *Financial Times*'s Ian Shuttleworth, reviewing a later, London, production, it was 'another example of Eno's ability to send the intellect and emotions in opposite directions simultaneously'.[35] Charles Isherwood's *New York Times* review of the Signature Theatre production spoke of it as 'moving and mesmerizing', admiring its 'sculptured lyricism' and 'poker-faced humor'.[36] For John Lahr, in *The New Yorker*, it was 'a clown play that capers on the edge of the abyss'.[37]

Commissioned by Yale Repertory Theater, his next play, *The Realistic Joneses*, opened in April 2012, though he had started writing it in 2008 and tried parts out in readings to friends. Suddenly, here was a play with a naturalistic setting, set in a semi-rural town, featuring four middle-aged characters, neighbours, seen in a familiar context – porch, backyard, kitchen, grocery store. But, then, *All My Sons* begins with people chatting and joking in a backyard before the secure becomes insecure, while *Our Town* steps from the quotidian to the profound, indeed finding profundity in the quotidian.

The clue to what happens perhaps lies in the reading he did to prepare himself which included what he called 'Oliver-Sacks stuff about funny ways the brain can go wrong' and Alphonso Lingis's *The Community of Those Who Have Nothing in Common*, a book in part about dying and how 'the old standbys in language – like 'Tomorrow will be a better day! – actually don't apply and won't work any more',[38] that the knowledge that you are not alone in this is not a consolation. The title, meanwhile, was an indication that this play was to be different from his others, while Jones is a word associated with addiction and craving (supposedly referring to addicts who lived on Great Jones Alley, off Great Jones Street in New York). Here it was not to do with drugs but with a more fundamental craving for a meaning in life.

There is a certain legerdemain about a play which seems one thing only to transform into something else, persuading audiences to re-examine their own initial responses. It is a play in which humour and pain co-exist, the former in some ways a product of the latter. Not proclaimed as such, it seems at first something of an absurdist comedy as its characters throw language back and forth in a parody of a domestic drama, like table tennis players using an invisible ball. Meaning barely makes it across the net. Small talk is too small to communicate anything but the need to avoid a silence which carries its own threat, and there is a sense of menace to be put out of mind.

One couple have come from a town built on top of a leak of chemicals. There is equally something threatening here in this apparently reassuring place and in the lives of those whose chatter veers towards or away from revelation. The humour lies in banalities presented as profundities, in misunderstandings, a literalness denying language its depth, in gaps of understanding the funnier and more painful because not wilful. It is not, it appears, to be a play of three-dimensional characters whose past actions result in present conflict, the private and the public intertwined, the social and the psychological working towards resolution. These seem characters who have never quite managed the task of completing themselves, not too sure who they are or what their fate, like figures from late Albee plays or the family members who meet as strangers in the plays of T.S. Eliot, aware of a menace not to be faced. Except there is, it is revealed, a reason for the linguistic perversities. The absurdities, aphasic spasms, have their roots in something altogether real. If there is a sense of the absurd it lies far deeper than words, in the very condition of their existence.

The play features two couples, both with the last name of Jones. It opens with Bob and Jennifer, late at night, in the backyard of their modest house, with mountains in the background, postcard picture-perfect, engaged in a seemingly inconsequential conversation, even as Jennifer complains that 'we don't talk'.[39] She asks him what he fears most, whether there is something worrying him. Why is she asking him this? Why does he respond '*Sharply*?' The conversation continues, two instruments tuned to a different key.

They are interrupted by their new neighbours, John and Pony, bearing the gift of a bottle of wine. John claims to be an astronaut while explaining that 'I use the term loosely'. (17) So, not an astronaut. Indeed, later he claims to be in heating and air-conditioning, though incapable, it turns out, even of mending a broken lamp. When Bob, in a statement of the obvious, points out that other people had lived in their house before them John replies, 'Who knew the place had such an interesting history', (9) not, it seems, intending irony or condescension, conversation being disturbingly oblique, end stopped, not inviting further response. When Bob remarks that 'Moving is a pain', John replies, 'Staying still is no picnic, either.' (10) When John claims that he and Bob are not so different and Bob replies by saying 'we're probably very different', he responds by agreeing, 'me too, actually'. (13) 'I get what you're saying', says Bob. 'You don't get what I'm saying', (57) replies John. 'We ... stopped talking, me and Jennifer', Bob remarks, adding, 'I mean, we talk', (57) words beginning to swirl around, statements made and retracted or contradicted as if they can lead nowhere. These are figures, it seems, for whom nothing is clear, not even quite who they are, except that slowly it becomes evident why this is so.

Communication appears to follow a formula, social performance being simply that. They have a way of speaking past each other, the non-sequitur a preferred mode. Verbal gambits have a way of self-destructing. If 'you take the letters from the words "The United States of America," and you scramble them all up', John remarks, 'it doesn't spell anything. It's just gobbledygook, total nonsense'. (17) As Pony says of him, 'John and words – forget about it', (21) and not only John. Logic is no more reliable; John and Pony having bought their house because it is near a good school system not because they have any children but because John hates stupid children. (20)

The setting may be naturalistic, the dialogue is not. There is, though, a reason for the curious linguistic and behavioural traits on display since both men have an illness which effects the language centres, and much more – Harriman Leavey Syndrome (invented by Eno) being an irreversible and degenerative nerve disease. Leavey, it turns out, is the name of the specialist both men are consulting, both having, at one stage, gone blind. Suddenly the humour generated by misunderstandings, aimless responses, jumps in logic, has a rational and disturbing cause, the more so since it becomes evident that their shared illness will inevitably be fatal. It is a condition which leaves John crying in the night, and the two women struggling to deal with their husbands' decline. A play which had seemed one thing now becomes another. How, after all, to deal with a condition from which there is no reprieve, one of whose symptoms is a mind increasingly unable to process experience or articulate with clarity?

Bob gets by on denial, not wishing even to enter the doctor's surgery as he struggles to hold his fear at bay, even while he continues to deteriorate. Meanwhile, John has a seizure though

Pony hesitates to describe it as such as if naming it would be to acknowledge a truth to be denied. The two women are on the edge, Pony more so, the strain fracturing her equanimity as she, too, begins to evidence the same linguistic caesuras, logical jumps. Speaking to Bob of John she says, 'He's completely great … He sort of half disappears, sometimes, probably because I need him to, I guess, because I think sometimes I can only handle half a person, which is probably why I'm attracted to you. I don't mean attracted. Which, God, why can't I, you know, just, I wish I could have more focus.' (47) It is not he alone who half disappears as she wanders randomly back through her life confessing to feelings of 'Terror … Abandonment … Loneliness'. (74)

The question is what is the best strategy in the face of what they realize is an inevitability. Beneath the daily chatter, the arc of careers, consoling relationships, a sense of the beauty of the world, is a central truth accommodated to by relegating it to moments of sudden spiritual vertigo, or by clinging to a desperate hope. When Jennifer says that 'talking with someone can make you feel better,' he replies, 'What if, after you talk, the other person just stares back at you. With nothing in their heart?' (52) Consolation and despair are a sentence apart. 'Everything is going to be all right,' she assures John, only for him to reply, 'No one ever said that to me … When it might have been more true.' (54) Later, he remarks that 'words don't do it for me anymore', (57) suffering a neurological episode as words tumble out of him haphazardly.

Eno has always spoken of his plays as celebrating life. It is difficult to see *The Realistic Joneses* as fulfilling that ambition. When his characters visit a restaurant a man dies, a reminder of the destination towards which they are heading, an echo of Pozzo's cry from *Waiting for Godot*, 'one day he went dumb, one day I went blind, one day we'll go deaf, one day we were born, one day we shall die, the same day, the same second, is that not enough for you?'[40] Is there consolation in the fact that they share their plight, that wives remain with their husbands as they begin to fade away, living with no more than moments of contact, a broken kaleidoscope of memories?

Eno himself has said,

I had wanted for some time to just write a play that was about mortality … how we grapple with that … We are afraid of illness because we are worried about death and when we are worried about death we start thinking about mortality. And when you are thinking about mortality you are thinking about how do I want to live every day. These are the kind of things these Joneses are dealing with. They might not be dealing with them explicitly and they might not, by the end of the play, come to a super clear resolution as to what the best thing to do is. And that wasn't just by accident because I think that in trying to write and think about people with compassion you come to realise that there is no bad way to deal with a huge, awesome, unknowable mystery. There are different ways.[41]

The play, he explained,

concerns things that I have been thinking about – intimacy and fear of death. The fact that we all die and our fears or anxieties about it are potentially things that we could share and that could make us feel less alone, but I think sometimes we lug that anxiety around and keep it like a dirty secret, and that probably ends up making us feel a little estranged from other people. Almost like we're ashamed of the fact that we're going to die. That all sounds sort of morbid. I don't really mean it to be. People talk about the meaning of life; it seems like if you can get some kind of a handle on the meaning of death, then the life part might be a lot clearer. The point of all these considerations should be, in the end, to have the happiest, fullest life you can imagine … We all have to face this process – aging, sickness – that, in some ways, is the opposite of life, but, importantly, we are still alive while it is happening, and we have some time and a lot of choices about how to face it.[42]

In 2013, as part of the Actors Theatre of Louisville Humana New Plays Festival, by special arrangement with Signature Theatre, Eno presented *Gnit*, an anagram for Gynt (or, as Peter, in the play, says, a typo) it being, as he explained, a rough translation of Ibsen's *Peer Gynt*. It was something of a challenge, beyond the fact that the original ran for nearly five hours, with forty scenes and over forty characters, since that play was in verse and his in prose, shifts in the verse being significant in the original ('Why can't people read the thing as a poem?' Ibsen asked, 'That was what I wrote it as.'),[43] while it also targeted aspects of Norwegian society. Indeed, Ibsen suspected it was a play unlikely to be understood in other countries, though, as it turned out, he was wrong. As Ibsen noted, in a letter to his publisher, it was to be 'a long dramatic poem, having as a principal character a part-legendary, part fictional character from Norwegian folk lore during *recent* times'.[44] Later he would say that Peer Gynt was a real person who had lived around the turn of the nineteenth century, even as he confessed that little more was known of him than was to be found in Peter Christen Asbørnson's *Norwegian Fairy Tales*, so that he had felt free to invent.

It was not written to be performed but read, perhaps unsurprisingly since, among other things, he called for exploding boats, a sinking boat, a galloping horse, along with hoards of shit-throwing monkeys, embodied thoughts, leaves flying before the wind (though later it was, of course, staged, as he adapted it and persuaded Grieg to supply music). In that form it was not altogether well received, his friend and admirer Georg Brandes, as Michael Meyer, a translator of the play, pointed out, accusing Ibsen of misanthropy, self-hatred and belittling human nature since Peer Gynt is a lying fantasist, hubristic, a braggart, a coward, a rapist, stealing other people's stories, treated with contempt by those around him even as his ambition is to become Emperor of the World.

Gynt is a man who falls in with trolls, is dispossessed, possible redemption offered only by Solveig, the young woman who offers love, only for the trolls to intervene. Following the death of his mother he escapes to Africa where, now a middle-aged man, he is prosperous, having made his money from slavery, salving what he claims to be his conscience by supplying them with alcohol, while exporting Bibles and rum to China, convinced, as ever, that a man 'must live for himself and himself alone' not carrying 'the woes of others'.[45] He is hailed as 'The Prophet of Self'. (127) After travelling, he returns home to Norway only to be shipwrecked, surviving by denying another man safety on a dinghy until at last he comes towards death never having constructed the self in which he had believed. 'Life', he says, 'is a terrible price to pay for birth', (177) a Norwegian Beckett. Finally, Solveig appears with her message of human and divine love.

Eno shrinks the cast to six, having a single actor play multiple parts, and the running time to two hours. Pier becomes Peter and Solveig Solvay. Some elements are retained. Peter's mother suggests he would be better off marrying a local girl, Sarah, who she believes loves him, only to confess that she is marrying someone else that same afternoon. Peter duly carries her off.

As in the original, he declares that his objective is to go 'on a journey to discover, uncover, the authentic self'.[46] Eno's text, however, has familiar markers, particularly his fondness for sudden reversals. So, Peter's mother says that Peer is a good boy like his father only to confess that she had disliked and been deeply offended by him. For his part, Peter says that he will attend the wedding and get 'her idiot father's consent' only to add, 'I always respected him'. (12) A figure representing the whole town says, 'Interesting. That wasn't interesting. Well, it wasn't uninteresting. Yes, it was. No, it wasn't.' (19). This is so much a trope not only here, where it characterizes different figures, but elsewhere in Eno's work – statements made and contradicted or withdrawn, words suddenly evacuated of meaning – that it seems to stand for a defining sense of contradiction, stasis, irony as in *Waiting for Godot*'s famous neutralizing stage direction: 'Let's go. (*They do not move*).'

Here, as elsewhere, banalities can prove doorways to disturbing anxieties. Asked what she is afraid of, Solvay insists, 'I'm not afraid of anything' before listing, 'loneliness, choking, stroke, drowning, anything socially transmitted, the dark, weakness, guilt … going blind, history'. (18) Jokes are generated by misquoted phrase even as they have an element of truth about them. Peter lays claim to 'problem-causing skills', (19) even as he is a generator of problems running away with the bride-to-be.

There are knowing references to the original. A stage direction in Ibsen's play indicates '*A hillside, with great rustling trees. Stars twinkle through the leaves, Birds sing in the treetops. GREENCLAD WOMAN is walking on the hillside.*'[47] In *Gnit* this becomes, '"Tall peaks in the distance. Late day, the shadows lengthen. Amid mountain flowers and babbling brooks, a solitary figure approaches." That's a stage direction from some play I read in school'. (27) Trolls turn into the Green family, business people, anxious to mould him into their own form in a play which sometimes parodies, even mocks, the original with its indulgent lyricism and seemingly earnest philosophy, except that parody is already built into Ibsen's text.

Most of the African scenes are cut, as are other figures, and a gang of armed robbers introduced, but the most significant cut of all is that Solveig/Solvay is no longer waiting for him, having died before his return, so missing, too, are the hope and the faith. No wonder Peter turns to the audience and says, 'I wish this had been happier' (72). Eno's concern with the original was that Peer comes off too much as 'a lovable scamp', adding

> I thought it was important to write a play where we can really see the effects on other people … and how it can just be selfishness plain and simple and cause a lot of pain and a lot of worrying and a lot of suffering for other people. It was important to me, in adapting this, to show the costs of that and to show the … costs to … Peter.[48]

Why, though, did he choose to write a version of *Peer Gynt* at all? Peter's search for an authentic self, Eno has said, is

> something very present to me, concerning potential damage to the world that we might inflict in our own search for ourselves. That was one of the reasons I was taken with the play. I wanted to somehow make it into something that addressed more directly some of those questions about what is the cost to others if we go on a merry search for ourselves.

This in a country which celebrates individualism and the idea of the self-made man.

One thing that got me started was sympathy for both the character of Solveig, in the original play, and the actress who would play her. Solveig disappears for a couple of acts, about 30 years, and then comes on in the last few minutes to forgive Peer and tell him she's always loved him. I thought she deserved a little more dimensionality and agency. And, because of that original ending, in which there is some sweetness and light, I think the play is a little more misunderstandable than it needs to be – the Solveig stuff raises a larger question about what the play is actually about.

And then I started, along with kind of disliking him, feeling sorry for the character of Peer. Thinking of all this suffering and struggling he has gone through over the last two centuries, it seemed very sad to think that his point was being lost on us, or was outdated in some way. So, though my adaptation probably gets a little aggressive with the original text, it started out of something like love and sympathy. There are some important, hurtful, sort of "classic" things to learn from the play, but I think they can be learned in under two hours and with some laughs along the way.[49]

What he wanted, he said, conscious of a certain hyperbole, was

that people would find it to be the funniest, saddest, most meaningful thing they had ever experienced in their entire lives, which lives [would] improve immediately and vastly after they left the theatre having seen this play. That's my hope and that's my want. That's what I hope will happen when I go to see a play. I know that's absurd. And it's excessive but I hope that with all that hoping and wanting people would end up having a nice time, an enjoyable night in the theatre.[50]

Writing in November 2021, he noted:

Over the past 13 or 14 years of working on this adaptation of PEER GYNT, a grinding but real affection has grown in me for complicated Ibsen and his complicated play. So, nothing has pleased me more than to hear that people who really love and know the original play feel that– with 3 hours and 25 actors removed– something moving, funny, clear, and actionable has finally been revealed, re-interpreted, or created, in my adaptation. I have only read the first sentence of one review, which described Gnit as 'inward-looking,' which is really discouraging, as I spent so many serious years rethinking, reworking, and changing the original– which is famously and endlessly (maybe even hopelessly) inward-looking– in an effort to make something that is raucously, honestly, and yearningly OUTWARD LOOKING. The all-caps means I really believe I have done this.[51]

In 2014, Eno found himself presenting one play, *The Open House*, the second of his Signature Theatre works, while rehearsing another, *The Realistic Joneses*, for its Broadway opening at the 950-seat Lyceum Theater on 45th Street, the oldest continuously operating legitimate theatre in New York.

The Open House seemingly occupied familiar territory, if not for him, the family, supposedly the place of safety and security but in drama, from Sophocles to Shakespeare, Ibsen to O'Neill, Albee to Letts, the site of emotional danger, tension, pain, as characters deploy weapons, literal and psychological, in a war the more painful because of a memory of love. In his case it was to some degree rooted in his own sense of a family life which might have been other than it was. It is, he has said, 'a picture of the faceless and cruel indifferent force of evolution' whereby 'people are here and then replaced by other people who are similar but with one little trait changed, or alternate universes, alternate paths. If things had been slightly different might they have turned out like this.' He meant it, he insisted, to be 'a very optimistic statement about things. Certainly it's a statement about change and the possibility of change in many ways, a statement about change when it seems … there is no possibility for change.'[52]

It has the appearance of a realistic drama, with a reassuringly solid set, a family room, drained of colour. A son and daughter come together with their uncle (whose wife was killed in a tornado), to celebrate their parents' anniversary, though there is little celebratory about this gathering, their wheelchair-bound father emerging from time to time from behind his newspaper to make wounding comments, belittling everyone, seemingly taking pleasure in humiliating those to whom he is linked by blood or familial affinity. The room is charged with an emotional static. Attempts at contact are repelled. The dog has left, perhaps with good reason. There is, it seems, little open about this house. The curtains are closed, rather as in *August: Osage County* in which a hermetic house reflects those who have emotionally trapped themselves within it.

The father (characters being identified by their roles rather than names) delights in telling his children a story about encountering a beautiful woman, with whom he had spent an enchanting day, only to add that on the way back he had met their mother-to-be, 'talked a little, probably went out to dinner a few times' and then married her when her mother died of pneumonia.[53] It is a story with a deliberately dying fall which he has evidently told before, the rhythm of his cruelty evidently giving him a special pleasure, modifying it slightly but always travelling, with the same velocity, to the heart. In the face of his vitriol the mother offers an apparently emollient comment only for it to collapse under the weight of its own disturbing truth: 'your father loved you all when you were little. It was only when you started to talk.' (23) His virtue, she says, is that 'he never hit you'. (28) The negative is his habitual mode, his dark humour honed over the years, a reminder that hell can indeed be other people and that for a family, especially for one in American drama, it can seem that there is no exit.

The daughter has her own concern, a lump on her spine, as her mother also suffers from 'something women in my family are at fairly high risk for', (32) but sympathy is in short supply. The son, who has nightmares, rhapsodizes about his girlfriend because, 'I feel really calm with her'. (27) Even the uncle has a splinter which he has had for some time. As a family, they all seem to be walking the edge even as it is Father who commands attention. There is something of the toxicity of Pinter's *The Homecoming* or Shepard's *Buried Child* about *The Open House*, at least until something happens.

One by one they leave on various errands and then the change, which mother and daughter had fantasized about, occurs when there is a knock on the door and Anna enters, a real estate agent (the father, unbeknown to the family, having put the house up for sale so that open house has another meaning) played by the actor who also plays the daughter. Her first gesture is to open the curtains and reveal blue sky and green trees, a world beyond. She proposes that they should repaint a room which is as drab as they have allowed their lives to become. At this point they are joined by a would-be purchaser, Brian, played by the actor who had been the uncle now, like Anna, in a different costume. The mood lightens further, as does the room with bright flowers now on show. Anna massages Mother's wrist, relieving her of the pain she has suffered but forborne to mention.

A phone call interrupts bringing news of a traffic accident her daughter has suffered, a daughter for the first time granted a name. As Mother leaves, however, Tom enters, a landscaper, played by the actor who played the son, a man who, like other Eno characters, has a way of reversing himself in a single sentence, insisting that he does not 'really take drugs' except 'pot and cocaine and alcohol and stuff like that'. (49) He strips wallpaper to reveal something 'gorgeous but faded' underneath (51), a wallpaper originally chosen by Mother, evidence of a path not taken, the path which might have been chosen and which is, perhaps, represented by those who have come to a house which had seemed unchanging. The point of the doubling, indeed, is that in some ways this is if not a parallel world, then an alternative track. They are then joined by Melissa, Brian's wife, played by the actor who plays Mother, and Charles, her lawyer brother, played by the actor who played Father, Father having left in an ambulance after what may be a heart attack or stroke.

These characters have names which the earlier ones (a missing son aside) did not. They inhabit a world of colour, open a house that was closed, are capable of a healing touch. Like the wallpaper stripped away to reveal something altogether brighter, they have an energy that had earlier leached away. Even the dog returns. Two possibilities, two poles of experience, exist.

For Charles Isherwood, in *The New York Times*,

> The tentative, evanescent nature of life has been a recurring theme in Mr. Eno's work, and he rings a memorable variation on it here. While at first it may have seemed that the intimate brutality on display was of no consequence, 'The Open House' ultimately resolves itself on a quietly moral note: The poison of cruelty doesn't just cause people to disintegrate, but to evaporate completely, leaving no traces behind.[54]

Michael Billington, reviewing a British production in November 2017, was unsure 'whether Eno was being bleakly pessimistic or ironically optimistic' in a play which was 'often very funny', a 'skittish, mercurial variation on a familiar theme'.[55]

Ahead, lay his third play for the Signature Theatre, *Wakey, Wakey*, which he also directed. Signature's founder, James Houghton, was already dying when Eno wrote it (he died of stomach cancer in August 2016). It was, therefore, strangely appropriate in that it was itself a play about dying while also a celebration of life, not a solemn requiem but a 75-minute work (he mocks his audience by suggesting it will last three hours) recalling and enacting the messy, uncoordinated, improvised, but essentially present nature of a life open to pain but touched with beauty and humour alike, performed in the presence of others, a lifetime limited but whose fate it is to be preserved not in some metaphysical immortality but the living memory of others.

There is no doubt that the central character, whose name, Guy, is suitably both particular and general, is dying (probably, Eno explains in a note on performance, of cancer), and death and dying are hardly absent from Eno's work if also, as here, a neutralizing sense of possible transcendence. What the audience witness, though, is, for much of the time, a kind of one-man show in which Guy chats amiably with the audience, joking, telling stories even as he is in what is surely a hospice. This is an under-rehearsed stand up by a man who is sitting down in a wheelchair. His is an illustrated performance, complete with videos and music, word games, which he cues, a technology of which he is not a complete master, accidentally switching on the house lights at one moment, scrolling through the menu in search of a video he wants to show.

Recorded sounds from outside the theatre penetrate from time to time, the membrane between art and life deliberately presented as permeable. Rather as Eugene O'Neill, in *Lazarus Laughed*, envisaged the action spilling out of the auditorium at the end of the play so, here, Eno calls for refreshments to be laid on in the lobby, like a funeral feast but also as a way of, in effect, continuing the play, blurring the boundary normally presumed to separate assumed artifice from assumed reality.

There are moments when Guy asks his audience to think of someone who has changed their lives or simply to concentrate on 'a human being',[56] inviting them to step outside themselves, it being good to be 'able to picture someone else', (20) because it is all too easy to 'take almost everything in existence for granted'. The important thing, he declares, 'isn't what's gone or lost, it's seeing and knowing what's still there and how it can grow'. (21, 23). It is tempting to think that the play's title references the Brooklyn-based band Wakey Wakey whose best-known song was 'Almost Everything I Said the Last Time I Saw You', and whose lyrics insist on the need to step outside and open your eyes because, however bad things might seem, everything is going to get better.

Certainly, there is no sense of despair about a play which seems to offer a sense of grace, which invites its audience to wake up to a life they are too content to see drift by. We are, Guy says to the audience, 'here to say good-bye and maybe hopefully also better at saying hello. To celebrate Life.' (3) 'Is it now?' (1) he asks as the play begins, the ending already at hand as, for him, it is, as for those who watch, it will be. Guy has index cards, prompts for issues he wishes to raise, planned theatrical moments, memories, PowerPoint illustrations, fragments of his life, observations, admonitions, feelings, a jumble of thoughts pressing in on him as he reaches the end of his life, trying to pull things together, as several boxes on the floor presumably contain belongings which will soon not belong to him.

There comes a moment when he is joined by Lisa, clearly the nurse who will see him through to the end, to his end, though he fails to recognize her, a sign that things are beginning to close down. 'What was the topic?' (26) he asks, as Mr. Peters, in Arthur Miller's *Mr. Peters' Connections*, asks, 'what's the subject' as he, too, approaches his end struggling to understand how the pieces of his life might be fitted together, himself failing to recognize those he should. 'All this stuff is connected', (33) Guy observes. Life may have started with a plan but then came the necessary 'adjustments', so that it was not the acting out of a prepared script but a series of improvisations which, in the end, add up to meaning, as he pictures all those he had known as if they were brought together for a music festival and he was invited, at the last, to join them, his last words to the audience being 'Take care of each other.' (41). Lisa, without sourcing, quotes from Ignatius of Loyola at the moment he faced death: 'My birth is imminent. Forgive me, brethren … do not prevent me from coming to life.' (29) For him, life was to be in the next world. For Eno it is in this world.

The play does not end with Guy's death, however. Lisa places a bag of fortune cookies at the front of the stage for the audience, and puts on music before, '*A simple but mesmerizing video production begins*', (42) one featuring nature. Ultimately, Eno indicates, '*as much life and color and energy and humanness and diversity and joy should come into the theatre, via the video. Older people dancing, a child bearing a corner of a coffin, newly weds, children on a playground, all of it.*' For two and a half minutes he calls for 'a riotous and joyous scene'. A machine sends bubbles onto the audience, a spinning disco ball reflections. Balloons descend, the whole '*an incredible rock and roll show*' (42) as volunteers place juice boxes and party favours with signs inviting people to help themselves. What began with a dying man static in a wheelchair ends with a whirl of sound, light and action, a carnival.

In some sense, *Wakey, Wakey* concentrates into seventy-five minutes the theme underlying his earlier plays. Death and darkness exist. There is an acknowledgement of the contradictions, at every level, of human experience, language itself bearing the marks of these contradictions, along with a prevailing irony factored into existence. Yet he has always insisted that the theatre itself is a mechanism not merely for acknowledging this fact but for placing on stage the living evidence for communality, the intensity of lived experience, the capacity of language to break through its limitations, the possibility of finding a shape in the flux of events. Something arcs across the gap between what happens on stage and those who gather in expectation of an insight into other lives, a singular vision which can be shared, the theatre not being a comment on life but an expression, an embodiment of it, time here being shared, a fact underscored in this play by the characters announcing its passage.

Wakey, Wakey he has said, is 'about those things that we find a little bit hard to talk about, dying, people we love dying, which sounds pretty glum, but I hope and believe that it's a funny thing. In some ways it's a play about how to live a good life which I think is what a good play is often about.'[57]

For Ben Brantley, in *The New York Times*, it was 'a profoundly moving play' in some way celebrating 'life, irreducible and infinite in its finiteness'.[58] Perhaps it had a special significance given the death, a year previously, of Signature's founding artistic director.

There is a reiterative quality to Will Eno's plays. Different as they are, they tend to circle around the same fixed point, the contradictions inherent in human existence. He has a love of the circularities, deceptions and occasional opacities of language, as of its potential for the lyrical, for sudden connections. His characters debate with themselves and one another, seldom assured, frequently displaying an anxiety about relationships which never seem entirely secure. There is always, though, a humour which flickers through them, sometimes consciously deployed by the characters, sometimes a product of their lack of awareness. Always, though, there is a fundamental humanity to his work. Tentative in person, he is unwilling always to adjudicate between contending interpretations. *Wakey, Wakey* is surely an exception. Here, death has no sting. On the contrary, it is the fact of death which creates the urgency of realizing the significance, moment by moment, of life. That would be especially true of his next play.

In Walt Whitman's poem 'Unfolded Out of the Folds' he declares that first the man is shaped in woman and then shaped in himself. In *Leaves of Grass* he speaks of containing multitudes, also the knowing title of a Bob Dylan's song where he writes of being a man of contradictions, of many moods, today, tomorrow and yesterday the flowers dying like all things do, sleeping with life and death in the same bed. For Ralph Waldo Emerson, change was of the essence, contradictions to be embraced, consistency irrelevant or even despised.

The meaning of a life becomes clear only with its end, T.S. Eliot writing that the end is where we start from. A life only has shape in retrospect, finally, it seems, given the grace of form. A particular life is accreted as a 3D printer slowly reveals the shape it creates, slice by slice, even as it can only be understood when nearing its completion in the way that a drone's eye view can reveal configurations invisible from the ground. Perspective is all. A character in Romesh Gunesekera's novel *Reef* observes that all we have is memory of what we have done or not done, who we might have touched, even for a moment. Eno's next play raises the existential question of who we are. Heidegger supposedly once observed that 'every man is born as many men and dies as a single one', which I take to mean that when we are born there are a myriad of possibilities but that we die having defined ourselves. The reverse, though, could be equally true, moving not only from a single cell but a single unformed self which is not yet a self, to a complex being shaped by a myriad of experiences, scarred by loss, elevated by glimpses of transcendence.

Meanwhile, voices fade, faces once so familiar now misted over. As it says in Corinthians, we see through a glass darkly. Witnesses to our lives disappear one by one, no one left to ratify what we believe to be truths. Words begin to evade us, thoughts tracing a wayward path as time manages to both speed up and slow down. It speeds up as years come and go so much faster now, as those circling the earth on the space station see sixteen sunsets in a day, and sunsets have a greater significance than once they did. It slows down as does the body, signals from the brain seemingly determined to take circuitous journeys. Am I now what I was? Do we have a continuous self? What am I shedding at the end, what shadow do I cast, even as we are known and understood differently by those who witness the end and for whom we were never one thing?

Eno traces a life, which turns out to be many lives, through the variations, shocks and tribulations that life is heir to, but also those moments which seem to lack significance, the small change of life which turns out to be true currency. And is that life secure in itself, unique, given that its journey is common to all, shared across genders and races, across time? His new play would be a kind of memoir, not of himself but of an everyman or, indeed, everywoman, brought into the world, travelling to a known destination. There is a sense in which all memoirs are written backwards, the present recuperating the past in the hope that meaning will distil out, the telling of the tale revealing the purpose of the tale. His play would present audiences with a tangle of characters, shifting personas, leaps in time and consciousness, in the belief that a shake of the kaleidoscope would reveal if not a pattern then the fact that patterns inhere in the mechanisms of life, an act of faith, perhaps, not to be represented as a sentimentality even as that is the risk as a person is interred, this signalling more than the end of one individual, mind, heart and soul now stilled, memories eclipsed, relationships buried deep with the body.

In November 2019, Second Stage Theatre, in New York, staged *The Underlying Chris*, with a diverse cast 'so that the play resembles the world', encouraged by the opportunity for double casting. For Eno, his hope was that 'simply following the story will be an act of and an exercise in empathy for the audience', while conceding that 'Maybe that's true of all plays.'[59]

It opens with a prologue in which an eleven-year-old girl addresses the audience, reminding them to turn off their cell phones, pointing out the exits, and asking them not to take photographs. She then announces that the subject of the play is to be 'life on Earth', identity, change, continuity and renewal, 'a story about the moments that shape a life, and the people that shape a life, and the people who shape a moment. And the things we *don't* have names for. The essence, I guess, the spirit. And also mystery. And meaning.' (1–2) There is an echo of *Our Town*, whose heroine asks whether human beings ever realize life when they live it. In this case the central character is three months old when the play begins, referred to with a male pronoun, only to switch to a female one a moment later. He/she is Christopher/Christine and a succession of other names and racial identities.

There are echoes of Wilder, too, in the fact that *The Underlying Chris* is a work which foregrounds its own processes, not only by a direct address to the audience, and its incorporation of a play, but by drawing attention to the fact that we are watching actors, changing their appearance, the Chris character 'changing constantly in terms of gender, race, etc., this', Eno declaring, 'as much for the purpose of theatricality, energy, and surprise as for a social or political message'. (np) For Eno,

> every play I've written or thought about writing is somehow very much on the path to *The Underlying Chris*. This is definitely a play that brings into focus a lot of things that I as a playwright have thought about, and that I as a human being have struggled with. The notion of identity, in its most simple terms. What is the realist thing about me, what is the irreducible part ... it has felt like that rare thing where one's private pre-occupations and worries ... line up with some part of a national conversation.

Is identity a product of gender, race, sexual proclivity, the pressure of external forces, or psychological needs? Michael Ondaatje has said that we are made by what comes before us, before in the sense of personal and public history. By the same token identity is a product of time, Eno taking his protagonist through the decades, interested as much in nuanced moments as in major shifts, brutal traumas, sudden losses for the most part being relegated off stage. Do we, though, have an essential self, persisting through times? Eno's answer is that 'The play is about the essence of this character Chris, and how that deep-down [an] essential part of us remains, throughout the many changes and challenges and phases of life.'[60] The question is, how deep down?

The journey, then, is to be that of Chris 'through the world, through time and space', (2) from cradle to grave. In the next scene he is already ten, his father now dead, while in the following one she is twelve to fourteen and in hospital after a diving accident, her mother and uncle also dead in a car crash only for her to be adopted by her doctor having been abandoned by her uncle's sister-in-law who was to have looked after her. So, he/she ages, training as a doctor, changing with every encounter, later giving up medicine because 'It just wasn't who I was', instead becoming a therapist because 'Bodies come and go, but the spirit, that's what I was always interested in ... people's ideas and feelings, the part of people that moves through the world and changes but also lasts.' (34) As Christopher remarks, 'when I thought I was starting to *become myself* or *get somewhere*, I'd suddenly be somewhere else with someone else'. (28) So, what do we make of Eno's suggestion that 'an essential part of us remains?'

As a woman in her forties, she is married with a daughter. Then, as a man in his late fifties, having abandoned his career as a therapist, and precipitated a divorce, he is an actor rehearsing a play in a small community theatre. Though the play's dialogue is more than a little precious, it is not without its relevance as the character he plays asks, 'Was there a plan, and I ruined it, or refused it? Was there never a plan? Or is there one, a perfect, grand plan that I'll never be able to see, even though I stare and stare while the moss grows over my name?' (37) The director's remark that 'Transitions are always hard', (43) clearly has a relevance beyond the production.

In her mid-to-late sixties, Krista is in a park with her grandson as Christoph, in his mid-to-late seventies, arrives with daughter Joan 2, two worlds overlapping, both having daughters with the same name. Referring to her career as an actor (a man at the time), her grandson says,

'Mom said it would be hard for you to switch back and forth between different people', (48) a comment directed at the audience as much as the character as when Krista says, 'I sometimes feel surprised, being here – like I walked through the door into someone else's life.' (49)

By now decline has set in, Kit losing his driving licence, unable to pass the eyesight test but also less lucid than before even as his granddaughter recalls him saying that 'Water can be a cloud, or a snowball, or a waterfall, but it's always the same stuff, it's just in a different setting, or on a different day,' he adding, 'You might have changed here and there but you were you from the day you were born.' (54) So, there is, apparently, a core identity, a soul, which remains the same. Is that true of a country, constantly changing but ever the same? A small pain in the back felt by a young child is felt by all, a mark of their commonality.

At eighty-two, Christiana is now in an assisted living home, her eyesight poor. A mother enters with a young baby, the baby from the first scene, past and present together, beginning and end. Kris, now blind, and in his eighties, is up for physical therapy for his back. The final scene is set in a cemetery, the destination towards which this man/woman, in common with all, has been heading, the characters now gathered, including those representing the different ages of a person here reduced to a brief biography displayed on an easel, the name Chris misspelled.

A brief elegy expresses the essential optimism of the play which has displayed the ages of a man, who might as well have been a woman, or a person of any colour, or origin. As a character observes, 'Things are difficult, aren't they? Difficult and rewarding. It's quite an honor to be born, isn't it?' (71) And we are back with Thornton Wilder and Emily's encomium to life in *Our Town*: 'Oh earth, you are too wonderful for anybody to realise you', a play which, over the years, has been cast with an array of actors. It was staged in Manchester following the terrorist attack, the Stage Manager played by a British-Moroccan Muslim.

Eno's final scene, which gathers the whole cast, in its array of races and genders, for the most part plays against sentimentality, those arriving for the funeral, or engaging in arranging it, chatting about anything other than the man being buried, indeed who is already in his grave, the mistake over his name having overtones of farce. The final speech, however, by a man himself fighting back his tears, ends as he is handed a small paper cup from which he drinks saying, 'oh, that's nice. Apple juice. I was expecting water', as though what had seemed a bland and formulaic occasion were somehow elevated into a kind of humanist eucharist.

For Jesse Green, in *The New York Times*, *The Underlying Chris* was 'infernally clever … play'. Declaring 'it's annoying at first, like an anagram you can't decipher. But the cleverness eventually leads the story to an overwhelmingly emotional conclusion it might otherwise never have reached.'[61]

A month later, in December 2019, *The Plot* opened at Yale Repertory Theatre. Commissioned by Steppenwolf, it was dedicated to Martha Lavey, who had been its Artistic Director until 2015, dying following a stroke in 2017. The title is ambiguous given that its setting is a graveyard and that it involves more than one plot/conspiracy. Righty is a man in his sixties/seventies who is discovered beside a new gravestone having purchased a plot, except he already has another one, seemingly suffering from Alzheimer's, or perhaps being bipolar since he has purchased a boat trailer while seemingly not owning a boat. He is cared for by his wife Joanne. The graveyard, though, is not just a place of rest. A real estate developer, Tim, wants to acquire it on behalf of a somewhat mysterious buyer, helped by his assistant, Donna. He anticipates no problems dealing, as he is, with a man apparently barely in command of his senses and who can easily be dispossessed of his ninety-nine-year lease, buying him off with a condemned house and a nearby field. Things are not, however, as they seem, a trap waiting to be sprung.

There is, in fact, more than one plotter in *The Plot*, a play in which all the relationships we witness are transactional. Triumph consists of outmanoeuvring others, betrayal, deceiving, being natural instincts. Tim not only betrays/deceives Righty, but also his wife with his assistant. The magus, however, turns out to be the man others assume to be powerless: Righty. His financial acumen outstrips that of those who seek to take advantage of him. His Alzheimer's is assumed, but this involves his deceiving his wife, enrolling her, unwittingly, in his plot. If Tim lacks a moral compass, he, too, for all his triumph, perhaps lacks a sense of true north. His simulated illness also buys him a fully funded twenty-hour a week homecare worker.

Given that the action takes place in a graveyard, that the characters stand beside a literal reminder of life's undoing, that we give birth astride of a grave, there is, perhaps, a wider issue. As Joanne remarks, 'the reality underneath all this, is so strange – a person in a box in the ground. Night and day, rain or shine – dead, dead, dead. Cemeteries send out color brochures, as if it's like anything else.'[62] Not without justification, Donna asks Righty, 'this is what you decide to do with your time on earth? … I cannot believe the things people do', (45–6) adding, 'When you lie all the time, you sort of stop being a person.' (47) David Sedaris has said that all great art addresses the subject of death, tragedy, of course, being an ultimate denial as meaning is snatched from a darkening sky. But Sedaris is a comic writer. There are no jokes in *The Plot*, but Eno is drawn to the human comedy.

The play seems to end on a benign note as the land which was to have been given over to trailer trucks, is redeemed by the discovery of a rare salamander which makes development impossible, Donna now being enrolled in a new conservationist venture, along with a fifth character, Grey, until then something of an observer. The fate of the earth, it seems, is to take primacy. Yet has Righty really suffered a stroke, as he now seems to have done, or is he still a dissembler? Is his wife, as he hinted, perhaps herself showing signs of dementia? And what of the unseen character, in whose name the commercial venture had originally been pursued but is now behind an apparently environmentally friendly project, a god-like figure. He, it seems, is an ultimate magus, a master manipulator, a plotter. Do we search for meaning in the wrong place? Is there, in fact, a plot to existence? The inscription on a gravestone reads 'The Universe is fatal.' (254) On the other hand, there is a boat.

The seven-year-old who had wondered if anyone saw him, feeling that his existence was problematic to others, depending on, and arising from what he said, out loud, to people, and for whom the nature of identity would become a central concern, writes a play, *The Underlying Chris*, in which his central character comes into existence as he, the playwright, speaks out loud to an audience, his existence no longer problematic.

Theatre is artifice. Perhaps there is a degree to which that is equally true of life with its conscious performances, staged for those who believe such, or not, observers whose existence is necessary if we are to believe in our own. Speaking in the context of his monologue *Lady Grey*, but with equal relevance to another monologue significantly entitled *Mr. Theatre Comes Home Different*, he has said:

> The artificial nature of theatre just seemed to be the elephant in the room, and it seemed like a good idea to give the elephant a few lines. And I sometimes wonder if, if we can still have all the real and human feelings, in response to something that we are entirely aware

is fictional, maybe that's the beginning of a truer, deeper empathy? Or at least a version of empathy we can build on when the lights come up?

He does more than 'think about it a lot'.[63] It is, finally, an article of faith.

As to Samuel Beckett, there were limits to his admiration: 'he said that language was a stain upon silence … I do not see it as a stain … but rather as an amazing invention of humans.'[64] On the other hand, Beckett took pleasure in humour and paradox. Eno does no less.

CHAPTER 5
MARTYNA MAJOK: ON DISPLACEMENT

In the limited space of a 90 or so minute story, you need to make sure you are not reinforcing something damaging or dishonest about any one identity or experience … There's not one version of an immigrant story … You can tell whatever story you want to tell, but the folks who have gone through it will know.

I think when you get stuck, it's because you forget when you were in a position like the one the character's in, that you've separated yourself from who you're writing and the situation you're writing about … I have to go back to the times when that thing happened, or something like that thing.

… anytime you get to stage a play, you are given a platform to address a lot of people and there is an immense privilege in that. I think we have to be more responsible about what we make that conversation about. Just to recognise that not everyone has the opportunity to hear their story, let alone their words on that kind of platform.[1]

The British novelist Rose Tremain's advice to would-be writers is to write what you don't know, in other words reach out beyond your own experience, inhabit that of those remote from yourself. In an interview in December 2021, she said, 'I always say to my students, "Don't write about yourself because … You won't have learnt anything about the world, you won't have looked outside." So much of the learning I have done has been through research into the subjects I have chosen.' To her, there was a 'hideously narcissistic' trend by which the 'most accepted fiction is in the hands of people who've had rather exceptional, usually traumatic early lives, and that gives an authenticity … There is a story to tell.' At its most extreme there was a pressure not to intrude into the experience of others. In *Sacred Country*, she had written about a girl who thinks she is a boy. She doubts that that would be acceptable today when there is a tendency for people to patrol their own experience so that 'it is like walking through a forest with mantraps'.[2]

On the other hand, your own experiences are a resource, and writers are often drawn to mine them, to reprocess them, engage with them. That would be true of Tennessee Williams in *The Glass Menagerie*, *Vieux Carré*, *Small Craft Warning*, indeed, in one sense, in most of his plays. Of the last, he said that it was 'the responsibility of the writer to put his experience as a being into work that refines it and elevates it'.[3] He even stepped into his own work playing the part of a doctor who has lost his licence to practice, an echo of a playwright conscious of his waning appeal with critics. In *After the Fall*, Arthur Miller confronted his own private and public life. In Britain, Arnold Wesker's *Roots* replayed his early relationship with his wife, Dusty. In *South Downs* David Hare revisited his time at school. Of *Leopoldstadt*, Tom Stoppard said, 'Quite a lot of it is personal to me but I made it about a Viennese family so that it wouldn't seem to be about me.'[4]

For one American playwright, who would emerge in the second decade of the twenty-first century, the personal was central. This was in part because she wanted to stage the lives of those too often ignored or traduced, in art no less than life, and in part because she had been shaped, as, more crucially had her mother, by her experiences in a particular place which seemed to offer little in the way of physical or spiritual consolation, by the struggle of an immigrant family to survive, of working-class men and women to function in an environment and a culture not attuned to, or even acknowledging, their plight.

'I write,' she explained, 'about things that I have gone through, or that I am going through, for characters that are different from me but who have a certain experience in common with me. Externally we may seem different, but internally we're incredibly similar … I can only understand myself or talk about myself when I'm wearing a mask.'[5] Her plays are 'set in geographies I know well and peopled with characters that are composites of people I know … To quote Marsha Norman: "You've gotta write from your stuff." I think we writers write about what we know to understand what we don't.'[6] Perhaps that is where she meets up with Rose Tremain.

Martyna Majok was born in 1985, in Bytom, southern Poland, an ancient city which, in the post-war world, became heavily industrialized, polluted, with a declining population and a deal of poverty. Her mother went to America on her own, returning pregnant. When Martyna was still young, five, they moved to America to join what was now to be her stepfather and stepsister, though because of visa problems they shuttled back and forth for a time, spending summers in Poland. They settled in Kearny, New Jersey, a suburb of Newark, also industrialized or, more strictly, deindustrialized. Its population is 40 per cent Hispanic or Latino and Majok learned Spanish at school. Nearly 60 per cent of its citizens have both parents foreign born, and she grew up in a multi-cultural neighbourhood.

Of Kearny she has said, 'It's what you see in the opening credits of "The Sopranos." It's these bridges; it's these abandoned factories, which used to be factories that my mother worked at. Everybody I grew up with is pretty much an immigrant, and [their parents were] mostly single moms.'[7] Neither she nor her mother spoke English. She learned hers in part from watching the pre-school television series *Mr. Rogers* because, as she has said, he enunciated so well. The language spoken at home was Polish, her mother learning her English at work, an English never perfect but one shared by many of her community. For Majok, however, 'I see beauty and potential in what others might consider "broken" language … Sometimes a person's particular way of seeing the world felt like it translated more truthfully, directly, and poetically than maybe if it were spoken with perfect "proper English."'[8] What she heard, also, was a humour, sometimes inadvertent, sometimes a defence.

For a while the family was undocumented. Like all immigrants, they looked for an identity in a new country, for a sense of belonging, even as the terms on which that could come about were not always apparent. Displacement is not only a fact of geography. It can have to do with an alienation from a sense of oneself as the means of survival can seem at odds with a sense of autonomy, spiritual integrity. As she grew up, everyone seemed to come from elsewhere.

The Chinese artist and activist Ai Weiwei suffered deprivations as a child, exiled into a remote part of China where his bed was a dirt platform, and he was forced to clean toilets which consisted of holes over a cess pit. However, he found safety in his family even though they were at the bottom of the social scale. But he also said that it was positive to be poor, understanding, thereby, how vulnerable humanity can be. Majok, of course, did not suffer such an extreme of deprivation, though she and her family were displaced and did feel that they were seen as marginal, but deprivation there was. What there was not, was safety in her family. The actor Mark Strong, son of an immigrant, whose Italian father left home when he was too young to remember, had a working-class upbringing. His mother, moving from Austria, changed his name from Marco to Mark, herself, like Majok's mother, working in people's homes and in a factory. As he has said, 'there was no safety net', understanding that 'if I fucked up, there was no one to bail me out',[9] precisely Majok's understanding of her own situation.

Her upbringing was not entirely a happy one, given that her stepfather was prone to anger. Because of what she called the volatile situation in her home, she retreated into her bedroom to be safe. It was there she would write and draw. On one occasion she wrote something for elementary school about what was happening at home only to be sent to the nurse's office. When her mother found out she was terrified that she and her sister might be taken away from her so, on her return to school, Martyna told the teacher she had made it up.

She watched her mother deal with the problems of being an immigrant, working in factories and as a house cleaner, a private person whose philosophy was to remain invisible. She knew she could not look to her parents for help with schoolwork, their grasp of English not being sufficient. Nor would she be able to look to them for financial help as she grew up, though her mother was supportive. Like Ai Weiwei, however, she does seem to have gained an understanding of how vulnerable humanity can be and that is evident in her plays which, while focussing on those she knew best, explore human experiences which transcend her own. North working-class Jersey is her Yoknapatawpha county, her Thomas Hardy's Wessex, a place whose physical and moral particularity is crucial, but which deals with elemental forces.

At high school she was involved in a literacy programme, teaching English to immigrant parents who were struggling to learn the language at the same time they were teaching their children to walk and talk. As she has said, 'I became sensitive to language. It communicates so much about a person – the rhythm of how they speak, their sentence structures, whether they interrupt themselves.' As a part of that she offered dramatizations of common experiences they might have going to the store, to the bank and so on, along with a language they could practice. After a while, she explained, these became more elaborate, in retrospect recognizing this as the beginnings of something though at the time she did not think of this as playwriting since, knowing nothing of theatre, she thought 'a play was a movie they couldn't afford to make'.[10]

At the age of fifteen, in September 2001, she and her fellow pupils watched the Twin Towers fall from their school windows, a moment of trauma which, on a wholly different scale, she would feel on the election of Donald Trump not least because of what it would mean for immigrant communities such as her own, recalling that she broke into tears for several days.

It was at school that a teacher told her about a playwriting contest for students from New Jersey. She was the only one from a public school to be a winner, though she only went to the theatre in her last year at high school, using the forty-five dollars she had won playing pool. Her mother had brought home a pamphlet about the production, along with magazines she retrieved from work, material her employers had thrown away. It was, however, a crucial experience. The play was Sam Mendes's production of *Cabaret*.

None of her family ever went to the theatre. They were, she has said, simply struggling to survive. Now she was exposed to a new experience,

> In addition to being in a room where human voices are filling the space with so much life, it was a story that you can call 'pretty dark.' It has a 'tough' subject matter, but it was told with such humour, bawdiness and joy. There was a literal invitation in the beginning with 'Willkommen' that I really responded to. It wasn't compromising what it was about but was still inviting. I've taken that as a lesson for how to approach the act of making theatre.[11]

In her final year, looking through a list of universities, she came across the University of Chicago, 'I thought, "Oh, Chicago – blues and Polish people, that sounds awesome! I'll apply there, not knowing anything about the school."'[12] The only reason she could go was because she was offered a full scholarship. It was a year, though, before she was attracted to the theatre department.

At the University of Chicago, she acted in several student productions. It was there that she read Sarah Kane's plays, though not as part of a course. Kane, who studied under the British playwright David Edgar, writing her first play, *Blasted*, while at Birmingham University, only produced five plays, sometimes brutal, and committed suicide in 1999, having made previous attempts. When Majok saw a notice announcing auditions for Kane's *Crave* she signed up for it. *Crave* was so different from her other work, though, that Kane published it under an assumed name, even inventing a fictional biography. It is a play in which the characters have no names, only letters of the alphabet, while no gender is attached to them. There is no obvious plot and there are no stage directions. Even its initial director expressed some bafflement. It is a little difficult to see what Majok responded to unless it was the language, or languages, since the occasional speech is not in English.

She considered being an actor but even in her first year was conscious that she would need to be self-supporting and be able to help her mother. As her final year thesis, she wrote a full-length play, *wander/standing*, which she has described as terrible. As she explained to Joanna Socha, 'I found it incredibly difficult but, at the same time, I'd never felt quite as honest with myself as I had after I finished writing … So once I'd realised that I felt like that was the path to follow.'[13]

In her final year of college she applied for a fellowship specially designed for immigrant students, established by two Iranian immigrants. With a certain irony, it was called the Merage Foundation Fellowship for the American Dream, the irony being that, apart from Merage being pronounced mirage, Majok was fully aware that the dream was not available to many of those with whom she had grown up. There was a further irony, however, since she would later write the book for the Broadway musical, *The Great Gatsby*, copyright on the book having conveniently run out in 2020. The fellowship was to be spent during the first two years after graduation. She used the money while working as a cocktail waitress.

The fellowship paid $20,000 over two years, so perhaps not so ironic. Despite having a degree in English from the University of Chicago, her application to one institution required her, as a Polish immigrant, to take a test in English as a foreign language, with which I have sympathy since I was required to take a similar test when, many decades ago, I arrived in Kansas on a Fulbright. Evidently, being English wouldn't count. But then, the university also refused to accept any vaccinations I had received outside the country, especially somewhere with what they liked to call socialized medicine. Like Martyna, I had great pleasure in taking the test.

She was the only person to win a Merage scholarship to work in the arts, these usually going to those looking for careers in more lucrative professions, a path she thought she might have followed if she had not won the scholarship. The advantage of the Yale School of Drama programme, to which she now went, and her subsequent time at the Juilliard, was that, in contrast to other graduate programmes, they were both free (she receiving a stipend while at Yale) so that she would end up without a debt. During her time at college, however, she had several medical problems which would make her query whether she could afford to choose a career as a playwright, more especially since she had lost her health insurance.

The play she submitted as her writing sample when applying to Yale, *Mouse in a Jar*, is a somewhat bizarre, non-realistic work, set in an unfinished basement in New Jersey. It opens with a Polish woman, an illegal immigrant, cooking food, her leg bound around by a chain, the victim of a man, we never see, and with a daughter who herself becomes violent. The woman has no desire to get away. Beyond the fact of an illegal immigrant woman, subject to male violence, and with a daughter at odds with her, all aspects of Majok's life, this was not a dramatic direction she would go. The play began rehearsals in Chicago the day she left for New Haven. As a result, she was not involved in rehearsals or the production staged by Red Tape Theatre, committed to experimental work, and offering plays to audiences free of charge.

In 2011 came *the friendship of her thighs*, workshopped at Yale and then, through Yale, at the Playwright and Director Centre in Moscow, Russian not being a language she had mastered, in the process discovering that Russian directors were not happy to welcome writers, seeing themselves as auteurs. It won her a student feminist playwriting prize in 2011. Then came *rewilding* and later, in 2014, after *Ironbound*, and following graduation from Yale, *John, who's here from Cambridge* which would lead her to write *Cost of Living* which won her a Pulitzer Prize.

Along the way, she had worked at the Kennedy Center New Play Intensive, open to students, with its workshops which introduced her to the rigor of rewriting and which, in turn, opened the door to the National New Play Network which was committed not only to the production of plays but also to introducing writers to regional theatres, which in her case proved vital. Such is the complicated pathway for young writers to make their way. In the 1940s it had been possible for playwrights to see their first work staged on Broadway. Today they tend to snake their way through staged readings, development, small theatres, edging towards New York where even small theatres can attract the attention of reviewers.

When she left Yale, she asked herself, with a play in mind, "'If I quit now, what would I regret not having said?" It had to do with my mother's story.' As she told Nicole Serratore, she had tried to write that before, including a 'really bad' three-and-a-half-hour play. That was her thesis play *wander/standing*. In the end, though, she 'wrote it in five days, at fever pitch'. That play was *Ironbound*. As she explained, 'I had a cold table reading at the Lark and when we read it people laughed. They responded in an emotional way. That gave me hope in the story, in my choice to be a playwright, and that maybe there's something there. That was the play that got me my first New York City production and got other things going.'[14] The Lark, on 43rd Street, New York, one of whose board members was David Henry Hwang, was dedicated to the notion that playwrights are 'society's truth tellers.', with a special interest in those from marginalized backgrounds. As a result of the pandemic, it closed in 2021.

Her decision to become a playwright, barely surviving financially, living in a series of sublets, focussing on her work, slowly began to erode her connections with the family in Poland which, in turn, made her feel guilty, conscious of what immigrants sacrifice in cutting ties. When a family member died, she could not afford to fly to the funeral, a fact perhaps echoed in *Ironbound* in which a mother lacks the funds to attend her husband's funeral without help.

As she has said, 'I tend to write stories about people I grew up with or stories of my family.'[15] That would certainly be true of *Ironbound* which, following readings and workshop productions, was produced by the Round House Theatre in Bethesda, Maryland, as part of the Women's Voices Theatre Festival on 9 September 2015. Its New York premiere followed six months later, on 3 March 2016. It was a co-production of the Women's Project Theatre and Rattlestick Playwrights Theatre.

She explained that the reason for writing it was that she felt that 'stories of poor women were misrepresented or just not present. I wanted to see my own story on stage, my mother's story.'[16] Thus it was that while she explained that a 'lot of the circumstances are hers … Darja's personality is more mine', Darja being the figure at the centre of the play. Her goal, she said, 'was to show a character who for the most part, in my experience of consuming American pop culture, has been seen as stupid and just walks around with a funny accent: these horrible caricatures of what immigrants and poor people are. Writing from that perspective, you're constantly having to explain what living in that body is.'[17]

It is a play which features those struggling to survive, to understand the terms on which they can relate to a society they see from the outside, how they can register their existence when the lives to which they are seemingly consigned fail to match their needs or coincide with the myths which had attracted them to the country in the first place. There is a reason that money is not only a necessity but in some way the measure of things. That is what they saw and experienced. Her characters are no more fluent in the language of the system they serve than they are in a language which never quite seems to capture their feelings. Private lives, which they look to for consolation, are invaded by necessities which set the terms for their existence.

A series of conversations underline a desperation which time does nothing to alleviate. Relationships become negotiations as characters are drawn together by mutual need, even as mutuality is under constant threat. In the background is an abandoned factory in a state in which businesses have moved out, abandoning those who once worked there, their tenuous grasp on a national dream of possibility now ended, so many statistics, so many people with no voice. Darja recalls a woman in a factory caught in a machine, whose screams are heard by no one because of the noise. No one hears those whose cries of desperation are blotted out by a society which barely registers their existence.

Beyond that, the relationship between men and women is complicated by their often contradictory needs, exacerbated by their upbringing, itself shaped by external pressures. In a study by Tamar Jacoby and Brookings Institution senior fellow Isabel Sawhill, many of the problems of the working class (they studied Ohio rather than New Jersey) 'seem rooted in family breakdown – the erosion of marriage, single parenthood, mothers who live from boyfriend to boyfriend … It may be even more important than economic dislocation, and it's often what's behind inadequate working-class incomes.'[18] Condescension is, perhaps, a breath away, while arguably they are reversing cause and effect, but Majok is concerned to expose the fracture lines within the family, between men and women, the gap between the promises of society and the reality of daily living. She moves the action through time, thereby staging the slow erosion of hope, the closing down of options, the adjustments, abandonments, negotiations. When survival becomes a priority, security a distant prospect, clung to nevertheless, something else, it turns out, is lost along the way, including relationships. Yet Darja desperately holds on to some things, to a son who is damaged, a damage which in turn has rebounded on her.

Dominique Morisseau, whose *Skeleton Crew* explored similar territory, in a conversation with Majok, explained that 'We instantly connected over the loss of factories, and the dirt under the nails of the working class.' 'I was pulled to write *Ironbound* the way I did,' Majok replied,

> with a working-class immigrant woman as an intelligent and capable but flawed core of a story, because centre stage wasn't afforded to these types of characters I had access to growing up … They were a joke. Their English was a punch line … It's about who's telling the story and who's seen as the 'other' … When I first took a playwriting workshop in college, I'd bring in plays about my neighborhood back in Jersey that were written in dialect. I didn't even think of them as 'written in dialect' – it was just the way people spoke. People called them 'accent plays,' like, 'Here's another accent play from Martyna.' It was definitely an eye-opener about class. I was a scholarship kid and this was a new world to me. People didn't respond to the humor I was attempting – the characters' circumstances felt too dark.

When she started *Ironbound*, she assumed that no one would be interested. 'I thought, "Who's gonna care about a poor Polish immigrant?"'[19] In the end, at its premiere, three hundred people stood and applauded, her mother, clearly a presence in the play, beside her.

At the time she had been reading the Slovenian philosopher Slavoj Žižek, a Communist, a Lacanian, and in some ways a mixture of different philosophies and approaches. What she responded to, though, was his insistence that decisions were made in the name of capital. For her, he summed up what she had been feeling for most of her life, that 'growing up under capitalism can make people treat … people like commodities. We don't necessarily always treat people as human beings … We're just like, "What is the exchange? What can I get from you?"'[20] At the same time her own mother had grown up under communism in which private lives were required to conform to historical determinism (though Žižek himself rejected this), the state, rather than capital, invading private lives.

Ironbound, originally commissioned by a grant from the National New Play Network, is set in New Jersey. 'The Jersey I know,' she says in a note, 'is gravel and cattails. Empty quarter drinks and Buds litter parking lots. A marsh, a highway, bridges. Almost everyone is from somewhere else. And, yes, there's a reason they're not living in New York.' More precisely, it takes place at 'A bus stop at night, a quarter mile from a factory in Elizabeth, NJ., or where there used to be a factory, depending on the year.' It covers a period of twenty-two years.

Majok has explained that she used the factory as 'an anchor in time – because I'd seen what happened with these factories in Jersey over 20 years … In the 90s, the factories were full and running; in the 2000s, they were starting to shut down and outsource; in 2014, they're gone. They're ghosts. The factory I was writing about is now just rubble.'[21] Ironbound is a working-class area of Newark, west of the Passaic River, over which passes the Jackson Street Bridge connecting Harrison and Kearny where Majok was raised.

The central character, Darja, speaks with a Polish accent, her English scarcely fluent. She wears the clothes of a cleaning lady. It is the winter of 2014, in other words the time when Majok was writing the play. The scene is bleak, drained of colour. Darja, now forty-two years old and twice married, is fighting with Tommy, a postal worker. He is plainly someone she has settled for rather than loved. They have mutual needs, their options not obvious, but he has been sleeping around, she counting the ways, though not as in Elizabeth Barrett Browning where it was love that was the issue. Indeed, she has been accessing his phone for four years, thereby discovering his various betrayals. They have been together for seven years but their relationship has been, or has become, transactional and, indeed, she proposes he pay her $3000 for her to stay and perhaps buy a car so she can drive to work or use it to look after, and help, her 22-year-old son who is, it seems, an addict, has stolen her car and has been the cause of pain to her.

He insists, 'I respect you. You work hard. I respect you. It's not your fault where you were born. It's not your fault you were dealt a shit hand. All those Communists 'n Nazis 'n shit. But you came here. Home of the brave. Make a better – home of the brave! Even if you knew you'd be behind, you came … That, from me, gets you respect. So if you need money, I can give you money.'[22] At the same time, though, he has a compromising video which he claimed to have wiped but still retains. By degrees she lowers her bid for money from $3000 to $1000, an echo of Willy Loman, in *Death of a Salesman*, progressively lowering the money he says he needs to survive.

Theirs is a curious relationship. They have been together, seemingly circling around one another, never really committed. They share expenses, just getting by but always vulnerable. There can be humour in some of their exchanges, and this is a play which, despite its bleakness, is, from time to time, lit with a dark humour. It is a play based around conversations which reveal the erosion, over time, of her state of mind, her circumstances and physical being, as they do the state of the relationships which she sees as a shelter against what life throws at her. She looks for permanence, dreams of something more than a shared situation, indeed of a love in which she finds it difficult to believe.

The action then switches to 1992. Now, she is with another man, Maks, a fellow Pole to whom she is married. From moment to moment, he lapses into Polish. It is now summer, and the relationship seems genuine as they play a game, the winner of which gains a sexual favour. She flourishes a dress belonging to the woman for whom she works, even as he accuses her of stealing it. What they share, beyond affection, is what seem unrealizable dreams. He plays a harmonica and sings a Polish song, persuading her to dance with him, a brief interlude before Darja talks about the need for money, her continuing theme. He retains a certain optimism, thinking he might become a musician in Chicago. Music, for him, is a resource, an escape, while she, whose other job is working in a factory, tells him, 'I want more, Maks. I need insurance. Apartment. *Out* of basement apartment. Car. I want car.' (23) For Maks, 'we come *to* shit. But we have something. We are not just body. Lift. Pull. Push. We are more than this … You can burn money. Gone, two seconds. Money it's nothing. Is important. But is nothing. What's most important in this life it's this thing you have what no one can take from you.' (24) For him, it is music: 'People in this country need to know this so I don't fall from this world like nothing ever happen.' (25) He wants to leave his mark on the world and, as Arthur Miller said of Willy Loman, who does not want that. In one sense he is about to do that as it becomes apparent that Darja is pregnant, but if that is a hope for the future it is also a further problem not only because of their money problems but also because we have already learned what that child's future will be. Chicago is just a dream

The action then moves to 2014, and to winter. She and Tommy are still together, though have not been talking for two days. Despite the fact that he plans to take another woman to dinner, a married woman, she is not ready to leave him not least because not only has she lost her job, accused of breaking things, and not without cause also having set fire to the clothes of the woman for whom she works and who is married to a millionaire, but she has no prospect of another:

> Please tell to me how. You see peoples here they go to school years, *years* they go, and they don't have nothing now. What I can do? Even the ugly jobs they don't have no more. Look there. Look the factory there. Just empty and glass [a glass factory did, indeed, close]. No factories here, nothing. No car. What I can do?
>
> (29)

No longer able to pay her share, she tries to cling to him, but he has already moved on, the woman he works for being rich, even as he is only cleaning her pool. Meanwhile, he claims his other job at the post office is under threat, people no longer writing letters. Despite the truth of such jobs disappearing, this is one more way of avoiding offering help to Darja.

The play then moves back in time again. It is the fall of 2006. Darja enters, her face bruised. She gathers cardboard as a bed, and a car tyre as a pillow. She is thirty-four and preparing to sleep on the street. There she is encountered by Vic, a teenage schoolboy from an expensive Catholic school, a rent boy, but sympathetic, giving her money. It is clear she is not alone in having needs, even as his alienation is different in kind, child of rich parents for whom, as opposed to Darja, money means nothing. He seemingly rides through life untouched by need, casually humane but equally casually detached. Finally, she accepts the money as, for a moment, they connect. She makes a series of calls to her son telling him not to go home, waiting for a reply through the night. Finally, the phone rings. It is evidently him, though if it is what he will say remains unknown.

The action now moves forward to 2014 as Tommy arrives with some gas station flowers to apologize. She assumes, rightly, that his affair is over. He now asks her to marry him, even as she learns that Maks, her first husband and father of her son, has died in Chicago, this being where her son had gone, a son who had been in rehab and whose health insurance only has four years to run. Both are desperate. As proposals go, his lacks something:

> I don't exactly make bank. But I pay my bills. And yeah I've fucked up. Fucked around. Okay. But yer also not a model sorry and I still love the fuckin shit outta you. Yer logic's aggravation, yer English is ridiculous, and you are one straight up crazy fuckin – yer crazy, D, sometimes. But you got wonderful legs. And yer heart is good. You like goin to the movies. I LOVE goin to the movies. You need a car. I got a car. I can make you pasta. You could make me lunches. And it's good to know that someone's got the keys if I forget mine.
>
> (52)

She sets out her terms, half the rent, health insurance, her son living close by, the whole arrangement even in writing. He proposes they go to Chicago together, for the funeral and perhaps, therefore, to see her son before, suddenly, we are back in the 1990s as Maks appears, he also about to go to Chicago. She lets him go. As he disappears on the bus, however, he appears in what Majok describes as 'a different, rewritten reality', playing 'Sittin on Top of the World'. Suddenly everything disappears except a huge moon on a beautiful night as Maks now plays 'It's wonderful', before the stars disappear and we are back in the bleak world of 2014. The car horn sounds and she, who has been waiting for a bus, begins to walk towards Tommy, singing to herself, 'fuck this bus'. She looks around at where she has been and where she is. She leaves. There is nothing but a bus stop, except a final stage direction indicates, 'a new day begins'.

Is that moment earned? What had seemed impossible to her back in 1992 now appears more than a fantasy even as Tommy's sudden return to her is a result of his other options having run out. For Maks, Chicago would be the place he died. He did not end up sitting on top of the world. The lyrics of 'It's wonderful', meanwhile, which begin with a touch of ambiguity – addressing someone who cares about the singer 'a little bit' – goes on to celebrate a love which will be a doorway to heaven. Whatever Darja has found, whatever dreams she has, stop some way short of heaven. But she evidently decides to go to Chicago, not for the funeral of a man she did once love, or because Tommy offers continued survival, but because of the love she holds for her son, whatever he has done, however she has been implicated in his behaviour. In the end, survival alone is not enough. It must be in the name of something beyond itself. Whose new beginning is it to be, Darja's or her son's or, as she hopes, both of theirs? For Tommy, too, it is a new beginning, but it is not clear how real that will be, Chicago, incidentally, also being a place where factories had been closing for decades. The new day which begins offers no guarantee of redemption. It is, perhaps, simply another day.

The play carries an epigraph from Robert Pinsky, himself from a lower-middle-class family in small town New Jersey, a lover of jazz who saw in it a lifetime of suffering, thought and emotion expressed through a single phrase and hence here appropriate for a play in which a character could be said to feed suffering into his music. Pinsky is a playwright and poet, Majok choosing a stanza from his poem 'Jersey Rain': 'Now near the end of the middle stretch of road/ What have I learned? Some earthly wiles. An art./That often I cannot tell good fortune from bad/ That once had seemed so easy to tell apart.' It is a poem in part about the source of his writing, the place 'which stains and scours and makes things bright or dark'.[23] For Pinsky, his Jersey emerges from contending forces.

It is interesting that Majok should have chosen for readers to enter her text through his words since, on the face of it, her Jersey is resolutely bleak, except that, every now and then, a moon shines down and, every now and then, in the lives of those she chooses to present, there are moments when something else lights the dark, when a self-aware humour is shared even in the middle of contention.

In a review in *DC Metro Theatre Arts*, David Siegel referred to it as 'its own kind of agit prop',[24] but *Ironbound* is not a rallying cry for the working class of the kind which characterized Clifford Odets's *Waiting for Lefty*. It is an implicit critique of capitalism, outsourcing jobs and people from their lives, a system in which money is not just a currency. But the bleak, uncompromising environment of a dark factory, and a bus stop where the workers stand, like Vladimir and Estragon, waiting not just for a bus but a sense of purpose, fulfilment, meaning to arrive, goes beyond an attack on an unforgiving economic system.

The only wealthy character to make an appearance, Vic, is himself lost. He knows nothing of privation but also has a lack of direction, his random acts of charity hinting at a humanity which seems designed to balance his own sense of unearned advantage, except that life still seems something of a game to him. He is not an agit prop figure created by a playwright for his symbolic significance, a stereotype offered as an archetype. In theory he is what Darja, and, indeed, Tommy, aspires to, seeing money not just as a relief from penury, though it is that, but a language, a measure. When Maks objects that money is not everything, saying that what matters is what no one can take from you, Darja can think of nothing that cannot be taken from her. Vic, however, is lost in a different way, insulating himself. Life never cuts deep for him, as it does for Darja, and those with whom she would connect her fate. For her, life is something she survives, a trap from which, from time to time, she imagines she might escape, as she potentially does at the end. She is not a Mother Courage figure, happily cooperating with the system, offering up her son. She has a tensile strength, constantly tested. She is a mother courage of a different order, her choices often wrong, retaining, though, one unwavering loyalty to the son she will not surrender to his own frailties.

Asked what she really cared about, Majok replied, 'what matters to me ... what makes me so mad' are moments

> when I felt like I wasn't seen. Or that my circumstances were misunderstood. Or that I am judged – or my family's judged – in a certain way that makes me feel like I want to be like, 'No, actually: Here.' And the only way to do that is just to show that experience ... I can *tell* somebody a thing ... I can say as much as I want, but until you've seen a person *go* through the emotions on stage – the simulation of the experience – they're not gonna really get it.[25]

The Roundabout Theatre production prompted positive reviews. In *Broadway World*, Jennifer Perry greeted 'a deceptively simple, thought provoking, and elegant work of art'.[26] Reviewing the Rattlestick Playwrights production in New York, in March 2016, Charles Isherwood responded to what he saw as a 'perceptive drama, with ... bone-dry humor and vivid characters', which 'illustrates how vulnerable people like Darja are, hostages to the vagaries of chance, unless they can manage to climb out of poverty', observing that 'no amount of tough talk, no thick carapace of cynicism, can insulate a woman in her position from the hardships of the world she has to negotiate'.[27] When the play, still featuring Marin Ireland as Darja, opened at the Geffen playhouse in Los Angeles, in 2018, Charles McNulty offered two reasons for seeing it. One was Ireland as Darja, who he saw as a 'piercingly human ... a figure traditionally related to the margins of American drama – and society'. The other was the way the play 'illuminates the American experience through the immigrant's journey. At a moment when the issue of immigration is being used as a political football, it's easy for some to distance themselves emotionally from the debate.'[28]

As opposed to *Ironbound*, she wrote her next play, *Cost of Living*, while working at what she called survival jobs, including teaching. It has three epigraphs, two from the Catholic short story writer and essayist Andre Dubus, whose daughter was raped and who suffered a serious accident when trying to rescue two disabled motorists, saving one at the expense of his own leg which was amputated. He was abandoned by his third wife. The epigraph comes from his essay collection *Broken Vessels*. It concerns a husband and wife eating together, 'pausing in the march to perform an act together; we are in love; and the meal offered and received is a sacrament which says: I know we will die; I am sharing food with you; it is all I can do, and it is everything'. The second is from the same author, this time from his short story collection *Dancing after Hours*, many of the stories in which are laced through with violence and betrayal. The epigraph concerns the most ordinary of gestures, the return of a cart to a parking lot because 'if you do it for one guy, you do something else. You join the world … You move out of your isolation and become universal.' The third is from Powel Majok, to whom the play is dedicated. It is in Polish, the English translation being 'Why do we crumble like this? People are stupidly engineered.' Unsurprisingly, just how relevant these are becomes apparent in the play.

Cost of Living had its premiere on 29 June 2016, at the Williamstown Festival before opening, the following June, at the Manhattan Theatre Club. It is a play featuring two disabled characters which manages not to be about disability. As elsewhere in her work, she is concerned with class. For all her awareness of the special situation of immigrants, she is not concerned with identity politics, even as her characters are determined to construct themselves in the face of an environment which sends back no echoes, struggling with the fact of loneliness and the attempt to find ways to escape it, and that means, among other things, engaging with the role of sexuality. She is anxious to obviate condescension or pity on the part of audiences, more especially in a play in which disabled figures feature. One strategy for doing so is to allow them agency, power, as another is humour, an antidote to the moral seriousness with which disability might more usually be treated.

She writes about survivors, even as she acknowledges the pressures which make survival both necessary and challenging. There is always, as in this play, a sense of loss, as there is an attempt to understand how that is addressed. There is a wariness on the part of her characters, conscious of their vulnerability, their need to protect themselves. She writes about figures who refuse to be victims, even as it is a role in which others might cast them, to which fate seems to have consigned them. Her dramatic strategy is to stage conversations between two characters who simultaneously hold each other at bay while realizing that contact is what they need. Here the characters are Eddie and Ani, John and Jess.

Asked how the play came about, Majok replied, 'It mostly came out of grief and economic despair. I had just written *Ironbound* and moved to New York and everything fell apart.'[29] She has explained that the play began with a ten-minute monologue, written one night after getting fired from what she called a survival job. It was January, snowing outside. She had little money. Her family member had died in Poland. 'Eddie's voice', she has said, 'came to me that snowy night'. She wrote the scene in a single sitting. 'A few months later, I wrote about John and Jess. And then Ani. The characters came to me incrementally over a year. They're all composite of people I know … and aspects of what I was feeling that year.' She recalled, too, 'one of my survival jobs when I lived in Chicago' which was when she was employed as a 'personal caregiver for two men with disabilities … And I suppose when I started writing, I had been wondering about care. About the nature of helping others and being helped. I was thinking about need and survival – and not just in an abstract sense … I was thinking of the survivors in and around my life.'[30]

Cost of Living takes place, for the most part, in New Jersey. Majok called for two of the characters to be played by disabled actors, while all the cast members should represent the diversity of North Jersey. It begins with a Prologue, set in a bar in the Williamsburg district of Brooklyn, gentrified, known for its hipster culture, not the sort of place, it seems, for the figure who opens the play with a monologue, an unemployed, 49-year-old former truck driver, Eddie Torres, who has been doing community service as the result of driving under the influence. It is a speech addressed to someone for whom he buys drinks whenever he becomes maudlin, even as he himself only drinks seltzer while confessing that he has been tempted because his wife has died, the wife who killed the loneliness he now feels. He is in the bar because he has received a message which seems to come from his wife, her number having been reassigned. Whoever called, is to meet him here, except that nobody has appeared.

From December, the action moves back to September, and an apartment in Princeton, with 25-year-old Jess, a first-generation child of an immigrant, her own name being a consequence of her mother's inability to speak English, 'yes' being one of the few words she knew, her accent meaning that a nurse misheard it as Jess. Majok offers a portrait of her in an elaborate stage direction. She '*does not come from wealth nor does she try to seem it. Has a hard time keeping her feelings and opinions to herself. Which has, apparently, got her into trouble. Still, she can't help it. Or doesn't want to. She can take care of herself. She will put up a fight when she needs.*'[31]

She is in an apartment being interviewed by John, wealthy, good looking, about to begin graduate work, but also wheelchair-bound because of cerebral palsy. He has what Majok indicates is a halted way of speaking. She hands him a resumé which lists her work as a cocktail waitress in a series of bars, if also the fact that she graduated from Princeton, a combination he finds hard to believe. She obviously needs the job as he, equally obviously, needs help. There is a gulf of class, of money, between them, and a deal of suspicion on both sides, but they come to an agreement.

Meanwhile, in another part of New Jersey, in another apartment, this one not evidencing signs of wealth, anyway being largely empty awaiting work, is another wheelchair-bound person, Ani (Ania Lucja Skowrońska-Torres), a quadriplegic suffering from an incomplete spinal cord injury following an accident. Her movement is restricted to some of the fingers on one hand which are partially functioning. Again, Majok offers a description of her: '*She has her own ways and is fine with those ways and those that do not agree don't need to stick around – as many haven't.*' (34) As for Eddie, her ex-partner, who comes to collect some of his belongings, '*Their interactions used to have ease. Eddie muscles it now*', (35) and, indeed, he moves her hand, unbidden, while recommending various therapies he has encountered on the web. He plays music on his phone because he has heard it could be good for her, even dancing until he realizes that, of course, she cannot. When she says that he still can't dance, he replies 'Look who's talkin', both seeing the humour in this, evidence that they had once shared something. In fact, she has been told that when music plays, 'the body goes lookin for the things it's missing. The broken things. The shit that's disconnected. And it tries to bring everything back together. Like it used to be.' (51) For a second it suggests something more than therapy is going on, even though Eddie has deserted her for another woman, she, meanwhile, relying on his insurance for her treatment. and, indeed, his financial help for the apartment. He leaves. She practises moving her fingers and then sits alone.

Jess's first day of work involves her shaving John, requiring a degree of trust on both sides. When she reaches for him to change his shirt, however, he goes into spasm, nearly falling out of his chair. His response is as ambiguous as Ani's when he says that 'anytime I reach beyond myself, it's violence … it always feels beyond you. So you have to throw yourself – your arms, your hands – at what you want.' (65) On one level that is about his physical reaction to sudden movement; on another it is a statement of his response to need. Like Ani, he is isolated, alone, while looking for something to restore an equilibrium to his life, the connections he has lost and, indeed, a connection seems to be forged as each reveals something of themselves to one another.

A month earlier, in a conversation between Ani and Eddie (as he says, twelve years sober and nearly twenty-one years faithful, evidently falling at the last hurdle), it emerges that he had wanted her to hire him as a carer, at least for a week. To her, this is his attempt to clear his conscience, though he is there because, when a nurse failed to turn up, he was the emergency contact, even as she seems anxious to end all contact, insisting that she will send on his belongings rather than have him intrude. The question which hangs in the air is whether, when so much else has been broken, it is possible that there may even now be a residual connection. In two separate apartments a man and a woman circle one another, in one trust broken, in the other, slowly built.

For Ani and John, options have largely run out, their room for manoeuvre literally constricted, they being dependent on others not simply for their physical needs. Whatever strengths they have learned to survive, their strategies, tactics, in the end they rely on strangers or, in the case of Ani, one who has estranged himself. They are, though, not self-pitying, both capable of recognizing the ironies with which they must live, and humour is one of the bridges to other people. The parallel conversations slowly expose truths, vulnerabilities, not restricted to those confined to wheelchairs. Both Jess and Eddie have had their different struggles. They may both have been motivated by money but something beyond that is exchanged, privacies acknowledged.

It is now December and in John's apartment he is showering, wheeled into the shower by Jess. She lifts and undresses him completely before washing his hair, soaping his body, and rinsing it off. Majok directs that the audience should witness the entire act which '*takes as long as it needs*', an action which underlines the necessary intimacy involved, an intimacy which seems to have grown since October as they talk while she tends to him, an intimacy shared by the audience. When he washes his own genitals, she turns away. A stage direction insists, '*It's not awkward*', but '*Routine*'(85). For Jess, or the audience?

Now, it is she who takes the lead, telling him the story of her experience in the bar where she works and where she seeks to protect vulnerable women from those who would abuse them and her. 'Fuck rich people', she explains she had said of a rich man who asked who she thought she was, and who had the money. While she has to work, she insists, they were privileged, money meaning nothing any more than does she, even as she was supposed to be the support for her family, the net to catch them when they fell. Slowly, it becomes evident that John is drawn to her, no longer condescending, and she to him. Something, it seems, is happening, except that some gulfs may not be bridgeable, some understandings incomplete.

The action moves back months, and to Ani's apartment. She is being sponged in a bath by Eddie, intimately, even as she confesses she has begun a period. He continues nonetheless and, for all their supposed separation, has plainly not left, they talking to one another as if he has not. He shares a story with her that he has not before, wishing that he had learned to play the piano, running his fingers along her arm as if it were a keyboard. He tells her that he will tear up the divorce papers. They share a cigarette. Things have clearly not been going well between him and the woman with whom he had left. He suggests that he and Ani might try again. When he leaves the room for a moment she slips down in the bath, only for him to save her.

Back in John's apartment, Jess arrives dressed as if for a date and, indeed, has understood that he had invited her, only to discover that he plans to go with a fellow student. When she asks if she can spend the night there, he says he would rather not since she had taken soap from his bathroom and clearly feels she might take more. She runs out of the apartment, into the snow, humiliated, making a call to her mother on her cell phone, a call lapsing into another language as she expresses her love, apologizing to a woman who has gone back to her home country, too ill to stay in America. Whatever hopes she had had, suddenly destroyed.

In an extended epilogue we are in Eddie's apartment in the early hours of the morning. It seems that he has returned from the bar he had gone to at the beginning of the play in search of a woman who never arrived. He has found Jess sleeping in her car, the car, it turns out, that she has been sleeping in for weeks during the day, working at nights, saving money to send to her mother. She is still wearing the dress for what had turned into a non-existent date. He has invited her in for a blanket. Each is suspicious of the other, she that he expects something from her, he that she may steal something, even as there is nothing to steal, the apartment a jumble of boxes. He explains that his wife is dead, a confession once made which suddenly releases his anguish as he pleads with Jess to stay, offering to pay most of the rent, even as he admits he is out of work. So, two people, both lonely, both conscious of a sense of loss, both with a sense of desperation, find someone whose need matches their own. The play ends as they stand together in a fading light.

Will they stay together, as roommates or friends, for more than one cold night? Are a sudden encounter and decision likely to rescue them both from their isolation and despair? It was an ending that Majok had to write the play to arrive at. As she has said, 'The ending is where you learn what your play is about.' In the case of *Cost of Living* – a title whose ambiguity underscores equally the need of her characters for money and the price exacted for the business of getting by, the struggle for daily existence –

> I suspected that two characters ... would need to meet at the end but I didn't know how or who. Then I thought about who still needed the most. And I ended the play in their meeting – in what will hopefully be something very good for the both of them ... They couldn't have met any earlier. They both need to go through the play to be able to be open enough for where they get to at the end – and to move forward,[32]

even as how an unemployed truck driver and an equally unemployed woman who lives in a car will get by is not clear.

It is only in retrospect that the Prologue makes real sense as Eddie recalls the loneliness he felt when driving, nights alone in a motel room, his wife a lifeline, a lifeline snapped, he talking about her in the past tense, keeping the lights on in his apartment, in his isolation texting a wife who will never reply, a wife from whom he hints he was estranged. There are two immigrants in the play while he, with the last name Torres, clearly has his roots elsewhere, all of them on a journey. But this is not a play simply about displaced people, those having to adjust to disabilities. As Eddie remarks, 'We're all of us, in motels, on the road to somewhere we ain't at yet and that makes us feel feelings. Roads are dark and America's long.' (10) Even John, born to privilege if also to physical limitations, is negotiating his way through a life which requires him to accept a daily struggle, his wealth an insulation but not a solution.

Each of them is aware of the tenuous nature of their daily existence, suspicious that others may seek to take advantage of them, anxious to protect their privacy, their sense of themselves. At the same time, however, that very concern may be what holds them back from making the human contacts that could be their salvation. The play slowly strips them of their protective shells, as they reach out. Yet just how precarious that is becomes apparent. Eddie and his wife had begun to come together again before a sudden phone call ended their potential reunion. Jess and John appeared on the brink of a romantic, and even sexual, connection when it became evident that the space between them had not been closed. The coming together of Eddie and Jess is a desperate gamble, two lonely people sharing their loneliness, their need and uncertainty in a balance which may or may not be maintained.

There are more than two caregivers in the play, those who administer it being themselves in need of it, care, indeed, being what all of them require what, on some level, everyone requires. Chance, misfortune, deprivation of one kind or another, have left them adrift, looking for some anchor in the storm. Those left stranded at the end are those whose care has helped sustain others, now turning, however desperately, to one another.

The issue throughout is trust and that applies beyond the confines of the play. As David Brooks observed, in a 2020 article in *Atlantic Monthly*,[33] levels of trust in America have been in precipitate decline. In 2014, a social survey found that only 30 per cent of American agreed with the proposition that most people can be trusted, the lowest social trust being among those most marginalized. Four years later, the figure for Black Americans was 15 per cent. Distrust of politicians, among other things, would lead to the election of Donald Trump who would himself go on to undermine trust in America's electoral system. It is not that Majok's play tackles these wider issues but her sense that those on the margin, those most vulnerable, treat others with suspicion, even as they are in need of the human solidarity they so desperately require to function, hints at the challenge to a solidarity necessary for any society to function and the difficulty of attaining it.

The play received positive reviews, though none quite as enthusiastic as that by Elise Marenson in the *New York Theatre Guide* for whom it was 'perfection', reawakening her 'belief in the poetry of theatre' and 'its purpose as the critical eye of human existence'.[34] Though Jesse Green, in *The New York Times*, felt that the misunderstanding between Jess and John was 'a big unforced error', nonetheless responded to 'moments of intense and complicated pungency' finding Majok 'exquisitely attuned to the many varieties of alienation hiding in plain sight', adding 'if you don't find yourself in someone onstage in "Cost of Living," you're not looking'.[35] Staged in London in 2019 at the Hampstead Theatre, it was reviewed by Michael Billington who, while having reservations about the opening monologue, which he found structurally clumsy, responded to a play which 'gets under your skin through its ability to provoke feeling without lapsing into sentimentality', and which 'argues, like John Donne, that no man is an island entire of itself but a part of the main'.[36] Interestingly, in both the New York and London productions, the part of Eddie was played by a Black actor, adding one more dimension to the relationship between him and Ani. In 2022, *Cost of Living* opened on Broadway.

Majok was sitting doing her taxes, having deferred jury duty, when, to her astonishment, she received a call explaining that the play had been awarded the Pulitzer Prize. One of the first texts she received, congratulating her, was from fellow Pulitzer Prize-winning playwright Stephen Adly Guirgis. The Pulitzer Committee awarded her play for, 'An honest, original work that invites audiences to examine diverse perceptions of privilege and human connection through two pairs of mismatched individuals: a former trucker and his recently paralyzed ex-wife, and an arrogant young man with cerebral palsy and his new caregiver.'[37] Her first call was to her mother, back in Poland, closing down the family home in which she had been born. It is not surprising that she was surprised given that she had barely emerged as a playwright. It was, however, one of a cluster of awards she has accumulated.

America is an immigrant country with, every now and then, a hostility towards immigrants. In that last respect it is hardly unique, more especially in the last decades. The immigrant can be seen as a threat, blamed for whatever problems are on the political agenda: crime, sickness, low wages, terrorism. At times, they are presented as an existential threat. And what happens once the immigrant arrives? A past has been abandoned in the name of something not always clear. A certain guilt may be involved to do with those left behind, even as adjustments are necessary to become fluent in the new culture. And does who they see themselves as being align with how they are seen by others? What does failure mean in a society which values success? In her next play, *queens*, eleven immigrants, all women, played by seven actresses, come together in an apartment in Queens, such questions implicit in their various stories.

She began writing *queens* in April 2016, the year Donald Trump was elected President, a man who succeeded in cutting immigration in half, though the play was being shaped before that. Nonetheless, as she wrote, so she became aware of the anti-immigrant rhetoric which was beginning to dominate social media, though, ironically, some of the settled immigrants shared that rhetoric, what she called the 'generation of comfort', and that is reflected in her play. One of the things she wanted to address was the mentality of 'pulling up the bridge'. As she has explained, it 'comes from a personal place for me … There's a Dreamer, because I grew up with a bunch of people who were undocumented … and people who weren't able to go to college … I have many masks in *queens* where I'm able to pull aspects of myself and my story and the stories that I've heard.' Rather than being designed as a timely intervention, 'those are the people I just grew up with'.[38]

The play has three epigraphs. one, from the American Pulitzer Prize-winning writer Nilanjena Sudeshna 'Jhumpa' Lahiri, born in London, the daughter of Indian immigrants, who arrived in America at the age of three. The name Jhumpa was given to her by her teachers who found her real name difficult to master. As a result, she was embarrassed, feeling that she was causing problems for others simply by being who she was. The epigraph, from her short story, 'The Third and Final Continent', is an expression of the extraordinary in the ordinary, the title reflecting the fact that America is the third country, and continent, the protagonist has lived in.

The second epigraph is from Junot Díaz' short story, 'Negocios', ('Business') about a Dominican Republic immigrant to America, conscious of the family he has left even as he struggles to make it in America. The key phrase is perhaps 'Life smacks everyone around', The final epigraph is from Max Frisch: 'We wanted workers, but we got people instead.' He was talking about the many guest workers in Europe, but it is a phrase which reflects Majok's determination to explore the nature of those too easily defined by their social status, by the roles to which they have seemingly been assigned.

The play takes place in what she calls 'Various parts of the world', though primarily in a basement apartment in Queens. It moves through time, between 2001 and 2017, 'nonlinearly'. The 2001 section occurs in the shadow of the fall of the Twin Towers, the helplessness of those who suffered there felt by a group of women themselves gathered by fate with no certainty as to their future. As one of them, Pelagiya, a Belarusian, herself afraid of flying, says, in a broken syntax, 'Everybody in the planes, nothing they can do, seeing the towers in front of, getting closer, at some point knowing what was gonna Maybe they see the people screaming that, crying that they about to And then they all gonna be nothing. Fire. Ashes. Falling from the sky. Dust. Floating down to the ground.' (43) The fact of the attack, though, makes them, in turn, vulnerable to those looking for scapegoats, who regard foreigners with the wrong kind of accent, terrorists. As Renia, a central figure, remarks,

> If someone speaks English with no accent, or if they sound French, German, something like people what don't really need to come here, then is different. But I open my mouth and whole history my country pours out. How much money I have, wars, history, everything pours out. Nothing like what happens to you happens to me but I talk only how much I need to here.[39]

'Self-pity', though, Majok notes, 'has little currency in these characters' worlds'. They 'say what's what and feel everything deeply but they know not to expect anyone to fix it … No one is a caricature.' (4)

The play in part focuses on Renia, who abandoned her family when seeking refuge, though that is something she shares with the others she lives with. By 2017, she owns the apartment building, though hers is not entirely a story of success. The shift in time scales enables us to chart how experience shapes character, the options and choices made along the way. One of the things which interested Majok was what the cost of a so-called better life is. As she has said, *queens* follows the choice which got Renia to this point and what she does when given the chance to help others. It also follows the story of a young woman, Inna, from the Ukraine, in search of the mother who abandoned her when young, mistaking Renia for that mother and punching her in the face on their first encounter. Renia has, indeed, abandoned her daughter, though not, she insists, Inna. In the course of a night, however, they assume a surrogate relationship, as Inna rents a room. They both have Slavic accents, though different ones.

This is evidently a place which many people, over time, have passed through, from different countries, all marked by the struggle to accommodate to a new place, a new language, a new sense of themselves. Just as railway stations used to have an office called Lost and Found, so they have lost something as they struggle to find something else, safety, acceptance, possibility, in a country with so much more to offer than the place they left, a land seemingly of plenty though access to it is problematic. Even their names prove a challenge, pronunciations differing so that they are not quite the person they were.

When Inna asks what work she can find, Renia explains, what had been clear from Majok's earlier plays, 'We take care homes. Us kinds people, we take care house. Men, they build them and women, they clean them. Take care children. Rest this country handles rest this country. But us, we do homes.' (14) When Inna asks for Renia's name '*a memory walks in*', and, for a moment, another figure intrudes asking the same question as the action moves back in time to 2001 when Renia, now in her early thirties, had been trying to rent a room in the same building or, more accurately, sublet since she will be sharing with others, all looking for somewhere to stay, all women who have connections with a range of countries (including Honduras, Afghanistan, Poland, Belarus, Syria, the Ukraine). They are, however, double immigrants in that, on arriving in America, they had settled in communities of people like themselves, only to leave because of problems, now living in a multi-cultural environment. At the same time

Majok was intent that they should not be defined only by their origins, nor even by their gender, though she was conscious that the stakes are higher for women. Nearly everyone in her own neighbourhood had been single mothers.[40]

One of the things they have lost is language and, through that, a certain understanding, identity. There are moments when they speak in Polish, Spanish, Ukrainian, untranslated, as otherwise they converse in broken English. One confesses that she followed a man simply because he was reading a book in her original language, a language whose alphabet was different from that which she now saw everywhere around her, spelling things out that, for her, still seem alien. Far from being a moment of emotional contact, however, it simply led to an attempted assault. So many dead ends. Words which once encoded emotions, subtleties of thought, find no real equivalent. Poems written in the original language do not translate. Referents have gone, a personal and public history, a whole culture. With time, connections with that past are eroded, promised contacts unfulfilled. The new country carries its menace even as the places they have left were dangerous and remain such, sites of natural disasters or a brutal politics. They are in a kind of no man's land where their old skills are not embraced, and where the sheer exhaustion of work blunts ambition.

For the most part they take care of children or houses as no one takes care of them, except those who share their situation. As to the title, this marks the location but also what Majok sees as the status of the characters she stages, women who may be marginalized in terms of the larger society but who command themselves, have strength, taking on a world largely indifferent to them, thus queens, albeit with a lower case. Some are documented, others not. One question remains, one which Majok has asked herself. Is this the life they had looked for? What might they have been if they had not taken the decision to leave a place, a language, a culture, a family, for a world in which they would not be embraced, homogenized, intruders, the object of suspicion?

The play moves around in time, but time has another significance. The cost of everything is related to the number of hours work necessary to pay for it. Even a party to say goodbye to one of the tenants, Isabela, represents work and with it a sense of suspicion. The level of a milk bottle is marked in case anyone takes some. They count their cigarettes. When one of them finds work for Renia she has to pay 10 per cent of her wage. The party, though, is a moment of solidarity as Isabela moves on apparently glad to be going but suddenly sensible that she is losing something, even as loss is a common factor. When they play music, she asks for it to be happy and sad, no happiness, it seems, without sadness. As she laments, 'I moved through this country. My child moved through me then I moved through this country for my child. Things is always moving … I'm always moving. How I'm always moving … ? I wanna sit one day.' (33)

When Aamani, from Afghanistan, retrieves alcohol from various hiding places, she recounts the stories of all those who had left the concealed bottles, stories of the work they did and their habits, one hiding cats from the street in her room, another writing two letters, one she sent and one she did not. This is a place of hidden stories. One, though, is of an educated woman who had fled her own country, hoping that her stay would be temporary, 'Now she works in midtown in fancy bathrooms, giving out paper towels and mints to women in dresses. Sometimes you have to live a whole new life. Because what your home was before, what her home was, that's not there now. And she loved so very much Before.' (45) For all of them there was a before, a time when they had a place and an identity. There is a reason, though, that Majok specifies that they are to have come from countries which, for the most part, have experienced traumas. Before may have a nostalgic draw but it was also not without its pain.

This is a building through which people move, though where to is never clear. As they do so they leave objects behind as though marking that they had passed this way. Isabela is returning to Honduras because her mother is ill but from where she will find it difficult to return, now lacking a sponsor and with no money, having sent what she earned back to her family. With a young daughter, she has not seen for years, she dare not chance an illegal entry while other members of her family have had to wait eight years for a decision on their immigration status, and are still waiting. Meanwhile, they all appear to have overstayed their visas. On this night, though, they wait up to see Isabela on her way.

There comes a moment, however, when another woman, Agata, intrudes, ushering in a conversation, with Renia, in Polish which is neither subtitled nor translated for the audience, though the tone is clear enough. She brings with her a bag of children's clothes, but also accusations. Renia has a husband and a daughter, not something she has shared with the other women. But Agata also brings news of Renia's mother who has died and already been buried. Every crisis brings this group of women together, suspicions laid aside. If Renia rescues a cat from the cold, this is a small gesture which hints at the function they have had for one another.

The play then returns to the present as Renia hands Inna clothes left years before by Isabela. Inna flourishes a picture of the mother for whom she has been searching, a photograph taken outside the building in which they are standing. As she sleeps so we hear a collection of telephone messages from the women who have left, messages to those they in turn had left in travelling to America, messages about missed birthdays, Christmases, with the plea, for those they call, to listen to the answering machines and, above all, not to erase the messages, not, therefore, to erase them from the lives of those they loved. The act ends as Inna screams, having woken from a nightmare, only to be embraced by Renia as a mother does a child.

The play's time shifting led some reviewers to regret a certain feeling of disorientation, more especially at the untranslated passages and transient characters in a canvas that Jonathan Mandell, in *DC Theatre Scene* felt overcrowded. The cast of seven is expanded in that actresses double, playing other women passing through, a device which the *New York Times* reviewer, Jesse Green, found a problem, interestingly suggesting that 'Ms. Majok would have done better to expand her scope … The material is so important, so ripe and multi-stranded that it might have been better off as a marathon or a mini-series.'[41] It was, he noted, not so much one play as several which is perhaps what attracted HBO to ask Majok to develop the play for a series. Perhaps, too, that is why the play remained unpublished in 2022.

Majok's next play, *Sanctuary City*, was set to open at the New York Theatre Workshop on 24 March 2020, except that by then Covid-19 had led to the shutdown of theatres. The play features three characters, two known only by letters, G (female) and B (male), the other called Henry. Presumably the characters are identified by initial letters so that they can be cast with actors of any national origin or ethnicity. The first two were born in other countries and brought to America when young. Henry is first generation, born of immigrant parents. All, Majok says, 'have American mouths' while all were raised working class. It is set in Newark, 'or thereabouts', and takes place between 2001 and 2006. She insists, however, that while the countries of origin can change according to the actors, nonetheless none should be of Western European origin or ethnicity, or from countries of greater liberalism than the United States, 'especially as it relates to marriage equality in 2006 or earlier'.[42] She adds, 'These characters have grown up within working class multicultural America. They have connections, feelings, and knowledge of their countries of origin' (or, in Henry's case, his parents' country), but Majok avoided specific references to encourage wider, more inclusive casting across subsequent productions, which need not replicate the casting of the original. (3) Her motive was in part to give opportunities to actors from different backgrounds, even as that would give a different spin to the stories told. As significantly, she insisted that productions should, 'Avoid sentimentality and self-pity. They have no currency in these characters' world.'

In 2001, the Dream Act was introduced, creating a pathway to citizenship for those brought to America as children. In 2010, Congress failed to pass it, two years later Obama announcing a temporary programme (DACA: Deferred Action for Childhood Arrivals). Predictably, Trump tried to end it. Given that her own family had, for a time, been un-documented, *Sanctuary City*, which features Dreamers, drew heavily on her own experience and that of those she knew. One character, in particular, mirrors aspects of her own life as the child of a mother working for naturalization, along with an abusive father.

Newark is one of the cities across America which declared itself a sanctuary city, which meant that it did not cooperate with ICE (U.S. Immigration and Customs Enforcement agency). While Mayor Ras Baraka would refer to its agents as slave catchers, in 2018 the city managed to hold, in the county jail, one of the largest daily populations of immigrant detainees in the country. For those in *Sanctuary City* there is no sanctuary, nor is there for the estimated 12 million undocumented immigrants.

Majok's characters tread the edge, constantly aware of their vulnerability, simultaneously struggling to maintain their invisibility, a permanent underclass, while trying to navigate their way to acceptance, inclusion. Personal relationships may offer not merely consolation but a route to a new life. They may also, however, carry their own threat. Meanwhile, there is the fear of discovery. This is America seen from the perspective of those who arrived in hope only to discover the price of entry.

The action begins in the winter of 2001 as G knocks on the window of B's room, before doing so again the following spring. B's mother is going back to her home country because of trouble at work and because of the attack on the Twin Towers which shows that everything is possible. G, at seventeen, who has been in American for more than half her life, has plainly been beaten by her stepfather, and not for the first time. Majok gives G a speech which precisely mirrors her own experience: 'Last time this shit happened, (remember?, my eye?), Miss Romano saw, sent me to the nurse, nurse called my mom, mom said I fell, then she freaked the fuck out on me when I came home. She said to say I fuckin fell, whatever. Said to say I always fall, I fell. Which I think they'll buy *once*.' (9)

G's mother is fearful that if the authorities investigated, if the man she lives with reports her, as he has threatened to do, she could be deported having long had a fake social security number. B and his mother are illegal immigrants, having overstayed their visas by nine years, like others existing in the shadow of 'that place on Fish Kill Road', an actual correctional facility in South Kearny. Deported, they would not be allowed back for a decade.

B's mother has asked him to go back to her old country with her, but he is afraid that he will end up with the same 'shitty jobs' his mother has had to do to survive. He would also not be able to go to college because he would need financial aid and any application would reveal his immigration status. What are B's options, or, indeed, G's? He enumerates them. 'Keep workin at the restaurant? Moppin floors? Washin dishes? Go to war? See if *they're* checkin papers.

Ship out with all the seniors still failin algebra. Be like a fuckin, high school reunion – in Afghanistan.' ((18) Time moves on. It is now 2002 and G's mother has secured a restraining order. The two of them are moving out, except that, like Majok's mother, she has already acquired another man in her life. Meanwhile B's mother has left the country.

A year later, G, now a citizen following her mother's naturalization, has succeeded in getting into college and realizes that she can help B become a citizen by marrying him. They rehearse the questions they may be asked if challenged, ever more absurd and intimate. The truth, though, is that while they have been together for years, even sleeping together in the same bed, they have had no sexual contact. He gives her a ring as she sets out for college in Boston.

Three years pass. G has come to see B in a small apartment, a place which 'belongs to people who work often and work late', filled with things inherited from people who have passed through. A gap, however, has opened between them, the planned marriage abandoned when G changed her mind seemingly afraid of what would happen if they were found out, dashing B's hopes of gaining citizenship and himself going to college. In fact, he has had a relationship with someone else, the someone, Henry, who now enters. They kiss. The relationship was a gay one. What they are unable to do is marry. Gay marriage would not be legal in New Jersey until 2013. At the time when the scene is set, 2006 moving into 2007, only Massachusetts had legalized it (in 2004) but gay marriage does not qualify someone for citizenship, or even a Green Card, something Henry, studying law, well knows also having coached his own parents for the citizenship test.

Henry questions why G had never considered a real marriage, suggesting that her own mother's experience had been a warning, that a fake marriage is as close as she will get. Though he is hostile towards her, both because he is unsure what might be involved even in a supposedly fake marriage, and because she had reneged on her agreement, he nonetheless agrees to appear as their witness. At the same time, it is apparent that the relationship between G and B had never simply been about securing citizenship, that there was a real attraction, as that between B and Henry has not been without its strains.

Sanctuary City is concerned with the price people pay in a society which requires them to deny themselves, which patrols the boundaries of the permissible. Majok's characters stare through a brightly lit window on the other side of which are displayed the prizes on offer for those who conform to the required models of behaviour, whose dreams are legitimized. It is a play in which love may betray or elevate, take more than one form, in which harsh realities co-exist with defensive fictions, concealment corroding the self. The gay man, the illegal immigrant, is obliged to hide in plain sight, existing in an alternative reality. Others have passed through the apartment leaving traces of themselves and where they are from as they move on, trying to stake their claim in a society for which they are barely visible. In opting for Henry, B has doubled his risk. It was only in 2003 that the Supreme Court ruled that homosexual conduct could not be criminalized.

As B remarks, his syntax reflecting the desperation he feels, 'I've been hiding and lying for the past 13 years of my For every For just basic human Because I didn't get some Some paper means I cannot be a full person here. I have had to hide who I am at every fuckin turn of my life … I've been lying so long I'm not even sure what's real.' (86) What he will not do is exclude Henry from his life if that is the price of maintaining the fake marriage which G was willing to offer. He decides not to go ahead with the plan suggesting that he might even leave the country and be re-united with his mother, with Henry accompanying him. For Henry, though,

'Wouldn't it just be more hiding? Another version of hiding. There. For you and me. I've done so much of that. For so much of my life. I lost too much of my life already to that. Even before this. I'm done with that.' (91) As he points out, if B leaves he would never be allowed back, while he himself would have no life there. There is blame whichever decision is made. Accordingly, he leaves as does G abandoning B alone in an empty apartment speaking a broken aria about the incompletions, the fragmented nature of his experience, not really knowing how it began, what decisions were made, by whom, and what the future holds:

> when did you
> decide
> what do you have in
> when did your
> relationship
> did your parents
> why or
> have you ever had
> have you ever
> …
> what are you gonna.
>
> (95)

The final note indicates that time goes by, '*years passing by a young man in a small city*'. Each of the characters is alone to face whatever fate he or she may have, not the only ones to be left alone. The play closed after previews. It was eighteen months before the lockdown of theatres ended. Meanwhile, someone had vandalized a poster writing 'This is about illegals', across it, leading Majok to comment, 'If a country has made a way of living impossible for certain people, how do we still care for ourselves and others when the rules and laws might not actually want those people to thrive?'[43]

Martyna Majok saw a series of plays staged in a remarkably short time, picking up an impressive series of awards along the way. All drew, to a lesser or greater extent, on her own experience. Her characters often meet as strangers in what remains a strange land, escaping from something, looking for something, struggling to articulate their feelings in a language which itself can seem isolating, even as there can be a curious poetry to a broken syntax, words freighted with meanings generated by the moment. There is a sense of loss, time and distance separating them from families which once offered them an identity that now has to be reconstructed in a world not attuned to their needs, financial, psychological, emotional. They keep an alternative world in their minds. Even if it slowly fades to transparency, it never entirely disappears. Were decisions made the right ones, more especially when those they turn to for consolation and aid can offer them nothing but menace?

Yet there are consolations on offer, if only in the fact that shared necessities can forge relationships with the strength to survive the pressures they experience. Moments of kindness stand out in part because they occur when they seem unlikely, a counterforce to what otherwise might seem an understandable alienation. The essence is to avoid sentimentality as it is to write against the stereotypes so readily available when considering those outside the assumed norm. At the same time, she has confessed that what she herself looks for in plays is an emotional response.

Hers are characters who exist on the edge, invisibility sometimes a product of their marginal existence, sometimes necessitated by their illegal status. Some have outstayed their visas, but outstayed something else as well, their grasp on the new reality insecure. If she writes about immigrants, inevitably she writes about identity but there is something else which is at risk of defining them, class. There is a reason the word 'money' recurs, its absence determining their actions, their freedom of action. She writes about survivors, not just those from other countries, but a gay man whose intimacies are patrolled, women, whose agency is more limited than that of the men they encounter who may at any moment strike out at them. She writes about the disabled who must negotiate where the limit of their freedom lies. Yet she also writes about love and its complexity. The cost of living may be the title of a play; it is also the subject of works which extend out from the circumstances of her characters.

Displacement is not only a factor of immigration, having to do with the terms on which individuals do or do not relate to the assumptions of the culture in which they live. On the eleventh of September 2001, American reality changed, certainly for those whose religious faith, or country of origin, marked them out. On a November morning in 2016 there were those who woke to find themselves in a world they no longer recognized as the election results became clear. It was certainly a day which shook Majok. In that sense, power is a subject, the power of those who shape everyday reality, the power of an economic system which requires an underclass to function, sustaining this by offering a dream of social mobility in fact more available in America's northern neighbour. There is a reason, though, that the play carries an epigraph from Harold Pinter's *Old Times* in which one character asks another what she does. 'Oh, I continue', she replies. So do Majok's characters. It is where their strength resides.

While it is true that, more than most playwrights, she draws on her own life, growing up where and when she did, hearing the voices she did, observing the struggles in her own home, as in the community around her, she has said, 'I go through the act of writing, which can be difficult and painful, in hopes that there's going to be something larger than myself on the other side.'[44] As she said, 'Write about what we know to understand what we don't'.

CHAPTER 6
DOMINIQUE MORISSEAU: POET OF DETROIT

My job is to speak the truth of my experience and my corner of the world. I can't be afraid of that truth or mute it in any way even as it becomes confronting for others or exposing of myself.¹

The one thing I can say I've learned to embrace, that I didn't always, is the idea of being a political writer … I've learned to embrace that I have a very strong social justice call to my work.²

We write because we are trying to articulate something or make sense of the world around us. It's hard to make sense of our current system of injustice and social rage, but it's important to give it voice and space.³

You are allowed to laugh audibly.
You are allowed to have audible moments of reaction and response.
My work requires a few 'um hmms' and 'uhn uhnns' should you
need to use them. Just maybe in moderation. Only when you need to vocalize.
This can be church for some of us, and testifying is allowed.
This is also live theatre and the actors need you to engage with them, not distract them or thwart their performance.
Dominique Morisseau. Rules of Engagement.⁴

Arthur Miller once remarked that all his plays were political. The works he wrote in the 1930s, on behalf of various left-wing groups, aside, that was largely true, though not in an ideological sense. What he meant was that he was engaged in a debate with certain values, myths, assumptions of his society and, it turned out, of the wider society beyond the shores of a country in his mind disinclined to acknowledge the relevance of history or to question its present realities. His were characters who bore the impress of the moment but equally of social habits presented as unquestioned truths. For him, the private and the public were conjoined, not to be surgically separated any more than could the present be from the past. Acts have consequences. As he was fond of saying, the chickens come home to roost, while the fish is in the sea and the sea is in the fish.

Miller found his way to theatre as a student at the University of Michigan. So, too, more than sixty years later, would a young woman, Dominique Morisseau, from a radically different background, different in terms of gender and race, born into a different America, but no less concerned to explore the impact on her characters of the social sea in which they swim. Where he was Jewish, a fact which seldom impacted on his drama (*Incident at Vichy* his adaptation of Fania Fenelon's *Playing for Time* and *Broken Glass* being clear exceptions) beyond a sense, which he also learned from the Depression, that everything could go away, she was Black and that would give her a subject and, at times, it seems, an obligation which extended beyond her plays into becoming an advocate for a change in how theatre in America is organized, calling for Black directors, dramaturgs, artistic directors.

In that, she was aware of a legacy, of one role model in particular, August Wilson, more especially his celebration of his home city of Pittsburgh in a cycle of plays. As she explained,

> I can't ever deny August's influence on my work ... I started writing the Detroit [Project] because I was reading August Wilson's work. I read his work back to back, and I read Pearl Cleage, who was from Detroit. I read her writing back to back ... I just thought, Wow, what his work is doing for Pittsburgh, how they must feel so loved, so immortalized in his writing, I want to do that for Detroit.[5]

She would dedicate the second play in her Detroit trilogy to Cleage because of her love of Black women and of the city.

In Wilson's work, white oppression was not his subject, merely the context in which his characters lived their lives. He was not a protest writer, though he did, he told me, see writing as involving him in a cultural war, even as the major political and social events in the decades his plays covered made no direct appearance. Hence, he said,

> There is a 1930s play, but it doesn't deal with the Depression ... I have a 1960s play, but I don't believe the words Black Power are ever mentioned, and it doesn't deal with Martin Luther King. So what? It deals with the people, people who live their lives in a certain social condition that could not have existed other than in those particular decades ... but the 1960s did not just spring out of nowhere. They were a direct result of the 1940s.[6]

So, as with Miller, past and present co-exist, private lives lived out in a social context.

He may have started out, in *Ma Rainey's Black Bottom*, to write a study of economic exploitation but decided that what he wanted to do was 'show the content of the lives of the people', even as he was aware that the music at the heart of that play is not only an expression of a particular cultural experience but also a bridge out into a wider culture. This was not the James Baldwin of *Blues for Mr. Charlie*, a writer torn between the Old and New Testaments, predicting the fire next time. It was a playwright for whom his Black characters, in their complexities, are centre stage, not to be defined in relation to a white society even as its parameters have been patrolled by those choosing to define culture in their own terms.

Cleage, who left Detroit at the age of eighteen, was the daughter of a civil rights leader and became a journalist, novelist, political activist, and playwright. She had been writing plays since 1981 and happily accepted the idea that in her writing she should write about the struggles of Black people, particularly women. Her 1993 book of essays was entitled *Deals with the Devil and Other Reasons to Riot*. She was not an unlikely inspiration for Morisseau which explains the epigraph to *Paradise Blue*: 'For Pearl Cleage ... Because of her love of black women in her work. Because of her love of Detroit. And because of her essay "Mad at Miles" – which gave me the ammunition and bravery to deal with community accountability in and out of my art.'

We live in an age in which people choose to define themselves in terms of race, gender, sexual preference, heritage, each element to be acknowledged and given equal weight. It is an approach to identity which can be inclusive or exclusionary, simultaneously an assertion of the mosaic nature of the national culture and an assertion of difference. In some senses it is an act of restitution, retrieving what has been disregarded, traduced. It is an assertion of what has been written out of the national narrative or seen as tangential to its central enterprise. For some, it is evidence of the fractured nature of the modern experience. For others it is a celebration of difference, a word which itself only makes sense if there is a presumed norm from which to deviate.

For Amiri Baraka, theatre was a revolutionary act, a racial assertiveness, until he became a Marxist-Leninist at which point race deferred to class. For Lorraine Hansberry and August Wilson, it was a way of celebrating lives under pressure but resilient, the former interested in the negotiation between two worlds, the latter in cultural resources with a history, the poetry to be found in everyday experience, the music not just a background to lives improvised in the face of a reductive template. For Wilson, who set his plays in the past, revisiting history was not only about reclaiming what was easily forgotten or suppressed, it was a necessary act to make sense of the present. Dominique Morisseau has said,

> It's taken me a while to embrace history, but that's not what I started out to do. I was interested in particular moments, but for me it was not about having a historical agenda. What I am really writing about is people, and those people transcend the time period they're in; they even transcend region. I'm writing about humanity, and that's everybody's entry into the plays.

Morisseau was raised in the College Park neighbourhood of Detroit which she has described as an affluent working-class area. Her mother's family had moved up from the South, like many other Black families in Detroit, her mother a teacher for forty years, as would be her daughter. Her father's family came from Haiti. Morisseau herself would marry a hip-hop musician, James Keys, a marriage which took place at the Charles Wright Museum of African American History, Wright being a surgeon and civil rights leader who had played a role in desegregating Detroit's hospitals.

The influence of all these elements is not hard to trace in her work. Her mother would take her to the theatre, while Motown was the background noise as she grew up, music, eventually, offering her a way into the historical periods she would visit in her plays. She later recalled being introduced to Shakespeare when in her sixth grade, and to African American drama at Cass Technical School in mid-town Detroit, a school named for Lewis Cass. He had been the 1848 Democratic presidential nominee and a spokesman for popular sovereignty, in particular for the right of each state to decide whether or not to approve slavery, leading many anti-slavery Democrats to leave the party for the Free Soil Party. So, perhaps, not the ideal name for a school when it came to Black students, though today it is nearly 83 per cent African American and 1 per cent white. Its alumni include Diana Ross and Lily Tomlin. As a child Morrisseau acted in plays and danced with Detroit's City Dance Company.

When she went to university, she originally had her eyes set on acting, even as she registered the lack of diversity when it came to casting. 'So,' she explained, 'I decided to write a play that was to star myself and the other two actresses-of-color in the department ... the first Black play produced in the Student Theatre. ... It sparked a huge movement of support from the student body.' As a result, 'I began to recognize the urgency in challenging the theatre to represent more under-heard voices. Playwriting became an important calling for me.'[7] She graduated with a BFA in acting. The play was entitled *The Blackness Blues – Time to Change the Tune (A Sister's Story)*, finding inspiration in Ztozake Shange's *For Coloured Girls Who Have Considered Suicide/When the Rainbow Is Enough*, not the only aspiring writer for whom that became an important text. She did not, though, abandon her acting among other roles appearing as Camae in Katori Hall's *The Mountain Top*.

Following graduation, she taught drama at her mother's school before leaving for New York where she was initially interested in dancing, meanwhile earning money from poetry slams to pay the rent. She then joined the Creative Arts Team at the City University of New York, an educational theatre programme, before, in 2011, working with the Emerging Writers Group at the New York Public Theatre, a programme, as its name implies, to support writers, offering staged readings of the work of new playwrights while they were free to watch rehearsals for Public Theatre productions.

At the age of eleven, Morisseau was inducted into a family secret. Her aunt Ainee, who they used to visit in Natchez, was the madam of a brothel whose clients were white. These were not terms which meant anything to her. It turned out, though, that Ainee was respected. 'This was especially remarkable,' she explained, 'for a black woman who owned her own business in the segregated South.' In 2011, in a production at the Zella Fry Theater at Kean University, New Jersey, she became Nellie in *Follow Me to Nellie's*, a play set in 1955.

'The reason people loved her is because she took care of so many of them … [she] paid hospital bills for those who couldn't pay them. She put some of her working girls through college. During the civil rights movement, she supported activists and posted bail when she had to – and that's the issue I've focussed on.'[8] It is one such activist, from the North, who has been registering Black voters (as Morisseau herself did) who, in *Follow Me to Nellie's*, hides in the house, falling in love with Na Rose, the only woman not part of the brothel. Her dream is to be a singer and is invited to be one by a blues band, refusing because of her loyalty to an ailing Nellie, even as the blues sound on a jukebox.

Beyond the house, however, there is an ominous sheriff and his son, drawn to Na Rose but equally a threat. Finally, violence invades what had seemed a no-man's land when the man they have been hiding is betrayed by one of the girls and the play moves away from domestic tensions to a violent confrontation. For Morisseau, what she wanted people to take away from the play was the idea that anyone can do something extraordinary, the civil rights movement having involved more than those whose names are associated with it.

The play attracted the attention of Michael Sommers, of *The New York Times*. Unfortunately, he was not impressed, finding Nellie 'scarcely fleshed out', the 'romance between Na Rose and Ossie "not written convincingly,"' the approach prosaic'.[9] Local reviews were more friendly. Ruth Ross, in *nj arts maven*, found it 'thought provoking' and 'a remarkable theatrical experience'.[10] It also won the annual Premiere Stages Play Festival Competition.

A year later, another play, originally developed in the Lark Playwrights Workshop, opened not in America but at the 75-seat Gate Theatre in London: *Sunset Baby*. In order to pay for the flight to England, she had to fund raise. The Gate's manifesto declares that 'Process is Political, Form is Political … don't portray the world, change it'. It is committed to 'amplifying the voices silenced by the canon.' *Sunset Baby* seemed to fit dedicated, as it is, to her father 'who dreams of revolution', and inspired by all 'the black activists throughout time that have shaped the world in which I live', even as 'I stand in recognition of their complicated struggles'. In particular, she was concerned to ask 'How do you build a world and a home at the same time? What gets lost in the struggle?'

She was prompted in part by the figure of the rapper, actor, songwriter Tupac Shakur whose work was in part concerned with social issues, who served time on sexual assault charges, but became known for his gangster rap and, at the age of twenty-five, was shot dead in a drive-by shooting. As Morisseau observed,

> One minute he'd be an intelligent orator breaking down the poverty mentality of a lost generation, and the next he'd be a contributor to a violent generational abyss. How can my generation be so brilliant and so self-destructive at the same time? That is the question that guides my play ... It is not a blame game. It is not about dis-crediting a movement or a people. It is about untreated wounds between the generations, and the hope for healing. It is about love.[11]

Just as *Detroit '67* and *Paradise Blue* were to be set at times of dissolution, staging the lives of characters whose dreams were fast fading, so in *Sunset Baby* Morisseau brings together figures for whom the old certainties have faded, certainties which were themselves suspect. The title may derive from a family photograph, but the sun is setting on careers, hopes, old convictions.

Even family connections are strained to breaking point and, indeed, seem always to have been under pressure. Kenyatta, in his fifties, a one-time Black revolutionary known as Ashanti X, who has served time in prison for the cause, now finds himself having to confront the human cost of his activism, a cost paid by his family. His wife, now dead, had become a drug addict, suffering from depression and, according to his daughter, Nina, from a broken heart. He is estranged from that daughter who is herself a drug dealer and robber, working to gain enough money to escape to Europe, or anywhere, with Damon, who has served time for murder. He, in turn, is estranged from the mother of his son, to whom he pays no child support while denied contact with that son by court order, even as he seems to know little of him. He is not only street smart but well read, invoking the theory of the criminologist Stephen Spitzer who distinguishes between what he calls 'social junk' and 'social dynamite', the one being those who have fallen through society's gaps, becoming dependant, accepting the roles they are given, the other those who fight back, the question being 'which one are you?'

The immediate cause for Kenyatta to see Nina is that she possesses letters which her mother had sent to him when he was in prison, letters that have meaning to him, but which could command a good price if sold, something which leads Damon to suggest they should sell them to finance their journey to Rio or London.

These are characters caught at a moment of change. Kenyatta is, Morisseau explains, 'navigating a softer version of himself', looking to recover something of what he had lost, his public commitment having been at the cost of personal relationships. Damon has 'lost his hardness and is on the brink of retiring from the game', (17) even lamenting the fact that gangsters no longer respect any code, not an entirely ironic stance. Nina has been left to her own resources, doing what she must in order to survive, and survival is a common link between these characters, as it is in her Detroit trilogy.

As Nina says, 'I never wanted this ... I don't want a hustle or no fast money. I don't want a movement or a cause. I want a home. ... I'm not alive here. I am not alive in this chaos.' (50–1) Damon offers himself as that family, 'the only family you got left'. (51) With a somewhat curious about turn, given that he had originally intended to steal and sell the letters, he urges her to attempt reconciliation with her father. Accordingly, she prepares for his arrival, but not before slipping a gun into her clothes. The meeting, in which he offers money for the letters, comes to nothing because neither can utter the word love, though it hangs in the air, what could unite instead dividing them.

He leaves behind photographs, but also a video, the recordings with which the play begins and ends, or nearly so. In these he tries to explain himself to himself, no less than to Nina. Having dedicated himself to changing the world he now needs to change himself, aware that the past cannot be denied. As for Nina, she reads the letters which instead of expressing her mother's accusation at being abandoned for the cause, sees that abandonment as her contribution to that cause, a declaration of love for the man Nina has held in contempt.

Instead of keeping the letters Nina posts them to Kenyatta and, instead of forging a relationship with Damon, takes her money and heads to the airport, the sound of her flight taking off blending with that of her doorbell buzzing, the relationship with Damon clearly at an end. Her choice, as she had read in one of the letters, is to 'heal or perpetuate'. (74) So, she turns her back on the life that had sustained her at the price of her soul, leaving to fulfil her dream.

As to music, always the soundtrack to Morisseau's plays, here it is that of Nina Simone after whom Nina's father had called his daughter: 'Feeling Good', 'Black is the Colour of My True Love's Hair', 'Love Me or Leave Me', 'Don't Let Me Be Misunderstood'. One of her songs, incidentally, was written by Langston Hughes, while she was a friend of Lorraine Hansberry. Nina Simon herself played a significant role in the Civil Rights movement even as her private life fell apart, being alienated from husband and daughter. She once shot a record company executive, moving to France as would Morisseau's Nina.

This is not so much a political play as one in which she explores the private impact of political engagement, not only the personal price to be paid for that engagement but also the nature of a commitment which may itself be morally ambiguous. Kenyatta had been involved in violence, even as there is violence on the streets. Nina and Damon carry guns. Shakur, whose music Morisseau admired, was equally capable of writing about the need for healing and for retaliation against the police. In at least two trials, one in Texas the other in Milwaukee, defendants charged with killing policemen implausibly quoted his lyrics as provoking their crimes, a police widow suing Shakur and his record company. For Morisseau, he was 'one of the most complex and brilliant hip hop artists there ever was'. (12) That complexity is what she probes in a play which explores the impact on more than one generation seeking to confront racism, to survive.

She is aware that she stands where she does not only because of Martin Luther King, and those who deployed passive resistance to claim basic rights, but because there were others who challenged the system even more directly, and paid the price for doing so, who went beyond rhetoric, arming themselves metaphorically or literally, advocating not assimilation to what they regarded as a suspect norm but the virtues of active rebellion with all the ambiguity that involved. She is not Nina, who sees criminality as a route to emancipation, but she is aware that her own freedom of action involves those who made sacrifices which were not theirs alone to offer to the cause. The play is in some senses Morisseau's attempt to understand those who wrestled with conflicting notions of right action.

The family, in *Sunset Baby*, is equally the seat of love and tension, a place of generational difference, offering a protective retreat but equally an exposed arena, intimate knowledge offering consolation or weapons to flourish. It is where emotional negotiations reflect different needs, a conflicting understanding of the world, power shifting over time, assumed authority challenged. Love may be its default setting, but its members are drawn together and pushed apart as what was once shared is placed under pressure. In *Sunset Baby* the family has been infiltrated by those forces until they assume primacy, and the effect is caustic. When the British spy Kim Philby was asked by his wife whether she or the Communist Party was more important to him, he did not hesitate: the Party. It was a question of conflicting loyalties. So it is in *Sunset Baby*.

At stake is what seems a betrayal of family in the name of a cause, with disastrous effects, except that a betrayed wife remains loyal, accepting the price to be paid for abandonment while celebrating the love which had brought her together with the man who follows his own dream of possibility. The play ends with an act of liberation, literal in that Nina chooses to leave a place which has become an emotional prison, making her what she would not wish to be, but also in the sense that she is free now of her anger and bitterness, reconciled in part to her father but also to what, in retrospect, might seem her parents' heroism. Both paid a price, but in the end it is because they did so that she can now lay claim to the freedom she thought lost, to become herself without the need for a suspect alliance.

Reviews were positive, notably from London's *New Statesman*, though its right-wing nature was evident.

> *Sunset Baby* is, first and foremost, a play about the personal and the political colliding, the tension between familial and social responsibilities. And at a time when America's first black president is facing election for a second term in office, the hustler's life that Nina and Damon are condemned to – and the very fact that so many are falling through the cracks of society at all – challenges the notion that Obama's presidency has brought about significant change for many African Americans.[12]

For *The Guardian*'s Lyn Gardner,

> US playwright Dominique Morisseau's three-hander may be a mite old-fashioned in construction, and is sometimes too schematic, but it's also smart, entertaining, and moving as it grapples with the tensions between past and present, one generation and another, while asking penetrating questions about the nature of liberation. Is it possible to be a good revolutionary and a good parent? Why are the gains made by one generation so often casually thrown away by the next? And what are the things we do for love?[13]

Ben Brantley, reviewing a Bank Street Theatre production, in *The New York Times*, welcomed a 'smart and bracing' play. 'The show's conventional story functions as a stress test for the people who act it out, illuminating their strengths and weaknesses as moral beings and, yes, survivors. During this process, each of them is seen with a remarkably clear gaze that avoids both easy cynicism and easy sentimentality.'[14]

In 2016, it was staged by St. Paul's African American Penumbra Theatre, dedicated to 'Art as Activism'. Again, reviews were positive while the *Chicago-Tribune*, reviewing the Chicago TimeLine production, declared that Morisseau was becoming a crucial American writer. For the *Chicago Theatre Review* it was a soul-shattering theatrical experience.

What's in a name? The events of July 1967, in Detroit, were described, depending on your perspective, as a riot, an uprising, an insurrection or a revolt. When a formal report on that year's events, the Kerner Commission, was published it preferred the word 'Disorders'.

Whatever the epithet, what was exposed was a racial fault line which had long existed. It was the worst 'disorder' for over a century.

On the 23rd of the month the Detroit Police Department raided an unlicensed after-hours bar known as a blind pig, on 12th Street on the Lower West Side. Inside, they found a large gathering of people celebrating the return of GIs from the Vietnam War. They arrested them all. It was a hot night. People were on the street. A bottle thrown through the window of a police car was all it took to set in motion violence which would lead to forty-three deaths and the burning of cities across America, to be repeated a year later on the assassination of Martin Luther King Jr.

In terms of its population, Detroit had been in freefall for more than a decade. Old neighbourhoods had been destroyed, including two Black areas, Black Bottom and Paradise Valley, both known for their music if also their poverty. They were demolished to make way for a freeway, I-375. There was high unemployment and de facto segregation in schools. Yet Detroit was also home to what came to be known as Motown, though following the riots it moved to Los Angeles. Among those recording for the label were The Supremes, a musical based on their lives later being written by a playwright who was herself born in Detroit and would celebrate the lives of those who lived there, explaining that she wished to 'put our experience into the American canon of theatre',[15] as her friend, the playwright, Katori Hall had done.

She may now be in New York but, fifteen years after leaving Detroit, confessed that her cell phone still retained a Detroit area code and that city would be the setting for a cycle of three plays set in Detroit. It began with *Detroit '67* which takes place at the time of the 1967 disturbances. Tellingly, the dedication to her trilogy, *The Detroit Project*, reads: 'Detroit is my family. My best friends. My husband. My first love. My creative genesis. My heart. This is for your imperfection. Your truth. And your ongoing survival through the decades, #lifelongdetroitgirl', while that to *Detroit '67* celebrates 'the indestructible spirit of my Detroit people who refuse to go up in flames'. The question is how that commitment, that acknowledgement, will work out in terms of characters who will embody the contradictions, and yet the spirit, of the city which is not merely to be the location of action.

Detroit '67 features five characters, four Black, one white. Whatever the tensions that will emerge, her description of them seems to emphasize what brings them together. Chelle, a Black woman in her late thirties, is described as having 'a loving heart'. Her brother, Lane, is 'loving'. Bunny, also in her late thirties, is 'joyful' while Sly, described as an 'honest hustler', is 'Fiercely loyal'. Only a white woman, Caroline, is 'mysterious', but even she is 'Beautiful, quietly strong, troubled, soft'. It could seem that sentimentality might be structured into those whose lives, it turns out, are embattled even as they try to insulate themselves from the forces which seem to define the parameters of their possibilities.

It is July. In Detroit. For those aware of the significance of the time and place, the fact of what happened then colours the audience response, though Morisseau herself, born in 1978, had to research the events of that summer. The action takes place in the unfinished basement of a two-story house at 1568 Clairmont Street, a real Detroit street where even in 2021 a nearby house was estimated as selling for only $110,000. There are pictures of Motown artists on the wall, along with those of Joe Louis, Malcolm X and Muhammad Ali. There is a picture of a black fist along with what is described as a very bad portrait of a brown girl.

Efforts are underway to transform a down-market, somewhat tawdry, space with a string of Christmas lights. It is, we learn, being prepared for what is hoped will be ticket-buying guests in search of somewhere to drink and listen to the music which is playing as the lights come up. A faulty record player is sounding out the Temptations' 'Ain't Too Proud to Beg', whose lyrics about a man begging a woman not to leave him, beyond being a comment on what turns out to be a fated relationship between a Black man and a white woman, perhaps has a wider significance in terms of a city in which abandonment is a fact even as it commands loyalty. The music in *Detroit '67* is not incidental to the play but an organic part of it. It is not just that the characters play music on a faulty record-player or an eight-track player. It is a part of their lives, reflecting the moment, their moods, needs, dreams, but also what brings them together.

It is a play in which music offers a counterpoint to the action, songs of love pursued, frustrated, embraced, even as in the social world there is little evidence of love, white police beating and harassing Black men and women, the neighbourhood beginning to burn along with the dreams of those who thought to find a way of staking a claim on a future not constrained by those who regard them as a threat or irrelevance. A student's future is in the balance, as is that of a family plotting different paths, held together by natural affection but with different strategies. At the same time, the arrival of a desperate young white woman creates an emotional interference pattern, disrupting assumptions as she embraces Black music and feels at home in this Black family, even as she herself is in search of an escape, even, potentially, bringing trouble on those who shelter her. For a moment, love, or its approximation, seems a possibility, but there is more than a community in flames. A Marvin Gaye song, which is played, speaks of the need to shelter in someone's arms.

Private and public dramas intersect. Things are falling apart. The question is whether there is a centre to hold. The bars raided by police are where people come together, some back from Vietnam where African Americans represented 23 per cent of combat troops, as two years earlier they had constituted 25 per cent of deaths.

Chelle's parents now dead, she plans to use the proceeds from selling their house for her son's college tuition at Tuskegee Institute. The parties, meanwhile, are to pay off the mortgage on her own home as well as contribute to her son's education. The problem, it emerges, is that her brother, Lank, has other plans. Without her knowledge, he sets out to buy a bar on 12th Street, where the riot would begin. There is more than an echo of Lorraine Hansberry's *A Raisin the Sun* in which the proceeds of a life insurance policy, following the death of the father, are to be used by Lena Younger, the matriarch of the family, to buy a house, while her daughter, Beneatha, sees it as paying for her medical training. Her son, Walter, though, wants to buy a liquor store with his friend who runs off with the money he has secretly invested. The play ends as a fractured family come together, sharing a single dream, the future not assured but grasped by those who had sought their own destinies, been guilty of betrayals, these finally set aside in the name of a newfound solidarity in the face of hostility.

In Hansberry's play, the issue is the purchase, or otherwise, of a house in the white area. In Morisseau's play, white flight to the suburbs leads to the sale of the bar: 'white folks all over town been tryin' to sell their property and move on out'.[16] In Hansberry's case, the sum at risk is $10,000; here, seven years on, it is $15,000. There are betrayals here, too, different dreams. The hostility of the white world is even more pointed than in *A Raisin in the Sun*. There is a similar move towards reconciliation, the sense that family wounds can be healed even if the divisions in society, brutally underlined by police beatings and the death of a central character, remain threateningly in place. The surprise is that Morisseau should say that it took her some time to understand that she was in essence a political playwright with a strong social call. It is evident in everything she writes, especially here at a moment when history is being played out in what many called a police riot.

Lank (his full name is Langston Hughes Poindexter, this clearly being a family with a sense of its cultural inheritance) has frequently been laid off from work, selling marijuana from his basement. Now he wants to have a legitimate business: 'Get us some business of our own – make them stop treatin' us like trash to be swept away. I'm tellin' you, we get a chance to get above ground, Detroit'll be a mecca.' (121) His father had worked in the Ford plant, but 'my heart', he explains, 'is into somethin' else ... Doin' for myself. Finding somewhere to really be somebody and have something that no one can take away from me.' (154) To do this, he joins with his friend, Sly, a numbers runner. For Chelle, this is just a 'hustle on the books', to which he replies, 'That's all any kinda business is', (123) an echo of David Mamet's *American Buffalo* and *Glengarry, Glen Ross*.

The preparations for the opening of their basement bar are suddenly interrupted when, late at night, Lank and Sly carry an unconscious white girl, Caroline, in having found her injured and barely conscious in the street, an act of kindness not without its risks. When she recovers consciousness the next morning, she explains that she has no money and nowhere to go. Against Chelle's better instincts, they offer her a bed in exchange for her working the bar at that evening's party. For another character, Bunny, 'ya'll got a white girl over here in the ghetto runnin' 'round under ya'll like some kinda maid ... Everybody gonna wanna see some of this.' (139) And not only the Black community it turns out, she having been beaten by her white policeman lover, a man whose corruptions she had witnessed which makes her a risk to be eliminated.

By degrees we become aware that beyond this house, preparing for celebrations, something is happening. Sly has been stopped by the police 'like I need some kind of pass to walk the streets', they asking where he was going, only losing interest when a radio call sends them off to a disturbance. Bunny, a family friend, a fixer, full of life, had been stopped being told that 'women like me up to no good', (141) aware that men and women alike had been beaten. For Lank, 'Ain't so long you can hit folks 'fore they start to hit back'. (142)

When news comes that the police have raided a bar, the area begins to burn. 'What kinda way is that to fight back?' asks Chelle, 'Runnin 'round burnin' up the city? That ain't hurtin' nobody but us'. (162) The question is whether the bar Lank and Sly have bought will be destroyed, the police evidently knowing the former's connection with Caroline. Lank is beaten but Sly, who told Chelle 'Don't be scared ... It's gonna get cleaned up soon. President Johnson himself gettin' involved. Say so right here in the paper', is killed, shot dead by National Guardsmen who had been joined by regular army troops. What had begun in the domestic world of a family planning for its future, in the basement of a small house in a poor neighbourhood, is now irremediably linked to the public arena. The sound of tanks rolling by displaces that of songs celebrating love and its frailties.

Lank had been drawn to Caroline, as she is to him, though his sister insists that 'you get around her and you get further and further away from reality. Forgettin' who you are and what this world can do to you.' (171) Under threat from the police, she leaves, a woman who does not share their race but who has never had a family, a place to call home, or a relationship which meant anything. For Chelle, 'You and him can pretend to be cut from the same cloth all you want. But outside this basement tell a different story. Lank got his eye on the sky but

Detroit ain't in the sky. It's right here on the ground. A ground with a lot of dividing lines. We on one side and you on the other.' (187)

In what is a crucial exchange, Caroline insists on the possibility of crossing lines, transcending 'all the zones and restrictions' only for Chelle to insist,

> You can disappear and reappear wherever else you want, in any zone you choose. Live a new life without permission or boundaries or some kinda limits to your skin. Can Lank do that? Can any of us? Everywhere we go, the lines are clear … You might dream the same. You might even feel the same heartbreak. But till he have the same *title* to this world that you got, you and him ain't gon' never be the same.
>
> (188)

One of his dreams dead, Lank is left with his plans for the bar. Now, Chelle decides to share his hopes for a place which she says should be called Lank and Sly's Feel-Good Chelle Shack. It is the family which now becomes central. The play ends as she sings and dances along with The Four Tops 'Reach Out, I'll Be There' played on the eight-track player which her brother and Lank had bought to fill the air with sound in their planned bar. The words embody the essence of a play in which, in the face of disappointment, of a coercive social world, there remains some consolation in human relationships:

> Now if you feel that you can't go on
> Because all of your hope is gone
> And your life is filled with much confusion
> Until happiness is just an illusion
> And your world is crumbling down, darlin'
> Reach out … Come on girl, reach on out to me.
>
> (197)

A stage direction indicates that she is 'definitely free'. But is she? After all, the public world remains resolutely what it was before. A year later, would come assassinations, with cities once again in flames. The police would go on beating and killing Black men. The dream of possibility is a bar, itself something of a retreat. Will there now be enough money to support Chelle's son in Tuskegee, and when he graduates will the world have changed? Vietnam had years to run. Motown would leave Detroit, if not the minds and imaginations of those who listened to its music. Music, indeed, is a space in which emotion and imagination can find transcendence even if, in the case of Black music, it is generated out of encoded experiences impermeable to those who live in a world remote from that of those who create it. And what of Caroline, an echo of Tennessee Williams's damaged Blanche Dubois, who has experienced the kindness of strangers but leaves without any real destination, the possibility of racial healing seemingly disappearing along with her?

Charles Isherwood, in *The New York Times*, was unimpressed, objecting to what he regarded as an 'overly tidy drama that uses the riots that roiled the title city as the background to formulaic stories about a brother and sister at odds and an interracial romance', a play which, to him, 'blends sentiment and racial history in roughly equal parts, with results that feel studied and disappointingly bland', having 'the diagrammatic feeling of an extended episode of a 1970s sitcom'. Caroline, meanwhile, 'is as much a device as a character: a convenient way for Ms. Morisseau to bring the issue of the city's stark racial divide from the streets into the basement'. She strikes him as a 'cipher'. As to the ending, 'even after tragedy strikes, you have the sense that all will be resolved with minimal lasting damage: just fire up some Motown, get those hips moving and everything will work out fine.'[17]

Given that this production was part of New York's Public Lab series, in association with the Classical Theater of Harlem and the National Black Theatre, and the beginning of Morisseau's career, this was not an encouraging response from the city's major newspaper. But was he right? It is surely hard to see it as formulaic, while the reference to a '70s sitcom is reductive without being insightful. As to the ending, with its apparent easy resolution, trauma being swiftly accommodated to family reconciliation, commitment to a shared dream, music celebrating love, this, staged in 2013, was to be seen by audiences nearly half a century after the events dramatized, a gap in time generating its own ironies. Perhaps tellingly, a review of the Detroit Public Theatre production by the *Detroit Free Press* saw it as 'timely', reflecting, as it did, issues still immediately relevant in a city in which gentrification remained a central concern. For Morisseau, the past is part of the present, hers, and that of the city she left but to which she returns in her work.

Detroit '67 won an Edward Kennedy Prize for Drama, an award for a new play or musical that explores the past of the United States, in order, as its terms of reference indicate, to participate meaningfully in the great issues of our day through public conversation, grounded in historical understanding. The award was worth $100,000.

The second play in the trilogy, *Paradise Blue*, which had its premiere at the Williamstown Theatre Festival in July 2015, moved the action to 1949 and the Paradise Club in Black Bottom, on the downtown strip in Detroit known as Paradise Valley. Once again, there are five characters: Pumpkin, 'Simple, sweet. Waitress, cook and caretaker of the Paradise Club'; Blue, the club's proprietor, 'Handsome, mysterious … Quietly dangerous … A gifted trumpeter'; Corn, 'Easy going and thoughtful … with a weakness for love. The piano man'; P-Sam, 'sweet-talker, hustler … The percussionist'; Silver, 'Mysterious, sexy, charming.'[18]

The play begins 'in darkness' with the sound of a trumpet, 'sorrowful, almost a dirge', a light coming up to reveal Blue as the note becomes 'the most beautiful … we've ever heard' before, as he smiles, 'overcome with peace' a gunshot sounds out. Then, we are in the nightclub, Pumpkin, as she sweeps the trash, reading a poem by Georgia Douglas Johnson, an African American poet and playwright from the Harlem Renaissance whose plays, like Morisseau's, feature music, a poem which speaks of a woman's broken dreams, a sense of entrapment, she responding to its language, what she calls its 'elegance', even as she seems not fully to register its relevance to her own situation:

> The heart of a woman falls back with the night,
> And enters some alien cage in its plight,
> And tries to forget it has dreamed of the stars
> While it – breaks,
> breaks,
> breaks
> on the sheltering bars.
>
> (10–11)

Later, she recites another verse which expresses a desire which she is not yet able to translate into action:

> The right to make my dreams come true
> I ask, nay, I demand of life,
> Nor shall fate's deadly contraband
> Impede my steps, not countermand.
>
> Too long my heart against the ground
> Has beat the dusty years around,
> And now, at length, I rise, I wake!
> And stride into the morning break!
>
> (66)

She is not yet ready to awake and sing. Eventually, though, rather than recite another person's words, she discovers her own, seeing beauty in herself but, alarmingly, it turns out, concluding that there is only one way to break out of the cage and release both herself and another whose struggles she seeks to end.

Gentrification was not an invention of the 1960s. It was a reality in 1949, the year of the Housing Act which called for slum clearance in the city. This followed the Detroit Plan of 1946. Under the slogan urban renewal, carried forward by Mayor Cobo, invoked in the play, those who had settled in the Black Bottom area were moved out to the 12th Street of *Detroit '67*. Black Bottom had been a mecca for Black music.

Slum clearance, though, offers only the context for a drama which focuses on a man, haunted by the past while searching for something he can barely articulate. Blue is the owner of the club, but things are falling apart. He has fired a member of his band and is negotiating to sell, an act which will prompt other owners to follow suit, effectively signalling the end of a Black community and the music which has been its mark. He will leave behind not only the members of his own band but a way of life. As Silver says, 'I heard of Black Bottom, Detroit.' Specially down this strip in Paradise Valley where folks got all their own business. If it's somewhere that colored folks is doing more than share croppin' and reapin' huge folks harvest … I ought to be there.' (26)

It becomes evident, though, that money is not the issue. The one resource Blue has is Pumpkin, who he loves but subordinates to a domestic life, a life with which she seems content, living at second hand even as she has a sense of something more. Blue's conflicting feelings are expressed in his trumpet playing as he aspires to a perfect sound which evades him, what the piano-playing Corn describes as 'Love Supreme. That's what we call it when you hit the perfect note that cleans your sins. Like white light bathin' him with mercy.' (73) Which sins they might be only becomes apparent with time as does a mercy which turns out to be implacable. For her part, Pumpkin's conflicting feelings are expressed in the contradiction between the poem she recites and the life she has lived. For her, the community is reassuring, a family, even as it defines the limits of her possibilities. For her, Paradise is not just a name. In her case it is an expression of her innocence, resisting the idea of conflict and sin until it breaks through her protective shield.

Into an already fraught situation comes a woman, Silver, who further disrupts what had only seemed to be a harmonious group. She has drifted from man to man, independent, with an eye on the main chance, confessing that she has shot her husband dead, still carrying a gun into whose use she inducts Pumpkin, the gun which might have been fired in the darkness as the play had begun and which will sound again at the end. She seems disturbingly well informed about the situation, herself offering to buy the bar: 'Everything's for sell', she tells Blue, 'Business. Land. Soul', (60) the implication being that in his case it is his soul that is on offer. If this is paradise, she is the snake, though the word used about her is 'spider'.

Nor is she the only one looking to buy. P-Sam (P for Percussion) strikes it rich on the numbers, an echo of the fortuitous money in *Detroit '67*, *A Raison in the Sun*, and Clifford Odets's *Awake and Sing*, in other words perhaps a rather too familiar a dramatic device.

Blue's pain, guilt, need are expressed in his music. We are told he 'plays a beautiful and painful melody – long, sorrowful notes', (43) but is 'too wrapped up in his pain' to continue, though, for Pumpkin, 'The pain is the sweetest part.' (43) Blue, though, insists that he cannot escape his father's demons, the father who founded the club and who was responsible for his mother's tears and, eventually, her death, strangling her believing the devil to be in her, himself ending up in an asylum. The murder was witnessed by Blue who inherited his father's skill as a trumpeter, but fears he may have inherited something else as well. 'That kind dead weight make a man dangerous. It can turn on you', (73) observes Silver who has reasons of her own for knowing so, confessing that 'my daddy had 'em in him. Husband too. Them feelin's of bein' trapped by yo'skin. Never allowed to get beyond where you at. Turns you mad. Only place you got to escape is that horn, ain't it. But horn only make it louder ... When you got demons that deep, they don't redeem you. They kill you in the soul'. (61) In her own case, her father had committed suicide. Blue's father, Corn explains, had reached for 'Love Supreme. That's what he was lookin' for and never found.' (63,73) Beyond his personal trauma, however, is the fact that, as Corn remarks of Blue, 'He just wanna be mighty but the world keep him small. Cost of bein' colored and gifted. Brilliant and second class. Make you insane.' (73)

For Morisseau,

> I wish we could feel what's hurting him, because hurt people hurt people. I do look at the hurt that Blue has faced and the abuse he has taken in his life and been a witness to as a black musician in the time period he's living in. What ... Corn says is the absolute truth – to be brilliant and second-class, you will be insane for the rest of your life. When we were in rehearsal, I would bring up the James Baldwin quote that I love because it speaks to Blue in a lot of ways: 'To be black and to be relatively conscious is to be in a constant state of rage'[19]

Blue believes that by moving on, leaving the place where he had witnessed murder, he can outpace his demons, something Silver insists he should do, but the evidence for such an escape in her own case is not strong while race cannot be outpaced. Her solution is to avoid commitment, have her literal and emotional bags ready to pack. Incapable of bearing children, she can leave no heritage, hardening herself, determined not to be vulnerable, a spider and not a fly.

As the play edges towards its conclusion so Pumpkin grows into herself, no longer reciting someone else's poem but creating her own, a poem not about broken dreams but her desire to save Blue, its words echoing the musician's search for the perfect sound:

I want to reach you purely
In truth and love sublime

She has, Corn remarks, found her own music, too late, though, to rescue the man she loves as she realizes that 'You just ain't right. I see now. You ain't never gonna be. You already gone.' (95) The only peace she can offer him, even as he finds the musical resolution he had sought, is by shooting him dead at the moment he achieves the sound he had looked for, the release for which he had yearned, the play ending with the sound of the shot which had opened it.

Detroit '67 had closed with renewed hope. *Paradise Blue* concludes, as Edward Albee's *The Zoo Story* had done, with a life saved by a life taken, a sacrifice designed to redeem but which cannot end with the act. What, after all, will Pumpkin's fate now be? The band will no longer be able to function without the man at its heart, and if the sale of the club may now no longer go ahead, the fate of Black Bottom is already sealed, history trumping such gestures even as the power of the music which brought them together will survive.

Reviews were mixed. Responding to its world premiere, at the Williamstown Theatre Festival, Laura Collins-Hughes, in *The New York Times*, found the figure of Blue disappointing, 'Peek beneath the surface of this violent, short-tempered bully, and there's not a lot there. If he's tormented by demons – which he is, in a cliché that Ms. Morisseau does not give a fresh twist – why should we care?' It was a play which 'culminates in a scene that reaches for poetry but feels purple instead, its failure to land partly because the other characters mean more to us than Blue does'.[20] The same newspaper, reviewing the play three years later at the Signature Theatre, preferred the other two plays in the Detroit trilogy finding everything 'overripe' in *Paradise Blue*, feeling that it 'so overplays its genre tropes that the characters feel like incoherent afterthoughts. Especially in the second act, as the plot tries to wind itself into a climax, they stop making sense', suggesting that though 'it engages powerful ideas in a format too weak to handle them, that's a more promising problem than the other way around.'[21]

Variety was equally dismissive, oddly regretting that urban renewal had not been more integral to what its reviewer regarded as a plot-thin drama. 'Lacking that kind of thematic core, the play restricts itself to being an atmospheric but insubstantial slice of dramatic life',[22] while the figure of Blue needed more depth, 'along with a richer sense of humanity', though it is difficult to know what to make of that last remark. The *Chicago Tribune,* responding to its Midwest premiere by the TimeLine Theatre Company, was altogether more receptive finding the play 'filled to the brim with complex, empathetic characters struggling and infighting as part of a community living under extreme duress'. For Chris Jones, it was 'one of Morisseau's most ambitious plays to date'.[23]

Paradise Blue is a fable, its characters playing their roles in a story about the struggle to survive in the face of an oppressive world. Most of them are musicians, music offering a structure, a resource, poetry in a prosaic world, a way of refracting experience, shaping it so that it offers a pure form in the face of psychological and social anomie. Blue, who some reviewers clearly felt underwritten, is an embodiment of those tensions. The transformation of Pumpkin, in a sense weaponized by Silver, is abrupt but has echoes of Steinbeck's *Of Mice and Men* as we are asked to accept that love may involve the taking of life, in Steinbeck's case as Lenny saves George from an imprisonment which would destroy him. In the case of Blue, he is caught at a triumphant moment of harmony and exaltation which, except for Pumpkin's violent but redemptive action, could only be followed by despair.

With the third play in the trilogy, *Skeleton Crew*, Morisseau moves from the rhythm of jazz to that of hip hop, from the dissolution of a community to that of an industry which in turn threatens the community. In 2007 there was a major recession. The play is set the following year. The city had grown on the back of the automobile industry, but that was now in decline. The year after *Skelton Crew* was set, Chrysler filed for bankruptcy. Four years later, the city itself did likewise. The financial cost was enormous. Morisseau is concerned with the human cost. Her own father had been a union man. Unions, once strong in Detroit, were now powerless. Not for nothing does she dedicate her play not only to members of her own family but to 'all of the UAW members and autoworkers whose passion for their work inspires me. And this is for the working-class warriors who keep this country driving forward. This is also for the politicians who echoed the negating sentiments, "Let Detroit Go Bankrupt."'

'Let Detroit Go Bankrupt', was the title of an op-ed piece in *The New York Times* by the Republican Mitt Romney whose father had worked in the industry but who opposed the government bailout which followed. When Morisseau was developing her play in 2014, at The Lark Play Development Center in New York, the situation had improved though the bailout itself had required job losses.

Skeleton Crew is set in the somewhat down-at-heel break room of a stamping plant, which makes body panels for cars. It is winter, 'somewhere around 2008', later clarifying this to January of that year before the collapse became even more evident. Gathered here are three working-class Black workers and their foreman, Reggie. Faye, in her mid-to-late fifties, is described as tough with 'a great compassion'. Dez, thirty years younger, is a 'hustler, street savvy' but also 'deeply sensitive'. The fourth character, Shanita, pregnant, is hardworking, 'Believes in the work she does ... a beautiful dreamer'. The break room is a space in which they can come together, away from the pressures of work, that work being conveyed as from time to time the sound of machinery reaches them, accompanied by hip-hop drum beats and what she describes as 'a cacophony of working class hustle'.[24] (207) In a play which she describes as realistic, she intrudes 'touches of the magical/ethereal', summoning up the rhythm of the plant, sometimes mechanically smooth at others dislocated, by the use of 'shadow puppets, choreography, video, a combo of all' (206), a choice which she leaves to directors and designers. She calls for silhouettes conveying 'the drone of workers on the line, operating stamping machinery. No clear people, just shadowed workers misted by the smoke'. (207)

This is not, though, the world of Fritz Lang's *Metropolis*, with its portrait of workers mechanically serving their overlords, the word 'drone' referring not to their status but the hum of work, broken from time to time, the entropy of the industry reflected in occasional breakages in production. Indeed, these are workers who take pride in their work even as there is evidence of decline, companies beginning to close or shed staff. Shanita declines a job in a copy shop, remote from the noise and dirt of the plant, because she takes pride in what they do, explaining, in an echoic language:

> The sound of the refrigerator humming. The sound of the machines running ... To me ... Sound like harmony. Like life happening. Production. Good sound ... Here, I feel like I'm building somethin' important. Love the way the line needs ... I'm building

something that you can see come to life at the end. Got a motor in it and it's gonna take somebody somewhere. Gonna maybe drive some important businessman to work. Gonna get some mama to her son's football practice. Gonna take a family on they first trip to Cedar Point. Gonna even maybe somebody's first time. Who knows. But I like knowing I had a hand in it.

(220, 240)

For Faye, with a linguistic harmony of her own, 'This beauty right here ... From a press machine on 12-line ... I'm telling you about having a son and bein' clueless. I'm telling you about not having the answers. Ain't never had 'em and probably never will. But whatever I'm doin', it's keeping me here' (235) except that theirs is the last small factory still standing, demand for its product disappearing with the industry it serves. Those who remain, a skeleton crew required as things run down, are afraid for their jobs but also fear leaving a place which had meaning to them. They contribute to making something. There is a product from their labour as well as a structure to their lives, except that that is precisely what is threated.

The break room is a retreat but, beyond it, and the factory, there are other problems. Faye, for all her confidence as a survivor, has long since been abandoned by the man who made her pregnant, leaving her with a son who grows up to be alienated from her. She is now in remission from cancer, even as she smokes. Remission, as she knows, is not cure. Having worked for twenty-nine years she is vulnerable, in terms of severance payments, if dismissed before it becomes thirty. She gambles and has lost her home, living in her car and, overnight, against the rules, in the break room. Yet she perseveres, albeit at her age having no alternative.

Dez, who plans to open a garage, carries a gun, aware of the violence in the streets. Reggie, who shares his background with those he formally oversees, has a mortgage and family to support. Shanita, pregnant, has no man to support her. Meanwhile, the decision has already been made to close the plant. The question is which of them will lose his or her job even as, surely in time, all of them will. They are in a lifeboat taking water.

Dez makes himself a candidate when thefts lead to inspections and Reggie discovers the gun he carries, choosing, however, not to inform on him. As co-workers, they form an impromptu family, including Reggie who does everything he can to protect the others. In a speech reminiscent of Tom Joad's in *The Grapes of Wrath*, Faye declares,

I know everything about this place, Dez. The walls talk to me. The dust on the floor write me messages. I'm in the vents. I'm in the bulletin boards. I'm in the chipped paint. Ain't nobody can slip through the cracks past me up in here. I can see through lockers. I know what you got in that bag you bring in here every day. But I don't expose it. Cuz everybody got their bag of shit. You got yours. I got mine.

(227)

The rhythm of this room is at odds with that of work except that there are dislocations in both. As the world collapses around them, these are figures for whom survival is a central concern, but survival is not only about retaining jobs as long as they can but the survival of a sense of self. The play, indeed, ends with an act of sacrifice, as Faye resigns to protect Reggie, otherwise about to lose his job, having put himself at risk to preserve the others, as Pumpkin had surrendered her freedom to protect Blue against himself.

The situation has potentially turned them against one another, each having reasons for clinging on to their jobs. In fact, they offer support. As Reggie says, 'Only way to get through it is to work together'. (289) As, for the moment, they return to work, the plant itself echoes this unity as the stage direction indicates that the silhouetted workers 'come alive. They begin working the line. Smoothly. Collaboratively. For the first time since the beginning of the play, the line has harmony.' Fay's spirit 'becomes embedded into the soul of the plant'. (290)

The irony, of course, is that we know what happened next. Such plants closed, those who worked there losing their jobs. The lines stopped. Morisseau's play is not, therefore, an intervention, in the sense of being a plea for public subsidies, political in the sense of a call for a transformed society, though I suspect she would sign up to that, and her plays are designed to reach out beyond the moment in which they are set. As with her earlier two plays, her central concern is to inhabit the lives of those who find themselves victims of situations they do not control while refusing to accept the role of victim.

She is concerned to place at centre stage those seemingly relegated to the margins, to hear their voices, detect the poetry in their lives and language, to understand their resources, their sense of pride even in the face of forces which might be thought to undermine it. Though their situation may set them against one another, she is concerned to stage the human desire for connection, a selflessness at odds with a society seemingly based on the autonomous self. Of the trilogy, she explained, it was not 'about trying to have a historical agenda. What I am really writing about is people, and these people transcend their time period they're in; they even transcend region. I'm writing about humanity, and that's everybody's entry point into the plays.'[25]

Her characters are all working class and Black, and that fact is central. They do find themselves in a particular place, at a particular time, in particular circumstances, but the struggle to retain an inner integrity, to forge meaning in the face of adversity, to march to their own drummer while reaching out to others, extends beyond this moment. She was not interested in writing a pathology of Detroit, having been affronted at university by the vision people had of it. What interested her was the resources brought to bear by those whose daily lives were shaped by external circumstances but equally by their own personal commitments.

Skeleton Crew is a realistic play, except for the fact that she deploys an expressionist technique to summon up the world of work which itself both determines and reflects the sensibilities of her characters. Once again, music does much the same, resonating with their social and personal situations.

The most accomplished of the trilogy, *Skeleton Crew* opened at the Atlantic Theater Company in January 2016, and finally provoked a positive review from *The New York Times*, Ben Brantley hailing a 'very fine' play, 'warm-blooded, astute … a deeply moral and deeply American play', in the tradition of Arthur Miller.[26] It went on to be one of the most popular plays performed around the country and in 2022 reached Broadway (receiving another enthusiastic review from the *New York Times*) in a season in which, uniquely, seven plays by Black writers were scheduled. She has confessed that it might not be the last play in the sequence.

Between the production of *Detroit '67* in 2013 and *Paradise Blue* in 2015, she worked on another play, commissioned by Penn States School of Theatre where she had a residency, a work developed with student actors in which she responded to a public event in which race became a central issue, but which resulted in conflicting accounts, in trials and public demonstrations. Jena, named for the place in Germany where Napoleon won a victory, is a small, very small, town in Louisiana (population just over 3000). The slogan with which it greets people is 'Jena: A Nice Place to Call Home'. Its high school slogan is: 'Giants in Academics, Character and Athletics'. In December 2006, there were those who doubted both claims. It has a newspaper with the somewhat perplexing title *The Jena Times Olla-Tullos-Urania-Signal*, these, however, being nearby towns, thus justifying a newspaper. This would be the first to carry news of the events which would eventually be reported nationally and internationally.

Jena is 87 per cent white. One of its first teachers had been a veteran of the Confederate army. The school is 90 per cent white, though in 2021 its principal was Black. In 2006, Black students tended to sit together while whites sat under a tree, known to some as the white tree. At an assembly a Black student asked if it was alright for Black students to sit under it. Told they could, he and others did so. The next day three rope nooses were discovered hanging from the tree. Were they hung there as a deliberate reminder of lynchings, or was this a student prank? There were, however, other incidents, fights, confrontations. On 4 December, six Black students attacked a seventeen-year-old white Jena High School student, Justin Barker, beating him unconscious. Was this, as they later claimed, because of the nooses hung from the tree? What followed were trials, the initial charges reduced to simple battery. A campaign on their behalf was waged, a protest march bringing some five or six times Jena's population to the town, including Al Sharpton, Jesse Jackson and the rapper Ice Cube. Eventually a civil suit was filed and a settlement against the six agreed.

This was the event which Morisseau decided to dramatize. *Blood at the Root*, whose title derives from Billie Holiday's 1937 song, 'Strange Fruit', was written quickly. The idea of responding to events in the news by 'using them in the poetry of the piece' had occurred to her earlier when she was working for the educational theatre company Creative Arts at City University of New York. One of the things which attracted her to the case was that she was struck by the fact that the young people involved showed 'their lack of sensitivity around things like nooses and the lack of exposure to the history of racism. I felt they had been failed and I wanted to put the power back in their hands.'[27]

In her author's notes, she explains that the play is built on the idea of 'devised production', by which she means that the work on the page is really a starting point, and that the ensemble is intended, along with the director, to put its own signature on the work. She offers the example of the tree which could be built out of the bodies of the actors while an actor might deploy dance in a work which should be 'Hip-Hop inspired'. Also important was that the 'language of this play should drive. There is a rhythm to it that flows and moves as poetry.'[28]

It could have been a documentary play, restaging the events at Jena, here renamed. It could have been an agitprop drama, a rallying cry for the Jena 6. After all, she dedicates the play to 'the resilient young men who make up the Jena 6'. In fact, it is neither. *Blood at the Root* is not a protest play, except in the sense that it protests a lack of awareness by those involved. Half the principal characters are Black, half white. The school principal can be any race, as can the students.

Friendships cross racial barriers. The white Asha, herself raised in part by Sharon, a Black woman, when her own parents divorce, offers to support the Black Raylynn's campaign to be class president, a bid to break what had been accepted as no more than one of the unspoken rules of a school which becomes a microcosm of the wider society. After all, here, Black and white students separate at mealtimes. For the Black Justin, editor of the student paper, it is just the way things are, not wishing to engage with the issue, his assertion of the need for budding journalists to remain neutral an expression of his own unwillingness to commit. The white students are responsible for the nooses hung from a tree which they regard as their territory, while the Black students have attacked a white young man, Colin, who it seems is gay, they having exchanged insults. Where the scales are not balanced is the response of the authorities which seek to try the sixteen-year-old De' Andre, responsible for the attack, as an adult.

The characters are each given their own aria, explaining themselves. Thus, Asha declares that 'If actin' Black mean bein' like Sharon … Mean findin' family and love in places you wunn't expectin'. If it mean not being angry unless you got good reason … Then maybe we should all be "actin Black" mo' often.'[29] It is the white Colin, victim of an assault he may or may not have provoked, who is given a speech which most directly expresses Morisseau's feelings, not simply about this event in a small southern town, but more widely. Having watched a documentary on the Civil Rights movement, *Eyes on the Prize*, he says,

> 'Nice to know how thangs used to be and that thangs as they is now come from somethin'. It all got roots … It feel halfway comfortin' knowin' it ain't just start with us. That it been this way. That somebody's been plantin' these awful feelings in the soil somewhere … And it got me thinkin' … what kinda crop is the folks after us gonna dig up? Is it still gonna be from the same ol' soil? Or is we ever gonna plant somethin' new?'
>
> (37)

In *Blood at the Roots* there are solos, recitatives, contrapuntal dialogues, choruses, broken speeches, harmonies, discordances. Even De'Andre's ironic lament from his jail cell takes the form of Hip Hop, the other prisoners picking up the beat as he calls out,

> Nod to the officer, never get smart
> Hold back the defiance/ keep the rage in ya heart
> Don't matter you right
> Don't matter you true
> Black face/ male body / ain't gon' listen to you
> Don't matter you hurtin'
> Don't matter ya pain
> Black face/ male body / you always to blame.
>
> (73)

Yet it is a white woman, Toria, who in her soliloquy, explains that she descends from a long line of abolitionists, that her forebear had moved slaves north, that she comes from people 'that believe freedom doesn't happen by itself. Ain't just for one group. Can't be free if everybody around you is chained. If we don't know how to connect to a struggle besides our own, we're all screwed … everybody always got a part to play in whatever world they livin' in at the time. Every generation.' (74)

It is not so much that Morisseau is intent on balancing the scales but that she is suggesting there is greater complexity to lives than is allowed in the context of racial confrontations. The past shapes the present but the past is neither stable, being re-invented by each generation, nor always quite as it appears even as it holds the key to present attitudes and values.

The play ends as the students call for de'Andre's release and he is, indeed, released. Morissesau indicates that 'He embraces the freedom through movement in space. A celebration', even as Colin approaches Raylynn and the tree is now illuminated with a multitude of nooses, reminding us, Morisseau adds in a stage direction, '*of what can never be forgotten*'. (76) The final word is 'Tomorrow', even as the last thing illuminated is the nooses. What happened to the real De'Andre? He later confessed that he had struck the white victim and described Jena as a racist town.

To say that Morisseau is concerned with language is hardly to distinguish her from other playwrights except that in the context of race and, here she suggests, of sexuality, it has a distinct force. As she has observed, 'Language can be a tool of empowerment and a tool of oppression. Language is a weapon. We don't carry the same sensitivity around certain words that others do, so we can dismiss them and not care. Our great unifier is not only in our actions, but our language and how we use it with each other.'[30] In her case it is also in the rhythms of speech, the musical soundtrack which expresses the particularity of individual lives and the cultural resources on which her characters draw. It is not, though, that she writes to address an audience defined by race. As she explained, 'I don't write to exclude anyone. To write about a specific experience is not an exclusionary practice.'[31] Her approach to writing is dialectical, being anxious to allow space for contending points of view, for the debates which go on within the characters as well as between them.

It is tempting to feel that as a former teacher she is in the business of educating and has said that she would not be the writer she is had she not had that experience. Certainly, she chooses to explore what can seem a disregarded past, but what primarily concerns her is to invite audiences to inhabit the lives of those who find themselves at moments of crisis shaped by private and public forces alike. They often bear the scars of their own social and psychological experiences. If there is an underlying theme it has to do with love, in its contradictions, and with survival, which itself has a cost. Behind this, she is interested in power, in relationships no less than society. If there is a specific momentum it lies in the direction of redemption, itself not easily won.

Reviewing a Howard University production in 2017, John Stoltenberg, in *DC Metro Theatre Arts,* insisted that 'Dominique Morisseau's *Blood at the Root* is a breakthrough contribution to the conversation on race in America and a unique instance of how art can inspire young people to conscientious action against injustice.'[32] Mary Ann Johnson's review of the Theatre Alliance production, two years later, in *MD Theatre Guide,* could scarcely have been more positive:

> Every once in a while, a play comes along that is so electric and alive and thought-provoking and mesmerizing that you want to shout about it from the rooftops. This is one such play ... This is a show that uses the Jena, Louisiana, incident not to reconstruct what happened (accounts vary), but as a jumping off point to feel how explosive and divisive everything still is.[33]

Following *Skeleton* Crew, 2017 saw the premiere of a play, commissioned by Steppenwolf Theatre, in which she addressed education directly. Prompted in part by her reading of Michelle Alexander's *The New Jim Crow*, a book which examines the criminal justice system, she was struck by the degree to which some Black pupils are liable to go straight from school to prison, hence the title: *Pipeline*.

At its heart is Nya, a single mother, a teacher, committed to her pupils but struggling to hold things together, anxious, above all, to see her son, Omari, succeed, even willing to see him educated in a private school (something of a surprise to Morisseau who had originally been thinking of the public system). He is described as bright, tender, honest, but feeling rage without release. After all, who is he, coming from his particular background but finding himself remote from it? In the same school is his girlfriend Jasmine, who Morisseau suggests can be either Black or Latino and who resents being the only poor girl of colour in the school, convinced that she would have been better off if she had stayed in her own community. She and Omari have been sent there not simply because it is assumed the school offers a better education, but because of their parents' fear, the fear of what their fate might be if they were in the public school system. Omari's father, Xavier, successful, a marketing executive, struggles to relate to his son on an emotional level while alienated from his former wife.

The other characters are a white woman, Laurie, who teaches in a public school, holding her own but not secure from the violence which can break out in the class and beyond, and Dun, a Black school security guard, described as genuine and thoughtful.

As a teacher in several boroughs of New York, and having taught in both public and private schools, Morisseau was familiar with the world she dramatizes while her mother, to whom she dedicates the play, was a public school teacher. She summons up the sounds and sights of a school system in which teachers do their best to encourage students who carry tensions into the classroom having passed through metal detectors at the school gate in a building patrolled by security guards. Some, we learn, suffer from mental illnesses, others are on Ritalin. Cars have been stolen from the school's parking lot. She calls for camera phone video clips of school violence to play in the background.

The school where Nya teaches is not insulated from the community from which her pupils come, nor from the pressures they have inherited and encounter. Sudden anger explodes into petty violence even as they are inducted into literature, especially Gwendolyn Brooks's poem, 'We Real Cool', which in eight brief lines charts the decline from school to early death, an admonition, a lament. Nya points out that two different publishers, one white, one Black, present the poem differently, one seemingly inhabiting its meaning through its layout, the other choosing a conventional form. As Nya recites, so a distant Omari, isolated in his own light, echoes it, neither aware of the existence of the other. The fear is that he may enact its dark logic. As Jasmine remarks, they are at risk of becoming what others assume them to be.

Nya and her ex-husband, separated by much but united in their concern for their son, recognize his anger. Xavier insisted that he should go to a private school because it is where he imagines he will be insulated from danger and set on a path to success. Omari's anger, though, is something he carries with him. He finds it impossible to relate to his father, who pays his school fees, sends regular cheques, attends the requisite events but is not part of his emotional life. It is not that Xavier is trying to buy love but that he fails to recognize his son's need for an emotional connection. When Omari strikes a teacher, things come to a head. He explains that he had cracked when, the only Black boy in the class, he was asked about the motivations of Bigger Thomas, in Richard Wright's *Native Son*, a man who murders a white woman. It is not that the teacher fails to understand that there was a context for this act of violence, but that Omari interprets his being singled out as evidence of the role he is being asked to play. This may be the immediate reason for his attack (in fact a violent push); it is not its cause. What is, is no clearer to him than to his parents, who briefly come together to deal with the fallout from his action. Even his girlfriend, Jasmine, who offers love, fails to understand him. Deeply alarmed, Nya experiences a panic attack, no less susceptible to pressure than her son.

It is Dun who remarks that the rage and resentment which seem to fuel some of the pupils are a legacy of an uninspected past. Omari's problem, like Bigger Thomas's, is that he does not feel he belongs anywhere, that he lacks the space to be himself, free of the assumptions other people make of him, of an uninspected history. The rage he feels is not his in so far as it is a product of a world which seemingly offers him only the regression of Gwendolyn Brook's poem, the play ending, or nearly so, with images of young boys walking to school in handcuffs, playground fights breaking out, what Morisseau calls a collage of chaos, except that, as ever in her work, there is the suggestion of a possible redemption as Omari insists that he can do better and his mother grasps his face, Brooks's poem playing against his acknowledgement of his faults and desire for an acceptance of his imperfection.

There is guilt enough to share around. None of the characters feel fully in control, convinced that in some way they have failed others and themselves. A white teacher laments that she cannot connect to her Black students, losing control of the class and herself. Nya, a single mother, cannot protect her son, driven to a moment of panic. Her ex-husband is aware that his strategies have not worked. Omari knows the pain he has caused, while Jasmine's attempts to rescue him from himself fail. Personal guilt, however, exists in the context of a society which has laid down its seemingly inflexible rules when it comes to those struggling to define themselves, to lay claim to the freedom they seek.

Pipeline is not an indictment of the public school system, nor of the privilege to be purchased by private schooling. The alienation felt by the pupils, the struggles of parents to protect and encourage their children, of teachers trying to inculcate knowledge in the face of an incipient anarchy, go deeper than institutional challenges, her characters responding to pressures which exist beyond the school gates, beyond the moment.

Reviewing the Lincoln Centre production at the Mitzi E. Newhouse Theater in 2017, Ben Brantley praised what he saw as its emotionally immersive approach, while finding it frustratingly unresolved, its final note of possibilities less potent than what struck him as its despair. It is true that her plays do tend to offer a glimpse of hope even at a moment when that can seem eclipsed, as if she has contending impulses, determined to offer a clear-eyed insight into the way things are while committed to a belief in the way things could be. *Pipeline* ends on that knife edge.

Sometimes plays have a long gestation. This was particularly true of one from People's Light, one of Pennsylvania's largest non-profit theatres (340 seats in the larger of two stages) located in Malvern, West Chester, the county seat of Chester County. Chester County is 82 per cent white, 6 per cent Black, a mixture of extreme wealth and poverty. *Mud Row* was the result of New Play Frontiers, a project designed to explore aspects of identity based on stories from the immediate region. Playwrights were invited to engage with the local community and thereby to increase and diversify audiences. For some six years, Morisseau engaged with the locality, especially the Melton Center which offers low cost or free programmes, community activities of all kinds.

As she would say, 'It is always encouraging to be in the presence of the people who call the Melton Center home. Their hearts move with the passion of people who are excited about building up the next generation. Our conversations served as much background food for *Mud Row*.'[34] Nor was this remote from the world she had known back in Detroit. 'It was the pride of the people that reminded me of my hometown … Because our communities across the nation, and the diaspora, are not so disconnected. We are all in need of the same things – respect for the land that we built, and honoring the people that sacrificed for us to have a sense of home.'[35]

She explored the area, recalling how she had arrived at the title, and absorbed the stories told to her by those she met:

> I remember an area by a railroad ... sort of a swampy area, and I was told in passing, 'Oh yeah, they call that Mud Row.' That was my entry point. I've made a fictional story that's a fusion of my own family history and oral histories of what I heard from the people that live in West Chester. I imagined those grandchildren, these young people today, [who inherit] these homes. I thought about how African American communities are set up, how things are passed down, sustained, or deconstructed, or gentrified externally and internally. For me, now, this play has also become about family and what ties bind us, regardless.[36]

The play opened only a few miles from where it was set.

Morisseau's interest in the past is not simply sparked by a fascination with exploring the history of Black experiences, an antiquarian impulse. For Elsie, one of two sisters in *Mud Row*, 'we got to know how we got somewhere, so we know how to get somewhere else'.[37] For her, there is an organic social, political, personal connection between past and present. *Mud Row*, like the subsequent *Confederates*, is set in two different time periods, thus establishing an implicit dialogue between them. A favourite rubric for examination questions invites candidates to 'compare and contrast', and here alternating scenes bring the 1960s and the present into proximity, facilitating that process. Is the present an iteration of the past, underscoring a continuity of challenges, attitudes, values, assumptions, or does the emphasis lie on change, progress, transformations? How does the public world impact on the private? How far does the individual shape that public world? The action focuses on a house rather than a home, a house like that in Tennessee Williams's *A House Not Meant to Stand*, in a state of some dilapidation. For Williams it was a metaphor for his society; so it is for Morisseau, the roots of a tree growing into its foundations, the foundations of a family but also of a wider society.

It is a play which debates differing approaches to past and present, accommodation as opposed to resistance, the terms on which survival is to be achieved. The sisters who feature are in effect aspects of a divided self negotiating a path towards self-respect. The family is divided by time and attitude but held together, no matter how tenuously, by a love which exists to one side of a contested history. The house, which provides the setting, represents continuity even as it marks contestation. The question of who owns it, legally or morally, is also a question of who owns history. The social context changes, but the challenges remain as generations feel their way forward, conscious of the past, as of the need to transcend it. It is a play which acknowledges wrong paths taken, equally out of hope and despair, while staging acts of reconciliation. It asks what belonging and community might mean while a home is sometimes a place of love, sometimes of contention, a protection against the world beyond even as the world beyond invades its sanctuary. Alternating scenes echo alternating approaches not only over time but within the self as much as between those held together by affection but pulled apart by differing commitments and hopes, hope persisting.

Mud Row opened at People's Light in June 2019. It is set, as Elsie explains in a Prologue, in 'the Colored area ... east of the railroad tracks. By Goose Creek. Where all the sewage from the town flows. One of the filthiest creeks to flow near West Chester ... Coloreds bein' the mud of the world ... livin' in mud-like conditions ... would naturally be in Mud Row.' (8) She and her sister Frances, who she addresses, come to life as if stepping out of a picture, as in fact they step out of time, the 1960s. Elsie is described as 'Poised. Proper. Soft. Desperate to find a sense of belonging', as Frances is 'tough. Fighter. Persistent. Not easily contained, especially when they believe in something'. (5) Elsie aspires to moving up, invoking DuBois's talented tenth, her sister seeing activism as the route to change, the two united, though, in their relationship. In the age of civil rights protests, one sister steps out into the world, determined to effect changes, to engage. The other takes an inward path.

The scene ends as '*a flash happens! They are frozen in photograph – forever hugging*'. The action then springs forward in time, the house now seemingly some five years abandoned, with a clutter of furnishing, including a black-and-white television.

Regine, granddaughter of Elsie, and her husband Davin, enter. Having inherited it, she plans a sale. Her sister Toshi has other plans, squatting in it. She is a former drug addict, her boyfriend, Tyriek, a former thug, though 'looking for a second chance at life', (5) as is Toshi, straight for nine months or, as she insists, nine months and six days, they having stopped stealing credit card numbers and running e-mail scams. They detect that someone has been intruding on the house, unaware it is her sister, before the scene moves back to the 1960s, history being reanimated as Frances makes protest signs.

Elsie sees her relationship with a student as part of her desire to move up the social ladder, in the process becoming pregnant. Meanwhile, their secret is that their father deserted the family, and their mother was, in Frances's words, a whore, something Elsie conceals from the man she hopes will lift her into a different world, as she does the fact that her mother was burned to death by the Klan. Again, there is a flash as the scene changes, a flash which Morisseau describes as immortalizing them.

Regina and Davin now return discussing the value of what they have inherited. There is a tension between them, however, she echoing Elsie's concern with the elite, he being concerned that what they realize are squatters might be in need, part of a community with a history of struggle. He values the past; she looks to transcend it.

Back in time again, we see Frances in what is described as 'a historical moment', surrounded by hate signs ('Go home nigger'). There are sounds of a mob as Elsie addresses her unborn child insisting that she will be educated and respectable, severing a link to a dubious past even as the man responsible for her pregnancy has beaten her when she confessed to her family background, the fact that she had lied to him. For Frances, any child 'will either carry my fate or your frailty', insisting that 'I'll fight anybody tellin' us we ain't fit for more than the gutter. And now you gon' fight too. Like it or not, that's what we got in our blood.' (45) What they have in their blood is evident as, in the present, Toshi, Elsie's granddaughter, is prepared to fight for the house until she discovers that it is owned by her sister, capitulating, feeling that redemption is beyond her.

In a final scene, Frances explains her dedication to the cause and regret at her sister's decision to opt for an insulated private life, privileging social status over engagement, as a flash '*immortalizes ELSIE in her wedding dress*' and '*FRANCES bandaged and ready for protest*'. The lights come up on Toshi and Regine '*as if they are watching their grandmother and great-aunt*'. (80) Regine, it turns out, has decided not to sell but to share, while Toshi and Tyriek are committed to contribute half to become part owners. As in the earlier period, sisterhood trumps other concerns, a house once again becoming a home. The stage is flooded with colours, spreading, a stage direction indicates, '*out into the world*'. (83)

The debate at the heart of the play is scarcely even-handed. In the 1960s, one sister plays her part in the civil rights movement, being beaten in the name of the cause, and hence validated by history. The other, who chooses upward mobility, lies to secure her hold on the world to which she aspires, and is beaten by the man she marries, a marriage, into a resentful family, which is occasioned not by love but pregnancy. There would seem to be no doubt which one chooses the right path to follow. To balance the scales, in the present the upwardly mobile sister is able to gift her sister the chance for a new start, supported by her liberal husband. But it is the other sister, this time not an activist but a product of wrong choices, whose transformation lies at the heart of the play's celebratory ending, an ending marked by the synaesthesia deployed throughout, colours being invoked and displayed reflecting the mood, psychology, feelings of characters who carry a symbolic role.

Writing in the *Philadelphia* Enquirer, Cameron Kelsall, commented on the 'care, humor, and deep emotional connection' Morisseau brought to 'her portrait of life in the historically black enclave of Chester', finding that she 'gives exquisite voice to four women occupying the same four walls – and in doing so, an entire community sings'.[38] Its run was extended.

In the American Civil War, both sides relied on spies. The northern operation was run, for some time, by the Pinkerton Agency. Initially, Thomas Jordan, a veteran of the Mexican American war, recruited Rose O'Neal Greenhow, a white woman and member of the Washington elite, to spy for the Confederacy, providing key information about the forthcoming battle at Manassas. She was not the only white woman to serve the Confederacy in this way. The South, however, was not alone in using women as agents, Elizabeth Van Lew being among them. But there was another resource, escaped slaves and those who would masquerade as slaves to provide what became known as Black Dispatches. One such was Mary Elizabeth Bowser who was placed into Jefferson Davis's household. Invisibility, Southern assumptions about the incapacity of slaves, or those who presented themselves as such, became a weapon. That invisibility, however, extends to what we know of the role of such people.

Morisseau was approached by Oregon Shakespeare Festival's American Revolutions: the United States History Cycle, along with Penumbra Theatre, to write about the role of African Americans in the Civil War. It was part of their Archive Project. The project had been inspired by an article in *Atlantic Monthly* by Ta-Nehisi Coates entitled 'Why Do Few Blacks Study the Civil War?' It was a commission she happily accepted, asking,

> Why don't we know more about our own hand in our own liberation … and where is the vision of me in that moment? … When I think of the Civil War … black women are utterly invisible … in the documenting of those histories. Where were we? … I started to want to know what black women's role was in our own liberation … Abolition is given more to the hands of white abolitionists than it is to black liberation freedom fighters who were architects of their own movement, [and] where is the vision of me in that moment? … That is not just through Harriet Tubman and Sojourner Truth. There were so many black women who were rebels … There were many unnamed rebels.

Confederates, then, was not only to focus on a Black woman spy but precisely to ask 'where is the vision of me in that moment?' It was a question which led her once again to explore the connection between the past and present. As she explained,

> I wanted to tell the story about two women, one an enslaved rebel ... who was becoming a Union spy and fighting her way to freedom. And then another one, a black woman professor in a contemporary university who is also navigating her space in an institution of higher learning in search of her own liberation ... As the play goes on, the line gets really thin between the past and the present.

It is not just a question of recuperating a lost past, of identifying, or even just exploring, what the present owes to the past, though an acknowledgement of that is part of the thrust of the play, but of tracing commonalities. Again, as she has said,

> there is a strong connective tissue between Sandra and Sara ... how they relate to their own bodies, as women ... they both have something that causes them to have a complicated relationship to their bodies, as black women. They take that into everything that has defined them in their different worlds, and how they proceed, how they are trusted and how they can trust others ... how they are perceived by others, how much people do or do not ... project on them.[39]

Sara is a female slave, Sandra professor at a largely white private university. Their status, condition, possibilities, could not be more different, even as, in their different ways, they struggle to write their own stories. Both have to negotiate their roles in a world in which others have the power to define reality, project a master story, incorporate them in myths at odds to their own necessities. There is obviously a radical difference between the circumstances of the two women. As Morisseau has said, 'Getting free in the past, it's just getting free ... Like, you're actually in bondage.' Getting free in the present is a very different thing, even as they are 'united in the history of black women fighting for freedom. They're united in being the most socially expendable.'

> The kind of racism that Sara experiences – you could be hanged, you could be dragged, you could be murdered – that overt racism is not most people's experience of racism. There is the kind of racism that breaks the body, that attacks the body. Then there's the other kind that kills the spirit. The one I engage with most often is the latter. But the micro always leads to the macro. Microaggressions lead into aggressive actions.

The question is 'What does freedom look like now?'[40] The title is not only a reference back to the Civil War but to what makes the two characters confederate.

It is a play which deals with race, gender, class. She is, as she has said, interested in the extent to which, and the ways in which, her characters are architects of their own freedom, even as an awareness of the past is implicated in current experiences. One of the ways in which she underscores that link between then and now is requiring the cast to double up, the two principals aside. Six roles are played by three actors, shifting through time, raising the question of what has changed and what has remained essentially the same. This is further facilitated by alternating scenes from the past and the present, precisely the dialogue between the two periods which had fired her imagination and which she had used in *Mud Row*. Originally scheduled for 2020, it was delayed by Covid, and then delayed again, finally produced at the Signature Theatre in New York in March 2022, while scheduled for Oregon the following fall.

For those who wondered at the speed at which she produced plays, she replied, 'My job as an artist is to just be prolific. I always say I have a running queue of things I want to do, and I haven't got to half of them', quoting the advice of Chadwick Boseman, 'Dominque, you always gotta have nine irons in the fire.'[41]

Outside of theatre, she found herself part of the writers' room for the top-rated *Shameless*, an adaptation of the British show written by Paul Abbott, a comedy, satire, about a dysfunctional family. It took her some time to adjust. Television was an alien world, as were the characters who formed the basis of the family. She was the only person of colour in the room. Her first instinct was to walk away but by her third season felt a genuine part of a group she respected. Within the theatre, she wrote the book for *Ain't Too Proud*, the musical based on The Temptations, drawn to it both by the fact that they came from her home city and because, 'In addition to loving their music, I love their incredible human story that is not just about brothers trying to make their dreams come true, but a young group of Black men trying to become artists at a time when the country didn't even respect their human rights.'[42]

A poet, an actress, a playwright, somehow those are not separate talents. Her work is infused with poetry, a sense of the rhythms of speech, a lyricism rooted in the lives of her characters, music being laced through her plays, sometimes foregrounded, sometimes commenting on the action, sometimes prompting subconscious associations. As a writer, she regards herself as an activist, with respect to her own work, and its production, to the structure and practices of the American theatre and, beyond that, her society, feeling that the imagination is not only a route to transformation, but itself an agent of transformation.

When, in 2018, she received a MacArthur Fellowship she joined, among other fellow playwrights, Samuel D. Hunter and Annie Baker. Popularly known as Genius Grants, these are designed to recognize 'extraordinary originality'. Besides winning a Steinberg Playwright Award, an Edward M. Kennedy Prize for *Detroit '67*, and an Obie for *Skeleton Crew*, unsurprisingly, she has also won a Spirit of Detroit Award.

CHAPTER 7
ANNA ZIEGLER: TIME PASSING

Most stories are made up. And we make up stories to … help us understand our lives and what we're doing here. And to provide us with comfort and the feeling of being less alone. Anna Ziegler, *The Great Moment*.

Our perception of time changes our experience of time, changes *time* maybe. We have to believe this. That what we experience is, to some degree, what is. And so the experience of time speeding up is real. *The Great Moment*.[1]

Anna Ziegler went to the exclusive St. Ann's school in Brooklyn for twelve years, ranked by the *New York Observer* as the leading high school in New York. An independent, non-sectarian school 'for gifted children', it claims to be free of what it describes as 'the encumbrances of formal grading', dedicated instead to 'each individual's agency in determining who they are and what categories or labels, if any, they choose for themselves'.[2] Individuals seeking to define who they are and what labels they choose for themselves would become a central feature of many Ziegler characters.

St. Ann's, with a particular emphasis on the arts, faculty themselves often being writers or artists, helped shape her. Its founding headmaster (a man for whom the word 'inappropriate' seemed disturbingly appropriate, given his attitude towards language and sex), in a school originally created by an Anglican church, and who retired in 2004, was fond of claiming that he planned to turn out 10 per cent of the nation's poets. By general agreement his behaviour was often outrageous, but he mandated the freedom pupils were granted.

At St. Ann's, Ziegler was taught by Beth Bosworth, herself a graduate of NYU's School of Arts and Science. From her, she learned that she did not have to follow rules, essentially the philosophy of the school whose alumni include fellow writers Lena Dunham and Lynn Nottage, neither of whom could be said to have followed the rules. It was at school that she took a class on playwriting, presenting her one-act play, *An Off Night*, at the end-of-year festival. Subsequently, in her sophomore year at Yale, she took a course with Donald Margulies and another with Arthur Kopit.

When she was a senior in college, she applied to Arthur Kopit's playwriting workshop at Yale, but instead of submitting a play applied with a poem. She was accepted and, with Kopit's help and mentorship, joined the new Lark Playwrights Workshop in New York City (of which he was cochair) in the summer of 2001. Here she wrote her first full-length play. She later matriculated at NYU, where Kopit also taught, in its Dramatic Writing MFA programme. In the process, she transitioned from poet to playwright though, as with Dominique Morissau who followed a similar path, her drama would at times reflect her earlier commitment to the poetic.

Anna Ziegler is Jewish, and though many of the characters in her plays are themselves Jewish that fact is not always germane. She is interested in identity, but rather than exploring identity politics is concerned with the construction of the self, those whose lives never quite render up a clear meaning. And that frequently leads her to question the role of parents in shaping their children, and to question how children, in turn, impact their parents. This imbues time with a central significance. There is often an awareness of death in her plays, a destination which can either render life absurd or make inhabiting the present a necessity. She is drawn to final moments of reconciliation, redemption, even as she feels obliged to acknowledge the gravitational pull of entropy, as if she were debating with herself, her plays offering a dialectical field, their completions not entirely free of ambiguity. Many of her characters are thus conscious of the depredations of time, the unstoppable momentum which can breed a sense of purposelessness, even as the impulse to resolve is more than a fragile hope.

She sometimes takes public events as her subject, but not simply to restage them as if she were primarily interested in documentary theatre, instead looking beyond the moment, acknowledging the complexity of human responses. Arthur Miller called his autobiography *Timebends* because in it he shuttled between past and present, as Willy Loman does in *Death of a Salesman*. Ziegler does much the same in her work, frequently making it both a structural device and an assertion of causality, a generational pressure, memory unlocking truths even as they are contested.

Her plays are built around dialogues which are internal as well as external, audiences frequently acknowledged as if invited to adjudicate, to hear confessions, offer or withhold absolution. Some critics were concerned at what they took to be the neatness involved in the architecture of her work, loose ends seemingly tied up, discordant rhythms resolved, except that there is often a sense of an unexamined future beyond the fall of the curtain, in which such reassurances may prove unsustainable. There are betrayals in her plays, misunderstandings, gestures of love which console or frustrate. A former teacher, she has staged the lives of teenagers struggling to navigate their way through an uncertain life, existing in some no man's land between the assurance of childhood and the pressures of an adult world whose tensions they often observe if not fully understand, not least because age is seldom seen as bringing wisdom in private lives which exist to one side of public selves.

Whatever the circumstances of her characters, though – and her plays are varied, as are those characters – what she finds compelling are their struggles to make sense of things, whether it is a scientist trying to read the hidden code of existence itself, or people struggling to read unreadable relationships not least because who they are is in some degree a product of these relationships as well as of an arbitrariness with which they try to come to terms.

There is a humour to her work, which is also a value in so far as it implies characters not wholly in thrall to the circumstances in which they find themselves, though this can darken to irony, consciously deployed by characters, or structured into existence. Unsurprisingly, for a writer who began as a poet, there are also moments of lyricism which suggests the degree to which they can step outside the prose of the quotidian. Like most contemporary American playwrights, she has developed her plays over time, with the help of various organizations, and initially saw them open in small venues.

Soho Rep is a 65-seat theatre on Walker Street, New York, an organization with a record of assisting in the development of plays by new writers, including Young Jean Lee and Lucas Hnath. It was to this theatre that a new playwright, then twenty-five, raised in Brooklyn, turned for assistance in nurturing a play, a process which continued at the Sundance Theatre Lab. The playwright was Anna Ziegler; the play, *BFF (for Best Friends Forever)*. It would go on to have its premiere in 2007 at The DR2 Theatre in New York (named for Daryl Roth, a producer and investor), a 99-seat theatre in Union Square. It was a play which introduced some of the techniques and concerns she would deploy in her later work.

BFF takes place in 1991 and 2005 in Upstate New York and then New York City. At its heart are Eliza and Lauren, seen first, at the age of twelve, imagining their future. When Lauren says she has the 'feeling that everything happens at once ... That we're already grown up and walking around somewhere,'[3] the action jumps forward into that future, one not entirely remote from that projected by the young Lauren as we are introduced to a third character, Seth. And this would be a marker of her later plays as time shifts both disorient audiences and generate their own ironies.

The play's title derives from the pledge of Eliza and Lauren that they will always remain best friends, living alongside one another, relying on one another, not realizing that their teenage years will bring pressures that could tear them apart. Already, though, a gap has begun to open. Eliza's father has died and when she asks, 'do you ever feel like the hardest thing in the world is just waking up', (11) something intrudes into their otherwise vacuous chatter. Later, she confesses that 'when I'm alone it feels like there's no one else and there's nothing to come', (19) asking Lauren to confirm that she feels the same way, only for her to confess that she has no such anxieties.

Time, though, is not stable, as the action switches back to 1991. For Eliza, it is 'like we're outside of time ... Like this could be 1891 or 1691 and we have no idea what's coming next even though it's all bound to happen', (14) while in a sense she is frozen in time. Lauren has her first period, wants to wear a bra, to be moving on, even as Eliza learns from her mother the virtue of the status quo, the death of her father underscoring what can be lost with change. Lauren is interested in boys, Eliza told by her mother that such thoughts are premature. Lauren loves swimming, diving deep, feeling 'like time isn't passing', (22) even as out of the water she embraces time. Eliza prefers the shallows, resisting time's momentum. According to Lauren, though, her fear of water was a result of nearly drowning as a baby.

In the future they had imagined, Lauren meets Seth whose own father has died, something that he says has not affected him but to which, nonetheless, he returns, one time echoing inside another. He, too, explains that he looks for ways to escape time. Just as Eliza slowly seems to be under psychological pressure, so Seth, in therapy, confesses that 'I'm a worrier ... I've learned to stop writing out conversations though and focus on topics, ad lib from there.' (17) When he says, 'I like to think the kid I was still creeps in sometimes ... I daydream, pretend I'm a kid again', (21–2) it underscores a question implicit in the play, how far the past invades the present, the possibility (or impossibility) of a continuous self. There are echoes down the corridors of time. In one scene the young Lauren despairs because a boy has not called her back. In another, Seth is anxious when Lauren fails to call him. As a teen Lauren says to Eliza that she wants some time alone, as she later tells Seth, 'I want to be alone'. (27)

If Seth seems to share things with Eliza, Lauren begins to behave like her. She even assumes Eliza's name, the Eliza, we discover, who died of anorexia and for whom Lauren assumes she must have been responsible, hence keeping her alive by becoming her, at the same time unable to stay with Seth afraid that she might be responsible for his fate too. She carries Eliza with her because she feels her death was her fault, the best of friends proving anything but, she having abandoned the one person she swore never to betray, leaving her in her wake as she moved on to others.

As Lauren says, young girls can be cruel to one another, switching loyalties, so wrapped up in their own lives that they fail to notice other people's pain. In *BFF* that would seem to be no less true of those for whom life continues. All the characters are treading the edge, unsure of who they are, seeking confirmation from those who are themselves adjusting to loss, trying to understand feelings which can overwhelm. 'What do you think it'll be like to be grown up?' asks the young Lauren, 'do you think it will feel different than this?' (7) sensing that 'the years are gonna pass so quickly', even as she feels that 'everything happens at once … That we're already grown up and walking around somewhere and doing some job and we just don't know it.' (7)

BFF is a play which explores cruelty and compassion, hopes and disillusionments, the struggle by the individual to locate herself or himself against the onward rush of time. It is by turns lyrical and brutally direct. It is not without its contrivances, but, in the end, these seem to work, the most challenging being Lauren's taking on the name of her onetime friend as if thereby she can deny her death.

The New York Times was less than welcoming. For Anne Midgette, better known as a music critic, it 'just feels juvenile', straining credulity 'right from the first scene'. The language is 'of adult nostalgia', while the characters are 'set in motion more according to a psychological textbook than psychological credibility'.[4] Mark Blankenship, in *Variety*, found it a mixed bag, while noting that 'Anna Ziegler crafts several moments that exquisitely reveal the love and resentment between two best friends' adding that 'the elegance of individual scenes gets dulled by a structure dependent on flimsy tricks and dubious conclusions'.[5] Other responses were more positive, including the *New Yorker* whose reviewer found it an unmitigated pleasure.

For those intrigued by *BFF*, audiences had to wait less than a week for her next play, *Life Science*, which opened at the black box, sixty-seat, *Theatre 54* on West 54th Street. Once again, she writes about teenagers, this time a group of seventeen-year-olds, seniors in high school getting ready for college, one an Asian Jew, the rest white and Jewish. The action ranges from October 2006 to June 2007, three months after the play itself opened.

There are echoes of *BFF* in that these are characters struggling to understand who they are and how they relate to others and the world. For Dana, described as an alpha girl, outwardly confident, *Othello* is about identity, Iago trying to work out who he is, as *To the Lighthouse* is about 'Memory. How fast life goes. How sad and pointless it is'.[6] Leah, 'talkative, high-strung', also feels that 'life is going so fast'. (46) Again, as in *BFF* they contemplate their future, whether they will become what their parents are, while their shifting alliances in the present command much of their attention, petty jealousies, and insecurities assuming a disproportionate importance.

In many ways it is a comedy as they give equal weight to sexual relationships, less spontaneous than vaguely obligatory, and to geopolitics. Leah, whose parents argue over the fate of Israel, returns from a visit to Auschwitz with a desire not to be Jewish, even as she talks about a religious war which will leave her a new Anne Frank, holed up in an attic. Dana sees a television report of a Lebanese boy, Abdul, just five years younger than herself, who has lost his parents in an Israeli air raid, and decides to adopt him, bizarrely supported in this by her rich parents. Indeed, in some senses they are all insulated by their parents' wealth, coming from a world of investment bankers and plastic surgeons while planning their routes to ivy league colleges. They are playing at life as if these were games with no consequence, except that there is an undertow.

Mike, who we are told is smarter than he thinks he is, is afraid that when he gets to college 'I won't be "me" anymore', (40) as Leah confesses 'I'm not sure who I am and what I'm meant to do.' (43). In a television interview about her planned adoption of Abdul, Dana slowly falls apart, talking instead about her relationship to Mike suddenly confessing that Abdul will know 'how lonely I am, and how much I want to feel important in some small way', (44) even as in a letter Abdul explains that he is broken, missing his parents.

At the time she wrote the play, Ziegler was herself teaching at high school, hence, no doubt, not only her ear for the language of those she taught but also her decision to incorporate text messages which she indicated should be projected. The play is set in Bethesda, Maryland, known for its wealth, a place which took its name, ultimately, from the Bethesda pool in Jerusalem and, as noted, the characters are all Jewish though the degree to which that impinges on them varies. For Leah it generates a sense of precariousness, for Dana, guilt. For the others, it barely registers, beyond a sense of unease about identity. *Life Science* is not a major work. It does, however, demonstrate not just her facility with language, her fascination with the emotional pressures generated out of daily life, but also her concern with the struggle of her characters to make sense of themselves in a changing world and as they themselves change.

Ziegler grew up in a Reform Jewish home, visiting the theatre and, at school, writing poetry though, as she has noted, with a strong narrative element and full of dialogue. For a while she taught English at a Jewish school in Maryland where a colleague, a Muslim, found herself being questioned about his faith. If religion had in some sense been marginal to *BFF*, it is central to *Dov and Ali*, set not in Maryland but Detroit. Its first performance was in June 2008 at the 63-seat Theatre 503 in London, a home for new writing, a year later opening at Off Broadway's The Playwrights Realm, which focuses on early career writers, and which would later stage *A Delicate Ship*.

The issue of whether to follow rules lies at the heart of a play which stages a debate between an Orthodox Jewish teacher, Dov, whose father is a rabbi, and his Muslim student, Ali, having his own dilemma being in love with a Christian woman. Meanwhile, Ali's sister, Sameh, claims a freedom which challenges his understanding of the requirements of a religion which is absolute in its demands for obedience. An epigraph to the published version quotes the first line of the Qur'an: 'This Book is not to be doubted.' Both religions are of the Book. The problem is that they are, in essence, different books and Ziegler's characters try to negotiate between the freedom they wish to claim and the authority they feel obliged to obey at a human cost.

Asked why she often writes about Jewish characters, she has said, 'It's a way for me to explore what I feel about Judaism and the complicated relationship I have to it – sort of desperately wanting to be part of a community but not wanting to be a minority. There's a tension there.'[7] It is a tension, in *Dov and Ali*, which is equally applicable to a Muslim. In both cases, however, there is another source of authority figure, their fathers, absolute in their views.

The play is opened by Sameh, wearing a hijab, who introduces 'a new story that's also thousands of years old', which includes 'a confused teacher' and 'a precocious student', whose fathers offer a love which is 'opaque, hard to measure'. It sounds benign enough as 'once upon a time, they were friends. Sort of',[8] but the reason she presents this story takes most of the play to explain, though she makes appearances, unseen by the others, which hint at what is to come. 'I don't have anyone to talk to anymore ... I cannot speak unless I'm spoken to. Just so you know, Ali.' (8)

Ali enters, wishing to discuss the book they have been studying in class, William Golding's *The Lord of the Flies*. At issue, it seems, is whether an individual's death is necessary for the survival of the group. For Ali, it was required because the paramount need is the unity of that group. For Dov, his teacher, all being of one mind is dangerous because it is dissenters who prove vital, the book not being 'a call to do away with certain elements of our society that interfere with some kind of purity of spirit'. (9). And there, it seems, is the debate, Dov having abandoned his PhD on Utopian societies in literature, plainly having doubts about the particular society from which he comes, with its complex and often baffling edicts which he is inclined to breach. Some rules, though, it turns out, will prove inflexible, dissent having its limits, certainly when it comes to marrying a non-Jew. For Ali, 'Don't all Jews ask ... "Who am I?" "Why am I here?" "What am I meant to do?"'(9) while for Dov, that is a mark of everyone. Not so, Ali declares. His religion offers certainty. 'There has to be a rule book', (10) except why does he approach his teacher if he is certain? Once again, Sameh steps forward, unseen, explaining to the audience that she does so because 'she is tormented by events he can't speak of and doesn't understand'. (10) We have plainly not entered a story at its beginning.

Dov's other reason for abandoning his PhD is that, in love with the Christian Sonia, his observances of the customs, traditions, requirements of his faith are not what they were. For her, there are no rules, a cue for the reappearance of Sameh who declares that she has fallen in love with someone who does not believe in the Qur'an, and is an independent thinker, which her brother Ali translates as faithless. She declares that she has become a character in someone else's story, no longer free, subject to rituals, required to obey. She plainly speaks from another time, after an event yet to be revealed, her appearances, intrusions into an earlier time, suggesting a fundamental disruption of her life.

As the pressures build, both men break, bowing to fathers who represent a more fundamental authority. Dov cannot bring himself to admit he may be marrying outside the faith, while Ali commits an act of betrayal which he believes to be an act of obedience. Dov walks away from the woman he loves, while Ali informs on his sister leading her to be sent to Pakistan to be married to an older man and live her life at a remove, forced to submit where once she had rebelled. It is not only Jews who ask 'Who am I? Why am I here? What am I meant to do?' Sameh's cry of 'Be your own man' (30) finds no echo in Ali, who is nonetheless distraught at what he has done. As for Sameh, she now speaks of herself in the third person.

Only Dov feels his way towards redemption, asking himself 'who else am I if not *this* man, *this* person who's been brought up *this* way?' (47) only to call the woman he had abandoned now ready to break the rules, both he and Ali also breaking with the fathers who represent the power of the past to define present and future, who coerced their sons into believing obedience a path to salvation. It is possible, it seems, that Ali's break with his father may signify a more profound renunciation, except that he carries a burden, his sister paying the price for his own moral education.

The *British Theatre Guide*, responding to Theatre 503 production, found it an 'incredibly moving play that challenges notions of freedom, expectations and ultimately forgiveness'.[9] For Lyn Gardner, in *The Guardian*, while perhaps 'mapped out too carefully', it was 'an intense, intelligent and hugely promising play that plays out clashes of belief systems in the classroom'.[10] Responding to the New York production, Ken Jaworowski, while curiously objecting to the fact that 'the characters speak in precise sentences', the fact that 'their arguments are soundly constructed, their entrances and exits … impeccably timed' seeing this as offering figures who spout 'partisan viewpoints', concluded by noting that in 'a time of ceaseless snark and cynicism, its earnestness in asking bigger questions can be downright refreshing'.[11]

Variety offered a somewhat curious response: 'Watching "Dov and Ali" is a little like talking politics with a person who raises the subject but is too timid to have opinions. Playwright Anna Ziegler seems to believe it would be rude to come to any conclusions about Jewish/Muslim relations, the fundamentalist elements in either culture, or anyone's religious convictions.'[12] It was a tough ask and surely irrelevant to a play not concerned to arrive at conclusions but to stage the consequences of the struggle to find room for human feelings within the rigid confines of tradition and family edicts, to define oneself in ways not determined by history or religions for which the subordination of such feelings is regarded as evidence of faith.

In 2013, as part of a literary festival at the University of East Anglia, where, incidentally, Ziegler had won her MA in poetry, I brought together the Nobel Prize winner Sir Paul Nurse, and the Booker Prize winner Ian McEwan, to discuss science and literature, where they overlap, where they diverge. For Nurse,

> although we often separate science and the humanities, the intellectual processes involved are much more similar than perhaps we think … One thing that does interest me greatly is creativity and how that is common to the arts and to science … There is a period of time in a scientific enquiry when you really have no idea where things are going. You make some observations, you get some data, you get a bit of experimental evidence, and you have some sort of idea. Then you start walking in the fog … what you are doing is trying to imagine what would actually work … You have to imagine this, or you imagine that, and to get that to work you have to put different things together.[13]

For McEwan, 'novels track human fates through time and generally human fates through time come unstuck in some interesting ways. We have always been interested in conflict, misunderstandings, the misreading of each other, sometimes leading to reconciliations but sometimes not.' A link with science lies in 'the impulse to draw things together' that you thought did not belong together, that moment of surprise when you think "oh that actually belongs here with this" and as soon as it comes together several other moments of freedom are realised.'[14] A distinction, however, it seemed to him, lay in the fact that scientists 'are dogged by this terrible issue of originality and priority which we don't have in quite the same way. One thinks of Einstein racing to get to his general relativity with David Hilbert at his back or Darwin on that awful day when he received that twenty-page letter from Wallace.'

What mattered to Nurse was that

> I think a problem we sometimes have in conveying science is that we rush to the conclusion while what is interesting in science is the journey to that conclusion. What we don't tend to do in science is tell the stories of how you get there, which actually gets you into a much more human frame of mind. If you just focus on the outcome the individual never matters. We just don't tell those stories well enough … You could describe a novel in terms of reaching a conclusion but that is not the reason you would take that journey to read it.[15]

Unsurprisingly, the names of Crick and Watson came up in the context of what can be the competitive world of science, and their story is a familiar one as, belatedly, is that of Rosalind Franklin, whose role in the discovery of the DNA molecule was forgotten for many years. It was a story, though, which Anna Ziegler was prompted to tell when she was asked to write a play about three scientists (the others being Rachel Carson and Roger Young) by a small theatre company outside of Washington, DC. In the end, Franklin elbowed out the other two, as, in the real world, she herself would be as she failed to receive the recognition which went to others.

Acknowledging the fact that Franklin's story was, as Ziegler has said, inherently dramatic, what interested her was the character of a woman who not only had to fight for space to conduct her research, but for respect, a character with her own emotional limitations. It was a play originally commissioned and produced by Maryland's Active Cultures, opening in 2008, its director noting the number of scientists who came to see it. Two years later it was staged at the Ensemble Studio Theatre in New York's Hell's Kitchen, a theatre with a reputation for presenting the work of new writers, as part of the Alfred P. Sloan Foundation Science & Technology Project (apt for a play about scientists). Somewhat to Ziegler's surprise, given its humble beginnings, in 2015 the play was not only staged in London's Noel Coward Theatre, in the West End (London being a familiar enough location for many American playwrights early in their careers), but with Nicole Kidman in the principal part. It won the WhatsOnStage Award for the best new play.

Photograph 51 was not designed as a protest against the failure of Franklin to be awarded the Nobel Prize along with Crick and Watson. As she points out, she would not have qualified for it since the prize cannot be awarded posthumously. Franklin died some years before the award was given to two men whose achievement Ziegler was not concerned to challenge. What interested her was the character of a woman who did indeed play a significant part.

In *Hapgood*, Tom Stoppard had seen quantum mechanics as in some way reflecting the tensions between a public self and what he called a submerged self. In *Photograph 51* the double helix of DNA plays a similar metaphoric role. In Michael Frayn's *Copenhagen* the uncertainty theory itself becomes a metaphor for the unknowable nature of an encounter. In the discussion between Nurse and McEwan, indeed, the latter remarked that *Copenhagen* 'has a wonderful enactment of a parallel set of possibilities through a conversation between Niels Bohr and Heisenberg'.[16] Another facet of that play, however, is the game it plays with time and Ziegler's play has an epigraph from *Run* by Ann Patchett: 'Certain things exist outside of time. It was ten years ago, it was this morning … It happened in the past and it was always happening. It happened every single minute of the day.' For McEwan, 'We live in middle earth, don't we? Between the very large and the very small. I notice that a theoretical physicist is now proposing that time is the most real thing in the universe, and it is space that is illusionary. That would be a relief for novelists because time is of the essence in the structure of a novel.'[17]

In *Photograph 51* time is collapsed in so far as different moments are brought together, partly narrated in retrospect when the events described lie in the past, and partly unfolding in a present tense, the present of the events but also a different present, that of the audiences who from time to time are addressed directly, here and elsewhere in her work Ziegler delighting in breaking the fourth wall. As she has said,

> I love to play with breaking the fourth wall, and hopefully surprising the audience with a perspective that they didn't see coming because they were seeing one version of a

character and then suddenly they're telling us about another version of themselves. I think we are all many versions of ourselves ... Maybe that is ultimately what I am trying to find: that truthful composite of all of the sides of ourselves.[18]

At one moment Rosalind recalls her childhood, when her interest in repeated patterns foreshadowed a career in which that would become both her method and the object of her enquiry, while at another she is engaging in a sometimes-rebarbative dialogue with colleagues, by preference being private, subsumed in her work at the price of human engagement. As a woman and a Jew, she is alert to slights. In the first scene, the various characters who will constitute the drama appear, already commenting on what will follow, and on one another, often with a Stoppardian humour. Wilkins, a colleague, is inclined towards jokes, Rosalind, irony.

Beyond that, Ziegler is also interested in Rosalind's slowing of time in her approach to research as compared to the speed with which Crick and Watson proceed. If there is a race it is not one which motivates her in the way it does those who would seize the prize. If there is a race it is with herself, and that has its own deliberative pace. Scientific advance itself, of course, depends on a slow, sometimes very slow, accumulation of data, of hypotheses to be proved or abandoned, followed by a sudden breakthrough. It is that breakthrough which garners attention while it is the process which exposes the character of those who follow an idea, sometimes at a price.

Another epigraph is from the historian of molecular biology Horace Judson's *The Eighth Day of Creation*:

> As scientists understand very well, personality has always been an inseparable part of their styles of inquiry and a potent, if unacknowledged, factor in their results. Indeed, no art or popular entertainment is so carefully built as is science upon the individual talents, preference and habits of its leaders.

So it proves in Ziegler's play as Rosalind travels from Paris to King's College, London, to work with the biophysicist Maurice Wilkins who was working on x-ray diffraction with a graduate student Raymond Gosling. He assumes she comes as his assistant while she insists it is to be his full partner, this a woman who had become a scientist in the face of her father's objections. She is not inclined to accept the way in which women had been excluded from scientific ventures, especially, she notes, work on the atomic bomb, even as she disapproves of it, something which irritates Wilkins who did work on it and suggests that Jews – and Rosalind, as noted, is Jewish – should be grateful. Women, she complains, are even excluded from the University's senior common room while she tends to be addressed as Miss while Wilkins insists he should be called doctor.

He, it turns out, is no less of an obsessive worker than she, with no wife or children to distract him. Beyond the project on which she and he work, however, is a love of theatre. Famously, F.R. Leavis and C.P. Snow had engaged in mutual insults over the ignorance of those in the arts of science, and those in science of the arts. It was always a curious debate. Ian McEwan took a course in quantum mechanics while the Nobel Prize-winner Harry Kroto remained committed to graphic design to the end of his life even as his award was for his discovery of buckminsterfullerene. He, too, was a lover of theatre. Carl Djerassi, father of the contraceptive pill, also wrote plays, *Oxygen* and *Calculus* dealing with the struggle for priority among scientists, as well as teaching a course on Science-in-Theatre.

In *Photograph 51*, Wilkins and Rosalind meet in their enthusiasm for *The Winter's Tale*, as it happens a play in which a central character is seemingly replicated as in their work they were concerned with the process of replication. Both their grandfathers had memorized Shakespeare's plays. Where they, and an American graduate student, Caspar, who goes on to work with them, also come together is in their sense that there is beauty in the photographic images central to their undertaking. Paul Nurse, while saying that data trumps even the most beautiful idea, added that beauty 'is to do with a putting together of things you haven't seen before and there is an aesthetic buzz about that which I can't quite explain'.[19] Caspar, looking at x-ray pictures, declares 'they're beautiful – these shapes within shapes, shapes overlapping, shapes that mean more than they seem at first glance, but are also beautiful simply for what they are'.[20]

It is tempting to think that Ziegler is not only talking about putting things together that you haven't seen before, which is the scientific procedure, but also about the fact that this is the basis of metaphor and the overlapping dramatic strategy she deploys, while the characters she presents themselves mean more than they seem at first glance. Taking herself off to the Swiss Alps, significantly on her own, Rosalind remarks that 'the Alps seem larger and yet somehow less overwhelming than they have in the past, as though their vastness was made for me, as though the more of something there is to climb, the further I'll get to go … The mountains mean more than they seem at first glance but are also beautiful simply for what they are.' (220)

It is in that sense that the play is not primarily about telling a familiar story but seeing beyond the surface of her characters as the x-ray photograph reveals what is not otherwise observable. 'Are you there?' asks Gosling, looking for her in the laboratory, even as that is a question with more profound implications when it comes to someone who is a stranger to herself emotionally. 'We're simply not aligned', she says to him, referring to a piece of equipment but equally to her relationship to him and, indeed, all those others on the same quest. When Caspar suggests they might become a couple, she is merely baffled by his approach. She is like Sofia Helin in the Danish television series, *The Bridge*, emotionally detached but rationally focussed. As a girl she had prided herself on always being right, yet there was a residual doubt instilled in her by her father which makes her hesitant to proceed until certain of her data, even as photograph 51, in a sequence of photographs, finally reveals what looks like a double helix. Crick and Watson have no such doubts, even as their first model is disastrous. She puts the photograph in a drawer, freezing time.

Rosalind, Crick, Watson and Wilkins can seem like versions of Rosencrantz and Guildenstern or Vladimir and Estragon, vaudevillians discussing the meaning of life. 'I'm starting to think that there might come a point in life after which one can't really begin again,' says Wilkins, only for Watson to reply, 'That's right. It's called birth.' (252) except that they have a single-minded desire to win, life itself seemingly a competition, though Crick asks 'what is a race anyway? And who wins? If life is the ultimate race to the finish line, then really we don't *want* to win it … Or maybe the race is for something else entirely. Maybe none of us really knew what we were searching for. What we wanted.' (243)

On the face of it, they all know their objective, except that there is a level on which Rosalind vaguely senses something she has been missing, private needs which have nothing to do with solving a scientific problem, a human contact which evades her. Asked out to dinner by Caspar, she replies that she doesn't have the time. When she accepts the invitation, he says 'I hope I didn't take up too much of your time' (263) only for her to confess that 'I'm not sure anymore how terribly valuable my time is … Or maybe I haven't been … allotting it to the right things.' (264) And all this even as time is running out for her, the race no one wants to win finally ended as she discovers she has twin tumours, an ironic comment on the double helix which is the secret of life, she now accepting the fact that 'We lose. In the end. We lose.' (270)

Photograph 51, ostensibly a familiar story about the pursuit of the secret of life, is also a contemplation of mortality, of battles fought along the way, struggles for primacy, in gender no less than scientific esteem. It looks back through the lens of time, and in doing so explores felt urgencies as well as the notion of time squandered. X-ray photographs, blurred at first, become steadily clearer as do characters who circle around one another as though they were mutual mysteries to be solved, the double spiral of the DNA molecule a metaphor no less than an emerging truth. As Paul Nurse observed, of Arthur Koestler, 'Koestler had this idea that creativity is putting together things that were different and he made that very nice analogy to humour because so much humour is actually putting things together that spark something off.'[21] Bringing together different disciplines was the key to solving the riddle of DNA but here Ziegler's bringing together of her different characters is not only what generates the drama but also the humour which equally characterizes her play.

Beyond that, she has said that 'I've found that I'm drawn to stories that culminate in a character's need for forgiveness. I'm drawn to stories about regret and about the fallibility of memory. I tend to write about people who are doing their best despite making mistakes – and all of that is true of *Photograph 51*.'[22] It is true that her characters are doing their best despite their mistakes. The need for forgiveness? Regret? Forgiven by whom? Crick and Watson seem immune to regret, or the need to seek forgiveness, though perhaps they have need to do so, ethical concerns being laid to one side given their drive to succeed and the worthiness of their objective. More interesting in this context, though, is Ziegler's version of Rosalind for whom regret has been held at bay until the end when she glimpses the possibility that she may have paid a price for her single-minded devotion to an idea of her destiny. As to memory, all her characters are recalling what they choose to, or, in truth, what Ziegler wishes them to.

Reviewing the 2010 Off Broadway production at the Ensemble Studio Theatre, Eric Grade, in *The New York Times*, found it intermittently pedantic but largely satisfying. Five years later, the London production provoked greater enthusiasm. For Michael Billington, his only regret was that the play, intriguing, informative, was not longer, while Charles Spencer, in *The Telegraph*, noted,

> Were the play … simply to assert that Franklin was robbed of the prestige that was rightly hers – Watson and Crick were credited as co-discoverers, and she died in 1958, four years before the pair (and Wilkins too) received the Nobel Prize – it would serve a valid but rather worthy purpose. It's much more fascinating than that, though. It deals with timely feminist issues but also the key fundamentals of how we relate to each other, who we are, our tragic flaws. It deals with timely feminist issues but also the key fundamentals of how we relate to each other, who we are, our tragic flaws … A triumph.[23]

Ben Brantley, in *The New York Times*, spent much of his time praising Nicole Kidman, whose father was a biochemist and who was raised in and around science labs, seeing her performance as close to perfection while regretting that the play lacked the teasing layers or depths of *Copenhagen*. Four years on, reviewing a Chicago production, Chris Jones, in the *Chicago Tribune*, found it a terrific play, 'never dull for a second' saying that 'If this were a movie, there would be Oscar chatter.'[24] In his annual roundup, he named it the number one play of the year.

The year 2012 saw San Francisco's Magic Theatre premiere *Another Way Home*, originally entitled *An Incident*, following development, over a period of two years, at the O'Neill Playwrights' Conference, the McCarter Theatre and the Chautauqua Theater Company. It was inspired, she has said, by teaching John Guare's *Six Degrees of Separation*, responding to its tone and style, though surely little else. The play had changed in the process of development, characters being added and removed. It had, she explained, originally centred on prejudice, class and race. Class remains, though not as a central issue as she focusses on an upper-middle-class Jewish family, and the relationship between the parents, Philip and Lillian, and their children, Joey and Nora.

Another Way Home turns around the parents' visit to see their son, Joey, who is in summer camp in Maine, a visit recalled after the events as Philip and Lillian address the audience. It is already apparent that their marriage is under stress, she, as she sees it, having made sacrifices, abandoning her photography. For his part, Philip is unhappy in work which is clearly at the price of family life. Somewhere along the way they seem to have lost one another even as there are moments when they make momentary contact.

Joseph, who prefers the name Joey, is not easy having at various times been diagnosed with ADD, ADHD, autism and depression, while taking drugs such as Ritalin and Lexapro. Lillian has written to him daily, indicative of her concern and anxiety, except that he has never replied. Clearly, communication is not easy, neither parent quite knowing the language to use. Even as they try to talk to him, they themselves cannot stop bickering. Joey stands in contrast, in their minds, to their daughter Nora, a high achiever who attempts contact with her brother only to be rebuffed.

Joey's camp counsellor, Mike, who majors in drama at Vassar, is staging a production of Tom Stoppard's *Coast of Utopia*, abridged he points out, as well he might given that that play is a trilogy nine hours long. He seems assured beside Joey, except we learn that he had been raised by his grandmother, his parents an absence which he cannot address and will not admit to. There is, it seems, a current flowing in people's lives, invisible to the eye. His interest in acting, Joey suggests, is because it is about lying.

The play takes a different turn when Joey disappears and his parents, along with the rest of the camp, search for him through the night. Jolted out of his complacency, Philip 'realized I'd been alive fifty-eight years ... and I had no idea where they went. I had a wife and two children and an apartment and a decent job, and I was hardly a part of any of it. It was one of those realizations. I was fifty-eight years old.'[25] 'Life passes by in an instant and that scares the shit out of me ... all I can think about is all the time that's been lost, all this time we can't get back when we should have been ... I just can't take it anymore'. (47-8) Their daughter Nora says, 'I don't actually want to grow up, mom. I don't want my life to pass me by', (55) a sense of time passing, as noted, being a feature of Ziegler's plays, a structuring device but also a way of exploring shifting perceptions, experiences, causalities, anxieties. Time shifts generate perspective as her characters try to make sense of their lives, of responsibilities accepted or denied.

Asked why Joey failed to open and read his mother's letters, he replies,

> then all this time just comes pouring out! All this time … Like, time my mom spent writing the letter, time she spent worrying, time that hasn't even happened yet – like, all the things she wants to happen but which probably won't … With me. My life. Her life. Every day I think she's like 'that day wasn't good enough and now it's over' and like … What can I do about that?
>
> (59)

When Lillian explains why she stopped taking photographs, this is perhaps an explanation for Ziegler's methodology: 'what does a photograph really capture … Can it capture the absence of something? Of someone? I think I couldn't take pictures anymore when I finally realized how inadequate they are. That they … only remind you of everything you don't know.'[26] Not only is this a comment on the opacity of other people, and perhaps our inability to access our own inner motives and feelings, but a justification for Ziegler's entering the minds of her characters by having them address the audience directly.

For some critics, the willingness of characters to oblige by analysing themselves, teasing the meaning out of their actions, was altogether too convenient. Yet at some level these are all characters who fail to understand themselves, let alone those with whom they share what should be an intimate relationship. Even their confessions are approximations, leaving audiences to capture the absences. There is a loneliness where there should be amity, even as the play proceeds to a moment of redemption.

Joey returns and is embraced. He is still afraid that he is looking at life from the outside, his childhood fears not banished. Aware that his parents want him to believe that he matters, that existence itself does, he says, 'Maybe nothing does and we're all just trying to believe stuff matters to distract ourselves from the fact that we're just gonna die', (66) yet the experience has brought Philip and Lillian back together and the family are grouped together for a photograph, Lillian now picking up the camera she had laid aside as she says, 'I realize I see them; I really see them'. (71) But did she not say of photographs that they remind her of everything you don't know? Joey and Nora are about to leave home, the family assembled at the end of the play about to be disassembled, and that, too, would typify several Ziegler plays in which an apparent resolution carries the shadow of its opposite.

That same year, Ziegler, inspired in part by Sarah Ruhl's *Eurydice*, then turned her attention to the Greek myth of the Minotaur, re-imagining it, while taking pains to convey the essentials of the original myth for audiences who might not be aware of it. The original story involves King Minos of Crete, a son of Zeus and Europa, who declared himself king, proving his legitimacy by sacrificing a bull to the god Poseidon, asking him to send a new bull in return. The result was a beautiful white bull. Rather than sacrifice it, however, Minos settled for a lesser bull. Displeased, Poseidon makes Minos's wife fall in love with the bull. Desperate to consummate her desire, she commissions a wooden cow in which to disguise herself. The bull, object of her love, duly obliges. The result is the Minotaur, with a human body and the head of a bull. Minos responds by ordering a labyrinth to be built in which the Minotaur will be trapped forever, later requiring Athens, whose forces he had defeated in war, to send seven young men and seven young women annually to be fed to it. One year Theseus volunteers to be among their number, meaning to kill it, assisted by Minos's daughter, Ariadne, who gives him a ball of thread so that he can find his way back out of the labyrinth.

In a sense *The Minotaur*, which opened at the Synchronicity Theatre in Atlanta, in 2012, has an echo of *Dov and Ali* in so far as those who believe they have options are, as a trio of characters declare, 'reading from a script',[27] trapped in a maze like the Minotaur of the title. After all, how free, in a myth involving the gods, can anyone be? As the Minotaur observes, 'We can't change anything … my story will always be my story', (13) that being the essence of myths, except, of course, that Ziegler is on hand to subvert it. Once again, she provides epigraphs, one from the American physicist Alan Lightman's novel *Einstein's Dreams*: 'Such people stand on their balconies at twilight and shout that the future can be changed, that thousands of futures are possible.' The other is from the Jewish writer, and Holocaust survivor, Elie Wiesel: 'We are not the owners of our instincts. But controlling them, that is civilization.' (5) The play, in essence, stages a debate about the extent, or even the existence, of choice given that the terms of existence seem to be preordained, that freedom is no more than a word, the Minotaur speaking of 'the crime of having been born'. (41)

In other words, as in *Dov and Ali*, a central concern is with the extent of human freedom given the seemingly ineluctable nature of existence, and that is not the only link with her earlier plays. Once again, time is collapsed. Ariadne is 'eleven and fourteen and twenty-one … everything all at once … a memory that contains the future'. (10) Once again, the story is narrated as well as staged, in this case by a priest, a rabbi and a lawyer, which sounds the basis of a joke (and they tell one), the play being laced through with humour, perhaps especially if those watching are familiar with the original and therefore the games Ziegler plays, each innovation itself a declaration of possibility. Thus, the Rabbi enters dressed as autumn, the Lawyer as a bull and the priest as a wooden cow only to be dismissed by the Minotaur who himself takes on the role of narrator.

This is a story in which the Minotaur and Ariadne play Connect Four (and connection, and its failure, is a theme), and Minos is described as bringing spoils from his wars, including iPhones and Prada handbags, while Minos's original plan to return the bull to Poseidon is described as 're-gifting', evidently, the Lawyer observes, 'in favour then, frowned upon now', only for the Rabbi to confess that he had given away a slow cooker, presumably gifted to him, only to pay the price, not being 'invited for Chanukah for three years straight'. (13) In *Minotaur*, Theseus and Ariadne meet on a chatline for royals, exchange emails, enjoy watching television. Theseus does use yarn to find his way in the labyrinth, but in doing so eschews GPS or flashlights with triple A batteries. He and Ariadne use emoticons. A Johnny Cash cover of 'The First Time Ever I saw Your Face' plays in a smoky lounge.

The essence of a myth is that it remains unchanged, told and retold. The figures within it repeat their roles as Sisyphus rolls his rock uphill only for it to roll back down again and Prometheus's liver is pecked out by an eagle, regenerating each night only to be pecked out again. Here the Minotaur insists that none of them have any choices being trapped in a story, life itself being a labyrinth from which there is no escape. 'Nothing is ordained', declares Ariadne only for the Lawyer to reply, 'Are you kidding?' (51) Yet the Minotaur replies, 'Maybe stories are more flexible than I thought', (53) insisting that 'no one is just one thing'. (54) Theseus's heroism is to defeat the story. Theseus and Ariadne are no longer separated as they are in the myth and yet 'just before the lights go down a shadow of fear crosses Ariadne's face', (57) Ziegler ostensibly refusing to resolve the issue even as her thumb is on the scale.

She has said that the play is also about betrayal (Ariadne being the Minotaur's half-sister) and forgiveness, the durability, or otherwise, of love, though these are subordinate to the existential question at its heart. It is also, surely, about transformations, a fact reflected in its style as in the assumption towards which, and with whatever reservations, she drives, Elie Wiesel's desperate gamble on the possibility if not of redemption, then resistance to the unravelling of a sense of humanity, an escape from other people's stories by telling your own.

Ziegler obviously revelled in the writing of the play, its ironies, jokes, tilts at authority figures, visual gags, anachronisms, sheer inventiveness. She plainly gave herself licence to create a comedy laced with farce in which even her own seriousness is wilfully undermined.

Time and memory lie at the heart of *A Delicate Ship* which opened at the Cincinnati Playhouse in the Park in March 2014 before its Off-Broadway production at The Playwrights Realm. Its setting, indeed, is described as occupying 'a memory space that exists before and after the night when the action of the play takes place'. (3) Its location seems precise enough – an apartment in Brooklyn on Christmas Eve – or would but for the fact that that description is preceded by the word 'nominally'.

Readers enter the text through the refraction of a series of epigraphs, each, naturally, offering a clue to her sense of the territory we are about to explore. So, the American film maker Noah Baumbach is quoted as remarking that 'I'm nostalgic for conversations I had yesterday. I've begun reminiscing events before they even occur.' Kierkegaard observes,

> This is the simple truth ... to live is to feel oneself lost. He who accepts it has already begun to find himself ... Instinctively, as do the shipwrecked, he will look around for something to which to cling, and that tragic, ruthless glance, absolutely sincere, because it is a question of his salvation, will cause him to bring order into the chaos of his life. These are the only genuine ideas; the ideas of the shipwrecked. All the rest is rhetoric, posturing farce.
>
> (6)

Lila Azam Zanganech reports Dmitri Nabokov as saying, when asked why he had never married, 'life had slipped away too quickly' and that the perfection of his parents' marriage had made him feel it would be impossible to match what they had been. Beyond that, Ziegler offers two quotes from Auden, one observing that suffering can pass unnoticed against the banality of daily life, that even Icarus's fall, in Breughel's painting, could be irrelevant to those going about their business, a passing 'expensive delicate ship' sailing calmly on. The other quote has a chilling force as she notes that Auden had chosen to change a line of his poetry which had read 'We must love one another or die', to 'We must love one another and die.' (6–7)

All do, indeed, bear on what follows, a play in which nostalgia carries a toxic charge, even as the past is invoked to create a new present reality designed to lay down the basis for future nostalgia. A central character is seeking something to cling to with a disturbing ruthlessness as the apparent calm is disrupted, love clung to as the source of meaning even as it has the capacity for destruction. The quiet of a Christmas Eve is interrupted by a knock on the door. What, a woman in her early thirties asks, if she had not opened it. What shall I do now? asks the figure in Eliot's *The Wasteland*, in a section entitled 'A Game of Chess', hearing a noise at the door, adding 'Do you remember nothing?' In *A Delicate Ship* memory is a battleground and what to do now a question all three of its characters ask.

The play begins with them all present, though Nate, described in a note as 'a deeply wounded poet-type ... with an epically ranging emotional scale ... obsessed with his own self-hatred', addresses the audience, plainly in a different time, looking back and commenting on a conversation between two people. Sarah, Ziegler explains in a note, is 'sensitive and kind and indecisive ... who doesn't realize men are in love with her and struggles with fear in a way that makes her sidestep life a bit'. Sam is 'a dreamer ... who never wants to offend anyone ... honest and smart and tries very hard to fit in'. (3) Sarah then speaks, stepping out of the moment, introducing Nate with whom she had grown up, a man, she explains, who lives in the past to which she must return in order to bring him into the present.

The relationship between the two men has echoes of that between Jerry and Peter in Albee's *The Zoo Story*, one threatening, humiliating, the other seemingly passive, as it does of *Who's Afraid of Virginia Woolf?* in which caustic games strip away what only appears a surface equanimity. Power, however, shifts with time, time itself in some ways a subject as perspectives change, hopes and needs revised, reinterpreted.

On Christmas eve, on which the action takes place, Nate arrives, an unexpected intrusion as all three comment to the audience. What we are to watch is the playing out of a drama whose outcome is already known to those who have experienced it. They are, in other words, in a position to know what will happen as we, the audience, are not. It is Nate who invokes Kierkegaard: 'the only genuine ideas are the ideas of the shipwrecked ... the clearest thinking is done by people who are lost or suffering or lonely', (13) as, he insists, he is and as Sarah confirms is she. It turns out, indeed, that his salvation depends on the ruthlessness with which he seeks to bring order into the chaos of his life, by undermining the order of others, except that Sarah seems to be wedding herself to someone whose virtue is to be inoffensive, who offers a reassuringly predictable if unchallenging future. So, who is shipwrecked, the increasingly wild intruder or someone potentially wedding herself to a bland future?

Sarah, responding to Nate, but addressing the audience, confesses to her own sense of disappointment and anxiety. At thirty-three, she has been alone a long while. Her relationship with Sam has an air of desperation. There is a sense of being adrift, the past offering an apparently reassuring resource, seemingly secure, even as the past has its own ambiguities, never absent from the present which unavoidably it shapes. In 'Burnt Norton', part of *The Four Quartets*, T.S. Eliot speaks of time present and time past as present in time future, and time future being contained in time past, one consequence of which being that time is irremediable. What might have been exists as a possibility which is always present and may yet be. The poem speaks of footfalls echoing in the memory down passages not taken towards doors never opened. That thought traces through *A Delicate Ship* in which the characters dance around one another (Nate having once been an actual dancer) and the implications of their lives. Nate recalls the 'timeless life' of the college they once attended, while conscious that in another time their parents had lived that same life, their experiences reverberating in the mind. This is the poem which declares that humankind cannot bare very much reality, as Ziegler's characters cannot.

By degrees, the intimacy between Sarah and Sam is threatened by the previous intimacy of Sarah and Nate, relationships frequently involving exclusions, shared memories not available to others creating a barrier. To Sarah, Nate is a youthful companion, but, then, Ziegler had warned that she was 'the kind of woman who doesn't realize men are in love with her', as it becomes clear Nate is and as, in memory, they had once declared themselves to be.

Increasingly, Sam is irritated by this intrusion on what was to have been a romantic occasion, asking Nate who he is. 'I'm nobody, who are you?' he replies, a line (unacknowledged by Nate) from Emily Dickinson's ironic poem about the desirability of privacy, perhaps a reference which would be recognized by Sarah, what is shared between the two of them part of his strategy for excluding Sam, as he says, 'you must not know the same Sarah I know'. (21)

Sam's parents had divorced, as Sarah's had nearly done, while Nate confesses that he is a source of sadness to his. Sarah's father is dead. Something is missing. None of the three are entirely secure in themselves, Jews whose faith is irrelevant, whose past relationships have failed. 'I sometimes wonder why we can't just choose to be happy', laments Sam, (29) as Sarah 'always had to be holding someone's hand'. 'Her fear', Nate recalls, 'and her hope lived right on the surface', her greatest need 'to be loved'. (33,40) For his own part, he confesses that 'We often do things even though we know they're wrong', while that is what he is about as he proposes they play a game which involves 'getting to be someone else, or not knowing who you are'. (32).

In truth, it seems, Sarah does love Nate but the idea of joining herself to the anarchy he represents, his sense of desperation, is more than she can bear, even as fear of abandonment is what all three characters share. Nate is driven out and we are in the future as she and Sam look back, recalling that Nate had arrived with a poem, Auden's 'Musée Des Beaux Arts', about Breugel's 'Landscape with the Fall of Icarus', the poem invoked in the epigraph, relevant, they realize, because while the quiet pleasures of a Christmas Eve had been invaded, their seemingly placid lives turned upside down, the world beyond had continued, time passing as a ship's wake disappears.

For Nate, however, time stops. In some ways it had never moved forward from the moment, long before, when he had first seen Sarah, thinking she might be the answer to a question he could not articulate, seeing in her the beauty he senses might embody the happiness that had evaded him. Now, in a future which Sarah and Sam share, comes news that Nate has committed suicide, literally plunging down like Icarus. Still further in the future, though, Sam, now famous as a song writer, creates an album called Nate and Sarah, the song he is most proud of being called 'Love Song to Our Parents', a double act of reconciliation and restitution, except that, ten years further in the future, he and Sarah are no longer together, both now married to others. They seem to have achieved a certain equanimity, a settled status, yet something has perhaps been lost along the way. Nate was need personified, his desperate bid for love addressing the void which disturbed him, but beneath his aggression, the confusion he sewed, was a sometimes lyrical, always challenging, desire for something more than could be offered by a quiet evening enjoyed by two people whose love would prove too tentative to survive. For him, everything was at stake. He gambled and lost. He fell. They did not. But, like Icarus, he ventured more even as his presumption was what brought about his fall.

For Charles Isherwood, in *The New York Times*, it was Ziegler's 'quietly lyrical language', which he saw as having 'a luminous beauty', that impressed, along with 'her talent for creating characters whose complicated depths are just visible on their surfaces',[28] a play which was a story of love, pain and loss. Writing of a 2014 production, Rick Pender, in *CityBeat*, wrote that 'The Cincinnati Playhouse in the Park hit a home run with its world premiere of Anna Ziegler's *A Delicate Ship*.'[29]

By contrast, Elisabeth Vincentelli, in the *New York Post*, was not amused, seeing it as symptomatic of 'a certain contemporary American drama. Bred at elite universities and workshopped to death', finding it 'as overprocessed and tasteless as American cheese'.[30] She had obviously had a bad experience with American cheese. It is also not clear why elite universities should produce a 'certain' kind of drama. There are those who worry about workshops and development feeling, sometimes not without cause, that plays should be oven ready. On the other hand, there are many playwrights for whom this process has been invaluable. Her review, however, was an outlier.

Ziegler has explained that, in *The Last Match* (which opened in 2016 at The Old Globe Theatre in San Diego), she was drawn to write a play about two tennis players in part because she had herself been a player and because she was struck by the speech Andy Roddick gave on court at the US Open on the occasion of his retirement, a speech in which he expressed his love for the game. In fact, it was a very brief speech in which he acknowledged the support of the crowd, his parents and his team, hardly differing from the speeches made by many other players following a victory. There was another player, however, who might have informed the character she creates, Andre Agassi, who took part in the occasion honouring Roddick. In his autobiography, *Open*, he explains that his body had already decided to retire, offering an account of his back problems, treated by cortisone injections, precisely what Tim, Ziegler's character in *The Last Match*, suffers. His book also begins with his confession that he doesn't know who he is, and has spent half his life not knowing, an existential doubt which would have chimed with Ziegler for whom that doubt recurs in so many of her characters. Agassi's wife, like Tim's, was a tennis player (Steffi Graf), Roddick's was a model and actress. In fact, Ziegler has said that she had a number of players in mind, including Jim Courier, who in his last match paired with Agassi in doubles, retiring at thirty as did Roddick. All three had at one time been number one in the world. The play's other player, Sergei, is Russian, and Roddick did play against Russians (Igor Andreev, Yevgeny Kafelnikov).

What interested her, Ziegler explained, was the idea of someone ending a crucial part of his life at a comparatively young age, and the psychology involved in competitive sport saying, 'I think that the question of wanting is really central to the play. Can we ever satisfy our desire for more and better things? That's actually a theme that runs through my plays in other ways.'[31] She was about to have a baby when she saw Roddick make his valedictory speech, so that she was aware that she, too, was about to change 'because here was this person who was about my age, who was putting his whole life behind him, his identity was about to shift. I think something about that in connection with me also facing a shift in my life … got the seed for the play growing.'[32]

As ever with her work, it is worth noting the epigraphs to the published version. Here are two people, one in his mid-thirties, the other in his mid-twenties, but the epigraphs focus on the inevitability of death, if also resistance to it. Thus, Heidi Julavits, author of *The Folded Clock*, a meditation on time, relationships and identity, editor of *The Believer* magazine, is quoted as saying, 'When I want something – that to me is not youth exactly, but the opposite of death. That to me is a way to always feel like I am nowhere near the end.' Sarah Manguso, writer and poet, author of *Ongoingness*, a journal in part designed to address a sense of anxiety, writes, 'Let me put it another way: when I am with my son I feel the bracing speed of the one-way journey that guides human experience', a journey towards death, except that the final epigraph, from Tennyson's 'Ulysses', offers a consolation, echoed in the play:

> Though much is taken, much abides; and though
> We are not now that strength which in old days

Moved earth and heaven, that which we are, we are
One equal temper of heroic hearts,
Made weak by time and fate, but strong in will
To strive, to seek, to find, and not to yield.

(205)

As the match continues, from point to point, game to game, set to set, and the two players weigh up their opponents, register their fluctuating fortunes, they glimpse something beyond the immediate. So, Tim remarks, 'I take the first game so fast and in the moment you don't feel the pressure and the failure and the death and the ambition and the coming up short ... You feel you can do anything ... with everything in front of you', even as a certain entropy is evident, a career coming to an end.

Interleaved with the developing game are scenes with the two wives, Mallory and Galina, to some degree lives sacrificed in the name of success. Mallory, Ziegler explained, was not originally to have been a player, but it was that idea which helped her arrive at the nature of the relationship between her and Tim. 'That was the chip on her shoulder ... She didn't want to stop and yet she had to stop because she got injured. And now, she's ... forever in the shadow of this player who has the career she dreamed about and has to deal with all the gender ramifications of that.'[33] She is now a coach helping others to do what she no longer can.

Galina has not been a player, like Roddick's wife, it seems, a model and, like her husband, concerned for the state of her body, though for different reasons, while Mallory has left that other life behind. For Ziegler, this gives them a perspective which enables them to see a life beyond the game, a game, indeed, ultimately more serious. When Mallory announces that they are to have a baby, Tim remarks, 'for that moment you don't feel the pressure and the failure and the death and the ambition and the coming up short',[34] though a baby will one day die, as if death could not so easily be put out of mind. Galina asks Sergei whether playing tennis enables him to forget everything else, whether he can escape his own death. Behind them, meanwhile, are parents who have partly shaped them, either in emulation or in reaction, Sergei's being lost in a plane crash ten years earlier, their absence still felt, teaching him that 'we are all alone'. (193)

The play is structured around a match, a scoreboard keeping track of the game as advantage sways one way and then another. Ziegler's sympathy does not favour either player. Their contest is as much with themselves as with their opponents. The action moves in time and space, from the match to conversations with the players' wives, the public world of the contest interweaved with the private world of the family, each bearing on the other. There are moments when the audience is addressed, enrolled as confidants.

The end of a career means stepping back into time, a new awareness of another journey which has its end for, as Tim explains, 'I have to play. If I stop, I don't know who I am', (195) even as he is about to stop. Sergei has the same feeling: 'at the bottom of everything, an emptiness. We do what we can to run from this.' (196) When Mallory gives birth it, too, marks a moment of realization: 'I know all of a sudden that I will die. And I know with equal certainty that I am bringing a person into the world who will also die.' (193)

This is not Ziegler's only play in which a Becketian moment occurs, only for her to retreat from its absoluteness. So it is that, for the moment, the players are present, Sergei calling out 'I'm here ... I am alive'. (194) Fittingly, the play ends with the final set, the score five all, deuce. It is still going, Tim speaking of a vision of time speeding up, his son now a grown man, his own parents long gone, he in the middle, aware of the beauty of the world but also of a relentless rhythm of which he has only been a part, 'the autumn sun's setting, and the sky full of all these crazy colours and they spread out on the river, like a wreath, like a halo of light. Like the end and the beginning of everything'. (198) Ziegler may have opted for drama over poetry, but her work is often suffused with the poetic, an assertion of assonance, a consolation, language extending over a void.

Reviewing a Roundabout Theatre production in 1917, Ben Brantley, in *The New York Times*, found Ziegler 'fast becoming a master of swelling choral dialogue, in which urgent but lyrical phrases are intoned in a counterpoint … The routine back-and-forth of a hard-fought match finally approaches the ineffable radiance of one of those moments that tennis fans live for. Time seems to stop in such moments, even as it extends into eternity.'[35]

Streamed online in 2021, during the pandemic, it prompted Catey Sullivan, in the *Chicago Sun Times*, to welcome a play which 'uses tennis to explore themes that transcend sport: Failure, ambition and death, tennis as a metaphor for all. As the match progresses, "The Last Match" becomes both a joyful celebration of being alive and a grim look at the inevitable breakdown and decay of our bodies.'[36]

With *Boy*, Ziegler entered a contested area, and in the process set the actor at its heart a particular problem, ostensibly playing two different genders and ranging from the age of six to his twenties. If identity had been one of her themes, in this play it would be central. It began, she has said, with a Google search. She was looking for an idea which centred on gender, hoping for a commission from the Ensemble Studio Theatre/Sloane Foundation programme with its commitment to the development of plays which engaged with science. In doing so she stumbled on David Reimer's story. He was a Canadian, one of identical twins, who was born male but raised as a girl following a botched circumcision which irreversibly damaged his penis. His case was overseen by John Money, a psychologist at Johns Hopkins Hospital, who believed that gender is learned and can hence be changed. Reimer only gradually realized he was not a girl and began to live as a male at age fifteen. Urged, when young, to undergo an operation that would surgically construct a vagina, he later had operations to reverse the effect of early interventions. Reimer subsequently publicized his case to save others from following the same path. His twin developed schizophrenia and committed suicide as did David, shooting himself in the head. It led to an article in *Rolling Stone*.

Boy, the play which resulted, and which had its first workshop production in 2014, being further developed before its opening in 2016, could probably not, she confessed, have been written in the third decade of the twenty-first century when the issue at its heart had become the focus of sometimes vitriolic debates and even law cases. The story of

> David Reimer was certainly the inspiration for my play. It gave me a very general framework – boy loses penis, boy is raised as a girl, boy learns what happened to him and returns, at age fifteen, to being a boy. I set the play during the same time frame as the Reimer story because it is also a chronicle of where science was during those years – if the play were set now, for instance, no one would believe that such a decision could be made, and indeed, it likely wouldn't.[37]

On the other hand, I rather think it could, just such interventions, with the deployment of medications, now vigorously defended even as they have come under attack.

In England, a case was brought by a person who had undergone sexual re-assignment at an early age, taking his case to court. Keira Bell, a 25-year-old woman, was treated by England's only gender identity development service with puberty blockers when she was sixteen, before de-transitioning. A High Court ruling declared that anyone under sixteen was not capable of making a decision of such magnitude and that, in future, doctors of teenagers under eighteen would need to consult the courts for authorization of medical procedures. In 2021, the decision was overturned by the Court of Appeal. Authority was to rest with medical practitioners rather than the courts. An appeal to the Supreme Court was pending in 2022.

The play, though, as Ziegler explained, departed from the original:

> For instance, the John Money/David Reimer story seemed to lack the particular angle in which I was most interested – a story in which love is the blinding force, as opposed to greed or ambition or cruelty. I wasn't interested in writing a story about a villain and a victim, but in exploring the complicated terrain of mutual need, love and dependence between doctor and patient, and the problems that arise when someone is desperate to see an experiment succeed.[38]

That last remark, though, surely suggests that Dr. Wendell Barnes, the psychologist in her play, confuses the attachment he feels for the boy with his unthinking attachment to the theory into which his patient must be made to fit because she also speaks of the incredible betrayal at the heart of the play. Whose betrayal, though? Is it the doctor whose incompetence set the action moving? Is it the parents who, for most of the play, accede to an approach in which, in truth, they do not believe? Is it the man who manipulates more than gender? Is the play's title an assertion of fact or does it imply the choice of someone who for much of the time is offered no choice?

Boy is not, then, she has insisted, a direct attack on the psychologist, all the characters who surround Adam, the figure at its heart, being motivated by love, wanting the best for him. She speaks of their deep humanity and good intentions, however flawed they may be. though, in truth, while Wendell Barnes is committed to Adam, he is equally wedded to his theories remaining blind to the anguish of his patient who is an individual but also a case study which may burnish his reputation. As Ziegler has remarked, we see what we want to see.

She has spoken of a scene which in the end she abandoned but which explains something of her attitude to Wendell:

> There's a moment that's actually no longer in the play when the doctor, Wendell, who's been nursing resentment towards his own mother (who's also no longer in the play), realizes that he has failed his patient, a patient he thought of as his own child, and he says, 'I never forgave her – my mother. I thought one had to work hard to truly fail a child. I thought it was painstaking, deliberate work.' This idea keeps coming back to me these days. How blinded by love we can be to the real needs of our children.[39]

There is a reason that one of the epigraphs is from Mary Shelly's *Frankenstein* with its warning against scientific overreaching, while another is from the neurobiologist Stuart Firestein's *Ignorance: How It Drives Science*: 'There is no surer way to screw up an experiment than to be certain of its outcome.' His argument is that theories should follow data, suggesting that scientists can tend to fall in love with their ideas, this shaping the way they respond to data, rather than formulating a theory based on data, and that is surely what Wendell does. Perhaps interestingly, Firestein is married to a cognitive psychologist and worked in theatre for many years. Ziegler speaks of Wendell's love for his patient, but perhaps he has a greater love, for his ideas. Paul Nurse has said that 'we shouldn't be seduced by the beautiful idea unless there is data and testing to show that it still stands up. I think it is important because we are weak vain creatures and can be seduced by our own ideas. That, I think, is one of the weaknesses that scientists have.'[40]

Ziegler underlines the fact that acts have consequences but, while staying close to the actual case, omits the suicides which suggest that love and forgiveness, which she chooses to foreground, have their limitations. I am tempted to recall the fact that Anne Frank's diary is presented as a triumph for the human spirit perhaps because readers, and the writers of the stage play and film based on it, prefer not to address the abject and appalling end which she would suffer at Buchenwald.

By this stage in Ziegler's career, it is not surprising that the play moves around in time. Here, the stages of Adam's life are crucial as his options slowly narrow. Dates are projected, ranging from 1968 to 1990. The play opens in 1989 when he is launched on a tentative relationship with a young woman whose life has been less than wonderful. At this stage, there is no suggestion that anything is amiss, except that the action then quickly switches to 1973 when Adam was called Samantha and is six years old, responding to questions from Wendell who will shape her life, urging her to sit up straight and cross her legs, already beginning the process of re-inventing him as a her. Sometimes, he says to her, 'we have to do things we don't really want to.'[41] Earlier, the desperate parents had reached out to Wendell, not knowing what to do, only for him to tell them that they should raise their child as a female, already referring to 'her', urging them to 'let her live as a whole person as opposed to an incomplete boy', which 'could well do irreparable damage to the psyche'. (81)

Beyond that, the parents are told that they must never tell their son that he was born a boy, so that betrayal is structured into all the relationships. By the time Samantha is thirteen she is deeply uncomfortable with Wendell and her parents. She refuses a proposed further operation that would continue shaping her female genitalia. She refuses to see Wendell anymore. When Wendell finally meets Samantha again, after ten years have passed, she is no longer Samantha: she has changed so radically (having been restored to her male identity) that he no longer recognizes her. He assumes it is Samantha's twin brother who stands before him. And though Adam says, 'I don't know who I am', (125) he now reveals his complicated history to his girlfriend Jenny, who is relieved to finally know the truth. They had broken up because she could not understand why he could not sleep with her (he never having the courage to explain that his genitalia would not function normally). She accepts him as he is, and the play ends with their embrace.

There is a more profound question raised by the play, a question asked by John Milton in *Paradise Lost*, a poet invoked by Wendell, and quoted in an epigraph: 'did I request thee, Maker, from my clay/To mould me Man? Did I solicit thee/From darkness to promote me?' Adam, whose name is significant, being the first man, has to come to terms with who he is, how he has been shaped and what fate seems to have been reserved for him. It is no less true, though, of his parents who have played their role in shaping his destiny but who are themselves in turn shaped by that fact. Who determined what Jenny's life would be, that she should bear the marks of her upbringing and desertion? But, beyond that is the question of who anyone is, identity not being sharply defined, a product of biology and the random nature of experience, though for Ziegler the play made a strong case for nature over nurture, something she witnessed for herself giving birth while writing the play and witnessing that child's own responses.

In the end the story Ziegler chooses to tell is not that of a man who responded to the anguish of many years by committing suicide but of someone who finds his way back to himself. It ends on a note of tenderness which is not one of forgiveness or reconciliation but of grace. For Ben Brantley, in *The New York Times*, Ziegler was so concerned to resist the portrait of David Reimer chronicled by John Colapinto in *As Nature Made Him: The Boy Who Was Raised as a Child,* 'a grim portrait of a tortured soul … so determined not to be sensational or bleak' that the play 'bleaches itself of troubling complexity'.[42] In *The Guardian*, Alexis Soloski complained at 'a certain tidiness to the play, which while successful from a structural point of view, perhaps minimises the messiness of the issues it reasons, the unanswerability of the questions that continue to fascinate the playwright.'[43]

There is something to the idea that she resists too resolutely a bleak vision. Becketian moments pass swiftly as though that is not a path she wants to take. The description she offers of the characters in virtually all her plays tends to stress their positive, often redeeming qualities, even if they are then staged in their imperfections. Perhaps she loves them too much. She has been criticized before for her tidiness, the neatness of her constructions, intricate, as they weave through time before finally resolving. Yet even here, as she signs off *Boy* with a moment of consonance, we have learned enough to understand that wounds leave scars. What of the parents who realize that they have done damage? What of Wendell, whose work seems to have leached away and who has now lost a person he felt he had adopted as a substitute daughter only to discover that she is not a she anymore and has no desire to see him ever again? And what of Adam and Jenny? Will love really conquer all? Certainly, she accepts him for what he is, and does so with surprising alacrity, but he has effectively lied to her for years and love has failed her in the past, as it has him.

With her next play, *Actually*, produced by the Manhattan Theatre Club in November 2017, she continued her concern with identity, with respect to gender but also race, in the context of an issue then much in the news, as it continues to be, that being the differing interpretations of two people as one accuses the other of rape. It is set at Princeton, a university which, in 2014, was directed by the US Department of Education to change its requirement that there should be clear and convincing proof before a student could be convicted, instead requiring a preponderance of evidence, as Ziegler observes in an author's note to the published text, being known as 50 per cent plus a feather, a phrase used in the play. This had been the principle laid down under Title IX of the Education Amendment of 1972, but that had been challenged by twenty-eight Harvard law professors who objected to this lower standard in their own institution. As Ziegler notes, however, two months before her play was about to open, the Trump administration issued new guidance saying that universities could, if they wished, require clear and convincing evidence. Needless to say, rape, when only two people are involved, is difficult to establish, not least because those involved offer their own interpretation of what occurred. David Mamet's *Oleanna* explored somewhat similar issues as an accusation of sexual harassment turns into one of rape, the audience required to adjudicate.

For Ziegler, though, while the background against which the play was written was 'hugely important', it was also 'from my point of view, beside the point', she being interested in 'a larger and more timeless question about who we are as men and women and what forces drive our actions'.[44]

She was drawn to the subject because her lawyer husband worked at a college where he oversaw sexual misconduct cases and was involved in rewriting the college's policy. As she explained,

> There was a lot of angst and discussion in our house about that policy and about the problem on campuses. So, the play came out of this feeling that many of these cases are muddy and hard to piece apart. Of course, there are some that are absolutely black and white, but I was interested in the ones that weren't and in trying to come up with a situation that would make the audience or the reader question themselves and their own unconscious bias, and think about how difficult it is, given all the baggage we are carrying, to figure out what went into a moment between two people.[45]

The play features two characters in their mid-twenties; Amber, described as high-strung, charmingly neurotic, Jewish, and Tom, ostensibly confident with a deeper vulnerability, and African American. It begins at a college party, they both being freshmen on what is described as a 'sort of' first date. They have been drinking. It is Amber who raises the possibility of them sleeping together. Immediately, however, and for barely thirty seconds, they both turn to address the audience and talk about a hearing which seems like a trial, given the presence of two lawyers, before resuming their conversation, playing a game of Two Truths and a Lie in which they have to guess which is the lie, a harbinger of what is to follow. Among the truths she offers is that her father, a professor, had married his student, potentially a breach of rules, and that she herself was the product of that union.

There is more than one line crossed by these two, Amber assuming that being Black had given Tom an advantage in gaining access to the university, oblivious to any offence. She is equally casual, however, when, turning to the audience, she explains how a hearing, in which Tom's future at Princeton was at stake, came about: 'I didn't know Heather would tell anyone. She just came into my room and was like "Amber. People are saying you were *topless* at Cap last night" … And I'm like "that's the least of it. I mean, Thomas Anthony practically raped me." … And I knew immediately that I'd said something I couldn't take back', (6) even as she recalls only saying that 'things went pretty far' and that she had not actually said no. Is the word 'practically' to be the feather?

On the other hand, it turns out that Tom has a sexual history of his own, having had sex with his schoolteacher (who came onto him), explaining to the audience that she was then fired, for which he was blamed, a blame which his mother argued was because of his race. The audience, in other words, is already swayed one way and then the other before learning more about the central incident.

The addresses to the audience are effectively confessionals as, for a while, are Tom and Amber's increasingly intimate conversations, and what are, in effect, conversations with themselves as they seek to understand their own emotions. Amber's father has died, Tom's mother has cancer, two anchors no longer holding as they try to navigate their way, discovering their own flaws and the mystery of other people, struggling to understand those whose lives are closed to them.

In the hearing, every now and then their voices sound out together, the harmony they had found before, now revisited, both now newly conscious of their vulnerability, drawn to one another but aware they are playing parts in a drama not of their devising. The play ends by repeating the opening as Amber proposes the game of Two Truths and a Lie, requiring Tom to play if he wants to sleep with her, to which he replies with a question, 'who goes first?' (55) as a literal feather floats down between them. Did she, then, initiate what followed, or did he? What really happened? Or is that a question that can never be answered since they each recall it differently and even shift their ground, their own insecurities, doubts, shaping not so much their memories as their needs?

The point, though, as Ziegler insists, is not how the case should be resolved, who, if either, is guilty, who tells the truth and who lies, truth being literally irrecoverable given that each participant is confused as to motives, uncertain how to read their own feelings let alone those of others. Was silence consent or refusal? Why, Amber asks herself, has she always had difficulty saying no? Why could he not read her reactions for what they perhaps were? They had both been drinking to excess. Does that exculpate or inculpate Tom or, indeed, Amber? Ziegler has said that the choice to make one character Black and the other Jewish meant that 'because these are both characters who are in marginalized, victimized categories of people ... it's really hard for the audience to decide who to sympathize with ... there's this vacillation because they're both from traditionally victimized groups.'[46]

In the end, for all it is a play which reflects a contemporary, and vexatious, dilemma, in which rules, conventions and the law are necessarily required to intervene in the most private of circumstances, it is fundamentally a portrait of two people wrestling to understand how they relate to others and themselves, two people who carry their own psychological scars, sex being a liberation and the centre of a troubled search for meaning. Amber confesses that she had spent her 'entire existence feeling ... invisible', (47) hoping that Tom would gift her a sense of existence, asking 'am I the only one aware of the fact that I'm on this earth, in which case am I really on it? And if I don't exist then who is this?' (48) For his part, Tom declares 'I can't hide ... there is just nowhere to hide! ... I can't be anybody but who I am – this man in the world who everyone assumes will make a mistake, if they just wait long enough!' (47)

Structurally, the play resembles many of her others, the addresses to the audience, the interlacing of different times, the juxtapositions. As she has explained,

> A lot of the process of this play was figuring out where to break stories up and how to break them up. In many cases these two people are telling different stories at the same time. So, I wanted to think about what would be most interesting in juxtaposition that would then reflect on the other story in a thematic or more oblique way.

The two stories at its heart 'are woven together in this way in this night. Their stories are woven together forevermore. I think it was going to be a play about perspectives. I wanted to get in their heads. It didn't feel like a play that would work in more traditional dialogues or scenes. I wanted the audience to know what these people were really thinking.' It was, she has said, an attempt to recreate the interiority of the novel:

> In some ways, I always am thinking about novels when I'm writing plays. And also poetry. There's a way in which I'm trying to figure out ways to, as you say, create interiority that

remains dramatic, but is borrowing from first person narrative in fiction. I don't think that there are any dramatic rules that can't be broken as long as the writer is paying really close attention to how long the audience can sit in a certain kind of moment. So in that way, I feel like I am trying to understand what makes narration in a novel dramatic and apply it to the stage as well.[47]

At the same time,

I love ... surprising the audience with a perspective that they didn't see coming because they were seeing one version of a character and then suddenly they're telling us about another version of themselves. I think we are all many versions of ourselves, so I don't think there's necessarily a most truthful version, but maybe the composite is sort of truthful. Maybe that is ultimately what I'm trying to find: that truthful composite of all of the sides of ourselves.[48]

'Do I contradict myself', asks Whitman. I am a man of contradictions, says Bob Dylan in *Rough and Rowdy Ways*.

Jesse Green's response to a play in which the word 'actually' is required to carry a weight beyond its lexical meaning, was, in his *New York Times* review, to find it 'a rich and disturbing study, if one that is also manipulative. Balancing Amber's and Tom's points of view, as if with an eyedropper, the playwright seems less interested in the merits of the case than in solving the puzzle of her own narrative needs' even as he confesses, 'No wonder she stacks the decks so carefully' since she 'wants us to feel what it's like to live at that terrible crux' in a play that is 'not, after all, ... about rape' but 'about the failure of justice when it deals with unknowable midpoints instead of extremes. Amber and Tom are changed forever by events they can hardly recall, let alone judge. So how can anyone judge them?'[49] Hence, the eyedropper, the narrative needs being intimately involved in a balancing act which is simultaneously a narrative strategy and a thematic necessity.

Following the opening of *The Last Match*, Ziegler was commissioned to write a new play for San Diego's Old Globe Theatre. It started as a work about an arranged marriage in a Hasidic community but, as she explained, while she was working on it *The New York Times* published an email correspondence between the novelist Jonathan Safran Foes and the movie star Natalie Portman. This prompted her to write a second play:

My due date was coming up [she was about to give birth] and I couldn't see my way through either of (the plays) – I had maybe 30 pages of each. And at a certain point, as the deadline was approaching, I thought, 'Maybe they're the same play.' And I started to ... weave them together. And it actually didn't seem so crazy. It ... felt, in a strange way, that I was dealing with some similar territory. They were really both about these people who were ... looking for something more than they had.[50]

The result would be *The Wanderers*, so called because to her mind the characters were all on a kind of existential quest.

It opened at the Old Globe Theatre in 2018, and, interestingly, at the Gesher Theatre in Tel Avi the following year. It features two couples, Esther and Schmuli, ultra-orthodox Jews, who come together in an arranged marriage, strangers to one another, and Abe and Sophie, he Jewish, she described as Caucasian Jewish, half African American. Abe and Sophie are both writers, he successful, winning a Pulitzer and two National Book Awards, she less so. He insists that she has a resource as a writer descended from both Holocaust survivors and slaves, to which she replies, 'I don't want to write about myself. I write to get away from myself. Also, slavery and the Holocaust don't define me.'[51]

They are both children of mothers who grew up in a strict Hasidic sect, the Satmars, who reject modern culture. Their mothers both escaped from that life thus giving their children the freedom they now claim, though Abe's mother remained a governing spirit so much so that he raises his children in a religion which his wife claims he hates, to which he replies, 'Because that's what Jews do'. (21) They are happily married, in contrast to Esther and Schmuli whose own story is intercut with their own, except that in her opening speech, a look at the future, Sophie lets us know that eventually she decided to leave Abe. Why she does so, takes most of the play to discover not least because they seem happy, joking together until a particular joke turns sour. There is a fourth person, Julia, a movie star, but her status is unclear, existing through the email conversations she has with Abe.

Esther and Schmuli are ill at ease, knowing little about one another. He is shy, emotionally constrained, as he is by the rules of his sect. She is more open. They have children together, but he finds what he regards as her irresponsible liberalism an affront to their religion, she even listening to the radio and reading *Winnie the Pooh*, both forbidden. She recalls that her friend had fallen in love with an African American and left their faith, a rebellious spirit guiding Esther. For his part, Schmuli is not, though, unaware that there is more to life than is defined by his rigid faith, a beauty which goes beyond the confines of thought which he had received from his father, his grandfather, and back through time, even as he insists that walls are necessary to protect from vulnerability.

But when she talks of buying a computer and using birth control it is a step too far. He informs the rabbi, and her two daughters are taken away from her, she escaping with her son, Abraham – the boy who she named without the approval of the rabbi, the Abe who would go on to marry Sophie, two seemingly separate stories coming together. Could you have a Jewish story without guilt? Certainly, there is enough to go around in *The Wanderers*. It was the Jewish Isaac Bashevis Singer who once told me, 'I feel that a man without guilt is not a man at all.'[52]

Meanwhile, Abe enters into an email exchange with Julia, who had attended one of his readings and to whom he was drawn. She is apparently appearing in a film version of Philip Roth's *Everyman* in which the protagonist leaves his various wives. By degrees, the conversation becomes more intimate, he confessing to his dissatisfaction with his marriage, justifying his own selfishness saying, '*Of course* you have to be selfish. I mean, truly, what is there in this world to have faith in *besides* the self? Certainly not humanity, which is filled with real cruelty and the performance of cruelty, and death. Certainly not God – how can anyone believe in him? The ultimate in unreliability.' (31) When his father dies, it is to her that he turns, though this is the father from whom he had been estranged, whose actions led to the abduction of his sisters, leaving Abe suddenly adrift: 'It's horrible, Julia. Life is short, and full of illusion. There is no order to be made from madness.' (36)

Four years pass and Schmuli appears at Esther's door, offering forgiveness for an offence which in truth was his own, bringing with him a gift for the boy he wishes to see: *Winnie the Pooh*. There is a hollowness in both their lives.

Meanwhile, Sophie reveals that the emails had never come from Julia, that she had masqueraded as the film star. It turns out that she is a convincing writer after all. Who, then, betrayed who? Ironically, Abe was having an electronic affair with his own wife. Later, he mischievously opens an email exchange with his wife, masquerading as the newsreader Tom Brokaw for whom she had expressed admiration, explaining that he has finished a novel in which his parents reconcile, and she reveals that she has finished her book called *The Wanderers* based on the idea that it can take a lifetime just to grow up, 'to let go of a certain sort of galvanizing restlessness that leaves you always empty'. (66) When he attends a conference at which Philip Roth reads, the fictional Roth is asked how he would characterize himself. He replies with a statement relevant to more than this play: 'There is nothing I could say that would not be a fiction except that I am first and last the product of my parents.' (68) Abe ends by saying, '*Ein ba'al ha-nes makir b'niso*', meaning he doesn't know what he has done to deserve the miracles that happen to him, a phrase repeated by Schmuli, as Esther takes his hand. 'Let us feel how fortunate we are', he says, the final words of the play. *The Wanders* ends with reconciliations, a moment of grace.

Among the epigraphs to the text is one by the American journalist Margalit Fox which could be applied to a number of Ziegler's plays: 'The poet appears to have found his subject – the labyrinth of self-deceit into which we are led by, among other things, language itself, by the difficult reformulation of one's own story.' Here, storytellers, creators of fictions, play with language and are played by language, ensnared in one another's stories while trying to understand their own.

Another epigraph is from the Belgian psychotherapist, Esther Perel, daughter of two Polish-born Holocaust survivors, who has written about the tension between the need for love and the need for freedom, the sense that a vital clue to identity and meaning may have been missed:

> There is always a suspicion ... that one is living a lie or a mistake; that something crucially important has been overlooked, missed, neglected, left untried and unexplored; that a vital obligation to one's own authentic self has not been met, or that some chances of unknown happiness completely different from any happiness experienced before have not been taken up in time and are bound to be lost forever.

The road not taken is a reproach or an illusion, writing a route to truth or an evasion. Was there an alternative life? Is discontent structured into relationships, or must it be ignored as a barrier to living even as the struggle to understand others is implicated in the struggle to understand the self?

Given its Jewish characters, and that it was also produced at Theater J in Washington's Jewish Community Center, it is worth seeing how Jewish papers responded. Lisa Traiger, in *Washington Jewish Week*, found Ziegler's writing 'simply radiant' and the play 'smartly witty, dryly funny and fully engaging' with dialogue which 'sings in ways both artful and lyrical'.[53] For *The Jerusalem Post* it was a 'very accomplished, tightly knit Chinese puzzle of a play ... a treat'.[54] For the not notably Jewish *Broadway World, Washington D.C.*, it offered 'deeply complex characters' happiness, sadness, anger, fear, and jealousy',[55] welcoming the fact that it was to be produced Off-Broadway at the Roundabout Theatre Company, a production delayed by the pandemic until February 2023.

She now turned to myth once again, writing *The Janeiad*, in a sense a version of the *Odyssey* set in a present which mirrors a mythic past. The present is that of 9/11, the towers falling, Jane's husband, Gabe, trapped in one of them. She is waiting for his return as Penelope did for Odysseus, Penelope who now appears in the play in several different guises, Jane having been reading the *Odyssey* when the planes struck. When Jane remarks, 'I used to think I was waiting for my life to start. Now I think I'm waiting for it to restart. I hadn't realized it was actually going already,'[56] she expresses a thought that would be reflected elsewhere in Ziegler's work. For Penelope, waiting is 'our lot'. 'No one knew, no one can know what the world has promised us. What bills we will have to pay', (53) some bills literal enough, others harder to compute. The arbitrary blow of 9/11 gives way to that of Covid. As she says, 'I guess things have been shitty. In the world. In America. You know: Obama good, Trump bad. Terrorism bad. Russia bad. Global pandemic very very bad. Like something biblical rained down upon us', (54) the only balancing goodness she can think of being *Downton Abbey*. Beyond that lies the truth of the fact that 'There are all sorts of abandonments. Every day we abandon who we were the day before', (61) even as she herself has been abandoned, her life on hold. But, as Penelope, in the guise of a realtor, remarks, 'what is life but time and what is time but the hollow space between nothing and nothing. So fill it! Fill it, I say.' (77) But Jane feels as though she is not in charge of her own story sensing that someone else may be telling it, just as Penelope's life is subsumed in the story of Odysseus.

Time passes, a considerable time, until 2021, when, like Odysseus, after twenty years, Gabe returns in the guise of a beggar. In this theatrical gesture, the play suggests that Odysseus's 'return' might have been similarly fanciful, born out of the need of the one left behind. Out of that need, and hope, Jane created Penelope who has been her companion for twenty years, holding tight to the idea that Odysseus's return will mirror Gabe's. Except there comes a time when she no longer has need of her as a model, now living her own life, not in someone else's story, not in what has become the story, the myth, of 9/11. She is, she insists, the captain of her own ship. As the play ends, so she asks herself, 'knowing everything, knowing how it ends, would we do it all over again?' replying 'I know we would. And if *that* isn't the tragedy of all of our lives, I don't know what is.' (93) With that, she walks out into the world, 'into the unknown', no longer looking back.

The Janeiad is an affecting, poetic work in which 9/11 stands for the trauma of loss, those absences which seem to stop time, drain life of meaning, make moving on seem a kind of betrayal. Jane's sons grow up and move away. A once-full house is now empty. Hope seems corroded by an irony exposed by time. Yet denial, stasis, are equally corrosive, inimical to identity and a meaning which can only be generated by letting go, refusing to be defined by a past which can be mythicized. There is, perhaps, a personal dimension to her remark that 'I'm living my life, right now. The typewriter keys are clacking away … this is my book.' (86–70)

In 2019, Ziegler took a new play, originally commissioned by the Geffen Playhouse in Los Angeles, to the O'Neill Centre, with its playwriting workshop and writing residency. The play was *Antigones*, a contemporary version of the Greek tragedy. Where the original had focussed on a male body, that of Polynices, whose burial by Antigone had been refused by Creon, hers was concerned with the female body. As she explained,

> It now has a lot to do with a woman's right to choose, has much more to do with Antigone's body than the body of her brother, which the original focuses on, the burial

of her brother's body. That is not a component of this play. While it tells the Antigone story, there's also a very modern story of another woman woven through it … it's a story about how liberated women really are these days.

It 'has … to do entirely with the moment where we find ourselves, where abortion rights are threatened.'[57] Thus her Antigone, who has an abortion, quotes from a law book, the place marked by a post-it note:

> Common Law 32A – it is always the woman's fault if she gets pregnant because men can't be expected to be responsible, especially when the possibility of such extreme but also incredibly fleeting pleasure is so close at hand. To claim otherwise is punishable by death. 33B – Women are neurotic by nature and overthink everything. Common law 33B removes this burden by removing this particular choice. Which means: if you get pregnant, you must stay pregnant (until the pregnancy has run its natural course). To do otherwise is punishable by death.'[58]

By these laws a foetus is more valuable than its mother. Why these laws? Because Creon insists, there is a link between the woman's body and the body politic.

Antigones is laced through with humour, its language demotic, its references contemporary, Ziegler's ancient Greece having CCTV, cell phones and Whole Foods. It is also, at moments, lyrical. At the same time, it is in some sense a manifesto about women's learned behaviour, internalizing the prejudices offered as natural, passed from generation to generation. It is a declaration of the right to control a body which already bears the marks of experience, which has suffered monthly pains. 'This is my story. This is my body. And my body is the body of every woman', (64) Antigone declares, and what is true of her is true of the modern woman, Dicey, coming to believe that at least she has a choice whether to keep a baby or not, a baby she will call Antigone.

Choice, however, was precisely what was under threat. Two years after Ziegler presented her play at the O'Neill, Texas passed a law effectively banning abortion. A year later, the Supreme Court overturned Row v Wade, Ziegler's play foreshadowing it even as it reached back into myth. The plays ends with music playing, 'The Times They-Are-A-Changin', the final stage direction indicating that 'The actors look searchingly out at the members of the audience, hoping they are also experiencing the satisfaction of having changed'. (97)

The Great Moment, staged by Seattle Rep, which had commissioned it, is Ziegler's most personal work. Once again, time plays a central role. The word, indeed, recurs in the text. As Ziegler has explained,

> It was just the moment in time where I found myself. My children were little, my parents healthy, my grandfather 98 years old. I felt so keenly that the moment wouldn't last. That this was, perhaps (and not to be too dark about it), the end of a really great moment for our family – so I wanted to preserve it. Or to preserve the desire to preserve it, at least. Not to ward off loss so much as to crystallise what we'd be losing. My way of raging against the dying of the light, I guess. And to send a love letter to a moment in time out into the universe.[59]

Writing the play, the character based on the playwright remarks, may be a way of stopping her grandfather from dying. This is what Frederic Jameson called nostalgia for the present. In her case it is an attempt to slow time not just to shore it up against the future when change will disestablish relationships, but to seize the moment, examine it for its meaning, a moment which, for some, inevitably has echoes of the past even as processes are in train which will render it irrelevant, yesterday's music having a different rhythm and melody than today's. As a character in *The Great Moment* observes, this is the only now there is. There is, however, another nostalgia in the play, that of an old man, his friends now dead, who reaches back, the past offering consolations, a coherence fast disappearing as his mental faculties decay, what elsewhere in the play is called 'the envelope of time folding in on itself'.[60]

There is a reason, of course, why music from another era is played to those with Alzheimer's, and here a grandfather, increasingly adrift in the present, summons up memories of music from a time when time itself seemed to carry no threat. There is, though, a worse state, when memories cease altogether and the present has no meaning, and that fear exists in the play as we learn of a figure, a grandmother, who had forgotten those around her and, ultimately, herself. The grandfather recalls a 1944 film, *The Great Moment*, about the invention of anaesthesia by a man now forgotten. Ziegler's is a play concerned with the need to be alert to the moment, even its pain, an act of resistance against forgetting, against the anaesthesia of routine.

Ziegler's central character may have a different name, Sarah, but, a writer, it is clearly her. 'I'm a playwright', Sarah announces, 'if that isn't clear because, well, this is a play' (20), a fact made even clearer in that she is the author of Ziegler's own *The Minotaur*. Indeed, at one moment, referring to when the play will be in print, she remarks, 'Here we are on page 39 or page 57 depending on font sizes, and margins. You never really know how far along you are.' As it happens, it is on page 38 in the text I am reading, while the final remark applies to more than a text in a work in which there is no certainty when life will end.

The play was born out of her desire to observe, record, in the hope that words might themselves be a kind of sea anchor against the ebb tide of time. She may live in a country which leans into the future, pursuing happiness as if it is clear what that might be, but the future carries more than promise; there is a darkness necessarily put out of mind. The old have a secret which is not theirs alone, the young child already glimpsing it as those so familiar disappear. In the case of *The Great Moment*, she has said, the spark came from her grandfather's repetitions of the phrase, 'getting old sucks'. It made her wish to write it down so that she would retain his voice after he died. Sarah gives the precise time of writing. It is 23 December 2016, and she is thirty-seven, before the play moves forward to 28 April 2018 when her grandfather has turned one hundred, but, she points out, it will be later when audiences become party to her thoughts, itself an acknowledgement of passing time, as is the fact that she is carrying a child, counting down to the moment of another generational shift, a moment now imminent.

Her characters double up, the same actor playing a boy, a father, a grandfather as another plays a girl, a mother and a grandmother, one way of compressing time. 'You'll get used to it', Sarah says to the audience. Evan, three or four years old, asks a series of questions which set the tone for a play which addresses the fact of mortality, a mystery for a child and perhaps no less so for those approaching the end. Thus, he asks,

Is great-grandpa dead yet?
When will he die?

> What happens if a kid is hit by a car?
> Can a kid die?
> How does it feel to die?
> When will grandma and grandpa die?
> Were you the first person?
> What happens when forever ends?
> Will you be alive when I'm a grownup?
> Will you let me know when I'm an old man?[61]

More tellingly, he ends by asking 'Will you let me know when I'm about to die?'

Death is on the agenda because the grandfather is so old but, in a sense, as Sarah acknowledges, it is never off the agenda:

> People my age are starting to die. Three women I know from college have cancer. My husband's high school classmate died last year and everyone in their class went to his funeral, not boys anymore. But still, if we are relatively healthy, we blithely assume we will continue to live. That we are saved, somehow. Is there any way around that feeling?
>
> (24)

There comes a moment when the young Evan rebels against being incorporated into a play, his name, along with the rest of the family, having been changed. Just what is the legitimacy of shaping real lives into drama, the theatre ever having been a metaphor for life as life provides the substance for metaphor? Ziegler's generations are akin to Albee's characters in *Three Tall Women*, a line from which is incorporated into *The Great Moment*. In that play Albee traces different stages in a woman's life, effectively his own adoptive mother, explaining that 'I was inventing her while I was writing her. Even though a lot of the dialogue echoed exactly the things she said, I invented her character.' He himself appears in the play while declaring that 'I never put me on stage' admitting, though, that this was 'the closest I suppose anyone can accuse me of doing that but, at the same time, every character I write is filtered through my mind, my sympathies'.[62] 'I suspect', he added, that 'the fiction that I was talking about … is my translation of the facts into something a little more dramatically viable'. (6–7) So, too, with Ziegler for whom dialogue does indeed reflect actual conversations even as it is shaped by the imagination, as are characters who certainly have their models in family members but who serve a dramatic and thematic purpose. This is not a documentary play even as she insists she kept a record of the passing days and months.

If the play was designed to hold time at bay, it has its end, an irony itself held at bay by an ambiguity. Sarah and her son Evan are, she tells him, now together on a stage, the actual stage, looking out, a stage direction indicates, 'at the theater, at the audience, at the world, in wonder, taking it all in' as we hear the recording of a woman and child singing a verse of Steve Goodman's 'The City of New Orleans':

> *Good morning, America*
> *How are you?*
> *Say don't you know me? I'm your native son*

I'm the train they call the city of New Orleans
And I'll be gone five hundred miles when the day is done.

(62)

An image which recurs is that of a train which, Sarah says, brings us to this 'mysterious place and then takes us away again'. (60) A child has entered this life even as an old man is about to leave it. The train has a destination. At the end of the song, the stage goes to black. Time cannot be arrested, except, perhaps, in a play which, like the rhythm of life, will be repeated.

Writing in *Broadway World Seattle*, Jay Inwin objected to being required to watch someone else's therapy, lamenting the play's lack of extraordinary moments that 'amount to a message or meaning that is not widely known by our audience'. If its 'message' was that time is fleeting then audiences could derive that from *The Rocky Horror Picture Show*. Why, he asked, 'are you telling me all this … ? I guess the moral of the story is, if you're going to write yourself into a play, make sure what goes on in the play isn't something 90% of the world deals with all the time.'[63]

Moss Hart is credited with saying, 'if you've got a message, call Western Union'. Irwin, with his notion of art as a carrier of revelations, could be said to have missed the point. His regret at the absence of extraordinary moments is equally odd since Ziegler was precisely concerned to see the extraordinary in the ordinary. The *Seattle Magazine* saw a different play finding it 'startling in its simplicity', navigating 'the mundanities of life', responding to her turning 'her narrative scalpel on herself', adding

> Ziegler's hardly breaking new ground here, but she's telling her story honestly and beautifully, and wisely doesn't gin up 'conflict' for the sake of an inciting incident or whatever dramaturgical boxes playwrights are supposed to tick. Is real life boring? Yes. Is it also the most incredible experience – not to mention the *only* experience – any of us will ever have? Yes again. Learning to see or appreciate that in a new way is no small feat.[64]

The Wanderers, its New York premiere taking place at the Off Broadway Laura Pels Theatre in February 2023, won the San Diego Critic's Circle Award for Outstanding new play, *The Last Match* nominated for the award a few years earlier. *Photograph 51*, besides winning London's *What'sOnStage* award for Best New Play, was also selected as best new play by newspapers in Britain and America. *Actually* won the Ovation Award for an original play. She is currently working on a musical, *A House Without Windows*, while developing work for television.

An epigraph to *The Wanderers*, from the Pulitzer-Prize-Winning poet Mary Oliver, expresses the thought behind more than this play: 'Doesn't everything die at last, and too soon? Tell me, what is it you plan to do with your one wild and precious life?' Another epigraph, from the Jewish singer-songwriter Debbie Freedman, expresses the invitation which Ziegler offers to audiences: 'L'chi Lach to a land that I will show you Leich L'cha to a place you do not know', L'chi Lach being Hebrew for 'go forward' or 'go for yourself', which has been glossed to mean 'find within yourself the journey you are meant to have', Lech L'cha meaning 'Go forth'.

NOTES

Introduction

1. Herb Blau, *The Audience* (Baltimore, 1990), pp.1, 3.
2. https://www.broadwayleague.com/research/statistics-broadway-nyc.

Chapter 1

1. Gerard Raymond, 'Exorcising the Dark Side: Playwright David Adjmi Talks *Elective Affinities*', *Slant Magazine*, 4 December 2011. https://www.slantmagazine.com/house/article/exorcising-the-dark-side-an-interview-with-playwright-david-adjmi
2. Ibid.
3. Felicia R. Lee, 'Once a Boyhood Outsider, Now Reflecting on His Tribe', *The New York Times*, 16 June 2009. www.nytimes.com/2009/06/17/theater/17stunning.html
4. Daisy Bowie-Sell, 'Ayad Akhtar: The Petri Dish of British Theatre Is Overflowing with Rich Abundance', *What's on Stage*, 27 June 2017. www.whatsonstage.com/ … /ayad-akhtar-interview-indhu-rubasingham-guest-editor_4.
5. From Elective Affinities by David Adjmi. Copyright © 2011 by David Adjmi. Published in Stunning and Other Plays. Copyright © 2011 by David Adjmi. Published by Theatre Communications Group. Used by permission of Theatre Communications Group. David Adjmi, *Stunning and Other Plays* (New York, 2011), p.269.
6. Ari M. Brostoff, "The Damascus Affair," *The Tablet*, June 30, 2009. Tabletmag.com/sections/arts-letters/articles/the-damascus-affair
7. David Noh, 'Adjmi's Antionette', *Gay City News*, 13 November 2013. gaycitynews.nyc/adjmis-antoinette/
8. Hilton Als, 'Domestic Politics: David Adjmi on Household Race Relations', *The New Yorker*, 29 June 2009. https://www.newyorker.com/magazine/2009/06/29/domestic-politics
9. Felicia R. Lee, 'Once a Boyhood Outsider, Now Reflecting on His Tribe', *The New York Times*, 16 June 2009. https://www.nytimes.com/2009/06/17/theater/17stunning.html
10. David Adjmi, *Lot Six: A Memoir* (New York, 2020), p.148.
11. Julie Kanfer, 'Brooklyn Heights People: David Adjmi', *Brooklyn Heights Blog*, 28 October 2010. brooklynheightsblog.com/archives/23753
12. Adjmi, *Lot Six*, pp.162–3.
13. David Schmader, 'Triple-X-Ibsen', *The Stranger*, 9 January 2003. www.thestranger.com/seattle/triple-x-ibsen/Content?oid=13078
14. Heidi Schreck, 'In Dialogue: Suffer Little Children: The Sturm und Drang of David Adjmi', *The Brooklyn Rail*, 1 October 2015. brooklynrail.org/ … /in-dialogue-suffer-little-children-the-sturm-und-drang-of-david-a
15. Ibid.
16. Adjmi, *Lot Six*, p.338.
17. Ibid.
18. Raymond, 'Exorcising the Dark Side: Playwright David Adjmi Talks *Elective Affinities*'.
19. Ben Brantley, 'Privilege and Poison on the Upper East Side', *The New York Times*, 2 December 2011. https://www.nytimes.com/2011/12/03/theater/reviews/elective-affinities-with-zoe-caldwel …

Notes

20. David Cote, 'Review: Elective Affinities', *Time Out*, December 2011. www.timeout.com/newyork/theater/review-elective-affinities-off-broadway
21. John Heilpern, 'What Makes Political Theater Effective – Or Not', *New York Observer*, 7 August 2006. observer.com/2006/08/what-makes-political-theater-effectiveor-not/
22. Adjmi, *Stunning and Other Plays*, p.251.
23. Ibid., p.146.
24. Julie Haverkate, 'Other within the Other', *TCG Circle*, November 2011. www.tcgcircle.org/2011/11/other-within-the-other/
25. Charles Isherwood, 'He's Seen the Enemy, and It's Here at Home', *The New York Times*, 29 January 2008. www.nytimes.com/2008/01/29/theater/reviews/29evil.html
26. Frank Rizzo, 'The Evildoers', *Variety*, 27 January 2008. variety.com/2008/legit/reviews/the-evildoers-1200548651/
27. David Cope, 'David Adjmi: Will His Newest Play Be Stunning?' *Time Out*, 10 June 2009. www.timeout.com/newyork/theater/david-adjmi
28. Email from David Adjmi, 25 November 2017.
29. Lisa Traiger, 'A New Play Lifts Veil on Syrian-Jewish Community', *Forward*, 13 March 2008. forward.com/culture/12918/a-new-play-lifts-veil-on-insular-syrian-jewish-com-01460/
30. Cope, 'David Adjmi: Will His Newest Play Be Stunning'.
31. Adjmi, *Stunning and Other Plays*, p.5.
32. Felicia R. Lee, 'Once a Boyhood Outsider, Now Reflecting on His Tribe', *The New York Times*, 16 June 2009. www.nytimes.com/2009/06/17/theater/17stunning.html
33. Ibid.
34. Adjmi, *Stunning and Other Plays*, p.7.
35. Adam R. Perlmand, 'Stunning', *backstage*, 18 June 2009. https://www.backstage.com/review/ny-theater/off-broadway/stunning/
36. https://www.glpi.com.br/en/threes-company-parody-play-is-transformative-says-us-court/
37. David Adjmi, 'Some Thoughts on 3C', in *3 C* (New York, 2015), np.
38. Noh, 'Adjmi's Antionette'.
39. John Lahr, 'Love's Labors', *The New Yorker*, 2 July 2012. https://www.newyorker.com/magazine/2012/07/02/loves-labors-3
40. Larry Kunofsky, 'Larry Kunofsky on "3C" by David Adjmi', *New York Theatre Review*, 7 July 2012. newyorktheatrereview.blogspot.com/ … /larry-kunofsky-on-3c-by-david-adjmi-as.html
41. David Cote, '3C', *Time Out (New York)*, 22 June 2012. https://www.timeout.com/newyork/theater/3c
42. Charles Isherwood, 'Names Have Been Changed to Protect the Innuendos', *The New York Times*, 24 June 2012. https://www.nytimes.com/ … /3c-by-david-adjmi-at-rattlestick-playwrights-theater.html
43. Sydney-Chanele Dawkins, 'The Playwright's Playground: The Lonely and the Brave – an Interview with "Marie Antoinette" Playwright David Adjmi', *DC Metro Theatre Arts*, 25 September 2014. dcmetrotheaterarts.com/ … /playwrights-playground-lonely-brave-interview-marie-anto.
44. Ibid.
45. Meghan O'Rourke, '"Veronica": Two Girls, Alive and Dead', *The New York Times*, 23 October 2005. https://www.nytimes.com/2005/10/23/books/review/veronica-two-girls-alive-and-dead.html
46. Dawkins, 'The Playwright's Playground'.
47. Noh, 'Adjmi's Antionette'.
48. Raymond, 'Exorcising the Dark Side: Playwright David Adjmi Talks *Elective Affinities*'.
49. David Adjmi, *Marie Antionette* (New York, 2014), p.95.
50. Mark Pickell, 'Cap T Interviews Marie Antoinettte Playwright David Adjmi', *Capital T Theatre*, 5 March 2016. http://capitalt.org/wp/featured/cap-t-interviews-marie-antoinette-playwright-david-adjmi/5896
51. Dawkins, 'The Playwright's Playground'.
52. Email from David Adjmi, 25 November 2017.
53. Charles Isherwood, 'Moaning All the Way to the Guillotine', *The New York Times*, 12 November 2012. https://www.nytimes.com/2012/11/13/theater/reviews/david-adjmis-marie-antoinette-at-yale-repertory-theater.html

Notes

54. Julie Rattey, 'Marie Antoinette Reviewed', *America*, 19 November 2012. https://www.americamagazine.org/content/all-things-marie-antoinette-reviewed
55. Frank Rizzo, 'Marie Antoinette', *Variety*, 5 November 2012. https://variety.com/2012/legit/reviews/marie-antoinette-1117948692
56. Ibid.
57. Jon Magaril, 'Marie Antionette at Soho Rep', *Slant*, 15 November 2013. https://www.slantmagazine.com/theater/review-marie-antoinette-at-soho-rep
58. Everette Evans, 'Queen Rules in Stages' Clevertv "Marie Antoinette"', *Houston Chronicle*. 14 October 2014. Review: Queen rules in St'ages' clever 'Marie Antoinette'.
59. Adjmi, *Lot Six*, p.369.

Chapter 2

1. Natalie Tucker, 'Julia Cho, "Aubergine" Playwright', *DC Metro*, 15 January 2018. https://dcmetrotheaterarts.com/2018/02/15/interview-julia-cho
2. Jay Caspian Kang, 'The Myth of Asian American Identity', *The New York Time Magazines*, 5 October 2021.
3. Elizabeth Weir, 'Rising Playwright Julia Chi Premiers 99 Histories with Theater Mu and Intermedia Arts', *Talkin' Broadway*. talkin' broadway, 99 histories julia cho.
4. Tim Sanford, 'Julia Cho Artist Interview', *Playwrights Horizon*, 7 September 2016. https://www.playwrightshorizons.org/shows/trailers/julia-cho-artist-interview
5. *The Language Archive*, pp.230–231.
6. Mahira Kakkar, 'Julia Cho: A Playwright Drawn to "What Ifs"', *The Julliard Journal*, December 2007/January 2008. journal.juilliard.edu › journal › julia-cho-playwright-drawn
7. 'An Interview with Julia Cho', *2g (Second Generation)*. www.2g.org › an-interview-with-julia-cho
8. Julia Cho, *99 Histories* (New York, 2005), p.7.
9. Rainer Maria Rilke, *Letters to a Young Poet, Letter 8*, trans. M.D. Herter Norton p.72. https://monoskop.org/.../55/Rilke_Rainer_Maria_Letters_to_a_Young_... PDF file
10. Sanford, 'Julia Cho Artist Interview'.
11. Julia Cho, *BFE* (New York, 2005), p.10.
12. https://wearetherealdeal.com/2014/12/20/interview-with-actress-julia
13. Elyse Sommer, 'BFE', *CurtainUp*. www.curtainup.com › bfe
14. Anita Gates, 'Asian and Isolated in a Desert of Blondes and Coca-Cola', *The New York Times*, 1 June 2005.
15. Julia Cho, *The Architecture of Loss* (New York, 2005), pp.10.
16. Marilyn Stasio, 'The Architecture of Loss', *Variety*, 13 January 2004. https://variety.com/2004/legit/reviews/the-architecture-of-loss-1200537102
17. John Simon, 'Vanishing Acts', *New York Magazine*, 22 January 2004. nymag.com › nymetro › artsThe Architecture of Loss – Julia Cho – Ute Lemper – New York
18. Margot Jefferson, 'In Habitants of an Empty House Built with Greif and Longing', *The New York Times*, 14 January 2004. https://www.nytimes.com/2004/01/14/theater/theater-review-inhabitants
19. Julia Cho, *The Winchester House*, p.4 of unpublished text kindly provided by the author.
20. Julia Cho, *Durango*, in the *Language Archive and Other Plays* (New York, 2019), p.13.
21. Kathy Henderson, 'Before Paula Vogel's *Indecent* There Was *How I Learned to Drive*', *Playbill*, 10 May 2017. Error! Hyperlink reference not valid.
22. Mark Blankenship, 'Durango', *Variety*, 20 November 2006. https://variety.com/2006/legit/reviews/durango-2-1200511869
23. Elyse Sommer, 'Durango', *Curtain Up*. www.curtainup.com/durango.html
24. Dan Bacalzo, 'Piano Woman', *TheaterMania*, 6 March 2007. https://www.theatermania.com/new-york-city-theater/news/piano-woman_10242.html

Notes

25. Julia Cho, *The Piano Teacher* in *The Language Archive and Other Plays*, p.97.
26. Charles Isherwood, 'In a Quiet Suburb, a Quiet Life Darkened', *The New York Times*, 19 November 2007. https://www.nytimes.com/2007/11/19/theater/reviews/19pian.html
27. Jeffrey Walker, 'The Piano Teacher', *DC Theatre Scene*, 12 February 2014. https://dctheatrescene.com/2014/02/12/piano-teacher
28. Julia Cho, *The Language Archive* in *The Language Archive and Other Plays*, p.194.
29. Charles Isherwood, 'A Linguist at a Loss for Words Regarding Love', *The New York Times*, 17 October 2010. www.nytimes.com › 2010/10/18 › theater
30. Tim Treanor, 'The Language Archive', *DC Theatre Scene*, 20 February 2012. dctheatrescene.com › 2012/02/20 › the-language-archi
31. Chris Jones, 'In "Language" Love and Finding the Right Words', *Chicago Tribune*, 25 February 2014. www.chicagotribune.com › entertainment › theaterIn 'Language,' love and finding the right words – Chicago Tribune
32. Sanford, 'Julia Cho Artist Interview'.
33. Christopher Bigsby, *Writers in Conversation with Christopher Bigsby*, vol. 6 (Norwich, 2018), pp.147–8.
34. Sanford, 'Julia Cho Artist Interview'.
35. Ibid.
36. Ibid.
37. Ibid.
38. Julia Cho, *Aubergine*, in *The Language Archive and Other Plays*, p.301.
39. Charles McNulty, 'In "Aubergine," Julia Cho Turns Choked-Off Emotions into a Tale of Sustenance', *Los Angeles Times*, 1 March 2016. www.latimes.com › entertainment › artsReview: In 'Aubergine,' Julia Cho turns choked-off emotions…
40. Charles Isherwood, '"Aubergine," A Stew of Regret and Impending Loss', *The New York Times*, 12 September 2016. https://www.nytimes.com/2016/09/13/theater/aubergine-review-julia-cho.html
41. Julia Cho, *Office Hour*, in *The Language Archive and Other Plays*, p.366.
42. Jesse Green, '"Office Hour" Is the Play That Goes Bang', *The New York Times*, 8 November 2017. https://www.nytimes.com/2017/11/08/theater/office-hour-review.html
43. Michael Feingold, 'Julia Cho's "Office Hour" Grapples with Violence and Empathy', *The Village Voice*, 16 November 2017. www.villagevoice.com › 2017/11/16 › julia-chosJulia Cho's 'Office Hour' Grapples With Violence and Empathy
44. Donald Brown, 'Teacher's Threat', *New Haven Review*, 28 January 2018. www.newhavenreview.com/blog/index.php/2018/1/teachers-threat
45. paulavogelplaywright.com/new-blog/2017/12/1/office-hour
46. Antonin Artaud, *The Theatre and Its Double*, translated by Mary Caroline Richards (New York, 1958), p.41.
47. Mahira Kakkar, 'Julia Cho: A Playwright Drawn to "What Ifs"'. *The Julliard Journal*, December, 2007/January 2008. journal.juilliard.edu › journal › julia-cho-playwright-drawn

Chapter 3

1. Alexis Soloski, 'In This Play about Race, "People Need to Feel Uncomfortable"', *The New York Times*, 6 July 2018. https://www.nytimes.com/2018/07/06/theater/fairview-play-race.html
2. Lawrence Goodman, 'The Monstrous Unknown', *Brown Alumni Magazine*, 2 July 2013. https://www.brownalumnimagazine.com/…/2013-07-02/the-monstrous-unknown
3. Ibid.
4. Soraya Nadia McDonald, 'Pulitzer-winning Playwright Jackie Sibblies Drury Wants Her Audience to Feel Awkward', *The Undefeated*, 27 June 2019. https://theundefeated.com/features/pulitzer-winning-playwright-jackie

Notes

5   Goodman, 'The Monstrous Unknown'.
6   https://www.youtube.com/watch?v=m3efeYvcIA0
7   'Conversation with Playwright Jackie Sibblies Drury', *Howlround.com*, 21 January 2014. https://howlround.com/conversation-playwright-jackie-sibblies-drury
8   Ibid.
9   Quoted in Claudia Rankin, *Just Us: An American Conversation* (London, 2021), p.145.
10 Jackie Sibblies Drury, 'Empathy by Another Name', in *We ARE Proud to Present a Presentation about the Herero of Namibia, Formerly Known as Southwest Africa. From the German Sudwestafrika, between the Years 1884–1915* (London, 2014), n.p.
11 Ramona Ostrowski, 'We Are Proud to Present: Jackie Sibblies Drury', *companyone.org*. https://companyone.org/wp-content/uploads/2014/06/JackieInterview
12 https://www.neh.gov/about/awards/jefferson-lecture/arthur-miller-biography
13 Charles Isherwood, 'Acting Out a Blood Bath Brings Dangers of Its Own', *The New York Times*, 16 November2012. https://www.nytimes.com/2012/11/17/theater/reviews/we-are-proud-to-present-a
14 Michael Billington, 'We Are Proud to Present … review – "A Piran dellian take on a little-known genocide,"' *The Guardian*, 5 March 2014.
15 https://www.timeout.com/newyork/theater/we-are-proud-to-present-a
16 Goodman, 'The Monstrous Unknown'.
17 Jackie Sibblies Drury, *Social Creatures*, p.2. Text kindly supplied by the author.
18 Robe Weinert-Kendt, 'Writes Well with Others', *The New York Times*, 16 April 2013. https://www.nytimes.com/2013/04/17/theater/jackie-sibblies-drurys
19 Jackie Sibblies Drury, *Really* (New York, 2021), p.4.
20 'Undermain Theatre Presents *Really* by Jackie Sibblies Drury', *Undermain Theatre*, 6 April 2017. https://www.dmagazine.com/sponsored/2017/04/undermain-theatre-presents
21 Christopher Bigsby, *Writers in Conversation with Christopher Bigsby* (Norwich, 2013), p.136.
22 Ibid., p.133.
23 Ben Brantley, '"Really" Compares the Fixed Image with Life's Flux', *The New York Times*, 23 March 2016. https://www.nytimes.com/2016/03/24/theater/review-really-compares-the
24 Deb Miller, '"Really" at Theatre Exile', *DC Metro*, 2 February 2018. dcmetrotheaterarts.com › 2018/02/02 › review-really
25 Kadish Morris, 'Artist Kehinde Wiley: "The New Work is about what it feels like to be Young, Black and Alive in the 21st Century,"' 21 November 2021. https://www.theguardian.com/artanddesign/2021/nov/21/artist-kehinde
26 Clare Wrathall, 'Kehinde Wiley: "I took the DNA of William Morris and created Hybrids,"' *The Guardian*, 25 January 2020. https://www.theguardian.com › artanddesign › 2020Kehinde Wiley: I took the DNA of William Morris and created
27 Jack Sibblies Drury, *Fairview* (New York, 2019), p.6.
28 Christine Amapour, 'Jackie Sibblies Drury Discusses Her Play "Fairview"', 27 June 2019. https://www.pbs.org/wnet/amanpour-and-company/video/jackie-sibblies
29 Soraya Nadia McDonald, 'Pulitzer-winning Playwright Jackie Sibblies Drury Wants Her Audiende to Feel Awkward', *The Undefeated*, 27 June 2019. theundefeated.com/features/pulitzer-winning-playwright-jackie-sibblies-drury-wants-her-audien
30 Liz Appel, 'Theater Is Coded as a White Space – Jackie Sibblies Drury Is Changing That', *Vogue*, 5 June 2019. https://www.vogue.com/article/jackie-sibblie-drury-fairview-pulitzer-interview
31 Bridget Minamore, 'Fairview: The Pulitzer Winner Whose Creator Hopes That It Will Have a Shirt Shelf Life', *The Guardian*, 4 December 2019. https://www.theguardian.com/stage/2019/dec/04/fairview-jackie-sibblies
32 Alicia Menendez, 'Jack Sibblies Drury Discusses her play "Fairview"', *pbs.org*. www.pbs.org › wnet › amanpour-and-companyJackie Sibblies Drury Discusses Her Play, 'Fairview' – PBS.
33 Claudia Rankine, *Just Us: An American Conversation* (New York, 2020), p.197.
34 Ben Brantley, "Theatre as Sabotage in the Dazzling Fairview," *The New York Times*, 17 June 2018.

35 Charles McNulty, 'Playwright Jackie Sibblies Drury Daringly Deconstructs the Theatre of Black Identity in "Fairview" at Berkeley Rep', *Los Angeles Times*, 15 October 2018. Review: Playwright Jackie Sibblies Drury daringly. https://www.latimes.com/entertainment/arts/theater/reviews/la-et-cm…
36 Michael Billington, 'A Daring Challenge to the White Gaze', *The Guardian,* 5 December 2019. https://www.theguardian.com/stage/2019/dec/05/fairview-review-jackie
37 Jackie Sibblies Drury, *Marys Seacole*, p.1. Dramatists Play Service EPUB, 2022.
38 Victoria Myers, 'Jackie Sibblies Drury on *Marys Seacole* and More', *The Interval,* 19 Feburary 2019. Jackie Sibblies Drury on Marys Seacole and More | The Interval.
39 Rankine, *Just Us: An American Conversation*,p.319.
40 Ben Brantley, '"Marys Seacole" Puts Biodrama through a Kaleidoscope', *The New York Times*, 25 February 2019. https://www.nytimes.com/2019/02/25/theater/marys-seacole-review.html
41 Tullis McCall, 'Review of Lincoln Center's LCT Production of Marys Seacole', *New York Theatre Guide,* 5 March 2019. https://www.newyorktheatreguide.com/reviews/review-of-lincoln-center
42 Michael Sommers, 'Marys Seacole: Studying Maternal Care then and Now', *New York Stage Review*, 25 February 2019. nystagereview.com/2019/02/25/marys-seacole-a-bio-drama-studying
43 Frank Scheck, *The Hollywood Reporter*, 25 February 2019. https://www.hollywoodreporter.com/news/general-news/marys-seacole

Chapter 4

1 Joe Sola, 'Will Eno by Joe Sola', *The Believer*, 1 July 2008. https://bombmagazine.org › articles › will-eno
2 Darryn King, 'Will Eno's Deconstructive Theatre', *The Saturday Paper*, 8–14 October 2016. https://www.thesaturdaypaper.com.au/…/will-enos-deconstructive-theatre/147584520
3 John Bailey, 'An Interview with Will Eno', *Capital Idea*, 7 February 2010. apentimento.blogspot.com/2010/02/interview-with-will-eno.html
4 Will Eno, *The Flu Season and Other Plays* (New York, 2008), p.84.
5 Will Eno, *The Realistic Joneses* (London, 2014), p.8.
6 Chad Jones, 'Where There's a Will', *Theatre Dogs*, 7 September 2008. www.theaterdogs.net/2011/04/04/where-theres-a-will/
7 Alexis Soloski, 'Despair Is Looking Up', *The New York Times*, 19 February 2014. https://www.nytimes.com/…/will-enos-the-open-house-and-the-realistic-joneses.html
8 'Not From Here: An Interview with Will Eno', *Signature Stories*, Spring 2012. https://www.signaturetheatre.org/SignatureTheatre/media/…/SignatureStoriesVol2.pdf
9 Richard Patterson, 'Will Eno: A Very Human Thing', *Exeunt Magazine*, 11 September 2012. exeuntmagazine.com/features/will-eno/
10 http://xroads.virginia.edu/~hyper/walden/hdt02.html
11 Will Eno, 'Preface', *The Flu Season and Other Plays* (New York, 2008), p.74.
12 Eno, *The Flu Season and Other Plays*, p.81
13 Lyn Gardner, 'Tragedy: A Tragedy', *The Guardian*, 9 April 2001.
14 Kris Vire, 'Tragedy: A Tragedy at the Red Tape Theater', *Time Out (Chicago)*, 17 May 2011. https://www.timeout.com/chicago/theater/tragedy-a-tragedy-at-red-tape-theatre-theater-review
15 Samuel Beckett, *Samuel Beckett: The Complete Dramatic Works* (London, 1986), p.82.
16 Samuel Beckett, *Proust and 3 Dialogues with Georges Duthuit* (London, 1965), p.13.
17 Samuel Beckett, *Worstward Ho* (London, 1983), p.7.
18 Lyn Gardner, 'The Flu Season', *The Guardian*, 12 April 2003. https://www.theguardian.com › Arts › Stage › Theatre
19 Margo Jefferson, 'Psychiatric Patients and a Maze of Language', *The New York Times*, 10 February 2004.
20 Beckett, *Samuel Beckett: The Complete Dramatic Works*, p.37.
21 Ibid., p.33.
22 Will Eno, *Thom Pain (based on nothing)* (New York, 2005), p.16.

Notes

23. Mark Lawson, 'Will Eno – "It takes work to sound like a real person talking,"' *The Guardian*, 20 August 2014. https://www.theguardian.com/.../will-eno-title-and-deed-edinburgh-2014-monologue-
24. Lyn Gardner, 'Tom Pain (based on nothing)', *The Guardian*, 16 May 2004. https://www.theguardian.com/stage/2004/aug/16/theatre.edinburghfestival20041
25. David Gritten, 'Mesmerised by an Invisible Man', *The Daily Telegraph*, 11 August 2004. http://www.telegraph.co.uk/culture/theatre/3622069/Edinburgh-reviews-mesmerised-by-an-invisible-man.html
26. Charles Isherwood, 'Life's a Gift. Quick. Exchange It', *The New York Times*, 2 February 2005. http://www.nytimes.com/2005/02/02/theater/reviews/lifes-a-gift-quick-exchange-it.html
27. Will Eno, *Oh, the Humanity and Other Good Intentions* (New York, 2014), p.68.
28. Will Eno, *Middletown* (London, 2011), p.21
29. 'In the Middle of Middletown', *Steppenwolf Theatre Company*, 26 July 2011. YouTube.
30. Charles Isherwood, 'Word Woozy Roundelay in Average Town Ruled by Singular Sadness', 3 November 2010.
31. Chris Jones, 'Life, Death, and the Tricky Stuff in between', *Chicago Tribune*, 26 June 2011. http://articles.chicagotribune.com/2011-06-26/entertainment/ct-ent-0627-middleton-review-20110626_1_eno-middletown-practical-nurse
32. Will Eno, *Title and Deed* (New York, 2014), p.11.
33. 'Beyond Broadway: Will Eno's "Title and Dead"', *Broadway.com*, 5 June 2012. https://www.youtube.com/watch?v=m0tC24YUGwg
34. Lyn Gardner, 'Title and Deed – Devastating Monologue Channels Beckett', *The Guardian*, 6 August 2014. https://www.theguardian.com › Arts › Stage › Edinburgh festival 2014
35. Ian Shuttleworth, 'Title and Deed, Print Room Theatre, London', *Financial Times*, 19 January 2015. https://garestlazare.squarespace.com/.../Title-Deed-Print-Room-Theatr-e-London-review-
36. Charles Isherwood, 'A Stranger in Beckett Land', *The New York Times*, 20 May 2012. www.nytimes.com/2012/05/21/.../title-and-deed-by-will-eno-with-conor-lovett.html
37. John Lahr, 'At Two with Nature', *The New Yorker*, 28 May 2012. https://www.newyorker.com/magazine/2012/05/28/at-two-with-nature
38. Shannon Stockwell, 'The Weird but Ever-There Mystery: An Interview with Playwright Will Eno', *Words on Plays: American Conservatory Theater*, vol. 22, number 6. http://www.actsf.org/content/dam/act/education_department/words_on_plays/The%20Realistic%20Joneses%20(2016).pdf
39. Eno, *The Realistic Joneses*, p.8.
40. Samuel Beckett, *The Complete Dramatic Works*, p.82.
41. 'Will Eno the Realistic Joneses', *Samuel French*, 26 January 2015. https://www.youtube.com/watch?v=bTxuBqEIl_Q
42. Stockwell, 'The Weird but Ever-There Mystery: An Interview with Playwright Will Eno'.
43. Michael Meyer, 'Introduction', in Henrik Ibsen, *Plays Six: Peer Gynt, The Pretenders* (London, 1987), p.19.
44. Ibid., p.14.
45. *Henrick Ibsen, Plays 6*, p.92.
46. Will Eno, *Gnit* (New York, 2013), p.11.
47. *Henrik Ibsen, Plays 6*, p.62.
48. 'Will Eno Gnit', *Samuel French*, 26 January 2015. https://www.youtube.com/watch?v=kG-C_WCK_fc
49. American Theatre Editors, 'The 2013 Humana Playwrights Share Their Experiences at the New American Play Festival', *American Theatre*, 1 July 2013. http://www.americantheatre.org/2013/07/01/the-2013-humana-playwrights-share-their-experiences-at-the-new-american-play-festival/
50. 'Will Eno: Gnit', *Samuel French*. http://www.samuelfrench.co.uk/p/44438/gnit
51. http://willeno.com
52. 'Will Eno the Open House', *Samuel French*, 26 January 2015. https://www.youtube.com/watch?v=pBFTLOmV_bU

Notes

53. Will Eno, *The Open House* (London, 2014), p.15.
54. Charles Isherwood, 'When Dad Gets Mad, Learn to Disappear', *The New York Times*, 3 March 2014. https://www.nytimes.com/2014/03/04/theater/in-will-enos-the-open-house-dysfunctional-dynamics.html
55. Michael Billington, 'Sarcasm Rules Suburbia in Comic Portrait of a Bilious Dad', *The Guardian*, 30 November 2017. https://www.theguardian.com/stage/2017/nov/30/the-open-house-review-ustinov-studio-bath-greg-hicks-will-eno
56. Will Eno, *Wakey, Wakey* (London, 2017), p.18.
57. 'Will Eno on Wakey, Wakey and the Signature Theatre', 28 February 2017. https://www.youtube.com/watch?v=POdp0IMpu4M
58. Ben Brantley, 'Wakey, Wakey Stars Life and Death', *The New York Times*, 27 March 2017. www.nytimes.com › wakey-wakey-review-will-eno
59. Will Eno, *The Underlying Chris* (New York, 2020), np.
60. https://2st.com/images/pdf/Interviews/Will_Eno_Interview.pdf
61. Jesse Green, 'In "The Underlying Chris", You Are Who You Were', *The New York Times*, 21 Novembers 2019. https://www.nytimes.com/2019/11/21/theater/the-underlying-chris-review
62. Will Eno, *The Plot* (New York, 2020), p.63.
63. Chad Jones, 'Playwright Will Eno's "Lady Grey" at Cutting Bull', *SFGATE*, 2 April 2011. https://www.sfgate.com/performance/article/Playwright-Will-Eno-s-Lady
64. E. Kyle Minor, 'Will Eno's Mom-inspired "Plot" at Yale Rep Offers Blunt Negotiations', *New Haven Register*, 28 November 2019. Error! Hyperlink reference not valid.

Chapter 5

1. Corey Ruzicano, 'A Conversation with Martyna Majok', *Stage & Candor*, 7 June 2017. stageandcandor.com › conversations › martyna-majok
2. Rachel Sylvester, Al.ce Thomson, 'Rose Tremain on the Culture Wars', *The Times*, 4 December 2021. https://www.thetimes.co.uk/article/rose-tremain-interview-i-m-told-don-t-make-it-up-any-more-we-need-the-real-thing-568r8qbqd
3. Theodore P. Mahne, 'Small Craft Warnings' Captures Vitality of Tennessee Williams' Character', *The Times-Picayune/The New Orleans Advocate*, nola.com, 14 December 2015. https://www.nola.com/entertainment_life/arts/article_bdb59a16-c153.
4. Mark Brown, 'Jewish District Inspires Tom Stoppard in "Personal" New Play', *The Guardian*, 26 January 2019. Jewish district inspires Tom Stoppard in 'personal' new play | Tom Stoppard | The Guardian.
5. Rusicano, 'A Conversation with Martyna Majok'.
6. Peter Stamelman, 'Brooklyn Goes to Williamstown: An Interview with Playwright Martyna Majok', *Brooklyn Daily Eagle*, 22 June 2016. https://brooklyneagle.com/articles/2016/06/22/brooklyn-goes-to
7. Laura Collins-Hughes, 'Q, and A.: Martyna Majok, Putting Immigrant Lives on Center Stage', *The New York Times*, 17 February 2016. https://www.nytimes.com/2016/02/21/theater/q-and-a-martyna-majok
8. 'Everyone Was from Somewhere Else: An Interview with Martyna Majok', *Vilcek Foundation*, 23 January 2019. https://vilcek.org/news/everyone-was-from-somewhere-else-an-interview
9. 'Mark Strong on Life without a Father: "I got angry as I grew older. It took years to fix it,"' *The Irish Times*, 2 November 2021. Mark Strong on life without a father: 'I got angry as I got older. It took years to fix' (irishtimes.com)
10. Ruzicano, 'A Conversation with Martyna Majok'.
11. Jeryl Bruner, 'Martyna Majok Is a Prize-Winning Force with a Brand New Play', *Forbes*, 3 October 2021. https://www.forbes.com/sites/jerylbrunner/2021/10/03/martyna-majok-is
12. https://bstreetbengaged.wordpress.com/2018/10/05/martyna-majok-playwright-of-ironbound/

Notes

13   Joanna Socha, 'Pulitzer Prize Winner Martyna Majok Discusses Playwriting as a Career Choice', *W-Insight*, 20 May 2021. w-insight.com › 2021/05/20 › pulitzer-prize-winner
14   Nicole Serratore, 'Playwright Martyna Majok: "I want fluid to Leak from your Face. That's what I want Theatre to do"', *The Stage*, 17 March 2020. https://www.thestage.co.uk/features/playwright-martyna-majok-i-want
15   Jeryl Brunner, 'Martyna Majok Is a Pulitzer Prize-Winning Force with a Brand New Play', *Forbes*, 3 October2021. https://www.forbes.com/sites/jerylbrunner/2021/10/03/martyna-majok-is.
16   https://www.youtube.com/watch?v=tR4taiIYcZM
17   bstreetbengaged.wordpress.com › 2018/10/05 › martyna
18   Aimee Picchi, 'Five Traits of American Working Class', *CBS News*, 29 September 2017. www.cbsnews.com › media › 5-traits-of-americas
19   Dominique Morisseau, 'Maryna Majok Shines a Light on the Invisible in "Ironbound"', *American Theatre*, December 2016. https://www.americantheatre.org/2016/12/20/martyna-majok-shines-a-light-on-the-invisible-in-ironbound/
20   Tommy Smith, 'Shifting Shape: Ironbound's Martyna Majok', *The Brooklyn Rail*, March 2016. https://brooklynrail.org/…/shifting-shape-ironbounds-martyna-majok
21   Morisseau, 'Maryna Majok Shines a Light on the Invisible in "Ironbound"'.
22   Martyna Majok, *Ironbound* (New York, 2016), p.23.
23   Robert Pinsky, 'Jersey Rain', in *The Atlantic*, 18 April 2017. https://www.theatlantic.com/notes/2017/04/poem-of-the-day-jersey-rain.
24   David Siegel, 'Women's Voices Theatre Festival: "Ironbound" at Round House Theatre', *DC Metro Theatre Arts*, 16 September 2015. dcmetrotheaterarts.com › 2015/09/16 › womens-voices
25   Ibid.
26   Jennifer Perry, 'Round House Theatre's Ironbound Simmers Quietly', *Broadway World*, 16 September 2015. Review: Round House Theatre's Ironbound Simmers Quietly
27   Charles Isherwood, 'Ironbound Stars Marin Ireland as a Struggling Immigrant', *The New York Times*, 16 March 2016. https://www.nytimes.com/2016/03/17/theater/review-ironbound-stars
28   Charles McNulty, '"Ironbound" at the Geffen Playhouse: An Immigrant's Portrait, Painted with Piercing Realism', *Los Angles Times,* 9 February 2018. https://www.latimes.com/entertainment/arts/la-et-cm-ironbound-review
29   Emily Lovett, 'Path to Pulitzer: An Interview with Playwright Martyna Majok', *Chicagomaroon*, 22 April 2018. https://www.chicagomaroon.com/article/2018/4/22/path-pulitzer
30   'Interview: Playwright Martyna Majok on Grief and Hoping for Magic in Her New Play "Cost of Living"', *StageBuddy.com*. https://stagebuddy.com/theater/theater-feature/interview-playwright Martyna Majok.
31   Martyn Majok, *Cost of Living* (New York, 2018), p.19.
32   *StageBuddy.com*. https://stagebuddy.com/theater/theater-feature/interview-playwright Martyna Majok.
33   David Brooks, 'America Is Having a Moral Convulsion', *Atlantic Monthly*, 5 October 2020. https://www.theatlantic.com/ideas/archive/2020/10/collapsing-levels
34   Elise Marenson, 'Cost of Living', *New York Theatre Guide*, 8 June 2017. https://www.newyorktheatreguide.com/reviews/cost-of-living
35   Jesse Green, 'In "Cost of Living," a Familiar Alienation', *The New York Times*, 7 June 2017. https://www.nytimes.com/2017/06/07/theater/cost-of-living-review.html
36   Michael Billington, 'Adrian Lester Dazzles in Stirring Portrait of Poverty', *The Guardian*, 1 February 2019. https://www.theguardian.com/stage/2019/feb/01/cost-of-living-review.
37   www.pulitzer.org › winners › martyna-majok
38   'Martyna Majok and Danya Taymor on "queens"', *The Interval*, 20 February 2018. https://www.theintervalny.com/…/martyna-majok-and-danya-taym
39   Martyna Majok, *queens*, p.51. Text kindly supplied by the author.
40   Jan Simpon, 'Stagecraft: Martyna Majok, Queens', *Broadway Radio*, 24 February 2018. https://broadwayradio.com/blog/2018/02/24/stagecraft-martyna-majok-queens

Notes

41 Jesse Green, 'In "queens" 11 Immigrant Women and What They Left behind', *The New York Times*, 5 March 2018. https://www.nytimes.com/2018/03/05/theater/queens-martyna-majok-review.html
42 Martyna Majok, *Sanctuary City*, p.3. Text kindly supplied by the author.
43 David Gordon, 'Martyna Majok on Returning to Sanctuary City, 18 months after It Started Previews', *Theater Mania*, 14 September 2021. https://www.theatermania.com/off-broadway/news/martyna-majok-on
44 w-insight.com/2021/05/20/pulitzer-prize-winner-martyna-majok-discusses-playwritin…

Chapter 6

1 P.J. Powers, 'Interview with Dominique Morisseau', *TimeLine Theatre*, 24 February 2016. https://timelinetheatre.com/2016/02/interview-dominique-morisseau
2 Victoria Myers, 'An Interview with Dominique Morisseau', *The Interval*, 25 July 2017. www.theintervalny.com › tag › dominique-morisseau
3 Jacqueline E. Lawton, 'Interview: Dominique Morisseau', *ACT's 10 x 10 Festival Playwright Interview*, 7 March 2015. ATC's 10 x 10 Festival Playwright Interview: Dominique.
4 https://www.centralsquaretheater.org/2019-20-season/articles/from-the-playwright-dominique-morisseaus-rules-of-engagement/
5 Soraya Nadia McDonald, 'Tony-Nominated Playwright Dominique Morisseau Wants to Make American Theater Better for Black People', *The Undefeated*, 7 June 2019. theundefeated.com › tag › dominique-morisseau
6 Christopher Bigsby, *Writers in Conversation with Christopher Bigsby* (Norwich, 2000), p.414.
7 https://premiereplayblog.wordpress.com/2011/03/20/five-questions-for.
8 Peter Filichia, 'Follow Me to Nellie's Preview: Activist Hides in Brothel in Historical Drama', *NJ.com*. www.nj.com › follow_me_to_nellies_preview_a
9 Michael Sommers, 'Brothel's Guests: Love and Dreams', *The New York Times*, 22 July 2011. https://www.nytimes.com/2011/07/24/nyregion/love-and-segregation-in
10 Ruth Ross, 'Follow Me to Nellie's', *nj arts maven*, 17 July 2011. www.njartsmaven.com/2011/07/review-follow-me-to-nellies-premiere.html
11 Dominque Morisseau, 'Playwright's Note', in *Sunset Baby* (London, 2015), p.11.
12 Emily Wight, 'Sunset Baby: Review', *The New Staesman*, 3 October 2012. https://www.newstatesman.com/culture/2012/10/sunset-baby-review
13 Lyn Gardner, 'Sunset Baby Review', *The Guardian*, 20 September 2012. https://www.theguardian.com/stage/2012/sep/20/sunset-baby-review
14 Ben Brantley, 'Yes, Survival's Important. But then What?' *The New York Times*, 27 November 2013. https://www.nytimes.com/2013/11/28/theater/reviews/in-sunset-baby
15 Joe LaPoints, 'Stage Struck', *Hour Detroit Magazine*, 19 June 2013. www.hourdetroit.com › community › stage-struck
16 Dominique Morisseau, *The Detroit Project* (New York, 2018), p.118.
17 Charles Isherwood, 'Down in the Basement, Family Tensions Stir', *The New York Times*, 17 March 2013. https://www.nytimes.com › 2013/03/13 › theater
18 Dominque Morisseau, *Paradise Blue* in *The Detroit Project*, p.6
19 Bill Morris, 'Snapshots of Detroit: The Millions Interviews Dominique Morisseau', *The Millions*, June 15, 2018. See note 25.
20 Laura Collins-Hughes, 'Paradise Blue Rekindles Racial Drama in 1949 Detroit', *The New York Times*, 29 July 2015. https://www.nytimes.com/2015/07/30/theater/review-paradise-blue
21 Jesse Green, 'Downtown Renewal Means Trouble in "Paradise Blue"', *The New York Times*, 14 May 2018. https://www.nytimes.com/2018/05/14/theater/paradise-blue-review
22 Marilyn Stasio, 'Off Broadway Review: Paradise Blue', *Variety*, 15 May 2018. https://variety.com/2018/legit/reviews/paradise-blue-review-play

Notes

23 Chris Jones, 'Rich Paradise Blue Is Set in Faltering Jazz Club in East Detroit', *Chicago Tribune*, 5 May 2017. https://www.chicagotribune.com/entertainment/theater/ct-paradise-blue
24 Dominique Morisseau, *Skelton Crew* in *The Detroit Project*, p.207.
25 Bill Morris, 'Snapshots of Detroit: The Millions Interviews with Dominique Morisseau', 15 June 2018. https://themillions.com/2018/06/snapshots-of-detroit-the-millions-interviews-dominique-morisseau.html
26 Ben Brantley, 'Skelton Crew, a Tale of Autoworkers in Hard-Hut Detroit', 19 January 2016. https://www.nytimes.com/2016/01/20/theater/review-skeleton-crew-a-tale
27 Jose Solis, 'Interview: "Blood at the Root" Playwright Dominique Morisseau on the Power of Art, Language, and How Music Unites Us', *Stage Buddy*, 10 May 2016. stagebuddy.com › theater › theater-featureDominique Morisseau Blood at the Root – stageBuddy.
28 Ibid.
29 Dominique Morisseau, *Blood at the Root* (New York, 2017), p.33.
30 Jose Solis, 'Interview: "Blood at the Root" playwright Dominique Morisseau on the Power of Art, Language, and How Music Unites Us', *Stage Buddy*, 10 May 2016.
31 Ibid.
32 John Stoltenberg, 'Blood at the Root at Howard University's Department of Theatre Arts', 7 October 2017. dcmetrotheaterarts.com › 2017/10/07 › review-blood.
33 Mary Ann Johnson, 'Blood at the Root at Theatre Aliance', *MD Theatre Guide*, 4 March 2019. mdtheatreguide.com › 2019 › 03Theatre Review: 'Blood at the Root' at Theater Alliance
34 https://www.peopleslight.org/about/new-plays-projects/new-play-frontiers/mud-row-2019/
35 whyy.org/articles/mud-row-tells-the-story-of-black-history-in-west-chesters-east-...
36 www.broadwayworld.com/central-pa/article/Photo-Flash-Peoples-Light-Presents-Dominique-Morisseaus-MUD-ROW-20190627
37 Dominique Morisseau, *Mud Row* (New York, 2021), p.8.
38 Cameron Kelsall, '"Mud Row" at People's Light: Exquisite Production Lets an Entire Chester Community Sing', *Philadelphia Enquirer*, 1 July 2019. https://www.inquirer.com › arts › theater
39 Nataki Garrett and Dominique Morisseau, 'Oregon Shakespeare Festival: Confederates', *Literary Arts Archive*, 1 January 2022. literary-arts.org › archive › osf-confederates
40 Alexis Soloski, 'Dominique Morisseau Asks: "What Does Freedom Look Like Now"', *The New York Times*, 10 March 2022. https://www.nytimes.com/2022/03/10/theater/dominique-morisseau
41 Gordon Cox, 'Broadway Playwright Dominique Morisseau Reveals the Advice Chadwick Boseman Gave', *Variety*, 25 January 2022.variety.com › 2022 › legitBroadway Playwright Dominique Morisseau Reveals the Advice
42 Sergie Willoughby, 'Playwright Dominique Morisseau on The Temptations and the Making of Ain't Too Proud', *The Network Journal*, 5 November 2019. tnj.com › playwright-dominique-morisseau-on-the

Chapter 7

1 Anna Ziegler, *The Great Moment*, pp.23, 42. Text kindly provided by Anna Ziegler.
2 saintannsny.org.
3 Anna Ziegler, *BFF* (New York, 2008), p.7.
4 Anne Midgette, 'Friendship's No LOL Matter for Girls Becoming Adults', *The New York Times*, 1 March 2007. https://www.nytimes.com/2007/03/01/theater/reviews/01bff.html
5 Mark Blankenship, *Variety*, 24 February 2017.
6 Anna Ziegler, *Life Science* (New York, 2009), p.12.
7 Naomi Pfefferman, 'Play's Rape Case Not as Simple as Black and White', *Jewish Journal.com*, 3 May 2017. jewishjournal.com › culture › 218597.
8 Anna Ziegler, *Dov and Ali* (New York, 2016), p.7.
9 Rachel Sheridan, 'Dov and Ali', *British Theatre Guide*. www.britishtheatreguide.info › reviews › dova-rev

Notes

10 Lynn Gardner, 'Dov and Ali', *The Guardian*, 19 June 2008. Theatre review: Dov and Ali / Theatre 503, London – the Guardian.
11 Ken Jaworowski, 'A Jew and a Muslim, Firing Words after School', *The New York Times*, 12 June 2009. https://www.nytimes.com/2009/06/13/theater/reviews/13dov.html
12 Sam Thielman, 'Dov and Ali', *Variety*, 13 June 2009. https://variety.com/2009/legit/reviews/dov-and-ali-1200475163
13 Christopher Bigsby, *Writers in Conversation with Christopher Bigsby, Volume Six* (Norwich, 2017), p.270.
14 Ibid.
15 Ibid., p.274–5.
16 Ibid., p.276.
17 Ibid.
18 Victoria Myers, 'Anna Ziedler on "Actualy" and More', *The Interval*, 11 May 2017.www.theintervalny.com › anna-ziegler-on-actually-and-more
19 Bigsby, *Writers in Conversation*, p.272.
20 Anna Ziegler, *Plays One* (London, 2016), p.219.
21 Bigsby, *Writers in Conversation*, p.271.
22 Jennifer Rohn, 'Flaws and Forgiveness', 11 October 2015. www.lablit.com › article › 880.
23 Charles Spencer, 'Kidman Holds Us in Thrall', *The Telegraph*, 14 September 2015. https://www.telegraph.co.uk › theatre › what-to-seePhotograph 51, Noël Coward Theatre, review… – The Telegraph
24 Chris Jones, '"Photograph 51" at Court Theatre Delves into DNA's Forgotten Scientist, Rosalind Franklin', *Chicago Tribune*, 28 January 2019. 'Photograph 51' at Court Theatre delves into DNA's forgotten…
25 Anna Zeigler, *Another Way Home*, p.33. The text kindly supplied by Anna Ziegler.
26 Ibid.
27 Anna Ziegler, *The Minotaur* (New York, 2018), p.8.
28 Charles Isherwood, '"A Delicate Ship" Plumbs the What-ifs of Love and Heartbreak', *The New York Times*, 28 August 2015. www.nytimes.com › 2015/08/29 › theater
29 Rick Pender, 'A Delicate Ship (Review)', *CityBeat*, 28 March 2014. www.citybeat.com › 13005332 › a-delicate-ship-review
30 Elisabeth Vincentelli, '"A Delicate Ship" Is a Competent Love Triangle, but Overprocessed and Tasteless'. *New York Post*, 28 August 2015. https://nypost.com/2015/08/28/a-delicate-ship-is-a-competent-love
31 David Gordon, 'How Anna Ziegler Went from Poet to Playwright', *TheaterMania*, 1 November 2017. https://www.theatermania.com/off-broadway/news/interview-anna-ziegler
32 Victoria Myers, 'Gaye Taylor Upchurch and Anna Ziegler on "The Last Match"', *The Interval*, 18 October 2017.
33 David Gordeon, 'How Anna Ziegler Went from Poet to Playwright'. *Theatermania*, 1 November 2017. https://www.theatermania.com/off-broadway/news/interview-anna-ziegler-actually-the-last-match_82976.html
34 Anna Ziegler, *The Last Match* in *Anna Ziegler: Plays One*.
35 Ben Brantley, 'In "The Last Match" Tennis Is Not Only a Game', *The New York Times*, 24 October 2017. https://www.nytimes.com/2017/10/24/theater/the-last-match-review.html
36 Catey Sullivan, 'Hard Life Lessons Are Served up on and off the Court in "The Last Match,"' *Chicago Sun Times*, 2 May 2021. https://chicago.suntimes.com/2021/5/2/22415177/the-last-match-review
37 Richard Kelley, 'Anna Ziegler on the Blinding Power of Love, Gender Reassignment, Parenting, Betray and Boy', *Ensemble Studio Theatre*, 9 March 2016. www.ensemblestudiotheatre.org › est-blog-1/2016/3
38 Ibid.
39 Ibid.
40 Bigsby, *Writers in Conversation*, p.272.
41 Ziegler, *Plays One*, p.78.

Notes

42 Ben Brantley, 'In "Boy," a Man Deals with Gender Cards He's Given (Not Born With)', *The New York Times*, 10 March 2016. https://www.nytimes.com/2016/03/11/theater/review-in-boy-a-man-deals
43 Alexis Soloski, 'Boy Review – Transgender Drama Is Brisk and Fascinating but Too Tidy', *The Guardian*, 11 March 2016.
44 Anna Ziegler, 'Author's Note', in *Actually* (London, 2017).
45 Victoria Myers, 'Anna Ziegler on "Actually" and More', *The Interval*, 11 May 2017. www.theintervalny.com/interviews/2017/05/anna-ziegler-on-actually-and-more
46 Ibid.
47 Ibid.
48 Ibid.
49 Jesse Green, 'In "Actually," a Case of She Said, He Said and They Said', *The New York Times*, 14 November 2017. https://www.nytimes.com/2017/11/14/theater/actually-anna-ziegler-review.html
50 James Hebert, 'Old Globe Theatre's World Premiere "Wanderers" Weaves Together Disparate Stories', *The San Diego Union-Tribune*, 6 April 2018.
51 Anna Ziegler, *The Wanderers*, p.16. Text supplied by Anna Ziegler.
52 Christopher Bigsby, *Writers in Conversation, Volume 2* (Norwich, 2001), p.169.
53 Lisa Traiger, 'Lost Souls in Theater J's "The Wanderers"', *Washington Jewish Week*, 26 February 2020. https://www.washingtonjewishweek.com/lost-souls-in-theater-js-the-wanderer
54 Helen Kaye, '"The Wanderers" Nuanced Performances', *The Jerusalem Post,* 5 February 2020. https://www.jpost.com/Israel-News/Culture/The-Wanderers-nuanced
55 Brandon Horwin, 'BWW Review: The Wanderers at Theater J', *Broadway World Washington D.C.*, 26 February 2020. Review: THE WANDERERS at Theater J – Broadway World. https://www.broadwayworld.com/washington-dc/article/BWW-Review-THE
56 Anna Ziegler, *The Janeid*, p.27. Text supplied by Anna Ziegler.
57 Kristina Dorsey, 'Playwright Anna Ziegler Returns to Thew O'Neill with "Antigones"', *The Day*, 14 July 2019. https://www.theday.com/article/20190714/ENT10/190719893
58 Anna Ziegler, *Antigones*, p.18. Text supplied by Anna Ziegler.
59 Seattle Rep, 'The Great MomentPlaywright Anna Ziegler Talks Family, the Creative Process, and Her Work with Seattle Rep', *Seattle Rep*, 1 October 2019.
60 Anna Ziegler, *The Great Moment*, p.34. Text supplied by Anna Ziegler.
61 Ibid., p.3.
62 Christopher Bigsby, *Writers in Conversation with Christopher Bigsby, volume 1* (Norwich, 2000), p.3.
63 Jay Irwin, 'Seattle Rep's The Great Moment Is a Moment but Not So Great', *Broadway World Seattle*, 17 October 2019. BWW Review: Seattle Rep's THE GREAT MOMENT is a Moment but
64 Gemma Wilson, 'Seattle Rep's "The Great Moment" Gives Us Birth, Death, Aging – You Know, the Boring Stuff', *Seattle Magazine*. https://www.seattlemag.com/theater/seattle-reps-great-moment-give-us

INDEX

Abbott, Paul, *Shameless* 164
Adjmi, David 5, 85
   3C 5, 22–4
   Doppelgangbang 8
   early life and education 6–8
   Elective Affinities 5–6, 9–12
   The Evildoers 5, 12–18, 21
   as gay 6–8
   on German plays 9
   honours 24, 27
   Jewish (Sephardic) 6–7
   Lot Six 28
   Marie Antoinette 5, 24–8
   Strange Attractors 8
   The Stumble 27
   Stunning and Other Plays 6–7, 17–22
   Woody Allen's Fall Project 8
Aeschylus, *Prometheus Bound* 37
Africa/Africans 58, 60–1, 63
African American 19, 34–5, 64, 71, 73–5, 128, 139, 143, 145, 148, 160, 162, 188, 191
Agee, James, *Let Us All Now Praise Famous Men* 85
Ai Weiwei 114–15
Akhtar, Ayad 6
Albee, Edward 18, 22, 83, 94, 98, 103
   Three Tall Women 12, 42, 196
   Who's Afraid of Virginia Woolf 13–14, 37, 85, 180
   The Zoo Story 151, 180
Alexander, Michelle, *The New Jim Crow* 157
Als, Hilton 21
Angelou, Maya 61
Armstrong, Alun 59
Asbørnson, Peter Christen, *Norwegian Fairy Tales* 101
Asian 30, 35, 38, 40, 73–4, 168
Asian American 29–31, 33–4, 38, 52, 64
Asian American Political Alliance 29
Asian American Theatre Workshop 29
authentic/authenticity 13–14, 16, 60–1, 67, 74, 102, 113

Baker, Annie 164
Baldwin, James, *Blues for Mr. Charlie* 138
BAME (Black, Asian, Minority Ethnic) 73
Baraka, Amiri 139
Barthes, Roland, *Camera Lucida* 66, 68
Baumbach, Noah 179
Beckett, Samuel 84, 90, 93–4, 96–7, 112, 183, 187
   Krapp's Last Tape 91
   A Piece of Monologue 90
   Waiting for Godot 37, 88, 90, 92, 94, 100, 102, 178
   Worstward Ho 89

Bell, Keira 185
Benson, Sarah 72
Billington, Michael 63, 78, 105, 128, 175
Black Americans. *See* African American
Black Dispatches 162
Blankenship, Mark 168
Blau, Herb 2
Bohr, Niels 172
Boseman, Chadwick 164
Bosworth, Beth 165
Brantley, Ben 12, 28, 70, 78, 82, 107, 143, 154, 175, 184, 187
The Bridge TV series 174
British theatre 6
British Theatre Guide 170
Broadway, The United States 1–3, 71–2, 117
Brooks, David 128
Brooks, Gwendolyn, 'We Real Cool' 158–9
Brown, Donald 52
Browning, Elizabeth Barrett 120
Browning, Robert, 'My Late Duchess' 9
Brown, Simone, *Dark Matters* 76
Bush, George W. 11, 16, 25–7

Caldwell, Zoe 10, 12
Carmichael, Stokely 76
Carver, Raymond 84
Chicago Sun Times 184
Chicago Theatre Review 143
Chicago Tribune 46, 96, 143, 151, 176
Childress, Alice, *Trouble in Mind* 72
Chinese-American 29–30
Chin, Frank 29
Cho, Julia 30
   The Architecture of Loss 35–7, 40
   Aubergine 30, 33, 47–9, 52–3
   award/honour 46
   BFE 31, 33–5
   Durango 40–2, 52
   early life and education 31
   The Language Archive 30, 33, 44–9, 52
   99 Histories 31–4
   Office Hour 49–52
   The Piano Teacher 33, 42–4, 49
   The Winchester House 37
Cleage, Pearl
   Deals with the Devil and Other Reasons to Riot 138
   "Mad at Miles" 138
Coates, Ta-Nehisi, 'Why Do Few Blacks Study the Civil War?' 162

Index

Colapinto, John, *As Nature Made Him: The Boy Who Was Raised as a Child* 187
Collins-Hughes, Laura 151
Condon, Constance 31
Conrad, Joseph, *The Heart of Darkness* 11
Coppola, Frances Ford, *Apocalypse Now* 11
Coppola, Sophia, *Marie Antoinette* film 24, 28
The Cosby Show TV show 23, 73
Cote, David 12, 24
Covid-19 pandemic 1, 132, 164, 193
culture 2, 10, 18, 25, 32, 35, 44, 46, 63, 95, 131, 136, 138
Curtain Up 21, 35, 42
cynicism 13–14, 123, 143, 171

The Daily Telegraph 92
DC Metro Theatre Arts 122, 157
DC Theatre Scene 44, 46, 132
Deferred Action for Childhood Arrivals (DACA) 133
DeLillo, Don, *The Athlete in Rapture is Assumed into Heaven* 84
Detroit Housing Act (1949) 149
Díaz, Junot, 'Negocios' ('Business') 129
Dickinson, Emily 62, 181
Djerassi, Carl 173
   Calculus 174
   Oxygen 174
The Dream Act (2001) 133
Drury, Jackie Sibblies
   early life and education 55–6
   'Empathy by Another Name' 58
   Fairview 2, 55, 72, 75–8
   Marys Seacole 79–82
   people of colour 73, 75
   performers and role (rehearsal) 59–65, 67–9
   Pulitzer Prize 77–8
   race/racism (and genocide) 55–82
   Really 66–70
   Social Creatures 63–7
   We Are Proud to Present a Presentation about the Herero of Namibia, Formerly Known as Southwest Africa from the German Sudwestafrika, between the Years 1884–1915 56
Dubois, W. E. 73
Dunham, Lena 165
Durang, Christopher 31
Dylan, Bob 107
   Rough and Rowdy Ways 190

Edgar, David 116
Edinburgh Festival 6, 92, 96
Ehn, Erik 57
   Maria Kizito 56
Eliot, T. S. 15, 99, 107
   The Four Quartets 180
   The Wasteland 67, 89, 179
Ellison, Ralph, *Invisible Man* 76
Emerson, Ralph Waldo 107

Eno, Will 2, 83, 91
   and Albee 85
   awards/honors 89
   Behold the Coach, in a Blazer, Uninsured, 93
   The Bully Composition 93
   A Canadian Lies Dying on American Ice 84
   early life and education 83
   The Flu Season (The Snow Romance) 87–9
   Gnit 101
   inspired by Beckett (*see* Beckett, Samuel)
   Ladies and Gentlemen, the Rain 93
   Lady Grey 111
   Middletown 94–6
   Mr. Theatre Comes Home Different 111
   Oh, the Humanity and Other Good Intentions 92–3
   The Open House 103–5
   The Plot 110–11
   The Realistic Joneses 84, 98–101, 103
   Spokeswoman for Country Air 93
   Thom Pain (based on nothing) 89–93
   Title and Deed 96–7
   Tragedy: A Tragedy 85–9
   The Underlying Chris 108–11
   Wakey, Wakey 105–7
Evening Standard 78

Fanon, Franz, *Black Skin, White Masks* 73
Feingold, Michael, *Village Voice* 51
Fenelon, Fania
   Broken Glass 137
   Playing for Time 137
Financial Times 97
Firestein, Stuart, *Ignorance: How It Drives Science* 185–6
Flusser, Vilém, *Towards a Philosophy of Photography* 66
Foes, Jonathan Safran 190
Ford, Richard 84
Franklin, Rosalind 172–5
Frayn, Michael 68–9
   Copenhagen 172, 176
Freedman, Debbie 197
French Revolution 25, 27
The Fresh Prince of Bel-Air show 73
Frisch, Max 129
Fugard, Athol 8

Gaitskill, Mary, *Veronica* 25
Gardner, Lyn 87, 89, 92, 98, 143, 170
Gates, Anita 35
Gaye, Marvin 145
Gee, Emma 29
gender 71, 74, 79, 108–10, 116, 131, 137–8, 163, 175, 183–5, 187
genocide 43, 56–9, 62–3
gentrification 148–9
German/Germany 5, 9, 27, 44, 56, 60–3, 154
Giacometti, Alberto 66
Gilman, Charlotte Perkins 71

Index

Glaspell, Susan, *The Verge* 17
Goethe, *Elective Affinities* 9, 11
Golding, William, *The Lord of the Flies* 170
Goldsman, Akiva, *I Am Legend* 65
Goodman, Steve, 'The City of New Orleans' 196–7
Gosling, Raymond 173–4
Grade, Eric 175
Greenhow, Rose O'Neal 162
Green, Jesse 51, 110, 128, 132, 190
Gritten, David 92
Grossman, David 46
    A Horse Walks into a Bar 90–1
The Guardian 63, 71, 78, 87, 92, 98, 143, 170, 187
Guare, John 22
    Six Degrees of Separation 8, 21, 31, 176
Guirgis, Stephen Adly 128
Gunesekera, Romesh, *Reef* 107–8

Hall, Katori 144
    The Mountain Top 140
Handke, Peter, *Offending the Audience* 75, 82
Hansberry, Lorraine 76, 139
    A Raisin the Sun 145, 150
Hare, David, *South Downs* 113
Harris, Jeremy O., *Slave Play* 58
Harris, Kamala 73
Hartman, Saidiya 57
Hart, Moss 197
Heilpern, John 12
Hilbert, David 171
Hnath, Lucas 166
The Hollywood Reporter 82
Holocaust 45, 62, 178, 191–2
homophobic/homophobia 6, 22–4
homosexual/homosexuality 8, 16, 23, 28, 134
Houghton, James 105
Houseman, John 72
Hunter, Samuel D. 164
Hwang, David Henry 29, 117

Ibsen, Henrik 103
    A Doll's House 8
    Peer Gynt 101–3
ICE (U.S. Immigration and Customs Enforcement agency) 133
Ichioka, Yuji 29
identity 1, 30, 32–3, 35, 52, 73–4, 83, 97, 108–11, 114, 124, 131, 135–6, 138, 159, 165–6, 168–9, 182, 184–7
immigrants/immigration 1, 29–30, 38, 41, 47, 49–51, 74, 114–19, 123–5, 127, 129–30, 132–3, 136
Inwin, Jay, *Broadway World Seattle* 197
Isherwood, Charles 17, 24, 28, 44, 46, 49, 63, 92, 96, 98, 105, 123, 147, 181

Jackson, Jesse 73, 155
Jacoby, Tamar 118
Jamaica 55, 79–81

James, William 91
Jaworowski, Ken 170
Jefferson, Margot 37, 89
The Jeffersons show 73
The Jerusalem Post 192
Jews/Jewish 6–8, 17, 21, 137, 165, 168–71, 173, 176, 178, 181, 188–92, 197
Joad, Tom, *The Grapes of Wrath* 152
Johnson, Georgia Douglas 148
Johnson, Mary Ann 157
Jones, Chris 46, 96, 151, 176
Jones, Martha 72–3
Judson, Horace, *The Eighth Day of Creation* 173
Julavits, Heidi, *The Folded Clock* 182
Julliard Playwrights Programme 9, 31

Kane, Sarah
    Blasted 116
    Crave 116
Kang, Jay Caspian, *The Loneliest Americans* 29
Kelsall, Cameron 162
Kennedy, John F. 32, 60
Kerner Commission 143–4
Keys, James 139
Kidman, Nicole 172, 175
Kierkegaard, Søren 179
King, Martin Luther 76, 142
Koestler, Arthur 175
Kohler, Terri K. 76
Kopit, Arthur 165
Korean-American 29–33, 35, 47
Kroto, Harry 173
Kunofsky, Larry 24
Kushner, Tony 22, 31

Lahiri, Nilanjena Sudeshna 'Jhumpa,' 'The Third and Final Continent' 129
Lahr, John 24, 98
Lang, Fritz, *Metropolis* 152
language 11, 13–14, 16, 30, 44–8, 52, 59–60, 96–8, 107, 112, 114–16, 131, 135, 154–5, 157, 168–9, 192
Lavey, Martha 110
Leavis, F. R. 173
Lee, Chang-rae, *Native Speaker* 30
Lee, Felicia R. 7
Lee, Young Jean 166
Lehrer, Tom, 'Bright College Days' 14
Letts, Tracy 103
    August, Osage County 37, 104
Lewis, C. S. 37
Lightman, Alan, *Einstein's Dreams* 178
Lingis, Alphonso, *The Community of Those Who Have Nothing in Common* 98
Lish, Gordon 84–5
    Epigraph 84
Loman, Willy 120
    Death of a Salesman 59, 120, 166
Los Angeles Times 49, 78

Index

Lovecraft, H. P. 63
Lovett, Conor 84, 96
Lovett, Judy Hegarty, *Title and Deed* 84
Lowell, Robert 67

Magaril, Jon 28
Majok, Martyna 55, 79, 114
    awards/honours 117, 128
    Broken Vessels 123
    Cost of Living 123–8, 136
    Dancing after Hours 124
    on displacement/immigration 113–36
    early life and education 114–18
    Ironbound 117–24
    Merage Foundation Fellowship scholarship 116–17
    Mouse in a Jar 117
    queens 129–32
    Sanctuary City 132–5
Majok, Powel 124
Mamet, David
    American Buffalo 146
    Glengarry, Glen Ross 146
    Oleanna 187
Man about the House TV show 22
Mandell, Jonathan 132
Manguso, Sarah, *Ongoingness* 182
Ma Rainey's Black Bottom 138
Marenson, Elise 128
Margolin, Deb 56
Margulies, Donald 165
Matsu, Makoto 29
Maxwell, Richard 66
McArthur Foundation 1
McCall, Tullis 82
McEwan, Ian 171–3
McNulty, Charles 49, 78, 123
MD Theatre Guide 157
Mendes, Sam, *Cabaret* 115
Mertes, Brian 31
Midgette, Anne 168
Miller, Arthur 50, 85, 120, 154
    After the Fall 113
    All My Sons 44, 98
    The Archbishop's Ceiling 76
    Death of a Salesman 20, 40
    on Morisseau 137
    Mr. Peters' Connections 106
    Thomas Jefferson Lecture 61
    Timebends 166
Miller, Deb 70–1
Milton, John, *Paradise Lost* 186
minority group 1, 55, 74, 169
Moore, Michael, *Fahrenheit 9/11* 26
Morisseau, Dominque 1
    Ain't Too Proud 164
    Archive Project 162
    awards/honors 148, 164
    The Blackness Blues – Time to Change the Tune (A Sister's Story) 139
    Blood at the Root 155–7
    civil rights movement 140, 142, 156, 162
    Confederates 160, 163–4
    Detroit '67 141, 144–51, 154, 164
    Detroit Free Press 148
    The Detroit Project 144
    early life and education 139–40
    Eyes on the Prize 156
    Follow Me to Nellie's 140
    Incident at Vichy 137
    kind on others 140
    Miller on 137
    Mud Row 2, 159–62, 164
    Paradise Blue 138, 141, 148–54
    Pipeline 157–9
    Rules of Engagement 2
    Skeleton Crew 119, 152–5, 157, 164
    Sunset Baby 140–3
Morrison, Toni 71
Morris, William 71

Nabokov, Dmitri 179
narcissism/narcissistic 11, 13, 75, 113
National New Play Network 117, 119
New Play Frontiers project 159
New Statesman 143
news, television 86
The New Yorker 21, 24, 44, 78, 98, 168
New York Post 181
New York Stage Review 82
New York Theatre Guide 82, 128
New York Theatre Workshop 21, 132
The New York Times 1, 7, 12, 17–18, 21, 24–5, 28–9, 35, 37, 44, 46, 49, 51, 63, 65, 70, 73, 78, 82, 84, 89, 92, 96, 98, 105, 107, 110, 128, 132, 140, 143, 147, 151, 154, 168, 175, 181, 184, 187, 190
    "Let Detroit Go Bankrupt" 152
NHS Mary Seacole Centre 79
Nightingale, Florence 79–82
Norman, Marsha 31, 114
Nottage, Lynn 1, 165
Nurse, Paul 171–2, 175, 186

Obama, Barack 65, 71, 133
Odets, Clifford
    Awake and Sing 150
    Waiting for Lefty 122
Ondaatje, Michael 109
O'Neill, Eugene 98, 103, 194
    Lazarus Laughed 106
    Long Day's Journey into Night 37
online play 1, 184
Open (autobiography of Andre Agassi) 182
O'Rourke, Meghan 25
Orton, Joe 23, 66

Patchett, Ann, *Run* 172
Peña, Ralph 37–8
Pender, Rick, *CityBeat* 181
people of colour 73, 75–7
Perry, Jennifer, *Broadway World* 123
Pinsky, Robert, 'Jersey Rain' 122
Pinter, Harold 91, 94
    A Birthday Party 92
    The Homecoming or Shepard's *Buried Child* 104
    Old Times 136
Portman, Natalie 190
Postcards from America 9
Pound, Ezra 66–7
    Hugh Selwyn Mauberley (Part 4) 89

race/racism 2, 6, 19, 55–82, 138–9, 142, 155, 157, 163, 176
Rankine, Claudia 77
    Just Us: An American Conversation 81
Rattey, Julie 28
Reimer, David 184, 187
Rilke, Rainer Maria, *Letters to a Young Poet* 32–3
Rizzo, Frank 17
The Rocky Horror Picture Show 197
Roddick, Andy 182
Rogers, J. T. 57
Romero, George, *Dawn of the Dead* 64
Romney, Mitt 152
Ross, Diana 139
Roth, Daryl 167
Roth, Philip, *Everyman* 191
Ruhl, Sarah, *Eurydice* 177
Rushdie, Salman, *The Satanic Verses* 79

Sawhill, Isabel 118
Scheck, Frank 82
Schneider, Alan 94
Schreck, Heidi 9
Seacole, Mary 78–82
Seattle Magazine 197
Sebald, W. G., *Austerlitz* 66
Sedaris, David 111
Seldes, Marian 12
Serratore, Nicole 117
sexism 22–3, 74
sexuality 124, 138, 157
Shakespeare, William 6, 139
    The Winter's Tale 174
Shakur, Tupac 140–2
Shange, Ntozake, *For Colored Girls Who Have Considered Suicide/ When the Rainbow Is Enuf* 55, 139
Shaun of the Dead comedy 64
Shelly, Mary, *Frankenstein* 185
Shepard, Sam
    Buried Child 37
    A Lie of the Mind 87
Shinn, Christopher 85

Shuttleworth, Ian 97
Siegel, David 122
Simon, John 37
Simpson, O. J. 74
Singer, Isaac Bashevis 191
small theatres 2, 6, 53, 92, 117, 172
Snow, C. P. 173
Soderbergh, Steven, *Contagion* 65
soliloquy 2, 73, 156
Soloski, Alexis 84, 187
Sommer, Elyse 35, 42
Sommers, Michael 82, 140
Sontag, Susan, *On Photography* 66
Spencer, Charles 175
The Stage 78
Stasio, Marilyn 24, 35, 37
Steinbeck, John, *Of Mice and Men* 151–2
Stoltenberg, John 157
Stoppard, Tom 9
    Coast of Utopia 176
    Hapgood 172
    Leopoldstadt 113
    Professional Foul 44
Strong, Mark 115
Sturm und Drang (storm and stress) 9, 16–17, 28
Sullivan, Catey 184

Tan, Amy 29
The Telegraph 175
television news 86
Theatre Communications Group 3
theatre tickets (price of) 2, 40, 55, 90, 144
Thoreau, Henry David, *Walden* 68, 85
Three's Company TV show 22–4
Time Out 12, 24, 63, 78, 87
Tomlin, Lily 139
Traiger, Lisa 192
Treanor, Tim 46
Tremain, Rose 114
    Sacred Country 113
Trump, Donald 115, 128–9, 133, 187
Truth, Sojourner 162
Tubman, Harriet 162

Urbaniak, James 92

Van Lew, Elizabeth 162
Variety 17, 24, 28, 35, 37, 42, 151, 168, 171
Vincentelli, Elisabeth 181
violence 12, 16, 18, 35, 43, 49–52, 59, 63, 65–6, 140, 142, 144, 158
Vire, Kris 87
Vogel, Paula 47, 52
    How I Learned to Drive 38–42

Walker, Jeffrey 44
The Walking Dead TV series 64
Wallace, Naomi 72

Index

Washington Jewish Week 192
Welles, Orson 72
Wesker, Arnold, *Roots* 113
Wharton, Edith 18
Whitman, Walt
    Leaves of Grass 107
    'Unfolded Out of the Folds' 107
Wilder, Thornton 94–6, 109–10
    Our Town 94, 98, 108, 110
Wiley, Kehinde, The Yellow Wallpaper exhibition 71
Wilkins, Maurice 173–4
Williams, Tennessee 18, 84
    The Glass Menagerie 10, 31, 34, 113
    A House Not Meant to Stand 160
    Small Craft Warning 113
    A Streetcar Named Desire 7, 18, 20
    Vieux Carré 113
Williamstown Theatre Festival 124, 148, 151
Wilson, August 138–9
Women's Voices Theatre Festival 118
Woolf, Virginia, *Between the Acts* 2
Wrathall, Claire 71
Wright, Richard 76
    Native Son 158

Zanganech, Lila Azam 179
Ziegler, Anna 29
    Actually 187–90, 197
    An Off Night 165
    Another Way Home 176–7
    Antigones 193–4
    awards/honors 172, 191, 197
    BFF (Best Friends Forever) 166–9
    Boy 184–7
    characters/subject 165–6
    A Delicate Ship 169, 179–81
    Dov and Ali 169–71, 178
    early life and education 165, 169
    The Great Moment 165, 194–6
    A House Without Windows 197
    An Incident 176
    The Janeiad 193
    The Last Match 182–4, 190, 197
    Life Science 168–9
    The Minotaur 178–9, 195
    Photograph 51 172–5, 197
    The Wanderers 190–2, 197
Zinoman, Jason 21
Žižek, Slavoj 119
Zombies vs Strippers 64

www.ingramcontent.com/pod-product-compliance
Lightning Source LLC
Chambersburg PA
CBHW08093600426
44115CB00017B/2846